UNDERSTANDING
WOOD
FINISHING

UNDERSTANDING WOOD FINISHING

How to Select and Apply the Right Finish

BOB FLEXNER

Reader's Digest

THE READER'S DIGEST ASSOCIATION, INC.

PLEASANTVILLE, NEW YORK • MONTREAL

A READER'S DIGEST BOOK

Text copyright © 2005 Bob Flexner
Photographs and illustrations copyright © 2005 The Reader's Digest
    Association, Inc., except as follows: Photo 1-4 copyright © 2005 Michael
    Puryear; Photos p. 1, 1-6 copyright © 2005 Charles Radtke; Photos p. v(1),
    1-7 copyright © 2005 Bob Flexner; Photos 15-4 through 15-8 copyright
    2005 © Jim Roberson; Photos p. vii(2), p. x, 1-1, 1-2, 1-3, 2-3, 4-4, 4-5, 4-8,
    4-13, 4-14, 14-1, 15-2, 15-3, 15-9, 15-10, p. 205, 17-1, 17-2, p. 221, 17-3,
    p. 225, p. 226, pp. 228–232, pp. 234–236, p. 238, pp. 240–242, pp. 245–248,
    p. 271, 20-5 copyright © 2005 Rick Mastelli

Produced by arrangement with Image & Word, Montpelier, Vermont

FOR READER'S DIGEST
Copy Editor: Barbara Booth
Executive Editor, Trade Publishing: Dolores York
Project Designer: Jennifer Tokarski
Director of Production: Michael Braunschweiger
Associate Publisher, Trade Publishing: Christopher T. Reggio
President & Publisher, Books and Music: Harold Clarke

FOR IMAGE & WORD
Editor: Rick Mastelli
Design and Layout: Deborah Fillion
Photography, except where noted: Rick Mastelli
Photo 1-4: Sarah Wells; Photos p. 1, 1-6: Doug Edmunds; Photos 15-4
    through 15-8: Jim Roberson
Illustrations: Lee Hochgraf and Steve Buchanan

Cover design by George McKeon
Front and back cover photographs by Rick Mastelli

Library of Congress Cataloging in Publication Data
Flexner, Bob
    Understanding wood finishing : how to select and apply the right
finish / by Bob Flexner.—Completely rev. and updated
        p. cm.
        Includes index.
        ISBN 0-7621-0621-2 (hardcover)
        1. Wood finishing—Amateurs' manuals. 2. Stains and staining—
Amateurs' manuals. I. Title.

TT325.F53 2005
684'.084--dc22   2004065053

Address any comments about *Understanding Wood Finishing* to:
        The Reader's Digest Association, Inc.
        Adult Trade Publishing
        Reader's Digest Road
        Pleasantville, NY 10570-7000

For more Reader's Digest products and information, visit our website:
        www.rd.com www.rd.com (in the United States)
Visit Bob Flexner at www.bobflexner.com

Printed in China

1 3 5 7 9 10 8 6 4 2 (hardcover)

Contents

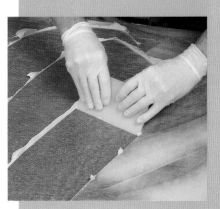

Introduction

I learned wood finishing in the mid-1970s from a couple of refinishers with a business down the street from my woodworking shop. Looking back, I realize that I became a pretty good finisher. I learned to spray lacquer and catalyzed finishes, use dyes, glazes, and toners, fill pores, and rub out finishes.

But I was simultaneously reading the woodworking magazines at the time, and gradually I lost my confidence. The more I read about finishing, the more confused I became—until by the early 1980s I stopped doing finishing altogether and began farming it out to others.

This continued for a few years, but I wasn't satisfied because I no longer had control. I was at the mercy of others, and I started getting complaints from some of my clients. I became very frustrated.

The dilemma I found myself in didn't make sense. Finishing couldn't be that hard. I had to figure out some way to make sense of it. So I started checking out finishing and refinishing books from the public library, and I redoubled my efforts to find information by reading woodworking magazines. No help. I just became more confused. It seemed that every time I thought I understood some explanation or procedure, I then read something that contradicted it.

The Breakthrough

One day I called my friend Jim, who had a good background in chemistry, to ask if he could explain why alcohol would separate furniture joints that had been glued together with animal hide glue.

"What's hide glue?" he asked. "It's glue that's made from animal skins," I explained. "Oh, protein!" he exclaimed. And he proceeded to tell me all about hide glue—all the information I had been unable to find in any of the woodworking books I'd searched through—how it worked, how and why it deteriorated, why it bonded without clamps, why alcohol would crystallize it and steam would dissolve it, and so on.

I was dumbfounded. For years I had been looking in vain for accurate information on the hide glue I used for restoring antique furniture. And Jim had known it all along—simply because he understood the chemistry of protein.

That conversation ended with Jim offering to take me over to the local university engineering library to see what we could dig up. I walked out with an armload of books dealing with hide glue.

Nearby the books on glues were several shelves of books on finishes, including books on the chemistry and technology of stains, dyes, solvents, oil, and wax. Several weeks later I went back and checked out a few of these books.

I don't have a background in chemistry or engineering, so I found these books difficult to understand at first. To further my education, I joined the national association of paint and finish chemists and attended some seminars and conventions. I spent countless hours talking to the chemists who actually make the raw materials used in our finishing products. I found these chemists to be much like the majority of woodworkers I've met: They love to share what they know with anyone who shows interest.

Slowly I began making sense of finishes. I found it remarkable how understanding each product and how it worked made its application obvious, and how this understanding helped me solve problems when they occurred in my shop. No longer did I have to learn everything by trial and error, a method that is hugely expensive and frustrating and one that requires a long-term commitment to succeed. (If you're not doing finishing on a regular basis, I don't see how you can ever get very good at it by trial and error alone.)

I also found it hard to understand why no one had taken this information and put it in a form that would be useful to woodworkers and finishers. No one had tried to bridge the chasm that divides finish chemists, who understand quite well what's true and not true about finishes, from those of us who use finishes. So I decided to do it myself with the first edition of this book, which was published in 1994.

The Half-Right Rule

The book was extremely successful—beyond my wildest dreams. But it didn't solve the problem. Published information on finishing is still confusing and contradictory. We are all still encumbered by what I call the "half-right rule." Half of what we read or hear about finishing is right. We just don't know which half!

Why is this? Why does the information about wood finishing continue to be so inadequate? Wood finishing is, after all, a very simple craft. It involves little more than transferring a liquid from a container to the wood using a rag, brush, or spray gun. Each of these tools is easy to master. (By way of comparison, think of all the tools you have to master to be good at woodworking.)

I believe there are two explanations. The first is that finishes are chemistry—they are molecules of various sorts put together to make a liquid with specific characteristics. So unlike woodworking and woodworking tools (which are physics), you can't see differences. You can't see the difference between varnish and lacquer, for example, not in the can, not even on the wood. In contrast, you know right away that a dovetail isn't a mortise-and-tenon and that a band saw isn't a table saw (even though it also has a table).

Not being able to see differences makes the second explanation possible and probably inevitable. It is that manufacturers of finishing products have a lot of room to mislead and exaggerate in their product naming and promotion. This results in your being misled and also in those people writing about finishing not knowing what is correct and what isn't. So there's no effective check on a manufacturer's natural inclination to make its products appear better and sometimes even different than they actually are.

I am convinced that the understanding of finishing would be far less a chore (and this book much smaller) if there weren't so much misinformation to debunk. You may well find that it will take more effort to unlearn what is wrong than to learn what is right.

The Secret Is That There Is No Secret

The reticence of manufacturers to provide good information is perhaps most evident in their reluctance to tell us what ingredients they are using. The excuse is usually that the information is proprietary. The manufacturer doesn't want to give away its "secrets."

At one time, manufacturers, and even the individual finishers and painters who made their own finishes, may have had secrets. But finish formulation has become a sophisticated science in the last 100 years. The essential chemistry of almost all finishing products has been thoroughly understood for decades.

There is very little that is new in wood finishes. And what is new has almost always been developed by the large chemical companies that produce the raw materials. These companies make their new information available to anyone who wants it, especially to the finish manufacturers who are potential customers. These raw materials' suppliers even provide the formulations for using their products. All the finish manufacturers have to do is mix the ingredients.

So all of the manufacturers of stains and finishes (as well as you and I) have access to the same information about raw materials and making finishes. Where this information doesn't flow is between the companies that put these raw materials into products and us, the users of the products.

Even among the companies themselves there's no secrecy because every large finish manufacturer has access to equipment that will analyze the content of their competitors' products. Every manufacturer can find out what every other manufacturer is selling. One of the pioneers of modern finishes William Krumbhaar, once said, "The real reason for secrecy is the necessity of concealing the fact that there is nothing to conceal."

Modern wood-finish suppliers, in fact, are little more than marketing companies following the best business practices for selling the maximum amount of product. With all the consolidation and cost cutting that has occurred during the last several decades, there are few, if any, people left at these companies who understand much about the products being sold. This explains why you get so little useful help when you call and why the directions on labels are often inaccurate.

Toward Understanding

So how do you overcome the dual realities that you can't master finishing by trial and error unless you practice every day, and you can't rely on what you are being told by the manufacturers or even in third-party books and pamphlets?

It's my experience that you do it by learning what the products are, how they work, and what they can be expected to accomplish. You don't need to go back to the original chemistry to do this because I've already done it for you. And this second edition benefits from a decade of refining and adding to the information I first presented.

My hope is that the information presented in this book will make it possible for you to succeed at finishing. I also hope that others will pick up where I have left off and develop the information further. There are, after all, an infinite number of ways to apply finishing products and an infinite number of effects. (There's only one accurate way to define the products, however.)

Above all, I hope manufacturers will begin to help us learn about their products. They can start by labeling their containers accurately and listing the ingredients on their labels. Nothing could go further to make wood finishing the easy craft it should be.

How to Use This Book

Books on finishing are difficult to read straight through because those parts you have no experience with are often difficult to follow. The information in this book is arranged linearly, in the order you actually apply a finish. But you needn't read the early parts to understand the later. A craft is not learned linearly. It's learned gradually, the conceptual understandings periodically buttressed by hands-on experience.

Turn to the sections of the book you're interested in. Try some of the finishes on scrap wood before you use them on a completed project. (You wouldn't attempt to cut your first dovetail joint on the actual drawer!)

As your skills improve, your interests will change, and you can tackle other sections. You'll find that all the materials and techniques used in finishing are interrelated. The more you learn about one subject, the better you'll be able to understand another.

Though finishing is easy to do, it is a complex subject. With so many variables, it's frustrating and often humbling. No matter how long you do it, you will continue to have problems. But that's what makes finishing fun. If it were straightforward, there wouldn't be a challenge. Everyone would be able to do it, and there wouldn't be any satisfaction when you accomplished something. In this way, it's just like woodworking.

Safety

Throughout the book I point out safety precautions you should take when using various individual finishing materials. Here is an overview.

Most of the materials used in finishing are bad for you. Solvents, such as mineral spirits, naphtha, and lacquer thinner, can cause dermatitis, dizziness, headaches, and nausea. Chemicals, such as lye, oxalic acid, and chlorine bleach, can cause respiratory and skin problems. Even the so-called "safe" strippers and water-based finishes contain solvents that are bad for your health if you breathe too much of them.

You should always protect yourself by arranging cross ventilation in your work area to provide a constant source of clean air. When you can't ensure a flow of clean air, wear a NIOSH-approved, organic-vapor, respirator mask. (NIOSH is the National Institute for Occupational Safety and Health. It is a federal agency that does research on matters concerning worker's health and tests and certifies respiratory protection.) In addition, you should wear gloves to protect your hands when they come in contact with the finishing materials.

But, in spite of these warnings, don't be afraid of using finishing materials any more than you are afraid of using woodworking tools. This is an important point, because it's becoming more and more common to read dire warnings about the hazards of using certain finishing products. Some of the warnings come from manufacturers of competing products. Some come from writers repeating the most extreme warnings they've heard without researching their validity. In some cases, if you didn't know better, you could expect almost certain death from products you can buy at any paint store.

Rely on common sense when using finishing materials just as you should when using power woodworking tools. Pay attention to your body. If you start to feel lightheaded or begin coughing, or if your hands become dry and chapped, protect yourself better. Since the risk of health problems caused by solvents and chemicals used in finishing increases with exposure (your body becomes sensitized), take greater precautions if you work with these products on a regular basis.

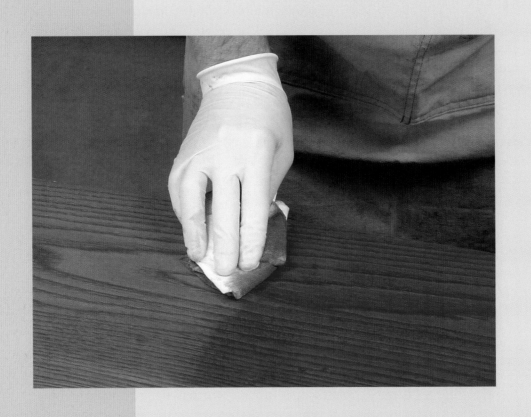

CHAPTER 1

Why Finish Wood, Anyway?

Why do we finish wood? It's an extra step, or steps, that most woodworkers don't find at all enjoyable. It's smelly and messy, and all sorts of things can go wrong. In addition, most woods look pretty good unfinished. Why bother? There are three good reasons for finishing wood: to help keep it clean, to help stabilize it, and to decorate it.

Sanitation

Wood is a porous material. It contains countless holes of various sizes. These holes can accumulate dirt and grime from handling, atmospheric contaminants, and food. Grimy wood is unattractive, and it can be a health hazard, providing a breeding place for bacteria. A finish seals the porous surface, making it less susceptible to soiling and easier to clean.

Stabilization

Besides being porous, wood is hygroscopic: It absorbs and releases moisture. Moisture within wood is called *moisture content;* moisture in the environment is either liquid water or water vapor (humidity). Wood responds to changes in the level of moisture around it. If you put very dry wood in water or in an area of high humidity, the wood will absorb

In Brief

- **Sanitation**
- **Stabilization**
- **Decoration**

moisture and swell. If you put wood that has a high moisture content in a relatively dry climate, the wood will release moisture and shrink.

These dimensional changes, commonly called *wood movement* do not occur consistently throughout a piece of wood. The surface of wood, for instance, responds more readily than the core. Wood swells and shrinks mainly across the grain; that is, in the width and thickness of boards, not appreciably in the length. And wood swells and shrinks more around the annular growth rings than it does perpendicular to the rings. The result of these different responses is that wood movement generates great stresses in wood and on the joints that hold pieces of wood together. The stresses cause splitting, checking, warping, and weakening of the joints. A finish slows moisture exchange, thus reducing the stresses and stabilizing the wood.

As a general rule, the thicker the coating of finish, the better it limits moisture exchange. This exchange does not have to be in the form of liquid water. It can be, and usually is, water vapor. Water-vapor exchange causes much damage to otherwise sheltered wood furniture and woodwork. It just does this more slowly than in wood subjected to liquid-water exchange.

Splits, Checks, and Warps

To understand better how moisture exchange causes splits, checks, and warps, look at Figure 1-1. A solid piece of kiln-dried wood is clamped securely so that it can't expand in width. Then it is exposed to 100 percent humidity for a period of time. The cell walls swell and the wood tries to expand, but it is constrained by the clamps. So the cell walls compress, changing from cylindrical to oval in shape.

If the board is released from the clamps and the humidity dropped to 30 percent, water evaporates and the cell walls shrink. But the cells don't return to their cylindrical shape: They remain flattened. So the board shrinks, becoming narrower than it was originally. If the board is reclamped and exposed again to high and then low humidity, it will shrink further. This phenomenon is called *compression shrinkage* (also *compression set*). It explains why nails and screws work loose in wood, and why the wooden handles of hammers and hatchets loosen over time, after continually absorbing and releasing moisture.

Compression shrinkage also accounts for splits developing in the ends of a board, checks in the middle of a board, and cupping (a type of warp) on the side of a board exposed to the most water (Photos 1-1 through 1-3). In each case part of the board comes in contact with water and tries to expand more than the rest of the board will allow it to. After a number of cycles of restricted

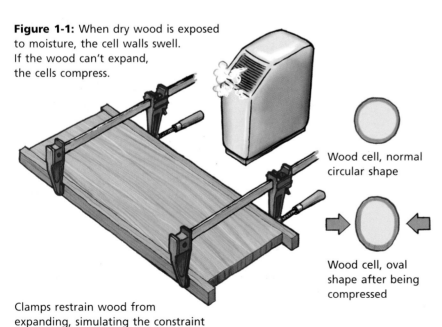

Figure 1-1: When dry wood is exposed to moisture, the cell walls swell. If the wood can't expand, the cells compress.

Wood cell, normal circular shape

Wood cell, oval shape after being compressed

Clamps restrain wood from expanding, simulating the constraint of metal fasteners, cross-grain construction, or simply differences in the moisture content between different areas of the wood.

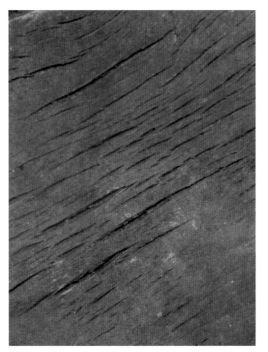

TIP

Understanding the concept of compression shrinkage leads to the counterintuitive, but effective, method for correcting warps caused by repeated exposure to water on one side. Hold the board in clamps so it can't expand; then wet the convex side (usually the bottom side of tabletops) many times, letting it dry after each. The convex side will be compressed and shrink, bringing the board flat.

Photo 1-1: When wood absorbs moisture, more is absorbed near the end than in the middle because the end grain is more porous than the other surfaces and because the end grain together with the nearby face grain presents more surface area. As a result, the end of a board is prone to expand more than the middle of a board. But the middle acts like a clamp on the end, causing compression shrinkage. After a number of cycles, the end of the board splits to relieve the stresses. You see this type of compression shrinkage on the ends of any boards exposed to repeated contact with water.

Photo 1-2: When moisture comes in contact with just part of a board, the wood cells in that part swell. But the surrounding wood acts like a clamp and prevents the swelling. This causes compression shrinkage and the resulting checks. You see this type of compression shrinkage on parts of tabletops subjected to repeated contact with water, as from a leaking potted plant.

expansion followed by full contraction, that part of the board changes shape or splits. Of course, these types of problems are less likely to occur if the finish is kept in good shape. Less water will be able to get to the wood.

Joint Failure

Joint failure also is accelerated by excessive moisture exchange—usually in the form of water vapor, not liquid water. The cells in wood are like soda straws running lengthwise in boards. The cell walls swell and shrink, changing the width and thickness of boards, but not

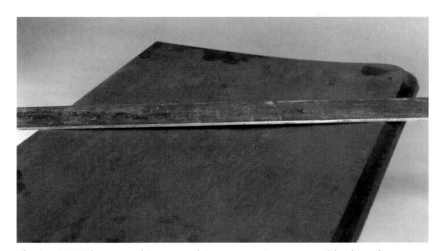

Photo 1-3: When wood is exposed to more water on one side than the other, the imbalance causes cupping. The side exposed to the most moisture has its expansion restricted by the thickness of the board, resulting in compression shrinkage. You see this type of compression shrinkage on decks and tabletops, where the cupping is almost always on the top side of the boards. This is so even though the direction of the rings would often indicate the opposite should happen, and even though the top may have been finished and the bottom not. Keep in mind that finishes on tabletops age and become worn, thus losing their resistance to water penetration. And it is the top that gets wiped with a damp or wet cloth after meals.

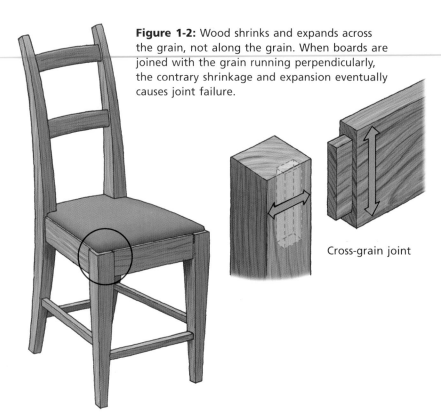

Figure 1-2: Wood shrinks and expands across the grain, not along the grain. When boards are joined with the grain running perpendicularly, the contrary shrinkage and expansion eventually causes joint failure.

Cross-grain joint

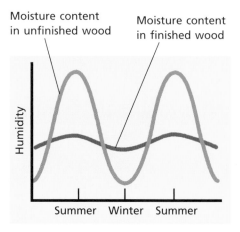

Figure 1-3: This chart shows how effectively a finish in good shape stabilizes the moisture content of wood through seasonal changes in humidity. Inhibiting moisture-vapor exchange effectively minimizes the stresses in wood that can be caused by wide swings in humidity.

Moisture content in unfinished wood

Moisture content in finished wood

Humidity

Summer   Winter   Summer

NOTE

No amount of finish or paint totally stops water-vapor exchange. For example, finished or painted wooden windows and doors shrink and let in cold air in the winter but swell tight in the spring and summer. A good finish reduces the extremes of variation that would otherwise occur during seasonal humidity changes, but it doesn't stop these variations.

the length. When boards are joined with the grain running perpendicularly, as they inevitably are in wood structures, the swelling and shrinking in different directions put great stress on the joints. As glue ages and loses its flexibility, the contrary movement in any cross-grain construction causes joint failure. This is why glued furniture comes apart in time, and why it makes no sense to claim that any glue will hold joints together forever (Figure 1-2).

The speed at which moisture exchange damages wood or breaks the glue bond in joints varies depending on the environmental conditions. Wood or furniture left outside in the weather develops splits, checks, warps, and joint failure much sooner than wood or furniture stored under cover. Wood or furniture stored under cover develops problems much faster than wood or furniture stored in a controlled environment (such as inside your house). Furniture moved from a damp climate such as New Orleans to a dry climate

such as Phoenix often develops joint problems within a year or two even if the wood is finished. The best environment for storing wood or wooden objects is one of constant temperature and humidity. This is the environment museums try to maintain.

A finish slows moisture exchange no matter what temperature or humidity conditions surround the wood. A finish makes the wood, or the object made of wood, last longer, and this is the problem with the "Do not refinish" message being conveyed by popular antique-valuation television shows, such as *Antiques Roadshow*. If many people heed this message, it will lead long-term to the destruction of a great deal of furniture (Figure 1-3).

Decoration

In addition to stabilizing wood and protecting it from dirt and grime, finishing wood is decorative. Even if you apply nothing more than a simple oil or wax

Photo 1-4: Two-part bleach was used to take the color out of the ash on the top of this coffee table. Black dye was used to ebonize the legs, also ash. Photo courtesy of the maker: Michael Puryear.

Photo 1-5: To accent the depth of the carving, glaze was applied to this ball-and-claw foot over the first coat of finish. The glaze was then wiped off the high areas to leave the recesses darker. Then the topcoats were applied.

finish, you are making a decorative choice. There are an infinite number of ways you can decorate wood, but all can be grouped into three categories: color, texture, and sheen.

Color

There are four ways you can apply color to wood. If you change the color through chemical reaction, it's called *bleaching* or *chemical staining*. If you apply a colorant directly to wood, it's called *staining*. If you apply a colorant between coats of finish, it's called *glazing*. If you add a colorant to the finish itself and apply it to the wood, it's called *toning* or *shading* if you can still see the wood through the colored finish; it's called *painting* if you can't. Each of these methods produces a different decorative effect:

■ Bleaching takes the color out of the wood, leaving it almost white (Photo 1-4). Chemical stains react with chemicals natural to the wood or added to the wood to change the color.

■ Stain applied to bare wood amplifies the figure and grain of the wood. Stain also highlights problems in the wood, such as scratches, gouges, machine marks, and uneven density.

■ Glaze, applied thinly and evenly to an entire surface, changes the tone of the wood's color and may highlight pores and recesses (Photo 1-5). Applied thickly, glaze can be manipulated with various tools to imitate wood grain, marble, or other *faux* (false) effects.

■ Shading, toning, and painting change the tone of the wood's color without highlighting pores and recesses. Shading and toning allow you to see the figure and grain of the wood. Painting totally obscures the wood's features. Shading changes the color tone only in the areas you want. Toning changes the color tone evenly over the entire surface.

A subtler, but still important, method of controlling color in wood is with the finish. Some finishes are perfectly colorless, while others add a slight

Photo 1-7: The grain in this Hawaiian koa and ebony chair was filled with paste wood filler. The finish was then leveled mirror-flat and rubbed to a satin sheen.

Photo 1-6: This bedside cabinet of mahogany, mulberry, and Port Orford cedar was finished with oil to bring out the natural color of the wood, followed by a thin coat of shellac, which gives a warm amber glow. Photo (above and on p. 1) courtesy of the maker: Charles Radtke.

thin-finish look is very popular. It's often called a *natural wood* look, and it is what you get when you finish with oil or wax. You can get the same look with film finishes, such as varnish, shellac, lacquer, or water base, as long as you keep them thin. Scandinavian teak furniture is finished with a film-building finish (usually conversion varnish) that is applied thin, not with oil, as is commonly claimed and believed.

By filling, or partially filling, the pores, you can completely alter the texture of the wood. You can fill the pores with paste wood filler or with many coats of finish that you sand or scrape back (Photo 1-7). The most refined finishes (for example, those commonly used on very expensive dining tabletops) have filled pores.

Sheen

Sheen is the amount of gloss the finish has. There are two ways to control sheen. The first is by choosing a finish that has the sheen you want built into it: gloss, satin, or flat. The second is by rubbing and polishing the cured finish to the sheen you want.

orange coloring (usually referred to as *yellowing*). Still other finishes, such as amber shellac, add considerable orange coloring (Photo 1-6).

Texture

All woods have a natural texture dependent upon the size and distribution of the pores. You can preserve this texture by keeping a finish very thin. This

CHAPTER 2

Preparing the Wood Surface

A quality finish is impossible to obtain if you don't prepare the wood properly. You probably know this already. I'm sure you've at least heard it. Most woodworkers dread the preparation steps, skip through them, and get a poor finish as a result. Others spend more time and effort than they need to scraping, sanding, patching, sanding, steaming out dents, sanding, and more sanding. Both extremes are probably due to a lack of understanding of what needs to be achieved.

The most glaring examples of how poor understanding leads to lower-quality work occur when the woodworker and the finisher are different people, and the communication between them is deficient. This situation is common in house construction, where cabinetmakers and trim carpenters often pay scant attention to the little things they can do to make the finisher's job easier and of better quality. "Oh, the finishers will take care of that," they'll tell you.

The usual cause for overpreparation is the belief that sanding to 400-grit or finer produces better results. The wood looks better when sanded to 400-grit, after all. Why shouldn't the finish on the wood also be improved?

When you have control of a project from beginning to end, you'll find that it pays to begin thinking of the finish from the start. In fact, the old wisdom holds that a good finish begins with the selection of the lumber itself.

In Brief

- Selecting the Lumber
- Sanding and Smoothing
- Sandpaper
- Dewhiskering
- Glue Splotches
- Dents, Gouges, and Holes
- Wood Putties

Photo 2-1: These four woods—pine, maple, mahogany, and oak—are each stained on the right side with the same stain. But they still look entirely different because the woods are different colors, and they have different figure and grain. Always choose a wood or woods that will give you the look you want at the end. In many cases, you can't make one wood look like another.

There are four steps in preparing wood for finishing:

1. *Selecting, cutting out, and shaping the lumber.* Many potential finish problems can be avoided by proper attention here.

2. *Sanding or smoothing the surface.* This is the most unpleasant operation for most woodworkers, so knowledge of the tools and some thought about what you're trying to achieve can go a long way toward reducing the drudgery and improving results.

3. *Dealing with glue that gets on the surface of the wood.* Glue will show up as light splotches through the stain and finish.

4. *Correcting surface imperfections in the wood,* such as dents, gouges, and splits, and filling gaps in the joints left by a less-than-successful glue-up. This step could be called "The woodworker's eternal quest for a wood putty that takes stain."

Selecting the Lumber

Woods of different species can vary greatly in grain pattern, and be impossible to make look the same short of painting them. For example, oak can't be made to look like mahogany, pine like walnut, or maple like ash. You need to think of how you want the object you are building to look when it is finished, and be sure that the species you are choosing can be made to look this way (Photo 2-1).

Even within a single species, wood varies greatly in color and figure. In some species there is a pronounced difference between sapwood and heartwood. You need to pay attention to how boards look when you're putting them next to one another in a project. The single greatest advantage you have over factories is in the attention you can devote to wood selection and arrangement.

Whether you're choosing boards at a lumberyard or from your own inventory, look through the supply and imagine how different grain and figure patterns would look if placed in various parts of your project. Be conscious of knots, splits, checks, and other defects, and determine how you will either use them to advantage or work around them. If you're using veneered plywood or plan to veneer the wood yourself, think of how the figure in the veneer can be used to best advantage. Above all, pay attention to color variations, such as those between heartwood and sapwood, unless you intend to paint the piece you're making.

For a table- or chest top, lay the boards out in different groupings, flipping and turning them end for end, until you find the best arrangement. Then mark the boards so you won't mix them up as you joint them (Figure 2-1). If you're making the top from veneered plywood, decide what part of the 4x8 sheet you can use most advantageously. On a chest-of-drawers, give the same attention to picking the drawer fronts. When people look at what you've built, they won't see the wonderful joints you've spent so much time and effort making. They'll see the design, which includes your choice of boards and their positioning, and they'll see the finish. You won't regret the time you spend selecting and arranging your wood.

Before you begin working your lumber, check to see that your tools are sharp and your machines are adjusted properly. Dull planer, jointer, or shaper knives and worn-out router bits will leave pronounced washboardlike mill marks in your wood that will require extra effort to remove. Chipped knives will leave unsightly ridges. Poorly adjusted machinery can snipe the ends of boards, and if the cutters on your machine tools are dull enough to burn or glaze the wood, your project could be ruined altogether (Photo 2-2). Always work toward the cleanest-cut, most mark-free surface possible.

Sanding and Smoothing

Of all the steps involved in making and finishing something of wood, sanding is the most universally detested. At the same time, curiously, it's the step that consumes the most wasted effort. There seems to be some mystique that the more you sand, the better the end product will be. But as an old finisher I knew used to say, "When you're in the bathtub and you're clean, get out!" Once the wood is smooth, the mill marks and other defects are gone, and the sanding scratches are fine enough so they won't show, there's no reason to continue sanding. You're finished. Your

Figure 2-1: Marking the boards you have laid out for a tabletop or chest top ensures that you won't get the boards mixed up as you joint them. Here are two ways to do it.

It will help to remember that just about the only reason you need to sand at all is **TIP** to remove the washboard-like mill marks left in the wood by planers, jointers, shapers, and to a lesser degree, routers. Before the invention of these machine tools, there was seldom any reason to sand; indeed, there was no sandpaper. Sanding is the price you pay for using machine tools to make your woodworking easier and faster.

Photo 2-2: Dull or poorly adjusted machine tools leave much more obvious marks than sharp, well-adjusted tools. Stain and finish highlight, rather than disguise, these marks.

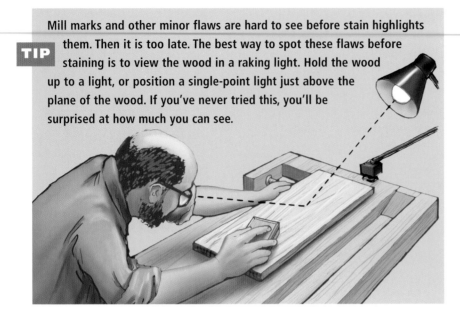

goal should be to reach this end with as little work as possible.

The tools used to smooth furniture parts before the introduction of machines were hand tools—bench planes, molding planes, and scrapers of several sorts. These tools are still available, of course, and can often be used very effectively to remove mill marks. In fact, for some woodworking projects, a finely planed surface can be regarded as a final surface. In some applications, the evidence of hand-plane work—ridges from the edge of the plane iron or hollows from a scrub plane—add character to a surface, evidence of a personal touch. And for any woodworker who can't afford or is uninterested in large power-sanding equipment, a simple tool like a scraper can be a godsend.

Whichever tools you use, you'll usually do a better job if you prepare all of the parts before assembling. You'll be able to secure each part to your workbench, where you can see what you're doing clearly in good light. And you'll be able to work in a comfortable position with any tool you choose. You'll also avoid the difficulty of trying to sand or scrape already-assembled, right-angle

joints, such as stiles and rails, or legs and rails, without putting cross-grain scratches in the perpendicular pieces (Figure 2-2). (Preparing the parts before assembly is not the same, however, as finishing the parts before assembly. Though there may be cases where doing this makes some sense, it usually doesn't.)

Turned and carved pieces shouldn't need any additional preparation. Turnings should be sanded (if at all) while still on the lathe. Most carvings should not be sanded at all, as sanding inevitably softens the crisp lines left by the carving tools.

Table and chest tops, sides, panels, rails, door and drawer fronts, and most moldings, however, will contain mill marks that should be removed. The most efficient tool you have, besides hand planes and scrapers, to accomplish this task is sandpaper.

Sanding Basics

The trick to efficient sanding is beginning with sandpaper coarse enough to cut through the flaws you want to remove with the least amount of effort—without creating larger scratches than necessary. This holds true whether you are using a machine or sanding by hand (Figures 2-3 and 2-4). In practice, the best grit to begin with is usually 80 or 100. If the problems are so severe that 80-grit doesn't remove them quickly, drop back to a grit that does, or use a scraper or plane. (See "Sandpaper" on page 12.)

On the other hand, if the problems can be removed with a finer-grit sandpaper, such as 120 or 150, you are wasting time and energy beginning with coarser sandpaper. (Many people begin sanding stripped wood with 100-grit sandpaper when no more than a light pass with 180- or 220-grit would be necessary to ensure that all the finish has been removed. The wood was sanded originally, after all.)

Beginning with the wrong grit is inefficient, but the most common error made in sanding is continuing to use sandpaper after it has become dull. Pay attention to what's happening. The cutting efficiency of sandpaper deteriorates fairly rapidly. You may cut your sanding time significantly by changing sandpaper more often.

Once the flaws have been removed, sand out scratches left by coarse sandpaper using increasingly finer sandpapers until you reach a grit that produces the size scratches you want. The scratch size makes a difference in color intensity when using a stain, particularly a pigment stain (Photo 2-3 on p.13). The best grit to end with is usually 150, 180, or 220. I usually stop at 180-grit. The goal is to produce a surface that does not show machine marks or sanding scratches after you apply a stain or finish. If you can make the scratch pattern even, you may achieve satisfactory results sanding only to 120- or 150-grit. Stationary sanding machines accomplish this best.

If you are using a vibrating or random-orbit sander, it's good practice to finish by hand-sanding in the direction of the grain, using the finest-grit sandpaper you used with the machine. This will remove the squigglies.

If you could sand just the right amount with each sandpaper grit, it would be most efficient to go through each consecutive grit—80, 100, 120, 150, 180. But most of us sand more than necessary with each grit, so we find that we actually spend less effort if we skip grits. This is especially the case when using sanding machines.

But sanding is very personal. We apply different pressures, use sandpapers to different degrees of wear, and sand

Figure 2-2:
Sanding Joined Right-Angle Parts

To sand parts that are joined at a right angle, sand the butted part first.

Then remove the crossover scratches by sanding the other part.

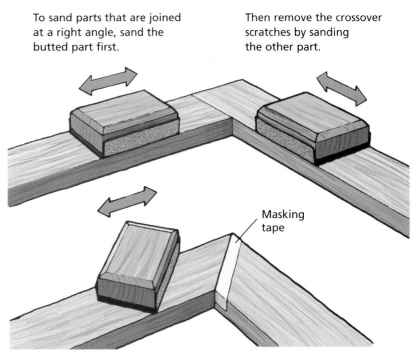

Masking tape

To sand mitered parts, place masking tape along the edge of one mitered part and sand the other part up to the tape. Then put the tape on the piece you just sanded and sand the other mitered part.

Figure 2-3: Sanding blocks are necessary for hand-sanding flat surfaces. The ideal dimensions depend upon the size of your hand. The dimensions indicated at right are about average. If your block is made from wood, glue on a 1/8- or 1/4-inch-thick piece of felt, cork (gasket cork is available from auto-parts stores), or rubber to reduce sandpaper clogging.

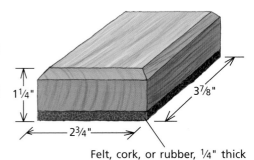

1 1/4"
3 7/8"
2 3/4"
Felt, cork, or rubber, 1/4" thick

Figure 2-4: You get the best use out of sandpaper by tearing the 9x11-inch sheet in thirds across the width, then folding each of the thirds in half (for use with a sanding block) or in thirds again (for use with no block).

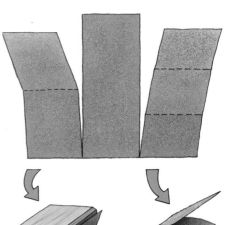
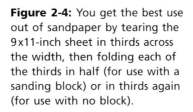

Sandpaper

If you count all the different sandpapers available for portable and stationary sanding tools, there are now enough types on the market to fill a book of explanations. Here are the three most important facts you need to know about sandpaper.

SORTING SANDPAPER BY COLOR

Sheet sandpaper, the type you tear into smaller pieces and use to sand by hand, is easiest to understand by color (photo below).

- Orange sandpaper is made with garnet abrasive and is available up to 280-grit. It is inexpensive and meant for sanding wood.
- *Tan* sandpaper is made with aluminum-oxide abrasive and is available up to 280-grit. It is more expensive than garnet, but lasts longer. It is meant for sanding wood.
- *Black (wet/dry)* sandpaper is made with silicon-carbide abrasive and a waterproof adhesive and is available up to 2500-grit. It is meant for sanding finishes using a water or oil lubricant.
- *Gray and gold (dry-lubricated)* sandpaper is made with silicon-carbide or aluminum-oxide abrasive and is available up to 600-grit. These sandpapers are coated with a dry, soaplike, zinc-stearate or similar lubricant so they don't clog easily. They are for sanding finishes, especially sealer coats and thin finishes that don't provide enough protection against wet lubricants. (To identify their dry-lubricated sandpaper, 3M uses the tradenames "Tri-M-ite" and "Fre-Cut"; Norton uses "Adalox" and "No Fil"; Klingspor uses "Stearate.")

SANDPAPER GRADING

There are two common systems for grading sandpaper: CAMI and FEPA. CAMI (Coated Abrasives Manufacturing Institute) is the traditional American grading standard. FEPA (Federation of European Producers Association) is the European standard and is identified with a "P" in front of the grit number. These standards are fairly equivalent up to about 220-grit. Then they diverge, with the "P"-grit numbers running higher than their equivalent CAMI numbers. You don't need to worry about the differences in these two numbering systems when sanding

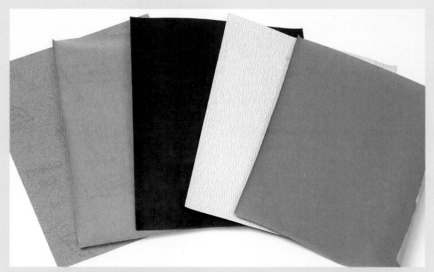

There are four types of sheet sandpaper useful to woodworkers. Each is recognizable by its color: orange (garnet) sandpaper is most useful for sanding wood; tan (aluminum-oxide) sandpaper is also most useful for sanding wood (aluminum oxide is almost always used on machine sandpapers); black (wet/dry silicon-carbide) sandpaper is most useful for sanding finishes using a lubricant; gray and gold (stearated silicon carbide or aluminum oxide) sandpapers are most useful for sanding-sealer coats or thin finishes.

Grading Sandpapers: Most available sheet sandpaper uses the CAMI or FEPA grading system. CAMI is the traditional American grading system. FEPA is the European system and is designated with a "P" in front of the number. Up to about 220-grit, there's not much difference in the grading systems. But above 220-grit, the grading diverges significantly, particularly in the black, wet/dry sandpapers used to level finishes.

APPROXIMATE EQUIVALENCIES OF THE TWO COMMON SANDPAPER GRITS

CAMI (U.S. Standard)	FEPA (European Standard)
800	P2000
600	P1200
500	P1000
400	P800
	P600
360	P500
320	
	P400
280	P360
	P320
240	P280
	P240
220	P220
180	P180
150	P150
120	P120
100	P100
80	P80

wood, but the differences become significant for the finer grits of wet/dry sandpaper used to sand finishes. For example, if you intended to use 600-grit on a finish and used P600 instead, you would actually be sanding with the equivalent of 360-grit. (See "Grading Sandpapers," below left.)

DISK BACKINGS

The most popular handheld sanding machine is the random-orbit sander, and there are two common types of sanding disks available for it: *PSA* (pressure-sensitive adhesive) and *hook-and-loop* (photo below). PSA disks are less expensive, but you can't remove a PSA disk, use another one for a while, and then put the original back on. So PSA disks are for production situations where you are likely to wear out the disk before you would want to switch to another grit. Hook-and-loop disks work like Velcro, so you can switch disks back and forth as much as you want.

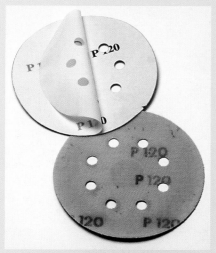

There are two types of sanding disks used with random-orbit sanders: PSA disks (top) use an adhesive backing and are less expensive; hook-and-loop disks (bottom) work like Velcro and are more expensive.

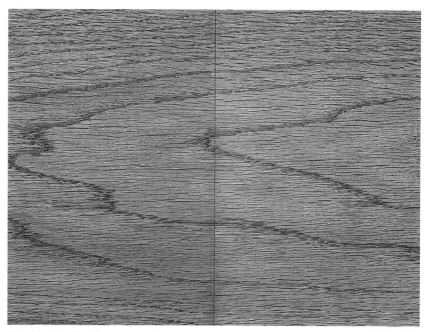

Photo 2-3: The finer the grit you sand to, the less a stain will color the wood. This is especially true with pigment stains because there is less space in each sanding scratch for the pigment to lodge. The lighter side of this board was sanded to 400-grit, the darker side to only 150-grit.

for various lengths of time. The only way to know for sure that you have sanded enough is to apply a stain and see if any machine marks or sanding scratches show. It's therefore wise to practice on some scrap wood until you get a feel for what works best for you.

If you are sanding by hand, always sand in the direction of the grain if this is possible (turnings and carvings are exceptions, of course), or you will surely produce cross-grain scratches that will show through the finish. It's also wisest to move the sandpaper with the folded edge facing the direction of travel. An open edge of sandpaper is more likely to catch under a sliver of wood and lift it, which will, at the least, tear the sandpaper and could jam painfully into your hand.

No matter how fine the final grit you use, you won't remove all of the tiny wood fibers that swell and make the wood rough to the touch if water is applied. If you intend to use a stain or

MYTH

You get better results if you sand to 400 or finer grit.

FACT

Before you apply the finish, wood sanded to 400-grit will have a higher gloss than wood sanded to, say, 180-grit, because 400-grit polishes more than 180-grit. But after you apply any film finish, you won't be able to see or feel any difference. Try it! You may save yourself countless hours of sanding in the future. See "Applying Oil and Oil/Varnish Finishes" on p. 73 to learn how to reduce sanding with these finishes.

finish that contains water, you may want to dewhisker the wood after your normal sanding steps. Wet the wood and resand it smooth after the water dries out. (See "Dewhiskering" below.)

As your final step, run the sandpaper lightly over every right-angled edge to remove sharp corners that could be dented easily, feel unfriendly to the hand, and might be too sharp to hold the finish. This is sometimes called *breaking the edges* or *softening the edges*.

Dewhiskering

Whenever water comes in contact with wood, the wood fibers swell, causing the wood to feel rough to the touch after it has dried. The swollen fibers are often referred to as raised grain. All stains and finishes that contain water raise the grain of the wood. Raised grain telegraphs through the stain or finish causing the surface to feel rough. It can also reduce the depth and clarity of the finish.

Raised grain will happen no matter how smoothly you sand the wood before you wet it. Since you can't prevent raised grain, the most effective way to deal with it is to make the fibers swell and then sand them level before applying the stain or finish. Once removed, the raised grain won't reoccur appreciably. Besides dewhiskering, this step is also called sponging, whiskering, and raising the grain.

After sanding the wood to about 150- or 180-grit, wet it with a sponge or cloth to the same extent as you will with the stain or finish. Just short of puddling is about right.

Let the wood dry overnight. Then sand off the raised grain with a sandpaper grit that smoothes the surface efficiently without sanding deeper than necessary. I try to use the same or one-number grit higher than the last grit I used. Dull (used) sandpaper is best because it is less likely to remove more than just the raised grain. If you don't have any used sandpaper lying around, you can make some quickly by rubbing two pieces of sandpaper together.

Sand lightly. You want to sand just enough to make the wood feel smooth again. If you sand any deeper, you will get below the wood fibers that have been swollen, and you'll raise the grain again when you wet the wood. (In practice, you'll always have some additional grain raising, but it will be significantly less.) Always sand in the direction of the grain.

Cleaning Off the Dust

Whenever the last step involves using sandpaper, you will leave dust on the wood. This dust must be cleaned off before applying a finish. There are four ways to remove the dust:

- Brush it off.
- Wipe it off with a tack cloth (a cloth made sticky by the application of a very thin varnishlike material that leaves a gummy residue).
- Vacuum it off.
- Blow it off with compressed air.

Brushing is usually the easiest and most convenient, but it kicks dust up in the air. If you aren't working in an efficient spray booth, you should wait until this dust settles before applying a finish.

A tack cloth is most efficient after brushing to remove the remaining dust on the surface. Your bare hand works pretty well too, as long as very little dust remains. (You shouldn't use a tack cloth with water-based stains or finishes. The varnishlike residue will hinder good flow-out and bonding. Use one of the other methods instead.)

A vacuum is the best way to remove dust if kicking dust into the air might create a problem in your finishing room. Otherwise, compressed air is the most efficient. Use compressed air outdoors or in a well-ventilated space, where the airborne dust will be evacuated.

Though it may seem logical that a better finish will be achieved if absolutely all of the dust is removed from the pores, I've never been able to see any difference.

Glue Splotches

No matter how hard you try to avoid it, it's likely that now and then you will get glue on the surface of the wood during glue-up. Either the glue will squeeze out of the joints as you clamp the pieces together, or you will transfer glue to the wood with your fingers. The glue seals the wood, preventing proper stain or finish penetration. You have to remove all the glue from the wood surface, or it will show up as un-evenness in color.

Here are some tips to help you avoid getting glue on the wood:

- Don't put excessive amounts of glue in the joints. Only when gluing up boards edge-to-edge should you apply glue liberally. In this case you will want squeeze-out to indicate not only that you've applied enough glue but that you've tightened the clamps adequately.

- Cut your mortises or dowel holes a little deeper to allow excess glue to collect at the bottom instead of being squeezed out. Also, chamfer the ends of the tenons and dowels and the mouths of the mortises and dowel holes (Figure 2-5).

- Have both a damp and a dry cloth nearby so you can remove any glue you might get on your hands as you work. Wipe your hands with the damp cloth, then quickly dry them so you won't wet the wood.

Even following these suggestions, you will still have glue seepage now and then. Here are two good ways to highlight it so you can remove it:

- Wet the entire surface with any liquid: usually water or mineral spirits. The liquid will soak deeper where there is no glue, leaving the areas that are sealed with glue appearing lighter (Photo 2-4). Water will raise the grain, so you will need to sand it smooth again.

- Add dye or an ultraviolet (UV) colorant (available from woodworking suppliers) to the glue before you glue up. Dye will show up clearly but will

Figure 2-5: Allowing for Excess Glue

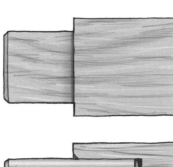
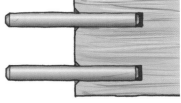

Cut mortises and dowel holes slightly deeper than necessary.

Chamfer the ends of tenons and dowels as well as the mouths of the mortises and holes.

Photo 2-4: Dried glue on the surface of the wood is often hard to see. You can highlight it by wetting the surface, usually with water or mineral spirits. (The upper part of this board hasn't been wetted.) The raw wood will absorb more liquid, leaving the glue-sealed area appearing lighter.

have to be thoroughly removed from the wood. The UV colorant will glow when exposed to UV light.

Removing Dried Glue from the Wood

Once glue on the surface of the wood has dried, there are only two ways to re-move it: Scrape and/or sand it off, or dissolve or soften the glue enough so it can be scrubbed off.

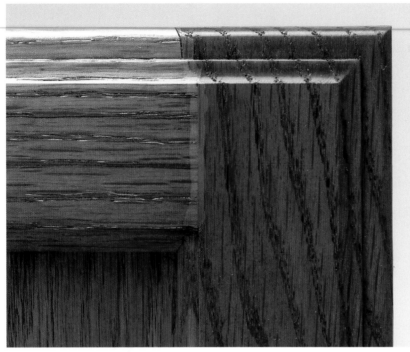

Photo 2-5: If any glue remains on the surface of the wood, it will prevent stain and finish penetration and will show up as a lighter splotch.

as water does, but they will require more scrubbing.

Whichever liquid you use, you will probably have to scrub a little to get the glue out of the pores. A toothbrush usually works, but sometimes you will need to use a soft brass-bristled brush. After cleaning all the glue out of the pores, sand the wood thoroughly to smooth any roughened grain. You can use a coarser grit of sandpaper if necessary, but be sure to finish with the same-grit sandpaper you used on the rest of the piece so the stain or finish colors evenly.

Other adhesives, such as contact cement, cyanoacrylate (Super) glue, and hot-melt glue, can be softened or dissolved using acetone. But epoxy, polyurethane, and plastic-resin (urea-formaldehyde) adhesives will have to be scraped or sanded off.

Removing Glue Splotches After Staining

Despite your best efforts, you may still have glue splotches after staining or finishing (Photo 2-5). Then what do you do? The solution is exactly the same as if you had caught the problem before applying the stain. You have to remove all the glue, and there are still only two ways to do this: mechanically, or with water or a solvent.

After removing the glue, you need to restain, and you may find that the new application of stain is lighter than the original. This could be because the stain that remained in the wood acted as a lubricant for the sandpaper, causing it to scratch less deeply. So even though you may have resanded to exactly the same grit as you used elsewhere, the stain colors a little less.

The easy solution to this problem is to apply more stain to the entire part (leg, stile, rail, even top) and resand everywhere while the stain is wet. Then

> **TIP**
>
> If you're using a water-based pigment stain over glue splotches caused by white or yellow glue, let the stain dissolve the glue. The solvent in these stains (glycol ether), together with the water, will break down the glue so it can be rubbed off with a cloth or scrubbed off with a brush. Simply leave the stain on top of the glue splotch for a minute or so, and then begin rubbing or scrubbing. Keep the area wet with stain. You should see the stain begin to "take" in less than a minute. (This trick won't work with any other type of stain.)

Mechanical Removal. Scraping and sanding are pretty straightforward in open areas. Use a chisel to get into tight areas around joints, scraping rather than carving away the wood. You have to remove the glue-contaminated surface, then resand the clean wood to the same grit you used elsewhere. This will ensure that the stain or finish colors the wood evenly.

Solvent Removal. You can soften white and yellow glues enough so that they can be scrubbed off by washing with water. Water works better if it is hot, and still better if you add vinegar to it. (Acids soften white and yellow glues, and vinegar is a mild acid.)

A number of commonly available organic solvents can also be used to soften white and yellow glues. In decreasing order of effectiveness, these include toluene (toluol), xylene (xylol), acetone, and lacquer thinner. These solvents won't raise the grain of the wood

Photo 2-6: To remove a dent, swell the wood flush by steaming. Thoroughly wet the dent with water, then touch the water with a soldering gun, the tip of a clothes iron, or a pointed metal object that has been heated over a flame.

remove the excess stain. Wet-sanding will even the scratch size over the entire part. If the part is then too light, wet-sand again using a coarser sandpaper.

If you still have a color difference that you can't live with, you may have to strip the entire piece, resand (it's not necessary to get all of the color out of the wood), and start over with staining.

Dents, Gouges, and Holes

No matter how careful you are, you will probably dent or gouge your wood somewhere in the preparation or assembly steps, and you may also have small holes, such as finish-nail holes, that you'd like to cover up.

Steaming Dents

Dents are compressed wood. They can usually be steamed flush, as long as the fibers have not been broken. Steam swells the wood fibers, filling out the depression. Dents are easiest to steam flush if the surface is horizontal. Put a few drops of water in the dent with an eye-

dropper, squeeze bottle, or syringe. Let the water soak in a little. Add some more water if needed, and then touch the water with a very hot object to turn it into steam (Photo 2-6). You can use a soldering gun, the tip of an iron, or simply a pointed metal object that has been heated over a flame (wipe off any deposited soot before touching the metal to the water).

Steaming out dents is not 100 percent effective or predictable. But it's nearly so. If you'll let the raised grain dry thoroughly before sanding it smooth, you'll usually get away with a mark so slight you can barely see it.

When the grain has been severed, however, it's often not possible to raise it flush again. Severed grain should be treated as a gouge. The wood will have to be either cut out and patched with another piece of wood or filled with a foreign material.

Wood Patches

If the gouge is large, a wood patch is best because it will be easier to disguise, and it will be fairly permanent (Photo 2-7). A wood patch is also best for filling splits in the wood and gaps left by

> For especially stubborn dents, cover the water-soaked dent with thin shirt cardboard. Then put a hot iron on top. **TIP** This traps the steam in the dent, forcing it down into the wood. CAUTION: It's often suggested that you lay a damp cloth over the dent and then put a hot iron on top of the cloth to create the steam. This method introduces steam to a much larger area than necessary and may result in a large area of moisture damage that will show through the finish.

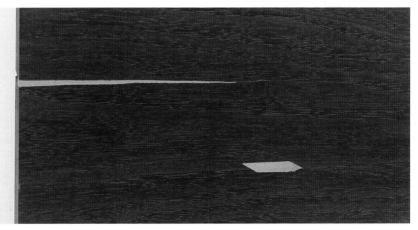

Photo 2-7: Patch large gouges and splits with wood of the same species and similar grain pattern. These patches are more permanent and easier to disguise than solid-colored wood-putty patches. (The split and gouge in this walnut board have been patched with maple for better visibility.)

TIP

> If the depression is deep, it's best to apply several coats of putty to build it level with the surface. One thick layer will take a long time to cure throughout and will probably crack from uneven curing. Let each application cure hard before applying the next.

poorly fitted joints. The patch, its grain aligned with that of the surrounding wood, will shrink and expand with the surrounding wood and be less likely to crack and come out at a later date. It will also color like the surrounding wood. Foreign materials, such as wood putty, are not flexible and are seldom permanent when used to fill large gouges, splits, or gaps. They don't color like wood, either.

The principle for patching a gouge with wood is the same as using a wood plug to disguise a screw hole. The patch will be less visible, however, if it is a diamond shape, or at least elongated, instead of round or square. Determine the shape you want and cut it out of another piece of wood that has a color and grain pattern close to the wood you are replacing. Trace the outline of the patch onto the surface you're repairing, and cut out the necessary wood with a chisel. If the damaged area is large, you can use a router together with a jig to control the cut more exactly. (Alternatively, you can cut out the shape in your damaged surface first, and then transfer the shape to the patch using tracing paper.) It's best to make the patch a little thicker than necessary so it protrudes from the surface of the wood when you glue it in. Trim it flush with a chisel, plane, or hand scraper after the glue has dried.

Patching splits in the wood or gaps in joints is straightforward. Simply cut some thin slivers out of the same type of wood, or use veneer, and insert the correct thickness into the opening. It's sometimes helpful to taper the sliver a bit so it will slide in easily and fill the gap. After the glue dries, trim the insert flush. This type of repair is usually easy to disguise and is almost as permanent as the surrounding wood.

Wood Putty

It's much less work to use wood putty to fill a gouge, split, or gap than it is to insert a wood patch. Wood putty can be quite effective for filling small defects.

Wood putty is simply a binder such as finish, glue, or gypsum (plaster of Paris), and some solid material such as sawdust, whiting (calcium carbonate), or wood flour (very fine sawdust). The binder cures and holds the solid particles together to make the patch. You may not have thought of it before, but most of the wood putties available commercially are the same as the finishes you use, only with some wood flour or whiting added to provide bulk. This explains why wood putties don't take stain well. Neither do finishes once they have cured.

There are three common types of commercial wood putties—those based on nitrocellulose lacquer, those based on water-based acrylic finish, and those based on gypsum. (See "Wood Putties" on facing page.) You can tell which kind you have by the instructions on the container:

- Nitrocellulose-based wood putties can be thinned or cleaned up with acetone or lacquer thinner (which contains acetone).
- Water-based-acrylic wood putties can be cleaned up with water until they harden.
- Gypsum-based wood putties come in powder form. You mix them with water.

Homemade wood putties are usually made from glue and sawdust. Take some sawdust, preferably from the same wood you are going to patch, and mix it with any type of glue. Epoxy, white glue, yellow glue, and cyanoacrylate all work well. Use a minimum amount of glue with a maximum amount of sawdust. If you use too much glue, the patch will be much darker than the surrounding wood.

Whichever wood putty you use, apply it the same way. Take a little putty on a putty knife (or dull screwdriver if the hole is small), and push it down into the hole or gouge. If the depression is not very deep, smooth off the top by pulling the knife across the surface. You want the putty to form a very slight mound so that when it shrinks as it dries, it won't leave a hollow. It's best not to manipulate the putty any more than necessary, because it becomes increasingly unworkable the longer it's exposed to air. Don't be sloppy. The binder in the putty is finish, glue, or gypsum, so it will bond to any part of the wood it comes in contact with, preventing stain and finish penetration and leaving a splotch.

Once the putty is thoroughly cured, sand it level with the surrounding wood. If you're working on a flat surface, back the sandpaper with a flat block.

Coloring Wood Putty

To match the surrounding area, wood putty patches can be colored in one of two ways:

■ Color the putty while it's still in paste form.

■ Color the patch after it has cured.

To color the putty itself, you can use *universal tinting colorants* (UTCs), available at most paint or art-supply stores. Universal tinting colorants will work with the three commercial types of wood putty as well as with homemade glue-and-sawdust mix. The color you want to match is the "background," or lightest, color in the wood after it is stained and finished. It may take some experimentation to arrive at that color. You can practice on some scrap wood. The trick is to judge the colors while they are still damp. At that stage, the colors will be close to what you'll get when the finish is applied. The color of the dry stain or putty will not be accurate.

It's usually easier to color the putty before applying it, but you can also get good results coloring a neutral patch. To blend a putty patch (whether colored or neutral) with the surrounding wood, you should apply your stain (if you're using one) and your first coat of finish (the sealer coat) to the entire surface. This will enable you to see the correct colors you want to imitate. (See "Sealers and Sealing Wood" on p. 116.) Once this sealer coat is dry, you need to paint in the grain and figure and adjust the background color. (For instructions on graining a solid-colored patch to look

NOTE
▼

Ready-made colored putties, usually identified by the names of the woods they are designed to imitate, are not meant to look like the wood after it's stained. These putties can often be used successfully without any additional coloring if you don't intend to stain.

Wood Putties

WORKING PROPERTIES

Nitrocellulose-based:
Dries very fast. Thins and cleans up with acetone or lacquer thinner.

Acrylic-based:
Cleans up with water until it has cured. Then cleans up with acetone, toluene, xylene, or lacquer thinner. Difficult to thin effectively. Often sold in tubes.

Gypsum-based:
Sold as a powder you mix with water. Does not redissolve once it has cured.

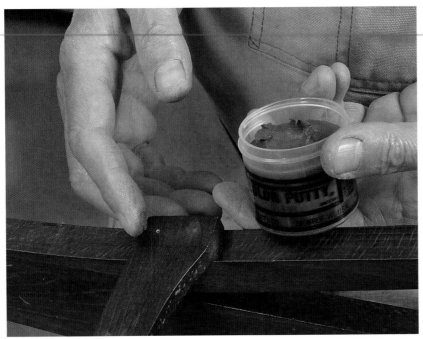

Photo 2-8: To use Color Putty to fill small holes, apply your stain (if you are using one) and sealer coat. Then take a little of a suitably colored putty on your finger and push it into the hole. Clean off the surface excess with a cloth or a clean finger and continue with the finishing steps.

Photo 2-9: To use a wax crayon to fill small holes, rub a suitably colored crayon back and forth across the hole until it is filled level. Then remove the surface excess with a cloth or a clean finger.

like wood, see Chapter 19: "Repairing Finishes.")

No matter what kind of putty you use to patch a gouge, and no matter how well you color the patch, it will probably show after a few years. The surrounding wood will darken or lighten differently from the patch, causing the patch to stand out. The only way to avoid this problem entirely is not to patch. The closest you can come to keeping the colors the same is to make the patch from wood taken from scraps of the board it is set into.

Color Putty and Wax Crayons

It's seldom worth trying to fill small nail holes or small gouges with wood putty. (The exception is on tabletops.) You'll make a mess around the hole, because the putty will stick wherever it touches the wood. It's usually easier to wait until you have applied a sealer coat or completed the finishing.

To fill small holes after applying the sealer coat, use Color Putty. Color Putty is a commercial version of traditional painters' putty: linseed oil and calcium carbonate (whiting) with pigment colors added. The product is widely available in home centers. Take a little of a suitable color on your finger and push it into the hole. Then wipe the excess off the surface, either with a cloth or with a clean finger. You can coat over oil-based Color Putty with varnish, shellac, or lacquer. You can coat over water-based Color Putty with any finish (Photo 2-8).

To fill small holes after completing the finishing, use a wax crayon. These are widely available in various wood tones. Rub back and forth over the hole using a crayon that is close in color. Then rub the excess off the surface with a cloth or your clean finger (Photo 2-9).

CHAPTER 3

Tools for Applying Finishes

There are only three tools used to apply finishes: rags, brushes, and spray guns. Included with rags are rubbing pads, included with brushes are paint pads, and included with spray guns are aerosols. This minimal toolkit is a principal difference between finishing and woodworking. In woodworking there are countless tools, with new ones coming on the market all the time. If you're a woodworker, you spend a good deal of time learning about the different tools, how they work, and the tricks they're capable of.

Finishing is very different. There aren't many tricks you can do with the three tools.

The sole purpose of using one of these finishing tools, other than to keep your hands clean, is to transfer a liquid finishing material from a container to the wood so the material is smooth and level. You could, after all, pour a finish onto the wood and spread it around with your hand. After the finish cures hard, you could sand it level, rub it with rubbing compounds, and achieve quite acceptable results. (See Photo 16-2 on p. 207.) But it is much easier if you apply the finish smooth and level enough in the first place so you don't have to sand at all, or at least very little, to smooth and level the surface.

In Brief

- **Making a Rubbing Pad**
- **Rags**
- **Brushes**
- **Using Brushes**
- **Common Brushing Problems**
- **Spray Guns and Equipment**
- **How a Typical Spray Gun Works**
- **Spray Booths**
- **Common Spraying Problems**
- **Aerosol Spray Finishing**
- **Compressors**
- **Common Spray-Gun Problems**

Making a Rubbing Pad

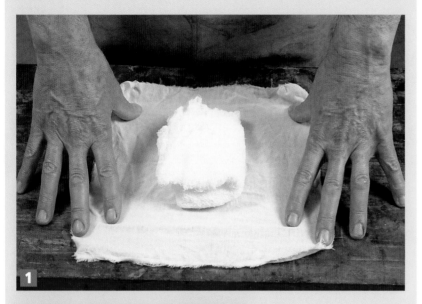

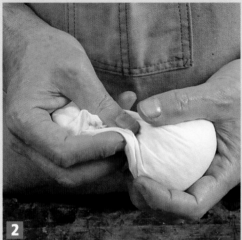

1 Spread out a small piece of well-washed, tightly woven, non-stretchable cotton cloth, such as a bedsheet, handkerchief, or cheesecloth, and put a soft cotton or wool cloth in the middle. Fold this inner cloth so it doesn't have wrinkles. If you're finishing a large surface, use a large inner cloth to make a large pad. Use a small inner cloth for small surfaces.

2 Lift the four corners of the outer cloth to a point and twist them.

3 Twist the corners tight so that the outer cloth is drawn taut around the inner cloth. The bottom of the pad should feel smooth and be free of wrinkles.

Here's what you need to know about these three basic tools.

Rags

The rags you use in finishing should be made of cotton. Polyester and other synthetic rags don't work well because they aren't absorbent enough. You can often substitute inexpensive paper towels for cloth rags if you don't have a large supply—especially when working with products that don't contain water. With products that do contain water you can substitute Scott Rags, a paper product available at many home centers and discount stores. These rags won't fall apart when they get wet.

By folding a cloth and wrapping it tightly in another cloth to create an unwrinkled bottom surface, you can make a great *rubbing pad* for French polishing and rubbing finishes. (See "French Polishing" on p. 131 and Chapter 16: "Finishing the Finish.") The pad can also be used to apply any film finish to any size surface, the only limitation being the drying rate of the finish. With a rubbing pad you can usually produce a finish with fewer marks than you can with a wadded or folded cloth. It's also less wasteful of finish than a cloth.

The inner cloth can be any type of cotton or wool: cheesecloth, T-shirt cotton, or sweater wool. The outer cloth should not be too stretchable: tightly woven cheesecloth, well-worn bedsheet, or an old handkerchief (my favorite). Wrap the outer cloth tightly around a wad of the inner cloth to make the pad, as shown in the sidebar at left. With a simple twist of the outer cloth, you can draw it tight during use to remove wrinkles from the bottom of the pad.

Photo 3-1: Left to right: chisel-edged, natural-bristle brush; chisel-edged, synthetic-bristle brush; square-edged, synthetic-bristle brush; foam brush; paint pad.

Brushes

Brushes are among the earliest finishing tools. Though the increasing popularity of spray equipment is making brushes less important, it's rare that a finisher doesn't own at least a few brushes.

Choosing a Brush

A good-quality brush is important if you expect good results. Good-quality brushes hold more finishing material (so you don't have to replenish the brush as often), and they spread the material more smoothly than poor-quality brushes. They're easier to use, and they last longer.

There are three types of brushes: natural bristle, synthetic bristle, and foam. There are also paint pads, which may be regarded as a type of brush because they are used in the same manner (Photo 3-1).

Brushes with natural and synthetic bristles are made of bristles glued together at the top with epoxy and held to a wooden or plastic handle by a metal wrapping called a *ferrule* (Figure 3-1). The quality of the handle, glue, and fer-

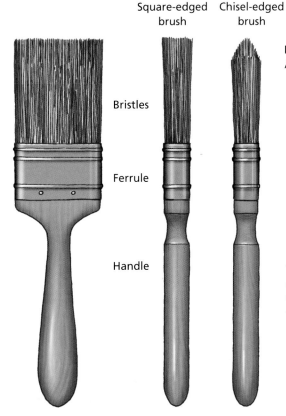

Figure 3-1:
Anatomy of brushes

Square-edged brush

Chisel-edged brush

Bristles

Ferrule

Handle

Three types of bristles (left to right): Non-tapered, tapered, and flagged

rule varies and usually corresponds to the quality of the bristles. You can almost always judge the quality of a brush by its bristles. There are three qualities to look for in good bristles:

- The bristles are arranged to form a chisel shape—that is, the brush is not cut off square.

- Each bristle is tapered—thinner at the tip than at the ferrule.
- The tips of most bristles are *flagged*—that is, split into several fibers.

Chisel-edged brushes (the center bristles are longer than the bristles on each flat side) do a much better job of applying a smooth coat of finish than squared-off brushes. Squared-off brushes are cheaper and are useful for applying stain, stripper, or bleach, where smoothness is not important.

Tapered bristles perform better than non-tapered bristles. The thickness of the bristles near the ferrule provides stiffness; the thinness at the tip provides flexibility and softness. Softer-tipped bristles usually apply a finish with less pronounced brush marks than do harder tipped bristles. (Compare the softness of various brushes by dragging the bristle ends across your hand.)

Flagging doubles or triples the number of bristle fibers that contact the surface. As a result, flagged bristles carry more finish and apply it more smoothly than bristles that are not flagged.

The difference between natural and synthetic bristles is the difference between hair and plastic. Hair softens and becomes uncontrollable in water; plastic doesn't. Therefore, natural-bristle brushes do not perform well in water-based stains or finishes; synthetic-bristle brushes do. Both types perform well with all solvent-based stains and finishes, though most painters and finishers prefer the results they get from natural bristles.

Natural-bristle brushes are made from animal hair. The best brushes for applying solvent-based finishes are made from the hair of Chinese hogs. Synthetic-bristle brushes are made from polyester or nylon, or both. Polyester adds stiffness. Nylon adds softness. For most situations, the best brush size for applying a finish is 2 to 3 inches wide with bristles 2 to 3 inches long.

There are hundreds of brush styles and qualities and no agreement as to which is best. Usually, the more you pay, the better the brush. Better means chisel-edged, flagged bristles, softer tips, with very few bristles falling out. My experience is that the finish used has a bigger impact than the brush. Some brands of finish level out better than others no matter what brush you use.

Foam brushes produce minimal brush marking, but they do tend to leave distinct ridges at the edge of each brushstroke, where more finish is deposited. Denser foam performs better than foam that is less dense. Foam brushes are inexpensive and, therefore, especially useful when you want to throw the brush away after using it rather than clean it. Foam brushes will dissolve in lacquer thinner and, depending on the type of foam used, also in alcohol. This means you shouldn't use these brushes with lacquer and you should test with shellac before using.

Paint pads have thousands of short filaments attached to a foam backing. They perform much like foam brushes, except that most are mounted in a flat plastic or metal holder, so they are useful only on flat surfaces. Because they hold a lot of finish and come in large sizes, they are popular with floor finishers. Like foam brushes, paint pads shouldn't be used with lacquer and should be tested with shellac.

Cleaning and Storing Brushes

You must clean and store your brushes properly after use, or they can become ruined for finish work. Shellac and lacquer are the only finishes that allow you

Using Brushes

Here are the essential steps for brushing a finish. Remember, your goal is to get the finish as smooth and level as you can.

1 If your brush is new, hit the ferrule against your hand to shake out any loose bristles. Even better, wash the brush before using it the first time.

2 Pour enough finish for the job at hand into another container, such as a coffee can or wide-mouthed jar. This way you won't contaminate your entire supply if you pick up some dirt with your brush.

3 Arrange your work so that you can see a light source reflected in it. This will allow you to see flaws as they are developing so you can correct them.

4 Clean the surface to be finished using compressed air or a brush if you are working in an efficient spray booth that will evacuate all the raised dust. Otherwise, use a vacuum or tack cloth. (See "Cleaning Off the Dust" on p. 14.) Just before starting to brush, wipe over the surface with your clean hand to remove any dust that might have settled.

5 Hold the brush by the metal ferrule, the handle resting between your thumb and index finger. Dip the brush into the finish so that about one-third to one-half of the bristle length is submerged in the liquid.

6 On large, flat, horizontal surfaces such as tabletops, set the loaded brush down in the middle of

a projected brushstroke and brush back and forth to stretch the finish out end to end. Brush with the grain so brush marks will be disguised. Lift the brush off each end in an airplane-taking-off motion, and set the brush back down in an airplane-landing motion. This helps avoid marks on the surface and runs down the sides. On very large surfaces you may need to set several brush loads down in several places and brush each out to get enough finish on the surface to stretch all the way to both ends. The goal is to create a thin coat of finish from end to end at least one brush-width wide. You can begin brushing at either the front or back edge of a horizontal surface. Just be sure to hold or position your container of finish so you won't be passing your finish-laden brush over, and dripping on, just-coated wood.

7 Once you have the finish stretched end to end, line up the brushstrokes and pop the bubbles by *tipping off*. Brush back over lightly from one end to the other, holding the brush almost vertical.

8 With each new brushload of finish, begin brushing a few inches ahead of your last stroke and work back into it and then away from it. Move fast enough to keep a *wet edge*—that is, the previous stroke is still wet enough so you don't put severe ridges in it. Clearly, you have to move faster with shellac and water base than with varnish.

9 On vertical surfaces, reduce runs and sags by reducing the amount of

finish in your brush. Do this by tapping or pressing the brush on the side or edge of the container. If possible, try to stretch out your brushstrokes from end to end, working with the grain, just as on horizontal surfaces. Look for runs and sags in a reflected light and brush them out as they develop.

10 On turnings, carvings, moldings, and other irregular surfaces, reduce the amount of finish in your brush so you don't cause runs or puddles in recesses. It's often easier to brush around a turning than along its length.

Brushing is very intuitive. Much too much is made of how to hold and move a brush. (I've probably made too much of it here.) If you do make a mistake, you can correct it very easily. (See "Common Brushing Problems" on p. 26.) The critical instruction is to work in a reflected light source so you can see what is happening.

Common Brushing Problems

Brushing is very intuitive, but problems can occur nevertheless. Here are the most common. For problems specific to the various finishes, refer to the chapters on these finishes.

	PROBLEM	CAUSE	SOLUTION
	Brush Marks	The brush is of poor quality.	Use a better-quality brush. (See "Choosing a Brush" on p. 23.)
		The finish material is too thick.	Thin the finish with the appropriate thinner. The thinner the finish, the less the brush marking—but the thinner the build.
		Either of the above causes.	Sand the surface level and rub to a desired sheen. (See Chapter 16: "Finishing the Finish.")
	Bubbles	Bubbles are the result of turbulence caused by the brush gliding over the surface. The finish is drying so fast that the bubbles don't have time to pop out on their own.	Work in a cooler room. The bubbles will have more time to pop out.
			"Tip off" (brush back over lightly, holding the brush almost vertical) to pop the bubbles before the finish skins over.
			Add the appropriate thinner or retarder to slow the drying.
	Dust Nibs	The air, work surface, finish, or your brush is dirty.	Allow the dust to settle, and wipe over the surface with a tack cloth or your hand just before beginning to brush. Strain the finish. Wash the brush in the appropriate thinner.
		Finish is drying too slowly.	Use a faster-drying finish.
		Either of the above causes.	Sand the surface level and rub to a desired sheen. (See Chapter 16: "Finishing the Finish.")
	Runs and Sags	You applied the finish too thickly.	Brush out the runs and sags before they harden. If necessary, remove some of the excess finish from your brush by brushing onto another surface or dragging the brush over the edge of a jar. Then brush the finish out thinner.
			Sand the surface level and rub to a desired sheen. (See Chapter 16: "Finishing the Finish.")
	Dragging	You're allowing the previous stroke to dry too much before connecting it with the next stroke. You're not keeping a "wet edge."	Work faster or in cooler temperatures if it is hot.
			Add thinner or a retarder.
			Use a slower-drying finish.

to fully reclaim a brush after the finish has cured. Soak the shellac brush in alcohol and the lacquer brush in lacquer thinner.

If you are planning to use the brush with the same finish later that day or the next day, you can store the brush in the appropriate thinner: mineral spirits for oil or varnish; alcohol for shellac; lacquer thinner for lacquer; and water for water base. Or you can wrap the brush in plastic wrap to shield it from air. If you store the brush in thinner, run a dowel rod through the hole in the handle (drill a hole closer to the ferrule if necessary) and suspend the bristles in the thinner so they don't rest on the bottom of the container (Photo 3-2). You can reduce thinner evaporation from the container by covering it with a plastic coffee-can lid. Cut a hole in the middle of the lid for the brush handle to pass through.

Cleaning any finish from a brush always includes the same last steps: Wash with soap and water and return the brush to its original holder, or wrap the bristles in paper so they dry straight and stay clean (Photo 3-3). The steps before washing are specific to the finish you are cleaning.

- Clean shellac in half-and-half household ammonia and water (the most efficient method), or by rinsing several times in denatured alcohol.
- Clean lacquer by rinsing several times in lacquer thinner.
- Clean oil and varnish by rinsing several times in mineral spirits, then rinse in lacquer thinner to remove the oily mineral spirits.
- Clean water base with soap and water.

If you use the brush solely for solvent finishes, you can rub a few drops of light oil, such as mineral oil, onto the bristles. The oil will keep them soft.

Don't apply oil to any brush you may use with water base.

Keeping brushes in good shape is more of a mental than a physical challenge; it takes only 5 or 10 minutes. Make cleaning your brush a part of your routine. You will feel so much better the next time you use the brush if it is soft and springy instead of stiff and difficult to work. If you keep a brush clean and the bristles straight, it will provide good service for years. Only when the flagged bristles wear away will you have to buy a new brush. Use worn brushes for less exacting tasks, such as applying stripper.

Spray Guns and Equipment

A spray gun turns a stain, paint, finish, or other liquid material into a fine mist—a process called *atomization*—and propels the mist onto a work surface. (See "How a Typical Spray Gun Works" on p. 28.) All spray guns will spray all but the thickest of liquids. Compared to rags and brushes, spray guns transfer liquids faster and leave a more level surface, but they cost a lot more and create more waste because of bounce-back and overspray (the spray that misses the target). This waste should be exhausted for health reasons and to keep it from settling back onto the work, and the equipment to accomplish this adds to the expense. (See "Spray Booths" on p. 30.)

You can achieve many of the benefits of spray guns without the expense by substituting aerosols. Aerosols are ideal for smaller projects and touch-ups. Many finishes, toners, and other useful products are packaged as aerosols. (See "Aerosol Spray Finishing" on p. 33.)

Photo 3-2: You can store a brush temporarily without cleaning it by hanging it in a container of the appropriate thinner or by wrapping it in plastic wrap.

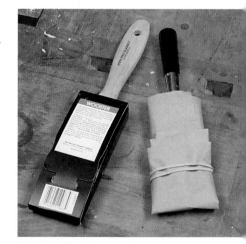

Photo 3-3: After you have cleaned your brush, wrap it in its original holder or in absorbent paper to keep the bristles straight and clean.

How a Typical Spray Gun Works

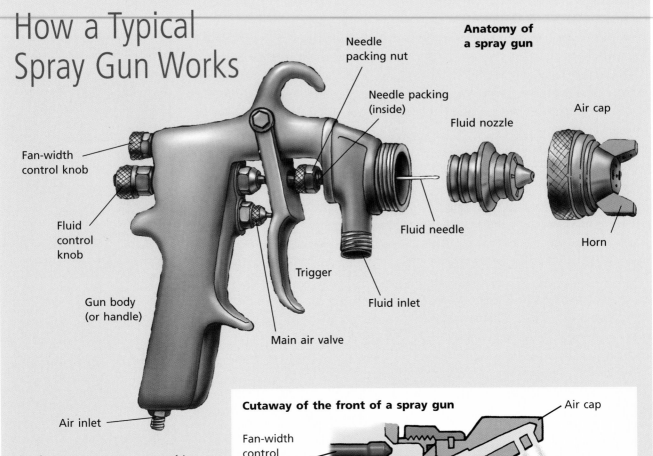

Anatomy of a spray gun

Needle packing nut

Needle packing (inside)

Fluid nozzle

Air cap

Fan-width control knob

Fluid control knob

Gun body (or handle)

Fluid needle

Horn

Air inlet

Trigger

Fluid inlet

Main air valve

Cutaway of the front of a spray gun

Air cap

Fan-width control needle

Fluid needle

Fluid nozzle

Fluid inlet

Air from a compressor or turbine enters the gun through the air inlet at the bottom of the handle. When you pull the trigger just a little, the air valve inside the handle is opened and air is allowed to flow through the gun and exit the small holes in the center and the horns of the air cap (shown as blue). (On "bleeder" turbine HVLP guns, air flows constantly, even without pulling the trigger.)

Pulling the trigger farther retracts the fluid needle, which allows liquid material to stream out the fluid nozzle (shown as yellow). The result is an atomized fluid stream in a shape varying from circular to oval in a plane perpendicular to the plane of the two horns.

Most spray guns have two control knobs on the backside of the gun. The upper knob adjusts the amount of air to the air cap and thus the width of the fan. The lower knob adjusts the amount of liquid exiting through the fluid nozzle. By screwing in the upper knob, you relax the fan width until it becomes circular. By screwing in the lower knob, you limit how far back you can pull the trigger, which reduces the amount of liquid exiting the gun.

Some turbine HVLP guns have only one control knob—the one that controls the trigger. The fan width adjusts automatically with trigger depression, and a more or less oval spray pattern can be created by adjusting the air cap or a template underneath the air cap.

Categories of Spray Guns

There are five categories of spray guns:

- Conventional
- Turbine HVLP (high-volume, low-pressure)
- Compressor HVLP
- Airless (hydraulic)
- Air-assisted airless

Conventional spray guns are the traditional high-pressure (commonly 35 to 45 psi) guns, powered by compressed air and in common use for a century. (See "Compressors" on p. 35.) The liquid material is supplied to the spray gun in one of three configurations as shown in Figure 3-2: siphon-feed, gravity-feed, or remote pressure-feed. Conventional spray guns have now been almost entirely replaced by HVLP spray guns.

Turbine HVLP is a technology that was introduced in the 1950s, but it didn't receive wide acceptance until the 1980s when tougher environmental laws made it make sense. Turbine HVLP uses a high volume of air supplied by a turbine blower instead of compressed air to atomize liquids. Reducing the pressure creates a "soft" spray with much less bounce-back and waste than occurs with high-pressure, conventional spray guns. Turbines with more fans, or *stages*, supply higher volume and pressure—up to around 135 cfm and 10 psi with a five-stage turbine—than turbines with fewer stages. (A three-stage turbine, 110 cfm and 6 psi, is adequate for clear finishes and is the most popular size.) The liquid material is supplied to the spray gun from a separate (remote) pressurized pot or from a pressurized cup underneath the gun (Figure 3-2).

Compressor HVLP is a technology introduced in the late 1980s in which compressed air is converted in the body

Figure 3-2:
Spray-Gun Configurations

Siphon-feed (or suction-feed) cup guns have a quart-size or smaller cup attached underneath the gun. Compressed air exiting the air cap creates an area of low pressure just in front of the fluid-nozzle tip. This draws the liquid material in the cup up the fluid tube and out the nozzle where it is atomized.
- CONVENTIONAL

Gravity-feed cup guns have the liquid material entering from a quart-size or smaller cup mounted on top of the gun. Gravity alone causes the material to flow through the fluid nozzle where it is atomized. Gravity-feed cup guns are replacing pressure-feed cup guns in popularity because of their better balance and efficiency (no air has to be diverted to pressurize a cup).
- CONVENTIONAL
- COMPRESSOR-HVLP

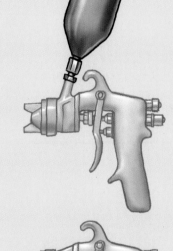

Remote pressure-feed guns have the liquid material entering at the fluid inlet through a hose attached to a separate pressurized pot. This system is the best if you do a lot of spraying.
- CONVENTIONAL
- COMPRESSOR-HVLP
- TURBINE-HVLP

Pressurized siphon-feed cup guns are specific to turbine and compressor HVLP systems. Because HVLP systems do not generate enough air pressure to create a low-pressure area to draw the liquid material up from the cup, the cup has to be pressurized. This is done by diverting some of the air from the turbine or compressor to the cup through a plastic tube from the gun.
- COMPRESSOR-HVLP
- TURBINE-HVLP

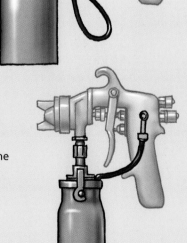

Spray Booths

Professionally equipped shops and factories use commercially made spray booths to exhaust overspray. Essentially, a spray booth is a box open at one end with an exhaust fan at the other and filters in between to catch overspray. Commercial spray booths have the following features:

- Steel construction for fire safety.
- Filters to catch and hold overspray before it gets to the fan.
- A chamber for collecting the exhausted air, making it possible for air to be drawn uniformly through a much larger area of filters than the simple diameter of the fan.
- A large enough fan to create an airflow of at least 100 cubic feet per minute, which is enough to pull overspray away from the object being sprayed.
- An "explosion proof" fan and motor to eliminate sparks that might cause built-up finish or solvent vapors to burn or explode.
- Side walls and a ceiling to create a work chamber or "tunnel" for directing the flow of air around the work object and through the filters.
- Ceiling and sometimes side lighting so the operator can see a reflection off the surface being sprayed.

Commercial spray booths are an essential tool for production shops, but these booths are too large and too expensive ($3,000 to $5,000 minimum) and require too much replacement air (heated or air-conditioned air to replace the air being exhausted) for almost all home shops. If you are using a spray gun at home on an infrequent basis and have to work inside to avoid cold, wind, bugs, falling leaves, and so on, you should consider building your own modified spray booth.

MAKING YOUR OWN

With a note of caution that doing any type of spraying in your house, with or without a spray booth, could affect your homeowner's insurance, here's how to build a safe, inexpensive spray booth that will be adequate in the volume of air and overspray exhausted for use with an HVLP spray system. Also, it will take up very little space. (See the figure on the facing page.)

The spray booth consists of a fan with a separate motor connected by a fan belt, one or more furnace filters, and plastic curtains. This design directs the flow of air around the work object and past the fan so that solvent fumes don't come in contact with the motor, and overspray doesn't build up on the fan blades.

Your choice of fan is determined by the amount of air, measured in cubic feet per minute (cfm), that you want to move and is a trade-off between better exhaust of overspray and reducing the need to supply replacement air. In other words, the more air your fan moves, the better the exhaust but the more windows you'll need to open at the opposite end of your shop and the faster the heat (or air-conditioning) in your shop will be lost. Generally, the larger the fan and the more sharply angled its blades, the more air it is capable of moving.

To mount the fan, construct a box from plywood or particleboard approximately 1 foot deep with both ends open. The dimensions of the four sides should be adequate to hold the fan at one end and furnace filters, which should be efficient enough to trap all overspray particles before they reach the fan, at the other.

Cut a slot on the top of the box large enough for the fan belt to pass through and mount a motor on the outside of the box adequate in horsepower to drive the fan. A $1/4$- to $1/2$-horsepower motor (1,725 rpm) would be typical. If you are going to spray solvent-based finishes, an explosion-proof motor is best. A standard TEFC (totally enclosed, fan-cooled) motor

of the gun to high volume and low pressure. Just as with turbine HVLP, compressor HVLP produces a soft spray with very little bounce-back and waste. In technical terms, HVLP spray guns have a higher *transfer efficiency* than conventional spray guns. Due to its soft-spray velocity, about two-thirds of the liquid material is deposited on the sprayed surface; conventional spray guns deposit only about one-third.

will do if you are going to spray only water-based finishes. Either way, the motor needs to be enclosed in a box to keep overspray from accumulating on it.

Place the box with the enclosed fan in a window, possibly resting on a stand just in front of the window, and seal the spaces between the outside of the box and the window opening. Then hang plastic curtains from the ceiling on either side of the fan running out 6 to 8 feet from the window wall. If the window is near a side wall, you could use it instead of a curtain as one side of your booth. You want the curtains to be wide enough apart so you can stand inside, or just outside, the tunnel when spraying.

The best curtains are heavy, fire-resistant "industrial curtain partitions" with supplied ceiling tracks. These are available from auto-body supply stores, Grainger's, or Goff's Curtain Walls. But you can use any type of plastic sheeting, noting that if the plastic is very light, it might be sucked in a little by the exhaust fan.

Mount the curtains to tracks on the ceiling so they can be pushed back when you aren't spraying and pulled out when you are. This way, you lose almost no space in your workshop.

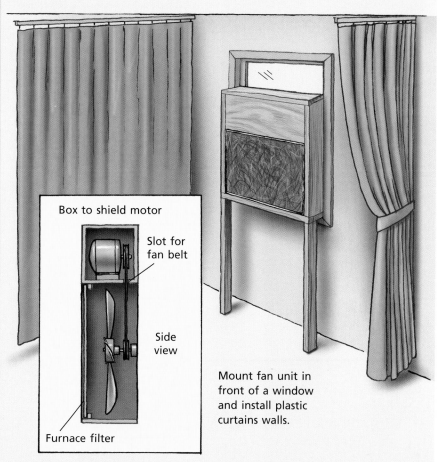

Box to shield motor

Slot for fan belt

Side view

Furnace filter

Mount fan unit in front of a window and install plastic curtains walls.

Though it won't be nearly as efficient in moving air as a commercial spray booth, this homemade spray booth is inexpensive, takes up very little room, and is safe as long as you keep all the parts clean.

For lighting, recess one or two 4-foot fluorescent fixtures between the joists in the ceiling as close as possible to the window, and shield the lights from contact with overspray by inserting glass plates between the lights and the ceiling. (The plates can rest on lips of the ceiling drywall.) For the best color balance, use full-spectrum bulbs.

To avoid a fire hazard with your spray booth, it's essential that you keep it clean. Sweep the floor after each job and clean or replace the filter often. If finish cakes on the curtains or fan box, clean or replace them.

By law in California, and widely accepted elsewhere, HVLP is defined as 10 psi of atomizing air or less at the gun's nozzle. Many finishers operate at higher psi, however, to improve atomization of thicker liquids. Liquid mate-rial is supplied to compressor HVLP guns from a gravity-feed cup above the gun, a separate pressurized pot, or a pressurized siphon-feed cup attached underneath the gun (Figure 3-2 on p. 29.)

Common Spraying Problems

Operating a spray gun is no more difficult than operating a router. But just as with using a router, problems can occur. Here are the common ones. For problems specific to the various finishes, refer to the chapters on these finishes.

	PROBLEM	CAUSE	SOLUTION
	Orange Peel	Inadequate air pressure.	Increase the air pressure. (This can be done only if you are using compressed air.)
		The finish is too thick.	Thin the finish with the appropriate thinner. You'll have to use this solution with turbine HVLP spray guns.
		You're holding the gun too far from the surface or moving it too fast, so you're not applying a fully wet coat.	Hold the gun closer or move it more slowly. Watch what is happening in a reflected light.
		You're holding the gun too close to the surface or moving it too slowly, causing the finish to ripple.	Hold the gun farther away or move it faster. Watch what is happening in a reflected light.
	Dry Spray	The finish is drying too fast.	Add the appropriate retarder to slow the drying.
		You're holding the gun too far from the surface or moving it too rapidly.	Hold the gun closer, move it slower, or add retarder.
		The overspray is settling back on your work after the finish has dried.	Add the appropriate retarder to slow the drying. Improve your exhaust system.
	Runs and Sags	You applied the finish too heavily.	Apply thinner coats.
		You're holding the gun too close to the surface or moving it too slowly.	Watch what is happening in a reflected light and make the necessary adjustments.
		You're not releasing the trigger at the end of each stroke when the stroke doesn't go beyond the object.	Release the trigger while flicking your wrist.
		You're not holding the gun perpendicular to the surface, so there is more buildup at the short end of the spray pattern.	Always spray perpendicular to the surface.

Some manufacturers provide a spray gun they call LVLP (low volume, low pressure). These guns can be used with smaller compressors, such as portable "pancake" compressors. LVLP is equivalent to HVLP, except that it puts out less liquid material.

Airless (hydraulic-atomization) spray guns are powered by a pump that pushes liquid material through a very small spray-nozzle orifice at up to 3000 psi. A very large volume of liquid material can be sprayed with airless systems, so they're often used by housepainters. The atomization is not as fine as with the other systems, however, so there is more pronounced orange peel. (See "Common Spraying Problems" on the facing page.) As a result, airless spray guns aren't often used to spray clear finishes onto fine woodwork.

Aerosol Spray Finishing

Most popular finishes are packaged as aerosols in sheens ranging from gloss to flat. These include polyurethane, shellac, lacquer, water base, and pre-catalyzed lacquer. Other useful products, such as sanding sealer, toner, and "blush" (white water-ring) remover, also are packaged as aerosols.

Aerosol finishes are the same as those you spray through spray guns except they are thinned much more to fit easily through the small orifice in the nozzle. You normally would have to spray at least twice the number of coats to get the same film build you can achieve with a spray gun. Application methods using aerosols are the same as those using spray guns. (See "Using Spray Guns" on p. 38.) For finishing large surfaces, you can attach an accessory trigger handle to the can to ease finger strain.

Whatever liquid an aerosol might contain, the cans themselves are pretty much the same, consisting of a nozzle (made up of a valve and actuator), a dip tube,

and a gas to propel the liquid through the dip tube and nozzle.

Before 1978, chlorofluorocarbons (CFCs) were used to propel the liquid, but these have been mostly eliminated because of their negative effect on the upper ozone layer. Most of today's aerosols contain liquefied petroleum gases (LPGs) such as propane, isobutane, and n-butane.

The nozzle on most aerosols has a simple cylindrical actuator that you push down to produce a cone-shaped spray pattern. Some have a small rectangular disk on the front of the actuator and can be adjusted to spray a vertical or horizontal fan pattern like a spray gun. Adjust the direction by rotating the disk using a pliers. These aerosols lay down a more even finish than the cylinder type.

With both types, you need to shake the can before using. If the can contains any solid material, such as pigment or flatting agent, you'll hear a ball knocking against the sides of the can as you shake. This ball helps put the solids into

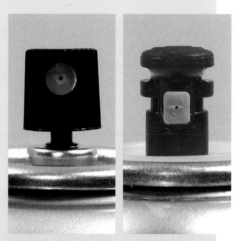

There are two types of aerosols. The more common type (left) sprays a cone-shaped pattern when you depress the actuator. The other type sprays a fan pattern whose direction is controlled by rotating the small disk on the front of the actuator with a pliers. This aerosol usually atomizes better and sprays a more even coat.

suspension. If you don't hear this ball knocking around, continue shaking until you do, and then shake for another 10 to 20 seconds.

When finished spraying, clean the dip tube and valve so the finish doesn't dry and clog them. Do this by turning the can upside down and spraying until no more liquid comes out.

Air-assisted airless and airmix systems are powered by both a medium-pressure (800 to 1000 psi) pump and compressed air. Approximately 80 percent of the spray pattern is achieved through hydraulic atomization, and 20 percent through the impingement of low-pressure air. These expensive systems are commonly used in factories and large shops to speed production with no loss in spray quality.

Choosing a Spray Gun

Unless you operate a professional shop doing a lot of spraying, you should probably be using a spray gun from among the first three categories. These spray systems are considerably less expensive, and the only quality you sacrifice is volume of liquid material that can be sprayed. This isn't very important unless you do a large volume of work, so I will concentrate my discussion on these systems.

Photo 3-4: To optimize a compressor-powered spray gun, open the control knobs for maximum fan width and trigger depression. Beginning with a low air pressure of about 10 psi, spray short horizontal bursts onto brown paper or cardboard, increasing the air pressure in 5-psi increments between bursts. When the runs on the oval-shaped spray pattern are approximately equal across the width, the gun is optimized for the viscosity of finish and the fluid nozzle, needle, and air cap installed.

If you are buying a new gun, choose between a turbine HVLP and a compressor HVLP. There is no reason to use a conventional gun unless you already have one and don't want to make a new investment. If you already own a compressor of adequate size, or you have need for a compressor to run other tools, choose a compressor HVLP. (See "Compressors" on facing page.) If you don't own or need a compressor, choose a turbine HVLP. Both produce excellent results. As with most tools, the more you pay, the more you can expect in terms of durability and performance. The quality of adjustment controls, for instance, can vary considerably.

Optimizing a Spray Gun

To achieve the best atomization possible from your spray gun, you need to adjust it for the viscosity of the liquid you are spraying and for the size of the fluid needle, fluid nozzle, and air cap in the gun. For example, a thick liquid requires more air pressure to achieve optimal atomization than does a thin liquid, and a large fluid needle and nozzle require more air pressure than a small one. (The larger or more viscous the stream of liquid, the more air pressure is required to atomize it.) Follow these procedures to adjust each type of spray gun.

Siphon and Gravity-Feed Guns. To adjust all compressed-air siphon or gravity-feed guns, turn both control knobs counterclockwise until the spray pattern is as wide as it will get; on most guns that will be until the threads begin to show. (Be careful not to totally unscrew the fluid-control knob.) This will give you the widest possible fan and the deepest possible trigger depression. Then turn the air pressure at the regulator down to about 10 psi. If you have a portable compressor (for example, a "pancake" compressor or one on wheels), there will be a psi regulator mounted on the compressor. If you have a large stationary compressor, you may have to purchase a separate regulator and mount it at your workstation (see drawing below).

Spray a short burst of finish horizontally onto brown paper or cardboard (the spray pattern will show up better than on white paper). Then open the air regulator by 5 psi and spray another burst. Continue opening in 5-psi increments until the runs are uniform across the oval spray pattern. At this point, the spray gun is adjusted to its optimum performance. Adding more air pressure simply creates more bounce-back and waste. It doesn't improve the atomization. (See Photo 3-4 on facing page.)

Compressors

Air compressor

Angled to drain condensation back into compressor

This is a typical setup for a stationary compressor and one workstation. The piping should be ³/₄-inch or 1-inch black or galvanized pipe, not PVA.

Regulator

Quick disconnect

Flexible hose connection

Automatic "spurt" drain

Antivibration pads

Drain valve

Oil, water, and particle filters

For additional workstations, simply add on to the angled pipe running along the ceiling.

There are three types of compressors: diaphragm (an example is a bicycle pump); rotary-screw (it provides a constant flow of air without a storage tank); and reciprocating piston. This last is the compressor that is used in almost all home and small shop environments.

Reciprocating-piston compressors consist of a motor, which is usually electric; a pump, which resembles an automobile engine with pistons and rods; and a storage tank. The larger the storage tank, the more air can be stored and the longer the rest periods for the motor and pump when the compressor is in use. Single-stage compressors compress air just once, typically to 125 psi (pounds per square inch). Two-stage compressors compress air twice: once to 125 psi and a second time to 175 psi.

Uniform pressure is created by pumping a large volume of air into a storage tank. Volume is measured in cubic feet, and the volume of air exiting the storage tank is measured in cubic feet per minute, or cfm. Volume and pressure work together, so every air tool, including a spray gun, has a volume and pressure requirement to work at optimal efficiency. A compressor-HVLP spray gun, for example, might require 15 cfm at 30 psi, while a brad nailer might need 2.4 cfm at 90 psi.

To choose a compressor to meet your needs, determine what tools you might use that require compressed air. Choose a compressor that supplies enough volume of air to fill the needs of your most air-hungry tool. If you are working with others who might be using an air-powered tool at the same time you are, get a compressor that provides 30 percent more air for each person. You can get by with less than double the amount of air per person because all tools won't be operating all the time.

Many home and small-professional shops use portable compressors (on wheels). These compressors come with a hose that has a quick disconnect at the operating end to attach to your spray gun. If you have a stationary compressor, you will need to run piping to one or more workstations. See the figure above for a typical setup.

Common Spray-Gun Problems

Here are the six most common things that can go wrong with a spray gun, together with explanations, causes, and solutions. The causes and solutions for each problem are arranged roughly in order of their frequency.

PROBLEM	EXPLANATION	CAUSE	SOLUTION
Fluid is leaking or dripping from the fluid-nozzle tip at the front of the spray gun.	The fluid needle in not seated well in the tip of the fluid nozzle.	The nut that holds the packing in place (located right in front of the trigger) is too tight. It presses the packing against the needle.	Loosen the nut a little.
		The packing has dried and hardened to the point that it doesn't allow the needle to close tightly.	Lubricate the packing with a non-silicone oil.
		There's dirt, paint, or finish in the tip of the fluid nozzle, preventing the needle from closing fully.	Clean the fluid nozzle.
		The fluid-nozzle tip or needle is worn or damaged, allowing liquid to seep through.	Replace the worn or damaged parts.
		The spring that pushes the fluid needle closed when the trigger is released is not working properly.	Replace the spring.
		The fluid needle is too small or too large for the fluid nozzle, causing them not to seat well.	Change the parts so they do seat well.
Fluid is leaking from the packing nut in front of the trigger.	The packing isn't sealing around the needle.	The packing nut isn't screwed on tightly enough to press the packing against the needle.	Tighten the packing nut.
		The packing is worn or dry.	Try lubricating the packing with a non-silicone oil. If this doesn't stop the leaking, replace the packing.
The paint or finish bubbles in the cup.	Air is backing up into the cup.	The fluid nozzle is too loose.	Tighten the fluid nozzle.

Guns with pressure pots. Spray guns with separate pressure pots require an extra step because the pressure of the liquid material to the gun has to be adjusted in addition to the air pressure at the gun. To set the pot pressure, begin by opening the control knobs on the spray gun all the way. Then shut off all the air to the gun and, with the pressure pot under pressure, pull the trigger all the way. Set the pressure on the pressure pot so the liquid stream shoots out of the gun approximately 8 to 10 inches before it begins to arc downwards into a container. (Usually, this is around 10 psi.) Then turn on the air to the gun and adjust it as just described. Increase the pot pressure if the spray pattern looks too dry or if coverage is too thin, and readjust the gun.

PROBLEM	EXPLANATION	CAUSE	SOLUTION
The spray is pulsating or fluttering.	Not enough air is being allowed into the cup or pot to replace the liquid material being sprayed.	The air inlet hole is blocked.	Clean the air inlet hole.
	Air is getting into the fluid passageway and mixing with the liquid material as it is sprayed.	The cup is being tipped too far.	Hold the cup more upright or add more liquid material.
		The liquid-material level in the cup or pressure pot is too low.	Add more liquid material.
		The fluid-needle packing is too loose or too dry.	Tighten the packing nut or lubricate the packing with a non-silicone oil.
		There is an obstruction in the fluid passageway.	Try backflushing with solvent or do a thorough cleaning. To backflush, press your finger over the center hole of the air cap and trigger a short burst.
		The fluid nozzle is loose or damaged.	Tighten or replace the fluid nozzle.
The spray pattern is heavy at the top, bottom, right, or left.	The air or the liquid material is being discharged unevenly from the spray gun.	There is an obstruction in the air cap or the fluid nozzle. To determine which, rotate the air cap one-half turn. If the disrupted pattern stays the same, the problem is in the fluid nozzle. If the pattern reverses, the problem is in the air cap.	Clean the part that is causing the problem.
		The tip of the fluid nozzle is damaged.	Replace the fluid nozzle.
The spray pattern is heavy at the ends or in the center.	The amount of air pressure is not appropriate for the viscosity of the liquid material.	There is so much air pressure that it splits the spray pattern.	Reduce the air pressure.
		There is too little air pressure to spread the spray pattern to its greatest width.	Increase the air pressure.

Turbine guns. Because you don't have any control of air pressure with turbine guns, you can't adjust them in the same way as compressed-air guns. You have to adjust the viscosity of the liquid material instead. If the spray pattern you get when you spray short bursts onto brown paper or cardboard with the control knobs wide open is not a full oval shape, the liquid is too thick and you should thin it until the spray pattern is correct.

If you want to reduce the fan width on any of these guns to spray a narrow surface, screw in the upper fan-width control knob. If this causes you to lose control because you're depositing too much material, reduce the amount by screwing in the lower fluid-control knob so you don't pull the trigger back so far.

TIP Instead of adjusting your spray gun to the liquid you're spraying, you can thin the liquid until the atomization no longer improves. The downside of doing this, of course, is that each coat you apply will be lower in solids, so it will take more coats to achieve any given film build.

Doing this doesn't affect the optimization of the spray gun. If the optimized spray gun doesn't spray as much material as you would like, you can increase the amount by installing a larger-diameter fluid nozzle with its equivalent needle. This will require that you reoptimize the gun because there is now more liquid material to be atomized.

Using Spray Guns

Using a spray gun is not difficult, but you should practice a little on cardboard or scrap plywood before tackling an important project. Here are the basic principles. (See "Common Spraying Problems" on p. 32, and "Common Spray-Gun Problems" on p. 36.)

- Arrange a light source so you can see what's happening in a reflection on the surface you're spraying. Without

this reflection, you might as well be spraying blindfolded. Your goal is to apply a fully wet coat, but not so wet that it runs.

- Clean the surface to be finished using compressed air or a brush if you are working in an efficient spray booth that will evacuate all the raised dust. Otherwise, use a vacuum or tack cloth. (Use a water-dampened cloth with water-based finish.) Just before starting to spray, wipe the surface with your clean hand to remove any dust that might have settled.

- Adjust the fan pattern of the spray gun wide for large surfaces and narrow for narrow surfaces.

- Plan a systematic spraying routine. On flat horizontal surfaces, spray the edges straight on, then at a 45-degree angle (partly on the edge and partly

Photos 3-5: Spray flat horizontal surfaces beginning half on and half off the front edge (a). Then overlap each stroke by half as you move to the back edge (b). End by spraying half on and half off the back edge (c). This way, you will deposit an equal amount of finish over the entire surface.

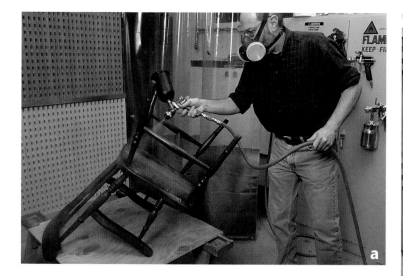

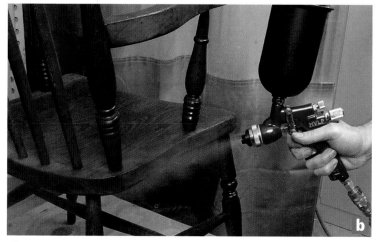

Photos 3-6: To spray a complex surface like a chair, begin by spraying the less seen parts first. Turn the chair upside down and spray the insides of the legs and insides and bottom sides of the stretchers (a). Right the chair and spray the outsides of the legs, topsides and outsides of the stretchers, and edges of the chair seat (b). Finally, spray the chair seat, back, and arms (if any) (c).

on the top). Finally, spray as shown on the facing page (Photos 3-5). On complex objects, spray the less visible parts first and finish with the most visible parts—for example, spray chair legs and rungs first, then the chair seat and back (Photos 3-6).

■ When possible, begin spraying a few inches off the wood and move onto it. Continue spraying a couple of inches off the other end before releasing the trigger. It's best to release the trigger (called "triggering the

gun") at the end of each stroke to reduce overspray and avoid hand cramping.

■ When spraying connecting surfaces, such as chair rungs, begin and end each stroke with a flick of the wrist to feather the spray as you pull back or release the trigger.

■ Hold the gun at a uniform distance from the object, usually about 8 to 10 inches (the approximate distance between the tips of your thumb and little finger when spread as wide as

> **TIP**
>
> Before beginning to spray an object, hold the gun at eye level and spray into the air so you can check the width of the fan and the uniformity of the spray. Adjust the knobs until the spray looks right, both in its width and uniformity. After you've done this a few times, you'll be able to adjust your spray gun fairly accurately using this method.

possible) and move it at a uniform speed.

■ Spray perpendicular to the surface, and don't rock the gun, as illustrated in Figure 3-5.

Cleaning and Storing Spray Guns

Cleaning your spray gun thoroughly is very important. If you leave finish to harden in the gun, the gun will become unusable, and it may be very difficult to get it clean again. Follow these steps:

Figure 3-5:
Proper Spraying

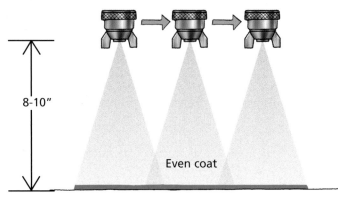

Correct position

8-10"

Even coat

For best results, hold the spray gun perpendicular to the surface you're spraying, and move it in a straight line over the wood.

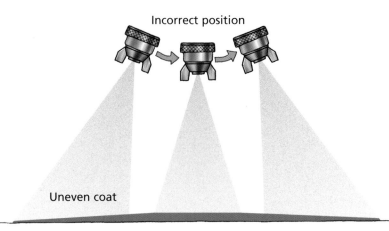

Incorrect position

Uneven coat

Angling or rocking the gun deposits an uneven thickness of liquid material.

1 Spray solvent through the gun after each day of use, or anytime you won't be using the gun for a period of time. This is especially critical with water base, varnish, and two-part finishes, which are difficult or impossible to remove once cured. You can usually leave lacquer in a spray gun and cup for a long period of time—even weeks—without any problems. The best solvent to use for all finishes is lacquer thinner, though water can often be used effectively with water-based finishes.

2 Remove the air cap and needle after each day of use. Leave them soaking in lacquer thinner or clean them and put them back in the gun.

3 Some finishers also like to remove the fluid nozzle and clean it. Doing this is especially wise when you finish a project and won't be using your gun for a while.

4 If you're using a cup gun, clean the cup thoroughly, including the gasket. If you're spraying finish through a pressure pot, clean it and the hose thoroughly. Run the appropriate thinner through the hose.

5 It's good practice to apply a drop or two of oil into the needle-packing nut after cleaning to keep it lubricated. You can buy small spouted containers of oil from spray-gun suppliers, or use mineral oil.

Staining
Wood

In Brief

- **Understanding Stains**
- **What Makes a Stain**
- **A Guide to Stains**
- **Chemical Stains**
- **Bleaching Wood**
- **Ebonizing Wood**
- **Using Aniline Dyes**
- **Matching Color**
- **Dyes and Fade Resistance**
- **Applying Stain**
- **Washcoating Before Applying Stain**
- **Washcoats**
- **Staining End Grain**
- **Common Staining Problems, Causes, and Solutions**

Of all the steps in wood finishing, staining causes the most problems. Because of such difficulties as blotching, streaking, color unevenness, and incompatibility between stain and finish, many woodworkers avoid the use of stains altogether. I'm convinced that the popularity of the "natural wood look" is at least partly due to the perception among woodworkers that stains are difficult to use.

Used properly, though, stains beautify wood, and they solve problems rather than create them. Stains add richness, depth, and color to wood. They help disguise problem areas and smooth color variations between different boards, and between heartwood and sapwood in the same board. They even allow you to make the color of cheap, uninteresting woods such as poplar and soft maple blend closely with that of higher-quality woods such as walnut and mahogany (Photo 4-1 on p. 42).

The most important quality of a stain is its color, and you probably choose a stain for this quality. It's doubtful that you are thinking about other important considerations, such as what the stain is made of, how fast it dries, or how it will behave on the wood. Manufacturers don't make this information easy to find out. Reading the label rarely tells you what to expect—except, of course, "professional results." This is unfortunate because ignoring the differences in stains, other than color, can lead to results you don't want.

It may sound silly at first, but stains are like saws; you have a number of choices. You wouldn't choose a table saw to cut a curve, and you wouldn't choose a jigsaw to cut a miter. In the same sense, you shouldn't use a wiping stain if you want the curls in curly maple to "pop," and you shouldn't use a dye stain if you want to prevent blotching in pine. Just as with saws, there is no "best" stain—just different types, some doing specific jobs better than others.

Woods differ, as well, and stains act differently on different woods. You need to take two universal characteristics of wood into account when choosing a stain.

The first is the color of the wood. Clearly, the same stain applied to pale maple and pink cherry, for example, or to yellow birch and brown walnut, isn't going to result in the same color.

The second is the figure and grain of the wood. There are four large categories of woods: softwoods such as pine and fir; tight-grained hardwoods such as maple, birch, and cherry; medium-grained hardwoods such as walnut and mahogany; and coarse-grained hardwoods such as oak, elm, and ash. Within each of these categories, you can fairly successfully match any two woods using some combination of bleach and stain. But trying to match woods of two different categories will never be entirely successful because of the differences in figure and grain. You should take these limitations into account when you're choosing the wood for your project. (See Photo 2-1 on p. 8).

Besides the differences in wood species, stains act differently on solid wood and veneer. Usually the solid wood stains darker; sometimes the veneer does.

Certainly, there are a lot of things to take into account when you are coloring wood. If you are going to use stains successfully, you need to understand how various stains and woods interact. It is the incorrect choice of stain, not so much the way it is applied, that causes most staining failures. (See "Common Staining Problems, Causes, and Solutions" on p. 68.)

Photo 4-1: Stains are often used to make cheaper, less-interesting woods resemble the color if not the grain of more-appreciated walnut and mahogany. Here, a walnut veneered panel is set in a beech frame that has been stained a walnut color.

Understanding Stains

There are a number of ways to classify stains. Understanding the ingredients, their properties, and how they interact with wood helps in predicting how a stain will perform. (See "What Makes a Stain" on p. 44.) Here are the qualities that make a difference:

- Colorant—Is it pigment or dye?
- Amount of colorant—Just a little or a lot?
- Binder—Is it oil, varnish, lacquer, or water base?
- Thickness—Is it liquid or gel?

Colorant

There are two types of colorant used in stains: pigment and dye (Photo 4-2). Pigment is finely ground natural or synthetic earth. Dye is a chemical that dissolves in a liquid. Everything that settles to the bottom of a container is pigment, and all the color that remains in the liquid after the pigment has settled is dye. (Dye settles only if there isn't enough liquid to put all the dye into solution.) Other ways pigment and dye differ, especially regarding application to wood, include the following:

- Pigment lodges only in scratches and pores large enough to hold it when the excess is wiped off. Dye penetrates everywhere more or less equally along with the liquid it is dissolved in (Figure 4-1 and Photo 4-3).
- Pigment obscures the wood when the excess is left on the surface. Dye is transparent when the excess is left (Photo 4-4 on p. 45).
- Pigment is very resistant to fading. Dye fades fairly quickly when exposed to strong ultraviolet sunlight and somewhat slower in weaker ultraviolet fluorescent light. (See photo in sidebar on p. 60.)

Photo 4-2: Manufacturers seldom disclose what type of colorants they have included in their stains (as if this should be a secret!). You may want to avoid using a dye, for example, because the object will receive a lot of sunlight (and sunlight fades dyes more than it does pigment). So you have to test yourself. To do so, allow time for pigment to settle. Then insert a stirring stick into the stain and see if you can pull up some pigment from the bottom of the can. If you can and the rest of the stirring stick is uncolored, the stain contains just pigment (left). If you can't and the rest of the stick is colored, the stain contains just dye (center). If you can and the rest of the stick is colored, the stain contains both pigment and dye (right).

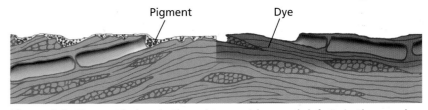

Pigment   Dye

Figure 4-1: Pigment lodges in the pores, scratches, and defects in the wood, accentuating them. Dye saturates the wood fibers with color, usually producing a more even appearance.

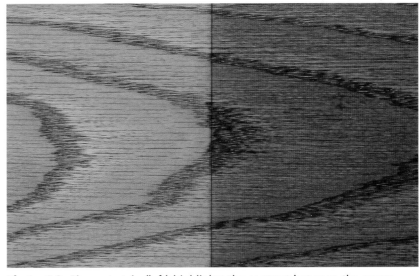

Photo 4-3: Pigment stain (left) highlights the contrast between the coarse grain areas and the dense areas in oak. Dye stain (right) colors the dense parts of oak, which reduces the contrast.

What Makes a Stain

Stains vary according to colorant (pigment or dye), amount of colorant, binder (finish), and thickness. Pigment can be used with any binder. Dyes don't require a binder but can be combined with one, as is done in combination pigment/dye stains. Each dye and each binder has a corresponding solvent or thinner.

	PIGMENT				DYE		
Binder	Oil[1]	Varnish[1]	Lacquer	Water base	No binder necessary		
Solvent or Thinner	Mineral spirits	Mineral spirits	Lacquer thinner, Fast-evaporating petroleum distillate	Water, Glycol ether, Propylene glycol	Water	Alcohol	Naphtha, Toluene, Xylene, Turpentine, Lacquer thinner
Other Formulations	Gel[2]	Gel[2]		Gel[2]	NGR[3]		

1. These can be mixed to make an oil/varnish binder.
2. Gel stains combine a colorant and binder with thixotropic agents that prevent the stain from flowing unless it is physically manipulated.
3. NGR (non-grain raising) stain is pre-metalized dye dissolved in glycol-ether solvents. It can be thinned with water, alcohol, or lacquer thinner.

TIP

To some extent, you can affect how dark a pigment stain appears on the wood by the grit of your final sanding. Coarser grits create larger scratches where more pigment can lodge. This makes the wood appear darker. Much less pigment can lodge in the scratches made by finer grits, so the wood appears lighter (Photo 2-3 on p. 13).

■ Pigment always has to be combined with a binder to glue the pigment particles to the wood. Dye can be used with or without a binder. This difference can cause confusion, and the names of the stains don't help a lot. (See "A Guide to Stains" on p. 48.)

Pigment. Until recently, all pigment was finely ground colored earth, mined in various parts of Europe and America. Now, most pigments are colored synthetic particles that resemble earth. Because pigment is opaque, it is used as the colorant in paint. When you pile enough pigment particles on top of each other, you can no longer see through to the wood. Because pigment is heavier than the liquid it is suspended in, pigment particles settle to the bottom of the container and have to be stirred back into suspension before use. Most commercially available stains contain pigment.

When the excess is wiped off, pigment colors wood by lodging in depressions, such as pores, scratches, and gouges. The larger the cavity, the more pigment lodges, and the darker and more opaque the cavity becomes. This is why pigment stains accentuate large pores, gouges, and cross-grain sanding scratches. Pigment lodged in sanding scratches that run in the direction of the grain is usually difficult to distinguish from the grain itself, which is why you should always sand with the grain (Photo 4-5).

Pigment can also color wood by building to a thickness on the surface. Building occurs when you don't wipe off all the excess stain, and it is equivalent to painting the wood with a thinned paint. You can control how much you obscure the wood by how much pigment you leave on the surface. Not removing all the excess pigment stain can produce a more even coloring,

Photo 4-4: The transparency of dye makes it possible to darken some parts of wood more than other parts without obscuring the wood as pigment stain does. Dye has been applied to the left side of this panel and pigment to the right side. The top half has only one coat, with the excess wiped off. The bottom half has been coated several times, without wiping off the excess. Note that the dye retains transparency. This characteristic allows you to use dyes to blend color variations between different woods, between different boards of the same species, and between heartwood and sapwood—all without obscuring the wood.

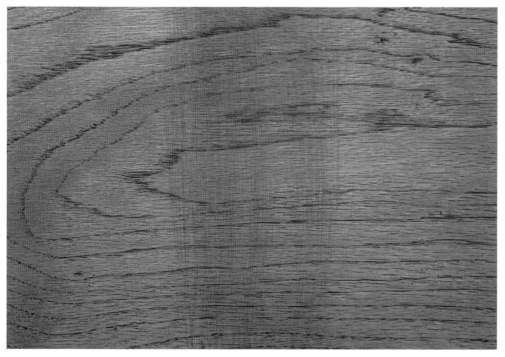

Photo 4-5: The pigment in pigment stains remains thick in all pores, gouges, and sanding scratches, making them appear much darker than the surrounding wood. This is the reason it is always best to sand in the direction of the grain. Sanding scratches don't stand out when they run with the grain, but they do stand out when crossing the grain.

Photo 4-6: Not wiping off excess pigment stain (right) leaves the wood muddied compared to the way it looks with the excess wiped off (left).

similar to paint, but the wood is muddied (Photo 4-6).

Dye is a colorant found in such common substances as coffee, tea, berries, and walnut husks. These and other natural materials, such as logwood, alkanet root, cochineal, and dragon's blood, were once used to color wood. (Chemicals are also used: see "Chemical Stains" on p. 49, "Bleaching Wood" on p. 50, and "Ebonizing Wood" on p. 55.) Now, far superior synthetic *aniline* dyes are available. These dyes are derived from petroleum (they were originally derived from coal tar), and they were developed, beginning in the late nineteenth century, for use in the textile industry. Unlike natural dyes, aniline dyes are available in an infinite range of colors and are considerably more resistant to fading. (See "Dyes and Fade Resistance" on p. 60.)

In the textile industry, aniline dyes are classified by chemical type or by how they are applied. Wood-finish suppliers classify dyes by the solvent in which they dissolve best. There are four types of dyes used in wood finishing:

■ Water-soluble dyes dissolve in water.
■ Alcohol-soluble dyes dissolve in alcohol.
■ Oil-soluble dyes dissolve in strong petroleum-distillate solvents, such as naphtha, toluene, and xylene, and also in turpentine and lacquer thinner.
■ Non-grain-raising (NGR) dyes dissolve in glycol ethers. (See "Glycol Ether" on p. 179.)

Water-, alcohol-, and oil-soluble dyes are usually sold as powders. The solvents for dissolving these dyes are widely available, and shipping and storage of the dyes are much easier in powder form. NGR dyes, on the other hand, are sold in liquid form. These dyes are also called *metal-complex* or *pre-metalized* dyes. Once they are dissolved in glycol-ether solvent, they can then be thinned with water, alcohol, acetone, or lacquer thinner (Photo 4-7). Though there may be an exception somewhere, you can assume that if a dye is sold in liquid form, whether or not it is concentrated, it is an NGR-type dye. Of course, if you thin what started off as an NGR dye with water, it is no longer "non-grain-raising."

- *Water-soluble dyes* are the best dyes to use on furniture, cabinets, and woodwork when you are applying the dye with a cloth or brush. The water solvent is very inexpensive and non-toxic, and water has a much longer "open" time than the other solvents, meaning that you have considerably more time to apply the dye and get all the excess wiped off.

- *Alcohol-soluble dyes* are used primarily for touch-up. They are dissolved in either shellac or padding lacquer and brushed onto damaged areas. (See Chapter 19: "Repairing Finishes.")

- *Oil-soluble dyes* are used primarily as a colorant in oil- and varnish-based stains. These dyes are seldom used by themselves to color wood.

- *Non-grain-raising (NGR) dyes* are best when spraying dye directly onto the wood and leaving it, or when combining dye with a finish to make a toner. (See "Toning" on p. 199.) These dyes are fairly toxic when sold in non-concentrated form because they contain a considerable amount of methanol. You should protect yourself by working in a room with good ventilation.

The working properties of all these dyes differ from the dyes in stains that contain a binder (oil, varnish, lacquer, or water base). Not having a binder makes color manipulation easier. You can remove some of the dye and lighten the color, even after the dye has fully dried, by wiping with the solvent for the dye. Each time you let the dye dry, you can then redissolve it and remove more of the color. This is only minimally possible with dyes that have been glued to

Photo 4-7: Dyes sold to wood finishers are classified by the solvent in which they dissolve. From the left, water-, alcohol-, and oil-soluble dyes are commonly sold in powder form. On the right, non-grain-raising dyes (those that dissolve in glycol-ether solvents) are sold in liquid form.

A Guide to Stains

It's one thing to know how stains differ. It's quite another to associate the differences with the names given to stains—both by manufacturers and by people writing or talking about stains. The confusion is made worse because of overlaps. Here's a guide.

Wiping stain
Can contain pigment, dye, or both. All contain a binder (usually oil, varnish, or water-based finish) that dries slowly enough so that excess stain can be wiped off in a fairly relaxed manner. Almost all consumer stains are wiping stains.

Varnish stain
Any stain, whether pigment, dye, or both, that contains a varnish binder.

Pigment stain
Any stain containing pigment, though many so-called "pigment" stains also contain dye. Pigment doesn't actually penetrate the wood, so stains containing pigment always require a binder to glue the pigment to the wood.

Oil stain
Any stain, whether pigment, dye, or both, that contains an oil binder.

Lacquer stain
Any stain, whether pigment, dye, or both that contain a fast-drying alkyd varnish or lacquer binder. These stains dry very fast, so they are often sprayed and wiped off quickly (sometimes by a second person).

Dye stain
Almost always dye that is dissolved in a liquid. No binder is needed because the dye soaks into the wood along with the liquid. Dyes are often included in stains with binders (with or without pigment), but these stains aren't referred to as dye stains— rather as pigment stains (incorrectly), wiping stains, oil stains, or water-based stains.

Water-based stain
Any stain, whether pigment, dye, or both, that contains a water-based binder.

Gel stain
Any thickened stain. The stain doesn't run and stays at the surface of the wood. Most contain only pigment, not dye.

Non-grain-raising (NGR) stain
A dye dissolved in glycol-ether solvent and often thinned with methanol. This stain is available only in liquid form and never contains a binder. Because of the rapid drying, NGR stains are almost always sprayed and left to dry.

Chemical stain
Any chemical that colors wood by reacting with chemicals naturally in the wood.

Shading Stain
The same as a toner—that is, pigment or dye added to a thinned finish. The difference is in how it is applied. Shading stains are applied to selected parts of a surface, while toners are applied to an entire surface. (See Chapter 15: "Advanced Coloring Techniques.") Some manufacturers label their pigmented toners "shading stain."

the wood by a binder. (See "Using Aniline Dyes" on p. 56.)

I find this quality of dyes invaluable for controlling color. Not only can I darken (or intensify) the color without obscuring the wood, or change the color by applying a different-colored dye, I can lighten the color quite significantly if I get it too dark. (To learn how to remove even more of the color, see "Bleaching Wood" on p. 50.) It's extremely difficult to remove all of the

CAUTION

▼

Don't mix chlorine bleach with sodium hydroxide (lye). The two will combine to produce a poisonous gas.

Chemical Stains

Some chemicals react with certain woods to produce color in the wood. Before the development of aniline dyes, these chemicals were sometimes used as stains in place of natural dyes or earth pigments. Some of the chemicals used were lye, ammonia (the process of coloring with ammonia fumes is called *fuming*), potassium dichromate, potassium permanganate, copper sulfate, ferrous sulfate, and nitric acid. If you've read much about finishing wood, you've probably seen some of these chemicals mentioned.

These chemicals pose two serious problems.

- They are dangerous to use. Most burn your skin on contact. They are generally bad for your health.
- They are difficult to control. If you get the wood too dark or the wrong color, it's often impossible to correct the problem by any method short of sanding all the color out and starting over.

Because aniline dyes can imitate any color produced by chemical stains, which have a limited color palette anyway, there's little reason

to take the risks using chemicals—with one exception. Potassium dichromate is very useful for coloring some woods in marquetry and other mixed-wood designs without coloring others.

Potassium dichromate darkens all woods that naturally contain tannic acid. These woods include mahogany, walnut, oak, and cherry, the typical woods used for the background and some of the darker pieces in a design. By applying a solution of potassium dichromate, you can darken these woods without affecting the color of the lighter woods such as holly, boxwood, and satinwood.

You can buy potassium dichromate crystals from specialty finish suppliers (see "Sources of Supply" on p. 300) and chemical supply houses. Dissolve the crystals in water and apply in the same way as an aniline dye. Experiment on scrap wood to determine the solution strength required to give you the intensity you want before you apply the stain to the design itself. Wear a dust mask when working with the crystals and gloves when applying the stain.

Bleaching Wood

You can put color in wood with stain. You can take color out of wood with bleach. You can use bleach to lighten most woods to an off-white color. Then you can finish the wood as is, or you can stain the wood to the color you want. Use bleach when you want to make the color of wood lighter than it is naturally, or when you want to neutralize the existing color in order to minimize its effect on the stain you want to use. You can also use bleach to lighten two different colored woods so you can stain them to a common color.

The procedure for bleaching wood is not at all difficult. The trick is to use the right bleach for the job. There are three types of bleach used in woodworking, and each serves a different purpose.

■ *Two-part bleach* (sodium hydroxide and hydrogen peroxide) removes the natural color from wood. It also removes dark stains caused by water, rust, alkalis, and some dye color.

■ *Chlorine bleach* removes dye color from wood and turns wood white unless reduced with a lot of water.

■ *Oxalic acid* removes stains caused by water, rust, and alkalis without changing the natural color of the wood. (Oxalic acid does remove oxidation, however, so it may lighten wood a little—back to its original color.)

Use two-part bleach when you want to lighten the color of the wood. Use chlorine bleach reduced with 5 to 10 parts water to remove dye with minimal effect on the wood's natural color. Use oxalic acid when you want to remove dark stains (other than ink) without affecting the wood's natural color.

All three types of bleach are often labeled "Wood Bleach" (photo below). This makes it difficult to know which you're getting. Here's the key:

■ Two-part bleach is always sold in two separate containers, usually labeled "A" and "B."

■ Chlorine bleach is sold as a liquid and labeled "sodium hypochlorite." It's also sold as household bleach, and in crystal form as swimming-pool bleach. (Apply chlorine bleach by wetting the surface and letting the bleach dry. Then wash with water to remove any residue from the bleach. There is no need to neutralize because the bleach itself is neither an acid nor an alkali.)

■ Oxalic acid is always sold in crystal form. (See "Using Oxalic Acid" on p. 286.)

Using two-part bleach to bleach wood requires four steps:

1 Pour some chemical from the container labeled "A" or "1" into a glass or plastic container. Never use metal. Both parts of the bleach will react with metal. Apply a wet coat of the chemical to the wood using a synthetic brush or a cloth. Work from the bottom up to avoid spots that might occur from drips onto uncoated parts. Be sure the coat is wet all over. Protect your eyes and your skin from contact with this chemical. It is usually sodium hydroxide (also called lye or caustic soda), which is extremely caustic and will burn you severely on contact. (Have some water nearby to wash it off your skin, just in case.) Sodium hydroxide will darken many woods considerably. Don't let this bother you; the next step will change things.

2 Pour some "B" or "2" chemical, usually hydrogen peroxide, into a glass or plastic container. Before the first chemical dries, apply the second on top. (Sometimes manufacturers reverse the order putting hydrogen peroxide in the "A" container and sodium hydroxide in the "B" container. It

There are three types of bleach used in wood finishing: two-part bleach (sodium hydroxide and hydrogen peroxide), chlorine bleach, and oxalic acid. Two-part bleach removes the natural color from the wood. Chlorine bleach removes dye color and also turns wood white. Oxalic acid removes water, rust, and alkali stains without affecting the natural color of the wood.

doesn't matter. It's the reaction of the two chemicals together that does the bleaching.) Use a separate brush, or thoroughly wash out the brush you used for the first chemical before using it in the second. You should see foaming as the two chemicals react, and the wood will lighten. Let it dry overnight.

3 Apply a mild acid, such as white vinegar mixed half with water, to the wood to neutralize the alkalinity of any remaining sodium hydroxide. Alternatively, if you are working outside, you can hose the wood with water, which will wash away most of the alkalinity. Let the wood dry overnight.

4 Sand the wood lightly with fine-grit sandpaper to remove the raised grain. Don't sand more than is needed to make the wood feel smooth, or you may sand through to unbleached wood.

You can combine two steps into one by mixing the two chemicals and applying them as one coat. If you do this, you must apply the mixture quickly or it will lose its potency (the reason the two chemicals are packaged separately).

One application of two-part bleach usually is enough. However, there are several ways you can try to lighten the wood further if that is called for:

■ Bleach the wood a second time.
■ Do your bleaching in sunlight (a mild bleaching agent in its own right).
■ Apply a second coat of hydrogen peroxide while the first coat is still wet.
■ Apply a solution of oxalic acid to the still-wet sodium hydroxide/ hydrogen peroxide application.

color, however. This usually requires a great deal of sanding.

For whatever reason, the brand of dyes (water-, alcohol-, and oil-soluble— not NGR) that gives me the greatest control of color is the W.D. Lockwood brand (Photo 4-8). Not only are these dyes available in a large variety of wood-tone colors, I find them invaluable for

Photo 4-8: It's much easier to adjust the value and hue of dye stains than of stains that contain a binder, especially with the W.D. Lockwood brand of dye stains. Adjusting the color is always more successful if you let the dye dry first. The middle section of these two sample boards was colored with a single coat of dye stain. Then on the top of the left board, I removed about half the color by wiping with a cloth wetted with the solvent for the dye (in this case, water). On the bottom part of this board I doubled the darkness of the stain by applying another coat and wiping off the excess. At the top of the right board I changed the red color to orange by wiping with a cloth wet with yellow dye. And at the bottom of this board I changed the red color to brown by wiping with a cloth wet with black dye. In each case, it was as if I had dissolved the dye to that strength, or a blend of dyes to that color, before I applied it.

Photo 4-9: Dye is far more effective than pigment for bringing the color of sapwood in line with that of heartwood when the stain is applied to the entire surface. Here, a walnut-colored dye was applied to walnut (right half) with a large swath of sapwood running down the middle.

What's in Watco?

▼

The walnut coloring in Watco and Deft Danish oil finishes is technically pigment, but it performs more like a dye. It is asphaltum, also known as bitumen or gilsonite. Asphaltum is simply fiber-free roofing tar that you can buy at most hardware stores. When thinned with mineral spirits, asphaltum makes an excellent walnut-colored stain. It's best, however, to combine it with an oil or varnish binder as is done in Watco, because on its own it doesn't dry.

matching color because of the control they give me. With other brands of dye, and with NGR dyes, it's more important to start off light and "sneak up" on the desired color by applying several coats, because it's more difficult to lighten the color if you get it too dark. (See "Matching Color" on p. 58.)

Another quality of dyes that I find valuable is their ability to unify most of the color difference between sapwood and heartwood. Of course, higher-strength dyes are more effective than weaker dyes. Simply apply the dye to the entire surface and the color of the sapwood is brought close to that of the heartwood (Photo 4-9).

You can combine dye with any finish that uses the same solvent for thinning as the dye does. You might find this valuable for "tweaking" the color of a manufacturer's stain or for "locking down" a dye when you intend to brush over it with that finish. For example, add

about 10 percent water-based finish to a water-soluble dye, and then you can brush over the dye with water-based finish without disturbing the color. The downside of doing this is that you lose the ability to manipulate the color after it has dried, just as with any stain that contains a binder.

Pigment/Dye Combination stains always contain a binder to glue the pigment part to the wood. Many woodworkers like this type of stain because the dye colors the dense parts of wood better than pigment alone. The downside of these stains is the same as that of dyes with no binder. The dye will fade in direct sunlight and fluorescent light (Photo 4-10).

Amount of Colorant

The difference made by the ratio of colorant (pigment and/or dye) to liquid is pretty obvious. More colorant creates a darker (more intense) color on the wood, and less colorant creates a lighter (less intense) color on the wood. You can add more colorant to any stain by adding more pigment or dye. You can remove pigment from a stain if you let the pigment settle first. You can remove dye from a stain by pouring some off after the pigment settles and then replacing it with thinner. The most effective way to lighten a stain, though, is simply to thin it with the appropriate thinner (Photo 4-11).

There's one other way you can control the amount of colorant in a stain, at least as it affects the wood. The longer you let a stain sit on the wood before wiping off the excess (as long as the stain doesn't dry in the process), the darker the stain will color the wood. The reason is not that the stain has penetrated deeper. All stains reach their maximum depth within seconds. The reason is that

Photo 4-10: Pigment stain (left) lodges in the large earlywood pores of oak, highlighting them. But it doesn't add much color to the dense latewood. Pigment/dye combinations (center) also highlight the pores, but the overall coloring between earlywood and latewood is more even. Dye stain (right) colors both earlywood and latewood the most evenly of any stain.

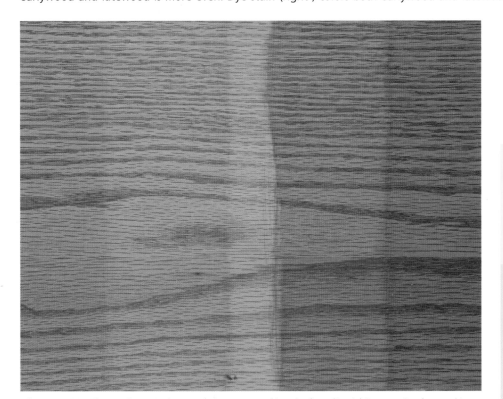

Photo 4-11: The ratio or colorant (pigment and/or dye) to liquid in a stain determines how dark the stain will be on the wood. Here, I've used a Pratt & Lambert walnut stain on the left and a Minwax walnut stain on the right—applying one coat of each on the inside and a second coat on the outside. (The center section is left unstained.) Both are pigment/dye combination stains but with different colorant-to-liquid ratios. It's easy to see the difference these different ratios make.

MYTH

The longer you leave a stain on the wood, the deeper the stain will soak into the wood and the darker the wood will become.

FACT

It is true that wood becomes darker if you leave a stain on longer, but it's not because the stain has soaked deeper. It's because some of the thinner in the stain has evaporated, and this has increased the ratio of colorant to liquid. Higher concentrations of colorant produce darker colors.

You can run into problems with a wiping stain that dries while you're trying to stain a large area. If the stain partially dries before you have a chance to remove the excess, you get streaking and blotching. The solution to the problem is to switch to a stain that dries more slowly. Stains based on an oil binder are, by far, the easiest to use if you intend to remove the excess from a large surface. Stains based on any of the other three binders may dry too rapidly to get the excess wiped off. These stains are the better choice when you want to move rapidly to the next step or when you don't intend to remove the excess.

thinner has evaporated from the stain, leaving a higher concentration of colorant on the wood. It's as if you applied a stain with a higher colorant-to-liquid ratio in the first place.

Binder

Binder is the glue that holds pigment particles to the wood (Figure 4-2). Without binder, the particles could be brushed or blown off the wood like dust once the liquid has evaporated. All binders are one of the four common finishes: oil, varnish, lacquer, or water base. (Shellac can be used to make a stain by adding alcohol dye, NGR dye, or universal tinting colorants (UTCs), but no shellac stains are available commercially.)

You can make your own stain by adding pigment to any binder and thinning if necessary: Use oil and japan colorants with oil and varnish. Use artist's acrylic colorants with water base. Use industrial tinting colorants (ITCs) with lacquer. Use universal tinting colorants (UTCs) with any finish, but you may

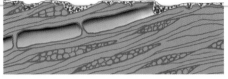

Figure 4-2: Binder glues the dustlike pigment particles to each other and to the wood. Without a binder, the pigment could be brushed or blown off the wood.

have to stir a bit to get them to suspend in oil and varnish.

The choice of binder doesn't have much affect on the way the stain looks on the wood. Rather, the binder determines how much time you have to wipe off excess stain. Oil binder cures slowly. Varnish and water-based binders cure moderately quickly. Lacquer binders dry rapidly. (Some "lacquer" stains are actually based on a very short-oil alkyd varnish, which is explained in Chapter 11: "Varnish." Because these stains act like lacquer stains and are commonly referred to as lacquer stains in the finishing trade, it's easiest to lump the two to-

Photo 4-12: Gel stains are thick and don't flow, so they don't penetrate into the wood. This can be advantageous when staining naturally blotchy woods such as pine.

gether.) Temperature and humidity affect the drying time of all stains. The higher the temperature and lower the humidity, the faster the stain will dry.

Manufacturers seldom tell you which binder they are using, but they do provide clues on the container:

- Stains using an oil or varnish binder list mineral spirits (petroleum distillate) as a thinner or clean-up solvent.
- Stains using a lacquer (or short-oil varnish) binder list active solvents in lacquer thinner or fast-evaporating petroleum distillates as thinners or clean-up solvents.
- Stains using a water-based binder list water as the thinner or clean-up solvent.

Some stains contain a higher-than-normal ratio of binder to colorant. These stains often are sold as a combined stain and finish (for example, Minwax Polyshades and any stain called a "varnish" stain). When using these stains, it's not necessary to wipe off the excess because the point is to get a build on the wood. These stains muddy the wood and are very difficult to use without getting pronounced brush marks and uneven coloring. I don't recommend them unless you have a specific need for a muted effect.

Thickness

The thickness of stains varies. Most stains are liquid, but some are thicker and are usually sold as gel stains. These are the same as gel varnish, but with a colorant included. (See "Gel Varnish" on p. 162.) Most gel stains are made with pigment in a varnish binder. A few make use of dye, and some use a water-based binder. All gel stains are unique in that they don't flow. Some are so thick that you can turn an open can of gel stain upside down and the stain won't come out (Photo 4-12). Gel stain

Ebonizing Wood

Ebonizing wood means to make the color of the wood black. It used to be done with chemicals. The most common ebonizing chemical was iron (nails or steel wool) soaked for several days in vinegar. You still see this concoction recommended in books and articles as the best ebonizing material. But it was replaced more than a century ago by black aniline dye, which is far more effective and easier to use.

You can use any black aniline dye—water, alcohol, oil, or NGR (non-grain-raising). But be aware that there are many shades of black (some are distinctly bluish), so be sure you use a shade you like. The only problem you might have is with water dye. It doesn't effectively color the pores of oak or other large-pored woods. If you use water dye, you may have to apply a black wiping stain over the dye (after it has dried) to get the pores black. You can apply the stain directly over the dye or over the sealer coat (like a glaze).

Sometimes you can get the dye concentrated enough to color the wood sufficiently with one coat after wiping off the excess. But it usually takes several coats. Allow each coat to dry, then wipe, brush, or spray on another coat until you achieve the blackness you want. You can also brush or spray on a coat and leave it—don't wipe off the excess.

The reason black dye works so well for ebonizing wood is that dye is transparent. You can make the wood totally black and still see the figure of the wood through the color. You could also use a pigmented stain or finish (in effect, paint) for ebonizing, but the stain won't make the wood very black, and paint will totally obscure it.

Black dye stain is the most effective stain for ebonizing wood. Here, I'm showing ebonizing on maple because the contrast is so striking. But if you really want the wood to resemble ebony, walnut is better, because it has a similar grain.

doesn't flow because it is made with a *thixotropic agent* that resists flow unless it is mechanically disturbed. Ketchup is an example of a thixotropic substance. You have to shake the bottle to get the ketchup moving so it will come out. When it hits your food, it remains as it landed until you spread it with your knife. Mayonnaise and latex wall paints are other examples.

Gel stains have been popular only for the last decade or two. Until very

Using Aniline Dyes

Water-, alcohol-, and oil-soluble dye stains are usually sold in powder form. You have to dissolve them in a solvent. Non-grain-raising (NGR) dye stains typically come already in solution.

Mixing Your Own Dye Stain

If you are mixing your own dye stain from powders, be sure to use the solvent (or solvents) specified by the supplier. Use water for water-soluble dye, denatured alcohol for alcohol-soluble dye, and naphtha, turpentine, toluene, xylene, or lacquer thinner for oil-soluble dye. Always use a glass or plastic container, because metal could react with the dye and affect the color. Follow the supplier's suggested powder-to-solvent ratio to get the supplier's intended color strength.

At first, having to mix the dye yourself may seem an inconvenience, but you will come to appreciate the greater control you have over the color. If you want it darker, add more dye powder or less solvent than the directions suggest. If you want it lighter, add less dye powder or more solvent. You can blend colors while they are still in powder form, but it is usually better to blend them after they have been dissolved. The color of the dye powders is seldom the same as the color of the dye when it is dissolved.

You can mix the dyes in any combination and between any brands, so long as they all dissolve in the same solvent. Measured amounts of one brand of dye and its solvent should produce the same color over and over. But to be safe, always dissolve more than enough dye to complete any given project. It's a good idea to strain the dissolved dye through a paint strainer or tightly woven cheesecloth to remove impurities and any undissolved dye, which could cause spotting.

Water dye will dissolve more quickly in hot water than in cold, and you will be able to dissolve more dye into hot water than into cold. But the dye dissolves in either. The dye can be applied to the wood hot or cold. But it's wisest to apply it everywhere at about the same temperature to avoid possible color variations.

Just in case your tap water contains mineral salts that affect the color of the dye, use distilled water. I've never had a problem with tap water, however.

Applying Aniline Dyes

It's wise to test the color of the dye on a scrap of the wood you are using. As with any stain, the color of the dye while still damp on the wood will be very close to the color you will get after you apply the finish.

As with any stain, there are two ways to apply aniline dye: Apply a wet coat and wipe off the excess before it dries, or brush or spray thinned coats and leave them. Build the color slowly to the intensity you want. Dyes are transparent, so you can continue to apply coats without obscuring the wood (Photo 4-4 on p. 45). Generally it's best to apply water-soluble dyes using the first method, and the other dyes, which dry much more rapidly, using the second.

Unless the object is small, water-soluble dye is the only dye that allows enough time to apply and wipe off before it dries. But water-soluble dye raises the grain of the wood, so you should dewhisker the wood first to get the best results. (See "Dewhiskering" on p. 14.) You can also "bury" the raised grain with your sealer coat and then sand it smooth.

As with other stains, you don't have to worry about grain direction when you apply a water-soluble dye, as long as you wipe off all the excess. Often, instructions tell you to apply the stain with a brush. I prefer a soaked cloth or sponge, or a spray gun, because these are much faster.

Coat an entire section at a time. Work rapidly so you get everything coated and wiped off before the dye dries. It's a good idea to work from the bottom up on vertical recently they were hard to find. Manufacturers didn't understand what they were good for. Bartley's was an early manufacturer of gel stain. The company included a can of cherry stain along with their cherry furniture kits, and their customers seemed very pleased with the results they got. Bartley's thought it was because the stain was so easy to use, so they began promoting it that way. Other companies figured out that gel stain was a very effective glaze. (See Chapter 15:

surfaces. This way if you should drip some dye stain, the drips won't cause spotting.

Leaving the Excess Dye

You can apply any dye without wiping off the excess, and you can apply as many coats as you want. Each new coat dissolves into the already existing dye, creating the equivalent of a higher dye-to-solvent ratio. The color will be darkened or changed depending on the specific dye strength or color you apply (Photo 4-8 on p. 51).

If you spray the dye onto the wood and don't wipe off the excess, it's best to spray highly thinned coats and gradually build the depth of color you want. That's the reason NGR dye stains are usually sold in a highly thinned solution. If you try to get the final color all at once, you may get it too dark, and it may be difficult to lighten.

The trick to brushing dye stain is achieving an even coverage. Brush out the dye in long strokes with the grain. Keep a wet edge—that is, be sure each brushstroke overlaps dye that is still wet. The dye should level out well—no brush marks showing.

If the dye stain appears streaky when it dries, wet a cloth with the appropriate solvent and wipe over the entire surface. Then wipe the surface dry. You will remove some of the color, but what is left will be evened out. You can apply more dye if you need to darken the color.

Techniques for Controlling Color

The great advantage of dye stains over stains that contain a binder is the control you have over the final color without the problem of muddying the wood.

- If you get the color of the wood too dark, wipe over the dye with its solvent to remove some dye and lighten the color.
- If the color is too light, apply more dye.
- If the color is wrong, apply a dye color that will correct it. The most common colors to apply are red, green, blue, yellow, and black (there is no white dye). (See "Matching Color" on p. 58.) Thin them out a great deal so you don't overshoot. If the color is then too dark, lighten it by wiping with the solvent for the dye.
- If you want to blend sapwood to heartwood, or a lighter species of wood to a darker species, first apply a dye to the entire surface. After it dries, apply a second coat (or a dye of another color or strength) to the lighter areas to blend them in if the first coat of dye didn't blend the colors well enough. This technique of matching different wood colors works best if you spray the dye. But it can be done successfully with a brush or cloth. You can also use a toner to blend the colors after you have sealed the wood. (See Chapter 15: "Advanced Coloring Techniques.")

CAUTION
▼

Certain aniline dyes, specifically those containing benzidine, have been linked to bladder cancer. To my knowledge, none of the dyes available to the woodworking community contain this or any other possible carcinogen. Nevertheless, you should treat aniline dyes with care. At a minimum, they can cause respiratory problems and allergic reactions in some people. Wear gloves and a particle mask when working with the dye powder, avoid making it airborne, and wear gloves when applying the dissolved dye stain.

Matching Color

Of all the steps in finishing, matching colors is the hardest. It's also the most difficult to describe. There are a few general rules, and I can provide some pointers. But experience is really the best teacher.

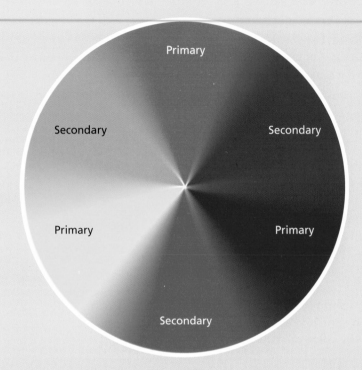

The primary colors are yellow, red, and blue. The secondary colors are orange, violet, and green. Each secondary color opposite a primary color is its complementary color, meaning that it cancels out the primary color. If you want to remove some of the red color on the wood or in a stain, apply or add some green. If you want to reduce a greenish caste on the wood or in a stain, apply or add some red.

GENERAL RULES ABOUT COLOR

- Learning pure color theory is helpful only to a point. Pure colors—yellow, red, and blue— are seldom used on wood. Colors for wood are closer to browns, a good example being the earth colors—raw and burnt umber, raw and burnt sienna, yellow ochre, and Van Dyke brown. In order to match colors, however, you have to look for the pure colors within whatever color is on or in the wood.

- Green is the complementary color to red. If you want to cool the color of a stain or the wood, add green. If you want to warm the color, add red.

- Mix a little blue rather than green with red to make a cordovan color.

- Black reduces the intensity of any color.

- Black added to orange, which is a blend of red and yellow, makes brown.

- Brown is the most important color in wood finishing. You can begin with brown and add black, red, green, blue, or yellow to get almost any of the common wood-stain colors. Adding white produces pastels.

- Light affects how a color appears. North light and daylight fluorescent bulbs bring out more of the green or blue (coolness) in a color. Incandescent (ordinary) light bulbs bring out more of the red (warmth) in a color. You can buy fluorescent bulbs that are fairly neutral, but they are usually quite expensive. They will have a color temperature of about 3500 degrees Kelvin (daylight bulbs are about 6300 degrees Kelvin; incandescent bulbs are about 2500 degrees Kelvin). You can also mix daylight fluorescent and the warmer incandescent bulbs to bring out both ends of the color spectrum. You should be aware that you can have a perfect color match under one light source and be noticeably off under another, because the different light sources pick up different aspects of the colorants. The best natural light to work under is north light, because it remains fairly constant throughout the day. But there is no agreement about which artificial light source is best.

- If you know the light source in which the object you are working on will be placed, do your color matching in the same light source.

ADDITIONAL PRACTICAL CONSIDERATIONS

- Always take the color of the wood into account. The wood's color affects the way the stain will appear. If you can, test your stain on a scrap piece of the same wood you intend to stain.

- Colors in both the wood and the stain change over time—usually as a result of light bleaching or oxidation. Different pieces of wood and different pigments and dyes change in different ways and at different rates. Achieving a color match is therefore often temporary.

- When mixing colors for a match, begin with small amounts of colorant (very little black, for example, goes a long way), and keep adding until you get what you want.

- Because you are almost always mixing blends of colors (rather than pure colors), you will develop your skills quicker if you build an inventory of colorants and always work from these. You will get used to the way the colors combine. Just be sure you're always working within the same systems—water/dye, oil/pigment, and so forth.

- Instead of beginning with pure colors and blending them to achieve a color match, begin with a commercial stain whose color is close, or begin with an earth color that is close. Then tweak this color using yellow, red, blue, green, black, or white (for a pastel). Lighten the color by thinning. Darken the color by applying a second coat. Brighten the color by adding yellow. Reduce the brightness of the color by adding black.

Photo 4-13:
Blotching is caused by stain penetrating deeper into some parts of wood than in others. It is common in woods with naturally uneven densities. Examples are softwoods such as pine (left) and fir, and tight-grained hardwoods such as cherry, birch, maple, poplar, aspen, and alder.

"Advanced Coloring Techniques.") So they began marketing the stain for graining fiberglass doors and other non-wood substrates.

I became familiar with gel stains in the late 1980s and found them a mess to use. They got all over everything and were difficult to clean up. Moreover, there was always a lot of stain left on the brush or cloth after I finished applying the stain, so there was a lot of waste. I stopped using gel stains.

Then I realized that because they don't flow, they are ideal for blotch-prone woods, that is, woods that absorb stain unevenly. Gel stains resist absorption; instead, they stay right at the surface of the wood, providing even color despite the wood's uneven absorptiveness (Photo 4-13). That's the reason

Dyes and Fade Resistance

The issue of fade resistance, called *lightfastness,* has been made confusing by manufacturers' claims—some making quite an issue over the lightfastness of their aniline dyes. Keep in mind that lightfastness is relative. Though some individual dyes, and types of dyes, are more lightfast than others, all dyes fade rapidly in direct sunlight (noticeably within several weeks). The differences in lightfastness among dyes is insignificant when compared to the excellent fade resistance of pigments.

If you are staining wood that will be placed in direct sunlight, even inside a building, or that will be placed in an office-type environment with fluorescent lighting, you should try to avoid using dyes altogether. On the other hand, dyes maintain their color quite well for many decades, and longer, in indoor conditions away from windows and fluorescent lighting. If you are finishing furniture, cabinets, or woodwork that will be placed in normal indoor conditions with incandescent lighting, you should not be worried about the type of dye you choose. All will hold their color well. Choose for other qualities, such as workability, cost, and odor.

I placed this panel with the right half protected with newspaper in a west-facing window for several months during the winter. I used every type of dye, including NGR and water-soluble. Though some did seem to fade more than others, obviously, you wouldn't want to use any of them on an object placed near a window.

purchasers of Bartley's cherry-furniture kits were so happy with the stain. It made the wood look good because there was no blotching.

Thus, gel stains are the easy one-step solution to the single worst problem in finishing, the only problem that can't be solved by stripping and starting over. Blotching is caused by uneven density in some woods, including softwoods, such as pine and fir, and most tight-grained hardwoods, such as cherry, birch, maple, poplar, aspen, and alder. Liquid stains penetrate deeper into the less dense parts of these woods. To remove blotching, you have to sand, scrape, or plane to below the depth the stain has penetrated. This is a lot of work, and then you still have the prospect of blotching to deal with.

Blotching is not always bad. The beautiful characteristics exhibited by stained curly and bird's-eye maple, for example, are the result of blotching, that is, uneven penetration. Burls also blotch, and blotching in walnut is appreciated by most people. You would rarely want to use a gel stain on these woods. You would use a liquid stain—in fact, a dye stain for the greatest "pop." There's no better example of how the choice of the type of stain you use is critical to the end result (Photo 4-14).

Applying Stain

Choosing the best type of stain to use on a project may be critical for getting good results, but the way you apply the stain can also make a big difference. There are basically two ways to apply stain:

- Apply a wet coat of stain and wipe off the excess before it dries.
- Apply the stain and leave it.

Generally, if you aren't using a spray gun, the first method is best. You will

Photo 4-14: Gel stain is perfect for pine because it doesn't penetrate. So it produces an even coloring, like the one shown at the top left. Liquid stain, which penetrates, accentuates pine's irregular densities, resulting in blotching, as on the bottom left. On a figured wood, such as bird's-eye maple, a gel stain (top right) masks the irregularities. A liquid stain (bottom right) emphasizes the irregularities, which we call "figure" but is the same phenomenon as blotching.

always get an even coloring on the wood as long as the wood has been prepared well and isn't naturally blotchy. If you are using a spray gun to apply the stain, you can use either method successfully.

The main concern in applying a stain and wiping off the excess is the time you have before the stain sets up too much to wipe off. Faster-drying stains, especially lacquer stains and all the solvent-based dye stains, dry exceptionally quickly. If you want to wipe off the excess of one of these stains on a large project, you should have another person doing the wiping right after you apply the stain. If the stain does get blotchy because it has begun drying, wipe over it with more stain, or with the thinner for the stain, to put it back in liquid form. Then quickly wipe off the excess (Photo 4-15 on p. 62).

MYTH

You should always apply and wipe off stain with the grain.

FACT

As long as you wipe off all the excess stain, it doesn't matter in what direction you apply the stain. (I usually wipe the stain rapidly onto the wood in all directions with a soaked cloth.) Nor does it matter in what direction you wipe the stain off. It is important only that you make a final pass with the grain, so that any streaks you might unintentionally leave will be less noticeable.

Photo 4-15: Fast-drying varnish, lacquer, and water-based stains are sometimes difficult to get wiped off before they begin to dry. This can result in blotching caused by the stain rather than the wood. If you experience this problem, apply more stain, or the thinner for the stain, and remove the excess quickly. For the next project, consider switching to a slower-drying stain.

Photo 4-17: Stains lighten when they dry. This could make you think that you haven't applied a dark enough stain. But the color comes back when you apply a finish, as shown on the right side of this example. The color of the stain while it is damp is pretty close to the color you will get when you apply a finish.

Photo 4-16: Lap marks are caused by brushing stain over an already dry stain, in effect applying two layers of color to that area. Keeping a "wet edge" and brushing out the overlap will prevent lap marks. Lap marks can also occur when spraying if the color is strong and your overlaps aren't even. It's best to thin the stain enough so that lap marks don't show.

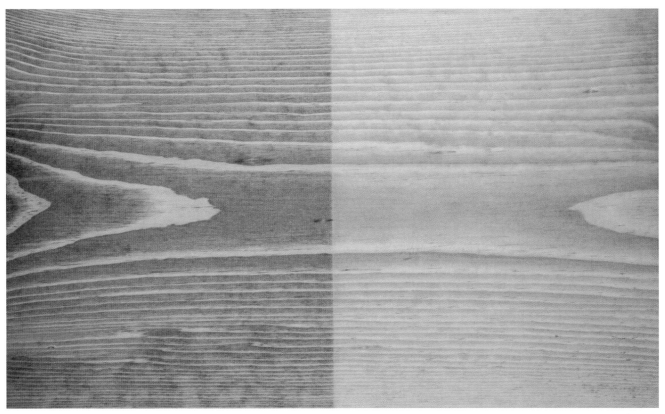

Photo 4-18: You can use a washcoat to eliminate blotching in naturally blotchy woods such as this pine board. But the price you pay is a lighter coloring, because the stain is kept from being absorbed into the wood.

The main concern in applying a stain and leaving it is getting an even coloring. Though an even coloring can be achieved using a brush (this is easier with dye than with pigment), it's much easier with a spray gun. Either way, it's best to thin the stain with enough of the appropriate thinner so you don't leave streaks or lap marks. The thinner you make a stain (meaning the more thinner you add), the more even the coloring. You may need to apply several coats to get the color intensity you want (Photos 4-16 and 4-17).

Washcoating Before Applying Stain

A washcoat is a thinned finish that is applied directly to the wood to partially seal it before applying a stain. (See "Washcoats" on p. 64.) Washcoats limit the ability of stains to penetrate into the wood, but they still leave the surface porous enough so some of the stain is retained after wiping off the excess. In fact, the easy way to distinguish between a washcoat and a sealer coat is by whether or not a stain still adds color even when you try to wipe it all off. If it does, the coating is a washcoat. If wiping with a clean cloth removes all of the color, the coating is a sealer coat. (See "Sealers and Sealing Wood" on p. 116.)

The principal use of a washcoat is to eliminate blotching in blotch-prone woods. Using a washcoat limits the amount of overall coloring, so it's generally not a good idea to use a washcoat on woods such as oak, mahogany, and walnut that don't present a problem (Photo 4-18).

The problem with applying a wash-coat to reduce blotching is that it takes some experimentation to get the solids content and application method right. If you are working on a large project, or if you do production work and need to deal with potential blotching, the experimentation is worth the trouble. Washcoating large surfaces before applying the stain is very efficient. But if you are staining a single project of small-to-moderate size, you will find that using a gel stain is considerably more predictable.

Wood Conditioner

A popular consumer washcoat is *wood conditioner*. Most brands are varnish thinned with two parts mineral spirits. You can easily make your own. Some

Washcoats

Washcoat is the name given to a thinned finish that is applied under a stain or between layers of color to gain better control of the decorating process. (See Chapter 15: "Advanced Coloring Techniques.") Washcoats are commonly used in the cabinet and furniture industries.

For most situations, a washcoat is any finish, sanding sealer, or vinyl sealer thinned to about 10 to 12 percent solids content. (See "Solids Content and Mil Thickness" on p. 108.) To get this solids content, thin each of the following finishes as follows:

- Thin shellac with denatured alcohol to a 1-pound cut.
- Thin lacquer half with lacquer thinner.
- Thin varnish with two parts mineral spirits to one part finish.
- Thin water-based finish with two parts water to one part finish. (If this doesn't flow out smoothly, use shellac as your washcoat.)
- Thin precatalyzed lacquer with two parts lacquer thinner to one part finish.

The goal of a washcoat is to achieve a very thin layer of finish, so if you tend to spray or brush thickly, you should use a thinner washcoat. You might even want to double the amount of thinner to make a 5 or 6 percent solids content. You may need to try several different percentages on scrap wood to find out what works best for you. You want the washcoat to be very thin, but not so thin that the next color coat goes through.

Here are the principal uses for washcoats:

- Partially seal problematic woods, such as those that tend to blotch, so they stain more evenly. (See "Washcoating Before Applying Stain" on p. 63.)
- Stiffen wood fibers so they can be cut off easily with sandpaper. This procedure is especially useful for evening coloration on end grain. (See "Staining End Grain" on p. 66.)
- Create a slick surface so paste wood filler is easier to wipe off or manipulate. (See Chapter 7: "Filling Pores.")

- Improve bonding through paste wood filler and glaze. (See Chapter 7: "Filling Pores" and "Glazing" on p. 194.)
- Form a barrier over a stain so the next coloring step doesn't smear the previous stain or mix with it.
- Improve the depth of finishes with several coloring steps by separating each step—and doing this with minimal build.

Once the washcoat has dried, you have to decide whether to sand or not. It will depend on the situation. Naturally, you will sand if you are using the washcoat to stiffen wood fibers. You should also sand if you are applying glaze over the washcoat, for a better bond and also so that more of the glaze color remains in areas where you wipe off the excess. But there is seldom a reason to sand in recesses. There is too much risk of sanding through, and these areas are usually a little rough anyway. Neither is there a reason to sand under paste wood filler. You will be sanding lightly anyway after the filler has dried to remove remaining streaks.

brands are water base (Photo 4-19). Because of the complexity of water-based finishes, you can't make an effective substitute yourself. (See Chapter 13: "Water-Based Finishes.")

Unfortunately, some of the most widely available brands of wood conditioner provide incorrect instructions on the label, and this has led to a lot of failures using the product (Photo 4-20). As with all washcoats, the thinned coating has to be allowed to cure fully before applying a stain. Otherwise, the stain simply mixes with the coating, which thins the stain and results in less blotching—but does not eliminate it. With varnish-based wood conditioners, overnight drying is best before applying the stain. On a warm day, you might be able to get away with only 6 or 8 hours drying. But varnish never

Photo 4-19: A number of companies offer washcoats to the consumer market. Most are varnish thinned with two parts mineral spirits (left). Some are thinned water-based finish (right). Unfortunately, the directions for using these helpful staining aids aren't always correct, leading to a lot of unwanted blotching.

Photo 4-20: Wood conditioner is a washcoat made with varnish or water-based finish. As with all washcoats, it has to be totally dry before it becomes fully effective. I applied a varnish-based wood conditioner to both sides of this pine panel. Then, following the directions on the can, I applied the stain "within 2 hours" to the left. On the right side, I waited overnight before applying the stain. The left side is blotchy, the right side is not.

cures adequately "within 2 hours," as the directions for these products indicate. Water-based wood conditioners need an hour or two, depending on the temperature and humidity, not the 30 minutes recommended.

There is no better illustration of why finishing seems so difficult to understand. Wood conditioner is a product promoted to solve the blotching problem, the single worst problem in finishing, and its major manufacturers provide instructions that don't work. At the same time, another product, gel stain, solves the problem consistently without any special instructions, and no manufacturer tells you this on the can!

Staining End Grain

The end grain of wood almost always stains noticeably darker than face grain that has been well sanded. The reason usually given is that the end grain absorbs more stain, but this is only one of the reasons. The other, and usually the more significant, is that the end grain has not been sanded well enough. The surface is still rough from the milling, so more stain is retained when you wipe off the excess. It's similar to what happens in the coarse grain of oak, where more stain is retained in the deep pores. The obvious solution, then, for getting end grain to color more similarly to face grain is to sand better (Photo 4-21).

But this is a lot of work, often too much work, especially on the bevels of raised panels where some of the crispness of the machining may be lost by sanding. There are two ways to make the end grain come out approximately the same color as the face grain:

- Spray the stain over the entire surface and leave it—that is, don't wipe off the excess.
- Washcoat the end grain to seal the pores and stiffen the fibers, making them easier to sand smooth.

Both methods are widely used in the cabinet and furniture industries, but both require a little practice to get right. To spray the stain successfully, it's best to thin it and make several passes. To

Photo 4-21: The primary cause of end grain staining darker than long grain isn't the stain penetrating deeper, as is so often claimed. It's the result of inadequate sanding. Crosscut sawing leaves a rough surface, which retains more of the stain when you wipe off the excess. On the right, the end grain of the oak was sanded the same as the face grain. On the left, the end grain was sanded more than the face grain—until it was perfectly smooth. (I continued to use the same grit sandpaper I used on the face grain; I didn't sand to a finer grit.) Then the board was stained.

washcoat just the end grain, wipe or brush a thinned finish onto it alone, and let it dry hard before sanding. Instead of finish, you can use thinned white or yellow glue, or you can use a commercial product called *glue size,* which sands more easily than common white and yellow glues.

On a blotchy wood, brush or spray the washcoat on both the end and face grain. Then sand the end grain smooth (Photo 4-22).

Photo 4-22: The top half of this birch raised panel was washcoated, and the end grain sanded smooth. The bottom half wasn't washcoated. The panel was then stained. The washcoating eliminated blotching in the face grain. The washcoating and sanding of the end grain evened the coloring so that it matches that of the face of the panel.

MYTH

A gel stain can be used to even the coloring on end grain just as it can be used to even the coloring on blotchy wood.

FACT

Unfortunately, this isn't the case, because most of the darker coloring on the end grain is caused not by deeper penetration (which gel stain limits) but by more stain being retained in the roughness after wiping off the excess. The end grain has to be sanded smooth if the stain is going to be wiped off.

Common Staining Problems, Causes, and Solutions

PROBLEM	CAUSE	SOLUTION
The stain didn't give you the color implied by the name on the can.	The name of the color on the can is a manufacturer's interpretation; actual colors will vary. You should test the color on scrap wood before applying it to your project.	Remove as much of the color as you can with the appropriate solvent or with lacquer thinner. Then restain with a color that will give you the result you want.
The stain highlighted washboardlike mill marks and tear-outs that you had not noticed before.	The stain penetrates unevenly into these mill marks. You should have planed, scraped, or sanded them out before you applied the stain (Photo 2-2 on p. 9).	Resand and restain. You don't have to remove all of the color before restaining.
The color came out differently from that of the store sample.	The piece of wood used for the store sample is not from the same board, the same tree, and maybe not even the same species of tree as the wood you're staining. Different colors, textures, densities, and grain patterns in different boards, and even in different parts of the same board, affect the color and overall appearance of the stain.	Adjust the color of the stain so it produces the color you want (see the solution below). It's best to test the stain on a scrap piece of wood first. You can adjust a color that's not right by adding compatible pigment or dye colorants and by thinning with the appropriate thinner.
	You may be applying the stain differently than the person (or the machine) that made up the store sample. You may have sanded the wood to a different grit, or you may have let the stain sit on the wood for a significantly longer or shorter time.	To darken the color, reapply the stain and don't wipe off all of the excess. To lighten the color of a stain that contains a binder, wipe with the appropriate thinner if the stain hasn't dried, or strip with paint-and-varnish remover. If the stain does not contain a binder, wipe with the appropriate solvent. Then build the color back to the darkness you want, possibly by applying several thinned coats and not wiping off the excess.
The color came out unevenly on doors, drawers, and other parts of the same furniture or set of cabinets.	The main reason stains appear different on different pieces of wood is that the pieces of wood themselves are a different color, texture, density, or grain pattern.	If the problem is different-colored pieces of wood, refer to the two solutions immediately above. If the problem is different texture, density, or grain pattern, there's not much you can do except paint the wood and apply a faux grain—not a very satisfactory solution.
	Stains can also appear different on solid wood and veneer.	Adjust the color on the lighter parts to match the darker parts. You could also apply a washcoat under the stain to get a more even coloring.
The end grain became too dark.	End grain is usually rough as the result of machining. So, more of the stain is retained when the excess is wiped off (Photo 4-21 on p. 66 and Photo 4-22 on p. 67).	Sand the end grain better before applying the stain; washcoat the end grain to stiffen the wood fibers so sanding is more effective; or spray the stain and leave it.

PROBLEM	CAUSE	SOLUTION
The stain came out blotchy on the wood.	The wood varies in density, causing uneven stain penetration (Photo 4-13 on p. 59).	You won't be able to get out all the blotchiness unless you sand to below where the stain penetrated. You can try masking the blotchiness by glazing, shading, or toning the wood. Use a gel stain or apply a washcoat to avoid the problem.
	Glue has gotten on the surface of the wood. The glue prevents even stain penetration. This shows up as light spots under the stain. The problem is common around joints (Photo 2-5 on p.16).	Scrape or sand off the glue. Restain. Blend any color variations by sanding the spot and the wood all around the spot while it is still wet with the stain.
	Some original finish remains on the stripped wood. The finish seals these areas, preventing even stain penetration. The sealed areas don't change color.	Restrip and restain. You don't have to remove all of the color before restaining.
	You didn't apply a sufficiently wet first coat of stain, or you didn't allow the first coat to penetrate thoroughly before you wiped it off. This occurs most often with lacquer and water-based stains. The wood appears mottled—lighter and darker in areas not characterized by uneven densities.	Quickly apply another coat of stain and let it remain on the wood longer before wiping off. If this doesn't fix the problem, you will have to strip the stain and start over. You don't have to remove all the color, just make it even.
	You're using a stain that dries too fast; you're trying to stain too large a surface at one time; or you're not applying and wiping off the stain fast enough (Photo 4-15 on p. 62).	Quickly apply another coat of stain or the thinner for the stain and wipe it off. If this doesn't work, you may need to use a paint-and-varnish remover to remove the stain.
The second coat of wiping stain didn't darken the wood.	The first coat sealed the wood enough so that you wiped off all the excess of the second coat.	Apply more stain and don't wipe off all the excess. This may obscure the wood a little.
Drips from a dye stain showed up darker after you applied the stain to the entire area.	The drips of dye stain have penetrated deeper into the wood than the rest of the stain because the drips were there first.	Apply more stain and let it remain wet on the wood long enough to penetrate to an equal depth as the spots. The spots will no longer show. Work from the bottom up and from already stained wood to unstained wood to avoid this happening.
The finish lifted some of the color and streaked it, or the stain bled into the finish, showing up as small spots of color over some of the pores.	The finish contains a solvent (usually lacquer thinner or water) that either dissolves the binder in the stain or puts the dye back into solution.	Strip off the finish and restain. Then either use a different, non-interfering finish or apply a barrier coat of shellac before applying your finish.

(continued on p. 70)

Common Staining Problems, Causes, and Solutions (continued)

PROBLEM	CAUSE	SOLUTION
The stain didn't dry.	The wood is an oily wood such as teak, rosewood, or cocobolo. The wood's oils inhibit the curing of all oil- and varnish-based stains.	Wash off some of the stain with naphtha, acetone, or lacquer thinner, and then restain just after the solvent evaporates. The solvent should have removed the oil from the surface so the stain will now dry.
	You left an oil-based stain too thick on the wood. Oil takes a long time to cure, especially if it is thick.	Allow longer for the stain to cure; remove the excess stain by scrubbing with fine steel wool and mineral spirits, naphtha, or lacquer thinner; or remove the excess stain with paint-and-varnish remover. Then restain and wipe off more of the excess.
The wood feels rough or fuzzy after you applied the stain.	The stain contains water. (Alcohol- and NGR-dye stains also raise the grain a little.)	Lightly sand off the raised grain with used 320-grit or finer sandpaper. Avoid sanding through. If you do, reapply the stain over the entire surface and wipe off the excess.
		Apply a sealer coat, which will lock the raised grain in place. Then sand it smooth.
The stain didn't get the wood dark enough.	The ratio of pigment to binder, dye to binder, or dye to solvent is not high enough. Or the wood is too dense to accept any more pigment.	Reapply the stain as evenly as possible and don't wipe off all the excess. This may obscure the wood a little if you are using a pigment stain.
The stain shows streaks through the finish.	Either you didn't wipe off all of the excess stain, or you brushed on a finish that dissolved and streaked the stain.	Strip off the finish. This will also remove the streaked stain. Then restain, being careful not to leave streaks, and refinish, possibly using a barrier coat of shellac.
The stain color intensified and got darker when you applied the finish.	When stain dries, the color gets lighter. It darkens again when you apply the finish (Photo 4-17 on p. 62).	If the color is too dark, you will have to strip off the finish and remove some of the stain. Stain that is still damp looks much like it will after a finish is applied. Once the stain is dry, you can approximate the look it will have when finished by wetting it with a liquid that won't mark or smear it, often mineral spirits or alcohol.
The finish turned off-white when applied over the stain.	The stain wasn't fully cured. The problem usually occurs with lacquer and shows up most often in the wood's pores, where the stain is thickest. The cause is applying the lacquer before all the thinner has evaporated from the stain.	You can try spraying the wood with lacquer thinner. If this doesn't clear up the problem, you'll have to strip and start over. Be sure to allow plenty of time for the stain to dry, especially on humid or cool days.
The water-soluble dye didn't color the grain in a large-pored wood.	The high surface tension of water kept it from penetrating well into the grain.	Wipe over with a wiping stain of about the same color, then wipe off all the excess. To maintain the dye color better, seal or washcoat the wood, and then wipe over with the wiping stain.

Oil Finishes

In late 1989, Jeff Greef, then editor of *Woodwork* magazine, asked me to write an article on tung oil. "Sure," I said. "That should be easy." Little did I know! It took me three months of experimenting and learning about oil and varnish to work through all the mislabeling and false claims. When I completed the assignment, I was able to show that most products labeled "tung oil" weren't tung oil at all; they were (and still are) varnish thinned about half with mineral spirits (paint thinner).

The difference is significant. Tung oil cures soft, so all the excess has to be wiped off after each coat. A tung-oil finish is therefore too thin to provide much protection. Thinned varnish cures hard, so it can be built up on the wood for good protection. I named this finish *wiping varnish* because it is thinned varnish and, being thinned, is easy to wipe on wood.

I also showed that many finishes with uninformative names such as Waterlox, Seal-a-Cell, Val-Oil, and ProFin were simply varnish thinned with mineral spirits. And I showed that products labeled "Danish Oil," "Antique Oil," "Maloof Finish," and some finishes labeled "tung oil," were blends of linseed oil (and sometimes tung oil) and varnish. I named these finishes *oil/varnish blend* for obvious reasons.

No wonder there had been so much confusion with the so-called "oil" finishes. Many people thought they were using oil when they were actually using varnish. Many others thought they were using a finish a lot more special than linseed oil and varnish mixed together. How did we in the woodworking community get into this sad mess, where we can't communicate accurately about the finish we're using?

The explanation begins with the romance associated with oil finishes and the misbelief that our woodworking ancestors preferred this finish to all others. It expands with the erroneous belief, promoted in magazines and in advertising, that oil protects well from inside the wood. And it culminates with manufacturers taking advantage of these myths and mislabeling their products to make you think you are buying something special.

Our Ancestors and Linseed Oil

One common rationalization for using oil as a finish is that eighteenth-century craftspeople used and valued oil for finishing—specifically, linseed oil. If you've done much woodworking, you've surely developed a profound respect for our ancestors' woodworking skills. It's not a big jump to assume that if these craftspeople were so good at woodworking, they must also have been good finishers. And if they used linseed oil, they must have chosen to do so because linseed oil made a great finish.

The idea that our forebears were skilled finishers pops up now and then in woodworking books and articles. It's often bolstered by the suggestion that if you follow their practice of rubbing coats of linseed oil into the wood once a day for a week, once a week for a month, once a month for a year, and then once every year thereafter, you will produce one of the most beautiful and durable finishes possible—maybe even better than anything that has been invented since.

This is all myth:

- It's myth that our ancestors thought linseed oil was a great finish. They used linseed oil, of course. It was inexpensive and available. But there is no evidence from surviving records, such as cabinetmakers' account books, that linseed oil was well thought of as a finish. On the contrary, most of the finer, eighteenth-century, city-made furniture was finished with wax, spirit varnish (made from alcohol-soluble resins such as shellac), or oil varnish (similar to our modern varnish).

- It's myth that our predecessors expended much effort applying linseed oil when they did use it. Rubbing linseed oil into the wood does absolutely no good, and it's pretty absurd to think of these cabinetmakers showing up at their clients' houses every week, month, or year to do another rubbing! There is some mention in cabinetmakers' account books of rubbing linseed oil, in combination with brick dust or pumice, to fill the pores of wood. But you have to get into the twentieth century before you find written reference to anyone in the eighteenth century rubbing oil alone into wood. (How could the twentieth-century writers have known?)

- It's myth that linseed oil applied in any manner is a durable finish. A linseed oil finish is too thin and soft to protect well against heat, stains, or wear. And linseed oil, no matter how you apply it or how many coats you apply, is quickly and easily penetrated by water and water vapor.

MYTH

Rubbing an oil finish into the wood increases penetration.

FACT

Rubbing warms the finish. The warmer the finish, the faster it cures. The faster the finish cures, the quicker the pores are capped off (sealed), which prevents further penetration. Though it's not likely that you would be able to measure the difference, rubbing a finish actually decreases penetration.

Applying Oil and Oil/Varnish Finishes

Oil and oil/varnish blend finishes are very easy to apply. In most cases, you just wipe them on the wood and then wipe off the excess. Here's a little more detail.

1 Prepare the wood. On new wood remove the machine marks and sand smooth to 180- or 220-grit. For tabletops it's a good idea to "dewhisker" the wood so water spills that work their way through the finish when the table is in use won't raise the grain of the wood. Dewhiskering also reduces grain raising that often occurs after several years of humidity changes and causes the initially smooth surface to feel rough. (See "Dewhiskering" on p. 14.)

2 Clean the wood. Remove the sanding dust with a brush, tack cloth, vacuum, or compressed air.

3 Apply the first coat. Flood the wood with the finish. You can use a cloth, brush, or spray gun, or you can dip the wood into the finish or pour the finish on and spread it around with a cloth. Let the finish remain wet on the wood for several minutes. If any dry spots appear, apply more finish. Before it becomes tacky, wipe off all the excess.

4 Remove "bleeding" before it cures. If any of the finish bleeds back out of the pores, continue wiping it off every hour or so until it stops. (See "Bleeding Oil Finishes" on p. 81.)

5 Apply additional coats. Allow the first coat to cure overnight. Smooth any roughness that remains by sanding with 280-grit or finer sandpaper. (Sandpaper is far more effective than steel wool for smoothing the first coat.) Clean off the dust and apply the next coat. You can combine the two steps by sanding the wood while it's wet with the second coat of finish. Wipe the wood dry. You can then apply as many coats as you want, allowing at least one day's drying time between each coat. But there's rarely a need to apply more than three or four coats.

6 Get the ultimate finish. Instead of sanding the wood to a very fine grit (as is often recommended) to get the ultimate smooth surface, sand between coats with very fine-grit sandpaper (for example, 600-grit). It will be much less work and produce the same result. For an even better result, sand while the wood is still wet with oil, then remove the excess. The oil will lubricate the sandpaper, creating a smoother-feeling surface.

MYTH

You can get a mirror finish by filling the pores with oil and sawdust.

FACT

This notion is based on the idea that sanding the wood while it's wet with oil makes a paste of oil and sawdust, which fills the pores. In reality, you can't avoid wiping most of the oil-laden sawdust back out of the pores when you remove the excess oil from the wood. So this is a very inefficient way of filling the pores. If that is your intention, using paste wood filler would be a better method. But the real beauty of an oil finish is its sharp delineation of the pores. This is lost when you fill, or even partially fill, the pores. If you want a filled look, you should use a film finish, such as shellac, lacquer, varnish, or water base, which will give you much better protection as well.

CAUTION
▼

Never leave oily rags bunched in piles. The absorption of oxygen, which brings about curing, generates heat as a by-product. When oily rags are piled up, the heat can't dissipate and may build up and cause spontaneous combustion. Always spread your rags out on a table or floor or drape them over the edge of a trash can (not on top of each other). When the rags are dry and hard, you can safely throw them in the trash. If you work with other people, you should have an approved air-tight or water-filled container in which to throw the rags. You can then have them hauled off and burned.

■ It's even myth that eighteenth- and nineteenth-century woodworkers were skilled finishers by today's standards. Surviving cabinetmakers' account books indicate that only minimal attention was given to finishing wood. Sophisticated wood finishing is a twentieth-century craft.

So the fact that our predecessors used oil now and then as a finish is no reason for us to use oil. They used linseed oil when they had nothing better. We have an entire array of finishes that are better in almost every way.

Oil Finishes and Penetration

Oil finishes are commonly referred to as penetrating finishes, not so much because they penetrate (all finishes penetrate), but to distinguish them from finishes that harden well enough so they can be built up on the wood. The use of the word "penetrating," however, has led to oil finishes often being marketed as protecting the wood from the inside. They are contrasted with film finishes, such as shellac, lacquer, varnish, and water base, which protect the wood by building a film on the surface of the wood. To assess the accuracy of the claim that penetrating finishes protect from the inside, you need to understand how penetration occurs and what value it has (or does not have) in protecting the wood.

Liquids penetrate wood by means of capillary action—the same way that water and nutrients rise in the live tree. It doesn't make any difference whether the liquid is on top, on the side, or on the bottom of the wood. If it is in contact with the wood, the liquid will work its way through the wood channels.

The trick to achieving deep penetration is to keep the surface of the wood wet for a while. You can put a straight-grained piece of wood into a jar containing a half-inch of oil finish, and the finish will eventually work its way up through the wood and come out the top. Only if the finish cures hard in the wood, preventing further penetration, or if it hardens in the jar, or if it evaporates (like water does) will the penetration be stopped (Photo 5-1).

But what good does penetration do, anyway? Very little. You can totally fill a piece of wood with a linseed oil finish, and it will do nothing to protect the surface of the wood from damage. Coarse objects will scratch the wood, stains will stain the wood, and water will smudge the wood almost as easily as if there were no finish in the wood. The only possible advantage gained by filling the wood with finish is to stabilize the wood from shrinkage and swelling caused by water-vapor exchange. You plasticize the wood by filling all the cavities with cured finish. But if you are looking for a finish to provide protection to the surface, the amount that a finish penetrates is of no significance.

Understanding Oil

Oil is a natural substance that is extracted from plants, nuts, fish, and petroleum. Some oils, such as linseed oil and tung oil, cure; that is, they change from a liquid to a soft solid by absorbing oxygen from the air. Oils that cure can be used as finishes. Other oils, such as mineral oil, olive oil, and motor oil, don't absorb oxygen and therefore don't cure. Because they don't solidify, they are ineffective as finishes. Still other oils, such as walnut oil, soybean oil, and safflower oil, are semi-curing: They cure very slowly and never very hard. They are only marginally effective as finishes.

Oils used as finishes have certain characteristics in common. They cure slowly compared to every other finish, and they cure to a satin (not gloss) sheen after you apply several coats. They also cure soft. This makes them impractical for use as finishes unless you wipe off the excess after each application. You can't build a thick, hard, protective film on the surface of the wood the way you can with film finishes. (See "Applying Oil and Oil/Varnish Finishes" on p. 73.) If you have any cured overspill around the cap on a can of linseed oil or tung oil, push your fingernail into it and notice how soft it is compared to other finishes.

Linseed Oil

Linseed oil is extracted from seeds of the flax plant. This oil, in its raw state, is an inefficient finish because it takes weeks or months to cure. So, to make it more effective, metallic driers are added. These driers are usually salts of cobalt, manganese, or zinc. They act as catalysts to speed the introduction of oxygen, and thus the curing of the finish. (Lead was once used as a drier but is no longer, because it is a health hazard.) With driers added, linseed oil is called boiled linseed oil, and it cures in about a day if the excess is wiped off. Unless you want an oil that cures extremely slowly, there's no reason to use raw linseed oil. (See "The Food-Safe Myth" on p. 76.)

Of all finishes except wax, linseed oil is the least protective. It is a soft, thin finish, so it provides no significant barrier against scratching. It is also easily penetrated by water and water vapor. Liquid water will work through a linseed oil finish and quickly cause a smudge, often within minutes (Photo 5-2). Water vapor will pass through a linseed oil finish almost as if it weren't there.

Photo 5-1: Slow curing is the characteristic that makes some finishes penetrate deeper than others. Linseed oil and tung oil cure the slowest, so they penetrate the deepest. They do this by capillary action. The linseed oil in this jar has risen completely through the oak and is coming out the top.

Photo 5-2: No matter how many coats of linseed oil you apply to the wood, or how you apply the coats, water will penetrate through the finish and smudge the wood in a very short time, as shown in the center of the board above.

In fact, old paints based on linseed oil performed well precisely because water vapor could pass through so easily. These paints allowed moisture to escape through the walls of houses without blistering the paint film. Modern alkyd-based paints blister easily because they form a much better barrier to water-vapor exchange. This is why water-based latex paint is recommended for use on the outsides of houses. Like linseed oil-based paint, latex paint "breathes."

Tung Oil

Tung oil is extracted from nuts of the tung tree, which is native to China.

The Food-Safe Myth

No myth in wood finishing is more ingrained in the psyche of woodworkers than the belief that oil and varnish finishes containing metallic driers are unsafe to eat off of, or to be chewed on by children. Woodworking magazines have gone to great lengths to spread this myth, recommending raw linseed oil, tung oil, semi-curing walnut oil, shellac (a natural resin), and products labeled "salad bowl finish" as the safe alternatives.

Companies selling salad bowl finish have prospered as a result of this myth. But consider this: Salad bowl finish is varnish! Wiping varnish, actually. And varnish cures at a reasonable speed *only* if it contains metallic driers. There are only a few of these driers to choose among, so all oils and varnishes use essentially the same driers as salad bowl finishes. Thus, the very finishes that are marketed to be food safe and are promoted in woodworking magazines as a solution to the problem are themselves every bit as guilty of containing the same driers as the oils and varnishes woodworkers are told to shy away from!

In fact, *all* finishes are safe to eat off of or be chewed on once the finish has fully cured. The rule of thumb for curing is 30 days, but warm conditions make curing happen faster. With all solvent-based finishes, you can determine that a finish has cured sufficiently by pressing your nose against the dry finish and sniffing. If there is any odor, the finish isn't yet cured. Only if you can't smell anything is the object safe for food or mouth contact.

The issue of metallic-drier safety begins and ends with lead. Lead is known to cause a number of health problems, especially mental retardation in children. For centuries, lead was used as the primary drier in oils and varnishes because it performs so well. Lead was also used in many pigments for the same reason. But there were two big differences between lead in pigments and lead in driers. In pigments lead made up as much as 50 percent of the volume, and pigments are crunchy. So when children chewed on paint (because the lead tastes sweet), they exposed themselves to a lot of the toxic lead. In oil and varnish, the tiny bit of lead drier (less than half of 1 percent) was enmeshed in the crosslinked matrix of the finish. So even if a child were to chew on a clear finish, exposure would be next to nothing. When lead was removed by law from pigments in the 1970s, it was also removed from driers used in oils and varnishes. So exposure is now zero.

To demonstrate further that metallic driers aren't a problem for food or mouth contact, consider the following:

- No Material Safety Data Sheet (MSDS), required by the government to list all hazardous or toxic effects of a product, warns against contact with food or children's mouths for any oil or varnish finish, or for any other finish.
- The Food and Drug Administration (FDA) lists all common driers as safe for food contact as long as the finish is made properly—that is, as long as the finish cures. (The FDA doesn't "approve" of finishes as some manufacturers claim. The FDA approves of ingredients and sets rules for testing that a finish cures properly.)
- You have never heard of anyone (adult or child) being poisoned by contact with a cured clear finish. If someone had been poisoned, you can bet it would have made the news!

Let's finally put this myth to bed and use other, more legitimate, criteria for choosing a finish.

Tung oil has been used for centuries in China, but it was not introduced into the West until the very end of the nineteenth century. It is now cultivated in South America and along the Gulf Coast. Even though more expensive than linseed oil, tung oil has established a firm position in the paint-and-coatings industry because it is one of the most water-resistant oils. Many high-quality varnishes are made with tung oil. But, contrary to what you might think, tung oil is seldom used as a finish in its own right.

Tung oil can be made fairly water resistant after five or six coats. But it is too soft and thin to resist scratching or water-vapor exchange, and it is a difficult finish to make look nice. The first three or four coats appear flat and blotchy on the wood and feel rough to the touch. Only after five or six coats, sanding between each coat, can you get an even, satin sheen. But the finish is still not as smooth to the touch as linseed oil.

In addition, tung oil cures very slowly—considerably faster than raw linseed oil but still slower than boiled linseed oil—so you need to wait several days between coats. This makes tung oil an inefficient finish to use.

Polymerized Oil

As previously explained, linseed oil and tung oil cure slowly by absorbing oxygen. The curing can be speeded up significantly by cooking the oils first in an oxygen-free (inert-gas) environment at about 500 degrees Fahrenheit until they thicken. This, or an equivalent process, is what is done with at least two products that you may be familiar with: Southerland and Wells Polymerized Tung Oil and Tru Oil. Tru Oil is widely available as a gunstock finish. These products act more like varnish than linseed oil or tung oil.

Cooking linseed oil and tung oil in an inert gas causes them to crosslink without going through the oxidation process. This changes the oils so that they complete their curing rapidly (faster than varnish) when exposed to oxygen, and it makes the oils cure hard and glossy. In contrast to normal linseed oil and tung oil, therefore, it's possible to build the oils to a thickness on the surface of wood.

These oils need a name. They are sometimes referred to as "heat-bodied,"

a vague term that simply means cooked and made thicker, usually in the presence of oxygen. Because the product that is sold to woodworkers is labeled "polymerized" oil, it makes more sense to call them polymerized oils. In this context, polymerize simply means crosslinking, and these oils have been partially crosslinked before you buy them, so the name makes sense. You have to be careful with the word "polymerize," however. It is often used by manufacturers as a marketing term to make you think that you are buying something special when you aren't.

There are two problems with using polymerized oil as a finish on large surfaces such as furniture. The oil cures fast, so getting it applied and the excess wiped off before it begins tacking up can be difficult; and you shouldn't apply the oil in thick layers like you do varnish, or tiny cracks may develop in the film. For small objects such as gunstocks, however, polymerized oil works superbly.

Understanding Varnish

To understand wiping varnish and oil/varnish blend, you have to understand varnish and how it differs from oil. (Varnish is explained in greater detail in Chapter 11: "Varnish.")

Varnish is made by cooking one or more oils with natural or synthetic resins. The oils used include curing oils such as linseed oil and tung oil, and semi-curing oils such as soybean oil and safflower oil that have been modified to cure better. The resins used were once natural, but they are now synthetic alkyd, phenolic, and polyurethane.

When oil and resin are cooked together, they combine chemically to form varnish, an entirely new substance

MYTH

The term "tung oil" in the name of a finish means that there is tung oil somewhere in the formula.

FACT

Not necessarily. In fact, most of the wiping varnishes sold as tung oil contain no tung oil. It would not make any difference anyway for truthful labeling. Even with tung oil in the formula, these finishes are still varnish, or blends of varnish and tung oil, not tung oil!

(Figure 5-1). Though varnish is made with oil, calling it "oil," as many manufacturers do, is just as ridiculous as it would be to call bread "yeast." (Bread is made by chemically combining yeast and flour.) Varnish cures much faster than oil. It also cures glossy (unless the manufacturer adds flatting agent to produce a satin or flat sheen). And it cures hard (again, check the overspill around the caps or lids of your cans of varnish or wiping varnish).

Most important is the hardness. This permits you to build varnish in relatively thick coats to a significant film on the surface of the wood. When varnish is built up, it protects the wood from all but the most severe scratches, and it forms an excellent barrier against stains, water, and water-vapor exchange.

Wiping Varnish Sold as Oil

Wiping varnish is simply varnish (any type, including polyurethane varnish) thinned enough with mineral spirits (paint thinner) so it is easy to wipe on

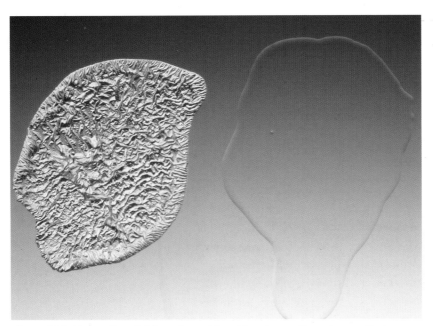

Photo 5-3: Tung oil and thinned varnish sold as tung oil are two entirely different products. Tung oil (left) cures soft, and it cures wrinkled if the excess is not wiped off. Thinned varnish (right) cures hard and smooth, so it can be built up for better protection.

HEAT

Resin + Oil ➡ Varnish

CAUTION: Don't try making your own varnish. It's very dangerous because of the possibility of fire.

Figure 5-1: Varnish is made by cooking a hard resin with a curing or modified semi-curing oil. This makes a substance that cures much harder, faster, and glossier than oil alone.

the wood. The amount of thinner can vary. Most commercial brands contain about one part thinner to one part varnish, but it's rare that you need this much thinner. (See "Wiping Varnish" on p. 155.) You can apply wiping varnish like an oil finish by wiping off the excess. (See "Applying Oil and Oil/Varnish Finishes" on p. 73.) Or you can apply it like full-strength varnish, leaving the excess. Of course, you can also remove just some of the excess before it's completely dry.

It's important to emphasize that wiping varnish is not labeled "wiping varnish." You can't buy it under this name. It will be mislabeled "tung oil," or it will be labeled with a proprietary name. There are three ways to know that you are buying wiping varnish:

■ Wiping varnish is necessarily packaged thinned, so "petroleum distillate" or "mineral spirits" (I've also seen it called "aliphatic hydrocarbon") will always be listed on the label. Tung oil is never sold thinned, so petroleum distillate is not listed.

■ Wiping varnish is watery thin and smells like varnish. Tung oil is thicker (like boiled linseed oil or full-strength varnish) and has a very distinct, pleasant odor that you will always recognize once you have smelled it.

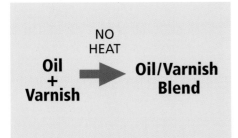

Figure 5-2: Oil and varnish can be mixed to make a finish with some of the characteristics of each. No heat is needed to achieve a thorough mix.

■ Wiping varnish cures hard and smooth after a day or two when left in a puddle on a nonporous surface such as glass or the top of a can. It takes a puddle of tung oil weeks or even months to cure, and when it does, it is wrinkled and soft (Photo 5-3).

Oil/Varnish Blend

Oil and varnish (including polyurethane varnish) are compatible, so they can be mixed. The resulting finish performs with some of the characteristics of each (Figure 5-2). The oil part of the blend reduces the gloss and makes the finish cure slowly. Application is therefore easy because you have plenty of time. (See "Applying Oil and Oil/Varnish Finishes" on p. 73.) But the oil also makes the finish cure soft (again, test the over-spill around the cap of an oil/varnish blend). This means that you cannot build an oil/varnish blend to a more protective thickness. The varnish part of the blend gives the finish more water resistance, hardness, and gloss.

As you would expect, the type of oil or varnish used, and the ratio of oil to varnish, makes a difference, though it is usually too subtle to detect. Because store-bought blends never tell you the types or ratios of oil and varnish used, you may choose to make your own. The

following generalizations should help you decide on a formula:

■ The higher the ratio of varnish to oil, the better the scratch, water, water vapor, and stain resistance—also, the higher the gloss. But if you get the percentage of varnish too high, you will lose some ease of application. A ratio of 90 percent varnish to 10 percent oil, for example, will perform very much like varnish alone. It will just cure softer. Begin by mixing half-and-half, and vary the formulation from there.

■ Using tung oil rather than linseed oil in the mixture will make the finish more water resistant. But the higher the percentage of tung oil you use, the more coats it will take to achieve an even, satin sheen.

■ Though there are significant differences in the qualities of the various varnishes you might use, the differences are difficult to detect when the film is so thin. Your choice of varnish is not very significant.

■ You can thin any blend with mineral spirits (or turpentine if you like). This will make the oil/varnish mixture easier to spread over large surfaces. But it will also thin the coating, so it won't seal the wood as well on the first application. And it will increase the likelihood of bleeding. (See "Bleeding Oil Finishes" on p. 81.)

Which Is Which?

Manufacturers use the name "tung oil" on all four types of finish discussed above: real tung oil, polymerized oil, wiping varnish, and oil/varnish blend. Manufacturers also use uninformative names such as Danish Oil, Antique Oil, Velvit Oil, Profin, Waterlox and Seal-a-Cell. In most cases, when you buy any of these finishes, you don't know what

TIP You can easily thin any varnish to make your own wiping varnish by adding thinner to the varnish until it is easy to spread with a cloth. The result will be less expensive but no less effective than a manufacturer-mixed wiping varnish.

MYTH
Watco Danish Oil makes the wood 25 percent harder, as the manufacturer claimed for many years.

FACT
I don't know how this figure was arrived at, because the product cures much softer than any common furniture wood. How could a soft-curing finish make wood harder?

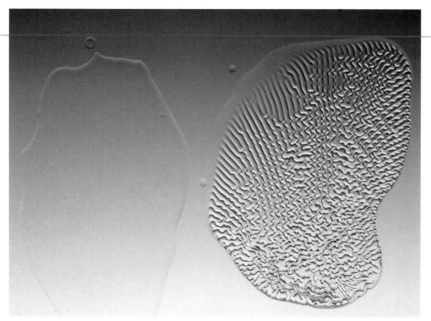

Photo 5-4: Sometimes you can tell if a finish is a wiping varnish or an oil/varnish blend from the overspill around the cap of the container. But if there is no overspill, pour some of the finish onto a piece of glass or other nonporous surface and let it cure for a day or two. If it cures smooth and hard, it is a wiping varnish (left). If it cures soft and wrinkled, it is an oil/varnish blend (right). Straight linseed oil and tung oil also cure soft and wrinkled, but they take many days or weeks to do so.

MYTH

Watco Danish Oil and Waterlox Original are the same type of finish, the difference in the two being resin content.

FACT

Watco and Waterlox are about as different as two finishes can be. Watco is a mixture of oil and varnish, so it never hardens. All the excess has to be wiped off after each coat or you will end up with a gummy finish. Waterlox is varnish, made by cooking an oil and a resin, so it cures hard and can be built up on the wood to any thickness you desire.

you're getting. You need to know how to tell which is which.

Straight oils—linseed oil and tung oil—have distinct smells. Once you've smelled one of these oils, you will always be able to recognize it. Both are nutty smells. Tung oil is sweeter smelling than linseed oil, which is more pungent. Neither of these oils is sold with thinner included, so petroleum distillate won't be listed on the container.

Wiping varnish, oil/varnish blend, and polymerized oil smell like mineral spirits because they contain a significant percentage of mineral spirits. So smell won't aid in distinguishing them. I don't know any easy way to tell if you have a polymerized oil except that it cures fast. There are three indicators you can look for to distinguish between wiping varnish and oil/varnish blend:

■ How fast the finish cures. Oil/varnish blend cures slowly. It can take up to

an hour or more to become tacky, depending on the ratio of varnish to oil. Wiping varnish becomes tacky in 20 minutes or less. (Times will vary with the temperature.)

■ Whether the finish is hard when cured. Wiping varnish cures hard. Oil/varnish blend cures soft.

■ Whether the finish wrinkles severely when it cures thick (Photo 5-4). Any finish containing oil (10 percent or more) will wrinkle when it cures in a thick film. Wiping varnish won't wrinkle unless the film is exceptionally thick. (See the table "How to Tell Which Finish You Have" on p. 82.)

Additional Confusion: Teak Oil

The confusion about oil finishes doesn't stop with straight oil, polymerized oil, oil/varnish blend, and wiping varnish. Some manufacturers market different "oils" for different woods. I saw the most outrageous example of this marketing ploy in a furniture store in Denmark. The store had an entire cabinet full of 2-ounce bottles of teak oil, rosewood oil, walnut oil, oak oil, birch oil, ash oil—a special oil for every type of wood furniture the store carried. Customers were instructed to use only the proper oil on each of the woods in their house!

Teak oil creates the greatest confusion in the United States. There are at least three different types of finish that are sold as "teak oil." There is mineral oil, which doesn't cure. There is a mix of wax and mineral oil, which also doesn't cure. And there is a mix of linseed oil and varnish, which does cure. (Somewhere there must be a wiping varnish I haven't found yet.) The teak oil that is sold by Watco, Behlen, and many Scandinavian furniture stores is an oil/varnish blend. This oil is essentially

Bleeding Oil Finishes

Oil finishes sometimes bleed back out of the wood's pores and form tiny puddles around the pore openings (photo below). If you allow the finish to cure, glossy scabs form, which are difficult to remove. You will have to abrade or strip these scabs off, and you can't do either without also removing the surrounding finish. So allowing any bleeding to cure creates a serious problem.

Bleeding occurs more often in large-pored woods and is caused by the finish expanding as it is warmed. Warming can occur if the wood is warmer than the finish when it is applied, or the wood is warmed during vigorous rubbing or in a move to a warmer location, especially if moved out into the sun. Bleeding no longer occurs after the pores are sealed—usually after the first or second coat has cured. Oil/varnish blends bleed the most, probably because of the added thinner and because they are naturally slow-curing (in contrast to wiping varnish, for example, which also includes added thinner but cures much faster).

To keep scabs from forming, wipe the bleeding off before it cures. Go back over the wood once every hour or so with a dry cloth until the bleeding stops. I usually apply the first coat of finish fairly early in the day, so there is plenty of time to get all the bleeding wiped off before quitting time.

There are two ways to deal with cured scabs.

- Obscure the scabs by rubbing and dulling them with fine steel wool or synthetic steel wool (Scotch-Brite). This often works well on medium- and small-pored woods, such as walnut and maple. But on large-pored woods such as oak it is almost impossible to remove all the gloss from the pores. If you are satisfied with the results you get after abrading, apply another coat or two of finish to replace the finish you've rubbed off. (You can combine the two steps by rubbing with steel wool after you've wet the surface with more finish.) As long as the pores are sealed, you won't have any more bleeding.

- Remove the scabs with sandpaper or paint-and-varnish remover. This will mean that you have to begin your finishing all over again.

Oil finishes sometimes bleed back out of the pores, cure, and form scabs on the surface of the wood. You should wipe off any bleeding before it cures, or you will have to abrade the scabs off or strip and refinish.

the same as other oil/varnish blends. Claims of UV protection are exaggerated because these finishes can't be applied thick enough for UV absorbers to be effective. (See "UV Protection" on p. 280.) Nothing is added to make these finishes better suited for teak or other oily woods.

Oily woods, such as teak, rosewood, cocobolo, and ebony, present a problem in finishing because the wood's natural (non-curing) oil inhibits the curing of oil and varnish finishes. (The oil may also prevent other finishes, such as lacquer and water base, from bonding well to the wood.) Because no oil finish

TIP If your oil or oil/varnish finish cures tacky because you didn't wipe it off well enough, scrub the finish with fine steel wool lubricated with mineral spirits, naphtha, or more of the same finish. In severe cases, use lacquer thinner. Then apply more finish and wipe off the excess.

contains anything to counteract the problems caused by the wood's oil, it's usually best to wipe the wood with a fast-evaporating solvent, such as naphtha, acetone, or lacquer thinner, just before applying the finish. This will temporarily remove the wood's oil from the surface. If it's applied quickly thereafter, the finish then has time to bond well and cure thoroughly before more of the wood's oil seeps back to the surface.

Choosing an Oil or Wiping-Varnish Finish

Choose the finish you want to use for these reasons: ease of application, protection, durability, and color. (See "Guide to 'Oil' Finishes" on p. 84.)

- *Ease of Application:* Straight linseed oil, tung oil, and blends of oil and varnish are very easy to apply because you have a lot of time. Tung oil is more difficult than linseed oil because

more coats are needed and sanding is usually necessary between all coats. Wiping varnish cures relatively fast, and polymerized oil cures even faster, so these finishes can be more difficult to apply to large surfaces.

- *Protection:* Finishes that are varnish or are polymerized offer more protection than straight oil or oil/varnish blend because the former can be built up to a thicker film on the wood. Tung oil provides better protection against water damage than linseed oil.
- *Durability:* Harder-curing wiping varnish and polymerized oil are more durable—that is, resistant to being damaged—than any finish that contains straight oil.
- *Color:* Straight linseed oil and tung oil yellow (actually "orange") the most. Linseed oil yellows more than tung oil. If you want to add warmth to the wood, these finishes are good choices. Oil/varnish blend adds some yel-

How to Tell Which Finish You Have

Clues	Raw and Boiled Linseed Oil	Tung Oil	True Polymerized Oil	Oil/Varnish Blend	Wiping Varnish
The label will almost always tell you correctly.	Yes	Yes	Yes	No	No
The label lists petroleum distillate (mineral spirits) as an ingredient.	No	No	Yes	Yes [1]	Yes
A thin coat gets tacky quickly under a blow dryer.	No	No	Yes	No	Yes
It cures soft and wrinkled when puddled on glass or on the lid of the container.	Yes	Yes	No	Yes [2]	No
It cures hard and smooth when puddled on glass or on the lid of the container.	No	No	Yes	No	Yes

1. Maloof finish is an exception. It doesn't contain mineral spirits.
2. Oil/varnish blend cures harder and wrinkles less than linseed oil or tung oil.

lowing, depending on the oils and varnishes used in the mixture. Wiping varnish and polymerized oil add the least color (Photo 5-5).

For most projects, oil/varnish blend and wiping varnish are the best choices. Oil/varnish blend cures to a satin sheen, while wiping varnish cures glossy unless the manufacturer has added flatting agent, in which case you should stir the finish before using, and you should leave a thin film so the flatting agent can be effective. (See "Controlling Sheen with Flatting Agent" on p. 110.) Wiping varnish is much more protective and durable because it can be built up.

Maintenance and Repair

Maintaining a thin wipe-on/wipe-off oil finish is usually more critical than maintaining any other finish except wax. Even slight wear will create voids, leaving bare wood exposed to spills. The best way to maintain a thin finish is to recoat it now and then, anytime it begins to look a little dry or show wear. Recoating can be done with the same finish you used originally, or with any other brand or type of finish as long as the original is fully cured. You can even use a wiping varnish over one of the oils, or one of the oils over a wiping varnish, though you may change the appearance when you do this (Photo 5-6 on p. 86).

As with any finish, oil finishes can be maintained with paste wax. Paste wax will raise the sheen of a dull surface and will reduce scratching significantly by making the surface slick. But once you have used wax, you should remove it with naphtha or mineral spirits before applying another coat of finish. Otherwise, the finish may cure softer and smudge easier.

(continued on p. 86)

Photo 5-5: Each of the panels above is finished with three coats of a finish that may be labeled or marketed as "oil." From top to bottom: linseed oil, tung oil, polymerized oil, wiping varnish, and oil/varnish blend. They produce quite different colors and sheens.

Guide to "Oil" Finishes

FINISH	Protection[1]	Sheen	Application	Cost	Color[2]	Penetration[3]	
Raw linseed oil	Poor	Satin	Very easy	Low	Dark	Deep	
Boiled linseed oil	Poor	Satin	Very easy	Low	Dark	Deep	
Pure tung oil	Poor until five or more coats	Dull until five or more coats	Very easy	Medium	Medium	Deep	
Polymerized oil	Potentially excellent if built up	Gloss	Easy on small surfaces	High	Light	Medium	
Oil/varnish blend	Medium	Satin	Very easy	Medium	Medium	Deep	
Wiping varnish (not an oil but often sold or marketed as oil)	Potentially excellent if built up	Gloss, unless flatting agents added	Easy	Medium	Light	Medium	

1. Indicates protection against water and water-vapor exchange.
2. Indicates the relative degree of color (darkness) the finish adds to the wood.
3. Indicates how deep the finish will penetrate if the surface is kept wet.
4. Indicates hardness, speed of cure, and sheen.

Raw linseed oil

Boiled linseed oils

Cure[4]	Comment
Soft and extremely slowly—weeks or months—to a satin sheen.	There's no reason to use raw linseed oil in finishing unless you have a specific need for a very slow-curing oil.
Soft and overnight when excess is wiped off—to a satin sheen.	Always wipe off excess, or the finish will be soft and gummy.
Soft and slower than boiled linseed oil—to a satin sheen.	Requires five or more coats, sanding between each, to produce a pleasing satin sheen. More water resistant than boiled linseed oil. Always wipe off excess, or the finish will be soft and gummy.
Hard and faster than wiping varnish—to a gloss sheen.	Very thick unless thinned with mineral spirits, which it usually is. Develops cracks in the film if applied thick.
Generally soft and very slowly, but varies depending on the ratio of oil to varnish. Produces a satin sheen.	Always wipe off excess, or the finish will be soft and gummy.
Hard and fairly rapidly—usually to a gloss sheen after several coats.	Can be built up to any thickness you want by leaving each coat wet on the surface.

Pure tung oils

Polymerized oils

Oil/varnish blends

Wiping varnishes

FACT

Lemon oil, an oily mineral-
spirits solvent with a lemon
scent added, is a very short-
lived maintenance product. It
is a furniture polish that will
help pick up dust, add
temporary shine to a dull
surface, and reduce scratching
until it evaporates—which it
will do within hours. The fresh
scent it imparts is a large part
of its appeal.

Photo 5-6: Lacquer darkens wood slightly, left. Boiled linseed oil adds a deep orange coloring to wood, right. (The center strip is unfinished.) This characteristic can be taken advantage of on many woods, such as this ribbon-stripe mahogany, to make them appear richer and deeper. This is especially the case if you apply a film finish over the top—in this case, the same lacquer that was applied to the raw wood. Be sure to allow the linseed oil a week or longer to cure before coating over.

TIP

If you realize, after you've
applied the finish, that one
piece of wood or a part
of a piece of wood is
lighter than the rest, you can
darken it with any dye stain
that uses alcohol or lacquer
thinner as a solvent. (See
Chapter 4: "Staining Wood.")
The solvent/dye solution will
bite into the finish enough so
that you won't remove the
color when you wipe on and
wipe off the next coat
of finish.

Woodworkers often cite the easy reparability of oil finishes as one of their primary advantages. Repairing a thin finish is often successful precisely because of its thinness. When you wipe an oil finish over the surface, it penetrates and darkens all scratches. Unless the scratches are severe, the new coat often disguises them. But the scratches haven't disappeared: The finish has blended in the color. Any finish can be repaired equally effectively if it is thin enough.

The problems that are difficult to repair in thin oil finishes are water smudges and color differences. Water smudges usually raise the grain of the wood, creating a visually different texture than the surrounding wood. Applying a coat of finish to the smudge seldom removes it from view. It usually helps to rub the surface with a cloth or steel wool, or to sand it lightly with 400-

or 600-grit sandpaper and then apply more finish. (You can also apply more finish and rub or sand while the finish is still wet, then wipe off the excess.) If this doesn't remove the smudge, continue applying more coats of finish to the damaged area until the two sheens blend.

Color differences can be caused by heat or spills staining the wood, by removal of patina (changing the color of the wood itself), or by eliminating the original stain. You can remove heat or burn stains only by sanding through the damage. You can sometimes bleach out spill stains with oxalic acid or household bleach. (See "Bleaching Wood" on p. 50.) You can sometimes fake patina with stain or bleach. And you can sometimes replace the original stain successfully. All of these problems can be difficult to repair to perfection.

CHAPTER 6

Wax
Finishes

Wax has been used for centuries, both as a primary finish for wood and as a polish over another finish. As a finish, wax has been almost entirely replaced by more durable oil and film-building finishes. For a discussion of when to use wax as a polish, see Chapter 18: "Caring for the Finish."

Wax is derived from all three classes of natural materials—animal, vegetable, and mineral—and some waxes are synthetic. All waxes are solid at room temperature. They are made into a paste (and sometimes a liquid) by dissolving them in a solvent. (See "How to Make Your Own Paste Wax" on p. 89.) Traditionally, turpentine was used because it

was the only solvent available. Now petroleum-distillate solvents are common. (See "Turpentine and Petroleum-Distillate Solvents" on p. 158.)

Until fairly recently, beeswax was the primary wax used because it was the only wax available. It is still the only wax in many commercial and homemade paste waxes. But now there are also a large number of natural and synthetic waxes, which are often blended by manufacturers. The waxes are chosen for cost, color, and slip resistance (for floors). But individual waxes also vary in hardness, gloss, and melting point, so the blend has to be adjusted to take these qualities into account.

In Brief

- **Using Wax as a Finish**
- **How to Make Your Own Paste Wax**
- **Applying Paste Wax**
- **Compatibility with Other Finishes**

Hardness, gloss, and melting point are related: The higher the melting point, the harder and glossier the wax. Here are some examples of natural waxes you may be familiar with, though manufacturers often use synthetic waxes that have similar qualities but are less expensive.

- Beeswax (taken from the hives of bees) melts at about 140 to 150 degrees Fahrenheit, is medium-soft, and produces a medium-gloss sheen. It is easy to use as a finish or polish.
- Paraffin wax (derived from petroleum) melts at about 130 degrees Fahrenheit, is softer than beeswax, and has a slightly lower sheen. It is rarely used alone as a finish or polish—although traditionally, butcher-block tables have been finished with paraffin.
- Carnauba wax (scraped from the leaves of a Brazilian palm tree) melts at about 180 degrees Fahrenheit, is very hard, and produces a higher shine than beeswax. It is very difficult to buff out when used alone.

In order to use very hard waxes such as carnauba, manufacturers blend in softer waxes, such as paraffin. The blending reduces the melting point, hardness, and gloss of the hard waxes. All common paste-wax blends melt in the range of 140 to 150 degrees Fahrenheit, the same as for pure beeswax. Therefore, all common paste waxes have about the same hardness and gloss. If you notice any differences, they are probably due to differences in the surfaces you've waxed, not to the paste waxes you've used. (Try applying two or more paste waxes to adjacent parts of a surface and see if you notice a difference.)

Major manufacturers of paste wax seldom use natural beeswax, either alone or in combination with other waxes. Beeswax is expensive. Also, beeswax has a grainy texture, which causes it to smudge easily. Pure beeswax polishes are usually made by small companies tapping into the mystique of beeswax being the traditional paste wax.

The only significant difference among commercially available waxes is the length of time you should wait before wiping off the excess wax. The waiting period depends on the evaporation rate of the solvent that was used to turn the solid wax into paste or liquid form. Some paste waxes, such as Johnson's and Briwax, contain solvents that evaporate quickly. Others, such as Minwax, contain slower-evaporating solvents. When all the solvent evaporates, the wax is solid again.

Wax becomes more difficult to buff off the longer you let it harden. If you want to apply wax to a large area before you start wiping, choose a wax with a solvent that evaporates more slowly. Unfortunately, you will have to discover the paste wax you like best by trial and error. Manufacturers don't provide useful drying information.

Some paste waxes are sold in colors. The colorant in the wax is dye or pigment. (See Chapter 4: "Staining Wood.") You can use a colored paste wax to stain the wood while finishing it or to color in nicks and scratches when polishing.

Using Wax as a Finish

In some ways wax is like oil and oil/varnish blends: It is easy to apply, produces a satin sheen, and dries soft. (See "Applying Paste Wax" on p. 90.) But a wax finish is even less protective than linseed oil. In fact, wax is the least protective of all finishes. It is the closest thing to having no finish at all on the wood.

How to Make Your Own Paste Wax

Commercial paste waxes are as good as anything you can make yourself. But you may want to make your own just for fun or to get a specific color or shine. Here's how to go about it:

1 Shred some wax or a combination of waxes into a container.

2 Add mineral spirits, naphtha, or turpentine in the ratio of ½ pint of solvent to 1 pound of wax.

3 Put the container in a pot of hot water, and let the wax and solvent combine, stirring as necessary. You can keep the pot of water hot by placing it on a heat source, but never put the container of wax and solvent directly over a flame or burner; it can catch fire.

4 When the wax has cooled, it will be the consistency of butter in summertime. If you want it thicker, add more wax and reheat. If you want it thinner, add more solvent and reheat.

5 You can add rottenstone or colorant (oil or japan pigments, or oil-soluble dye dissolved first in naphtha or toluene) to the dissolved wax to make it better at disguising scratches or to create different antique effects. Add enough colorant to make the wax a uniform color.

You can make your own paste wax by dissolving any solid wax or combination of waxes in turpentine or petroleum-distillate solvent (mineral spirits, naphtha, toluene, etc.). Heating will speed the dissolving, but don't put the container directly over a heat source; put it in water and heat the water. If the wax comes in bricks like the beeswax at left, grate it into the container of solvent. If it comes in flakes like the carnauba wax at right, simply add it to the solvent.

Wax provides no significant barrier against heat, water, water-vapor exchange, or solvents. The melting point of wax, around 150 degrees Fahrenheit, is too low to protect against damage from hot objects. Wax is soft, which necessitates wiping off all the excess, so a wax finish is not thick enough to be an effective barrier against water or water-vapor exchange. (However, a thick wax coating, as is often applied on the ends of boards, is a good barrier.) All common solvents, including those in liquid furniture polishes, dissolve wax on contact.

The only protection a wax finish provides is to reduce abrasive damage, such as scuffs and scrapes. Wax makes the surface of the wood slicker, so glancing blows tend to slide off rather than dig in. But reducing scuffs and scrapes is not a good reason to use wax

Applying Paste Wax

Paste wax isn't used much anymore as a finish for furniture, because it's not very protective or durable. It is, however, used as a polish over other finishes. (See Chapter 18: "Caring for the Finish.") Here is how to apply paste wax as a finish or as a polish:

1 Be sure the surface of the wood or finish is clean.

2 Put a lump of paste wax in the center of a soft, 6-in.-square cotton cloth and wrap the cloth around the paste wax.

3 Rub the cloth over the surface, allowing the paste wax to seep through the cloth and onto the surface. You can rub in any direction. You're going to wipe off all the excess anyway. The purpose of putting the wax inside the cloth is to control the amount you deposit on the surface. The less wax you deposit, the less you'll have to remove. If the wax is hard, knead it in your hand until the wax warms and softens.

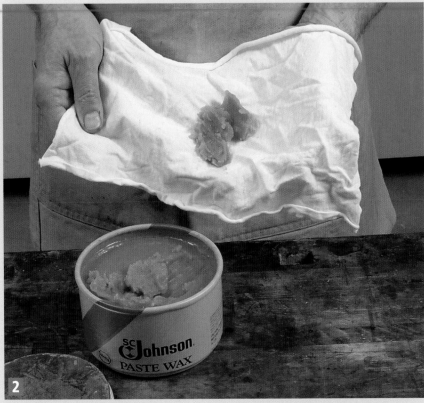

The easiest way to apply paste wax is to put a lump of wax in the middle of a soft cloth, wrap the cloth around the wax, and let the wax seep through the cloth as you rub it over the finish.

4 Allow most of the solvent to evaporate (the sheen will change from glossy to dull). The time this takes will vary, depending on the solvents used in the paste wax and the temperature conditions. Work on one small area at a time until you get a feel for the rate of evaporation.

5 Wipe off the excess wax with a soft, clean cotton cloth. If you catch the wax just as the sheen changes, the excess will be easy to remove. If you wait too long, you will have to rub very hard in order to build up enough heat (above 150 degrees Fahrenheit) to melt the wax so it can be removed. On the other hand, if you are too quick, you'll remove too much of the wax.

6 You can use a power buffer or drill with a lamb's-wool pad to remove the remaining excess wax and buff up a shine. If the lamb's-wool pad is smearing the wax and not removing it, the pad has become too loaded. You're no longer transferring the wax to the

TIP If you're using paste wax as a polish over another finish and you want to smooth and dull the finish at the same time you are applying the paste wax, you can apply the wax with steel wool. Rub with the grain so the scratches will be less noticeable.

TIP If the wax dries too hard to remove easily, you can apply more paste wax to soften the original wax and then remove the excess before it gets too hard. Or you can wash off all or most of the wax with a naphtha- or mineral spirits–dampened cloth and begin again.

6

If you don't remove the excess wax, you'll leave streaks of wax on the surface of the finish.

pad; you're just moving it around. Try to remove more of the wax with a cloth, and then buff again with a clean lamb's-wool pad. You have to *remove* the excess wax, not just spread it around. As long as you can smear the surface by rubbing it with your finger, you haven't removed all the excess wax.

7 You will usually get a better result if you apply more than one coat of wax, waiting at least several hours between coats. You are not building the wax with a second coat; you are filling in minute areas still left after the first coat. If the surface was dull to begin with, the improvement from the second coat is usually quite noticeable.

8 To maintain a wax finish or polish, dust it regularly with a feather duster or a soft cloth. On a wax polish (over another finish), you can dampen the cloth slightly with water to aid in picking up the dust. You can also use a water-dampened chamois. If the surface begins to look dull, rub it with a soft, dry cloth to bring back the shine.

If no shine reappears, apply another coat of paste wax. Because wax doesn't evaporate, you should not have to reapply wax on tabletops for many months, or on unused surfaces for many years.

9 If, after a number of waxings, you get so much wax on the surface that you can smear the wax

with your finger, then you have not been removing all the excess with each waxing. Apply a fresh coat of wax and rub off the excess, or remove most or all of the wax with naphtha or mineral spirits and buff what is left.

10 Softer woods are more difficult to finish with wax than harder woods, because the wax is absorbed more into the wood. You can keep applying coats until the sheen comes up and is even, or you can apply the wax with the help of heat to melt more of it into the pores. This will speed up the process. A hair dryer, heat gun, or similar heat source will raise the temperature of the wax above 150 degrees Fahrenheit and melt it. Just don't get the wood so hot that you scorch it.

11 If you are waxing a wood-turning, you can use a wax stick made of carnauba wax (like those made by Hut and Liberon) and apply the wax right on the lathe. The spinning will create enough heat to cause the wax to melt and transfer to the wood when you press the stick against it.

as a primary finish. Wood that receives the sort of use that requires scuff resistance will quickly become dirty if wax is the only finish. The dirt gets worked into the soft wax, and a dirty wax finish can't be repaired. It has to be stripped, and often the wood has to be sanded to get it clean.

The only reason to use wax as the sole finish is to keep the color of the wood very close to its natural color while giving the wood some sheen. Wax doesn't darken the wood as much as other finishes do, and it doesn't color it unless a colorant has been added to the wax. A wax finish may be very effective on a decorative, carved, or turned object that won't receive much handling. As the artist who created the object, you might choose wax for aesthetic reasons. A wax finish is better than no finish at all, but only because dusting is easier (with a feather duster, not with furniture polish or a damp cloth).

You may have seen instructions for wax finishes that suggest applying a coat or two of shellac, oil, or some other finish underneath the wax. This is an excellent practice for making a more durable finish than wax alone. But wax with another finish underneath to seal the wood isn't a wax finish. It's the other finish, with the wax being used as a polish on top of that finish. Wax is an excellent polish for use on any other finish. (See Chapter 18: "Caring for the Finish.")

Compatibility with Other Finishes

You'll come across formulas that suggest mixing wax with other finishes such as linseed oil, a mixture of linseed oil and varnish, or even mineral oil. Though it is possible to mix wax with these finishes, it is generally not a good idea. The resulting finish will be even softer than without the wax. In many cases the finish will be so soft that you will smudge it every time you touch it.

You can apply wax over any finish, but you can't apply every finish over wax. Only straight oil, oil/varnish blend, and shellac can be applied over wax. Oil and oil/varnish blend will dissolve the wax, making a mixture like the one described above. Shellac contains some wax naturally, so it will still bond to wood as long as most of the wax on the wood has been removed. (A large percentage of eighteenth-century furniture was waxed originally and then coated over with shellac in the nineteenth century.) Water-based finish will wrinkle when applied over wax. Lacquer, varnish, and polyurethane will cure softer and more slowly. In all cases the wax may weaken the bond with the wood or finish below.

CHAPTER 7

Filling
the Pores

In Brief

- **Filling Pores with the Finish**
- **Filling Pores with Paste Wood Filler**
- **Finish vs. Paste Wood Filler**
- **Oil-Based vs. Water-Based**
- **Common Problems Using Oil-Based Paste Wood Filler**
- **Using Oil-Based Paste Wood Filler**
- **Using Water-Based Paste Wood Filler**

All woods have a natural texture that results from the size and distribution of the wood's pores. Some woods, such as maple and cherry, have a smooth, even texture because their pores are small and uniformly distributed. Other woods, such as walnut and mahogany, have a coarse, even texture because their pores are fairly large and uniformly distributed. Still other woods, such as plainsawn oak and ash, have an uneven (alternately smooth and coarse) texture, because their pores vary in size, the spring-growth pores being much larger than the summer-growth pores.

The texture of the wood largely determines how the wood looks with a finish on it. The textures of maple and oak, for example, are so different that it is impossible to make one look like the other unless you paint the wood and then apply a faux-grain finish. In other words, paint the figure and grain on to the wood.

Though you often can't make one wood look like another, how you apply a finish can affect the wood's texture, as long as you're using a film finish. If you apply a finish thinly, the finished wood will have almost the same texture as the unfinished wood. If you fill or partially fill the pores of the wood while you're applying the finish, you can significantly change the wood's appearance. A *mirror*

Photo 7-1: You get very different effects on mahogany with its pores, as shown in the samples from left to right—unfilled, partially filled, and totally filled.

finish results when you totally fill the pores, so that there is no evidence of pitting in reflected light. You will often see this elegant effect on the tops of high-priced tables, but it doesn't require expensive materials or equipment to achieve (Photo 7-1).

There are two common ways to fill or partially fill the pores of wood—with the finish and with paste wood filler. Filling the pores with the finish is less problematic and, with small-pored woods, quicker. Filling pores with paste wood filler is faster with large-pored woods, less wasteful of finishing materials, and more stable, in that the filler shrinks less in the pores. Also, paste wood fillers offer a greater range of effects. (See "Finish vs. Paste Wood Filler" on p. 96.)

Filling Pores with the Finish

To fill the pores of wood with finish, you apply a number of coats of finish and sand them back until the dips in the pores come level (Figure 7-1). It's possible to do this with any finish that cures hard enough so it can be built up on the wood. Shellac, lacquer, varnish, water base, and all two-part finishes can be used to fill the pores. So can sanding sealer and catalyzed sanding sealer.

You can apply a number of coats and then cut them back all at once, or you can cut back each coat a little, until the surface is mirror smooth. Cutting back the coats all at once is more efficient. But if you cut back each coat of finish a little, you can simultaneously sand out dust and other flaws. Either way, be careful not to cut through the finish and dig into the wood. This is especially important if the wood is stained. If you do cut through, you may find the damage difficult to repair so it can't be seen—especially if the problem area is large. You may need to strip everything and start over. If you've never cut back a finish before, I recommend you practice on a test panel before you tackle an important project.

Using Sandpaper to Cut Back the Finish

Most finishers use sandpaper to cut back the finish. (It's also possible to use a scraper, but there's greater risk of cutting through.) If you're sanding after every coat, use stearated (dry-lubricated) sandpaper on the first couple of coats so lubricant doesn't get into the wood. After several coats you can use wet/dry (black) sandpaper and a liquid lubricant to increase efficiency. Here are some suggestions for how to proceed:

- Begin with 220- to 320-grit sandpaper. (See "Sandpaper" on p. 12.)
- To remove finish evenly on flat surfaces, back the sandpaper with a flat cork, felt, or rubber block.
- If you're using oil as a lubricant, you can add a little mineral spirits to make sanding easier. If you're using water as a lubricant, you can add a mild soap such as dishwashing liquid to reduce sandpaper clogging. I prefer oil and mineral spirits for most situations.
- If you're using a lubricant together with a random-orbit sander, pneumatic is much safer than electric.
- Use a plastic spreader to remove the sludge in various areas to check your progress. If you've applied a gloss finish (the best practice), glossy spots in the pores, indicating where you haven't sanded enough, will be easy to see (Photo 7-2).

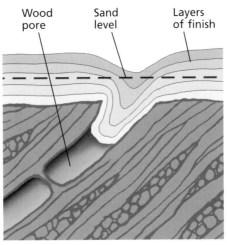

Figure 7-1: To fill pores with a finish, apply enough coats of finish to build the lowest point in the pitted pores up well above the surface of the wood. Then sand the finish back until all evidence of the pitting disappears.

If you're using varnish or lacquer and you want to fill the pores with easier-to-sand sanding sealer and reduce the chances of cutting through to the wood, apply a coat of the finish first. Then apply coats of sanding sealer and sand them back until you feel the resistance of the finish. This way, you'll leave the sanding sealer only in the pores, not built up on the surface where the sanding sealer could significantly weaken the finish film. (See "Sealers and Sealing Wood" on p. 116.)

Photo 7-2: To quickly check your progress sanding back a finish, clean the sludge from an area using a plastic spreader. If you haven't sanded enough, the dips of the pores will still show—especially clearly if you have applied a gloss finish.

- When you're satisfied that you have leveled the finish, sand with finer-grit sandpaper to remove the coarse-grit scratches. Continue through finer and finer grits or switch to steel wool or rubbing compounds until you achieve the sheen you want. (See Chapter 16: "Finishing the Finish.")

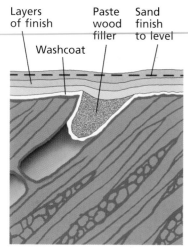

Layers of finish · Washcoat · Paste wood filler · Sand finish to level

Figure 7-2: To fill pores with paste wood filler, pack the filler material into the pores either over a washcoat (the best practice) or directly on the wood and wipe off the excess before it gets too hard. Then build a finish and level it with sandpaper to get a mirror-flat surface.

Filling Pores with Paste Wood Filler

Paste wood filler, also called *grain filler* or *pore filler*, is composed of filler material, binder, and usually a colorant. The filler material, which does most of the actual filling, is silica, calcium carbonate, clay, or microballoons (microscopic, hollow, glass-ball clusters made of silica). The binder, which glues the filler material to the wood, is oil or varnish (commonly referred to as "oil-based"), or water-based finish. The colorant is pigment. (Dye is not a good choice for paste wood filler because it may fade over time, leaving the pores lighter than the overall color of the wood.)

Paste wood filler is not the same as *wood putty*, which is considerably thicker and used to fill larger nail holes and gouges. There are, however, some brands of water-based wood putty that can be thinned with water so they double as paste wood filler.

You can buy paste wood filler in wood-tone colors from some manufacturers, or you can buy it without colorant (usually called "neutral") and color it yourself. Oil-based paste wood filler won't take stain well after it has cured, so you have to make it the color you want before applying it. Water-based paste wood filler usually takes stain fairly well, so you can still color it after application. (Be sure to check on scrap wood that the stain you intend to use colors the filler adequately.)

There are two ways to color paste wood filler: Add a compatible stain (oil stain to oil-based filler and water-based stain to water-based filler) or add concentrated colorants. It's best to add concentrated colorants because you lose control of the "flash-off" time with a stain. It will be the thinners in the stain, which you have no control over, that determine this time. Use ground-in-oil or japan-color pigments with oil-based filler. Use universal tinting colorants (UTCs) or artist's acrylic colorants with water-based filler.

You can apply paste wood filler either directly to the wood or over sealed wood (Figure 7-2). If you apply colored filler directly to the wood, the filler stains the wood in addition to filling the pores. If you apply colored filler onto sealed wood, the filler colors only the pores (Photo 7-3). In all cases, you get a better final result if you fill twice, waiting until the first filling is dry before applying the second.

Types of Paste Wood Filler

The binder in the filler determines which type it is—oil-based or water-based (Photo 7-4 on p. 99). Oil-based fillers have been in common use for a century. Water-based fillers have been in use only a decade or two. Oil-based fillers are easier to apply because you have a lot

Finish vs. Paste Wood Filler

Advantages of Filling the Pores with Finish	Advantages of Filling the Pores with Paste Wood Filler
Fewer application problems. Faster to fill small-pored woods such as maple and cherry. Can be used to keep the color of the pores very close to the overall color of the wood, whether stained or not.	Doesn't shrink as much in the pores, so pitting is less likely to reappear after several months. Much faster to fill larger-pored woods, such as oak and mahogany. Can be used to decorate the pores. (Use an entirely different color than the wood itself, or than the stained wood.) Can be used to create the appearance of greater depth in wood. (Use a color slightly darker than the color of the wood itself, or of the stained wood.) Less wasteful of finishing materials (finish and sandpaper).

Photo 7-3: The decision to washcoat wood before applying paste wood filler depends primarily on whether you want to color the pores the same as you color the wood or to color them differently than the natural or stained wood. Applying colored paste wood filler directly to wood (left) fills the pores and colors the wood. Applying paste wood filler over washcoated wood (right) puts filler, and thus color, only in the pores.

NOTE

There are possibilities other than paste wood filler for filling the pores in wood. These include nitrocellulose- and gypsum-based wood putty, plaster-of-paris, acid-catalyzed sealer, polyester, and other high-solids finishes. You can slow the drying of the nitrocellulose putty with lacquer retarder, and you can slow the drying of gypsum and plaster-of-paris with vinegar. You should color each before application because they don't take stain well. Acid-catalyzed sealer and polyester have a very high-solids content and sand easily.

more working time, but these fillers cause more problems when you apply a finish. (See "Common Problems Using Oil-Based Paste Wood Fillers" on p. 98.) Water-based fillers are more difficult to apply because they dry so quickly, but there are rarely problems applying a finish over them. (See "Oil-Based vs. Water-Based" at right.)

Oil-based paste wood fillers are by far the most common because solvent-based finishes are used far more than water-based finishes on high-end furniture worthy of being filled. (See "Using Oil-Based Paste Wood Filler" on p. 100.) These fillers vary in drying time depending on the ratio of linseed oil to varnish used. The higher the percentage of linseed oil, the more time you have to remove the excess filler. Of course,

Oil-Based vs. Water-Based

Advantages of Filling the Pores with Oil-Based Paste Wood Filler	Advantages of Filling the Pores with Water-Based Paste Wood Filler
Much easier removal of the excess filler.	Much shorter wait time before applying a finish.
More control over coloring the pores.	Can be stained after it has dried.
Better depth in most cases.	No question about whether the filler is ready to be coated over. It will sand powdery.
	Rarely a problem coating over with any finish.

Common Problems Using Oil-Based Paste Wood Filler

Oil-based paste wood filler is easy to apply, but problems can occur later during finish application. Here are the principal ones.

Problem	Cause	Solution
The finish wrinkles and doesn't dry hard.	You applied the finish before the filler was fully cured, and the oil in the filler got into the finish.	Strip the finish and filler material and start over.
Lacquer causes the filler to swell and protrude from the pores.	You applied too wet a coat of lacquer. The lacquer thinner in the lacquer attacks varnish and oil in the same way that paint remover causes oil paints to swell and blister.	Sand the surface level. This will have the effect of removing some of the filler that had been in the pores. Fill again, or apply additional coats of finish and sand them back.
		Strip the finish and begin again.
The filler turns gray in the pores when the finish is applied.	This usually occurs with finishes that thin with lacquer thinner. The cause is not fully understood but may be that the thinner remaining in the filler causes the lacquer to come out of solution.	You may be able to mask the problem with glaze, but you will most likely have to strip the finish and begin again.
The finish separates from the surface when a blow is struck.	The bond to the wood is poor.	Strip the finish and begin again. Apply a washcoat to the wood before applying the paste wood filler. The finish will bond to the washcoat through any residue that might be left on it.
		If you are using a water-based finish, let the filler cure longer before applying the finish.

more linseed oil also means you have to wait longer before you can apply the finish. (For more on the differences between oil and varnish, see Chapter 5: "Oil Finishes.")

Manufacturers provide little or no information about the drying time of their fillers, and weather also plays a significant role. So you can't know in advance what the working properties of the paste wood filler will be. You can learn only by trying different brands. If the filler hardens too fast for you, you can slow it by adding a very small amount of boiled linseed oil. Begin by adding no more than 1 teaspoon to 1 quart of filler. If the filler cures too slowly, you can speed it up by adding Japan drier.

Begin by adding a few drops to a quart of filler, and work up from there. It's always best, however, to find a brand of filler that gives you the working characteristics you want. Tampering with manufacturers' formulations can cause problems.

Some finishers cut out a step and use colored paste wood filler as both a filler and a stain. With oil-based filler, this is not the best practice. It's usually best to apply the filler over a thin first coat of finish called a *washcoat*. (See "Washcoats" on p. 64.) The reason for a washcoat rather than a full sealer coat is to keep the edges of the pores sharp, so less filler will be removed during the wiping process (Figure 7-3). There are at least six good reasons for washcoating before filling:

1 You have more control of the appearance. You can color the wood with one color and type of colorant (for example, a dye stain) and color the pores with another (the pigmented filler).

2 The washcoat provides a cushion so you are less likely to sand through stain if you should need to sand off streaks of unremoved filler after it has dried.

3 You can fill small sections at a time on large surfaces without getting lap marks, because you're removing all the colored filler except what is in the pores.

4 The washcoat creates a smoother, harder surface that makes wiping off the excess filler easier.

5 If something should go wrong—the filler becoming too hard to wipe off, for example—you can remove the filler with naphtha or mineral spirits without affecting the color of the stain underneath.

6 You get a better bond to the wood. The finish bonds better to the washcoat, which is bonded well to the wood, than it does to an oily surface on the wood left by the paste wood filler.

Two common solvents are available for thinning oil-based paste wood filler: mineral spirits and naphtha. (You could also use turpentine, but you gain no advantage over mineral spirits, and it costs more.) Mineral spirits evaporates more slowly than naphtha, so use it when you are filling a large surface and want more working time. Use naphtha on smaller surfaces when you don't want to wait for the evaporation. You can mix the two to reach a middle ground if you want. The choice of thinner has no effect on the

Photo 7-4: There are two types of paste wood filler—those with an oil/varnish binder (left), which use mineral spirits or naphtha for thinning and cleaning up, and those with a water-based binder (right), which use water.

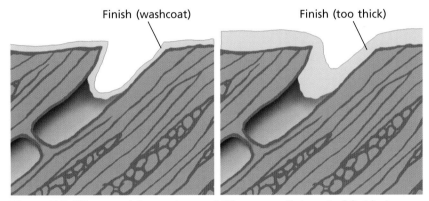

Figure 7-3: When applying paste wood filler over a first coat of finish, keep the coat very thin (called a washcoat) so the edges at the tops of the pores remain sharp (left). You will leave more filler in the pores when you remove the excess. If the pores are rounded over by a thick coat of finish (right), you'll pull much of the filler back out when you remove the excess.

ultimate curing time of the paste wood filler, only on how long before the filler becomes too hard to wipe off.

You can add any amount of thinner you want to the filler. The amount determines the working qualities. If you don't add any thinner, or if you add just a little, the filler will be thick and you will need to rub or press it into the pores of the wood. The filler will dry and set up quickly, so you can work only on small areas at a time. If the filler does dry too hard to wipe off, soften it by wiping with the thinner.

If you add a lot of thinner, enough to make the filler watery thin, you can brush or spray it onto the surface. If you

Using Oil-Based Paste Wood Filler

Although oil-based paste wood filler is the most commonly used, some woodworkers and finishers avoid it because of problems they've had or problems they've heard about. Application is actually uncomplicated, however, and the filler is quite forgiving because you can easily soften or remove it with its thinner for quite some time. Here are the basic steps for applying oil-based paste wood filler:

1 Stain the wood if you like and apply a washcoat of finish. (See "Washcoats" on p. 64.) You can leave this washcoat unsanded.

2 Add oil- or japan-pigment colorant to the filler if necessary to get the color you want. Stir the filler, and keep it stirred while you're using it.

3 You can use the filler right from the can, but it's easier to apply it thinned. Use mineral spirits for a longer working time, naphtha for a shorter time. If you leave the filler at a fairly thick consistency, you'll need to rub or press it into the pores as you apply it. You can do this simply by rubbing with a cloth, or you can use a plastic spreader or a squeegee. If you thin the filler to a water consistency, it will flow into the pores pretty well on its own. On larger surfaces it's easiest to thin to a water consistency, and there is less waste.

4 Apply the filler to the wood using a cloth, brush, or spray gun. (Use an inexpensive or old brush or

4

The most efficient method of applying oil-based paste wood filler is to brush or spray it watery thin on the wood to an even thickness. The thinner will "flash off" evenly across the surface, so there is an ideal moment to begin wiping off the excess. You want most of the thinner to evaporate out of the filler so there is less shrinkage back into the pores.

a dedicated spray gun.) If the filler is thick, rub or press it into the pores quickly after application. If the filler is thin, brush or spray it to an even thickness on the wood (see photo above).

5 Let the thinner evaporate to the point that the paste wood filler loses its shine. Temperature, air circulation, and the type of thinner used will govern how long this will take, but it's usually not very long. A soft, moist residue should remain.

6 Remove the excess filler by rubbing *across* the grain with a coarse cloth, such as burlap. (A cotton cloth may work also.)

Be sure the cloth is free of any dirt or grit that might scratch the wood. You rub across the grain to reduce the amount of filler you pull back out of the pores (see photo on facing page).

7 On turnings, carvings, and inside corners, use a sharpened dowel to remove the excess.

8 When the wood is clean, remove any remaining cross-streaks by wiping lightly in the direction of the grain using a soft cotton cloth.

9 Let the filler cure at least overnight before continuing. If the weather is cool or humid, let it cure longer.

6

When enough of the thinner has evaporated for the paste wood filler to have lost its shine, remove the excess by rubbing across the grain with a coarse cloth, such as burlap.

10 On large-pored woods, such as mahogany and oak, you'll get a more level surface if you *double-fill:* Apply paste wood filler a second time after the first coat has cured overnight. You can apply a washcoat of finish in between if you like.

11 Sand the wood lightly in the direction of the grain using 320-grit or finer sandpaper or a maroon or gray synthetic abrasive pad to be sure there are no remaining streaks running across the grain. Be very careful if you haven't applied a washcoat and have used the filler to stain the wood; it's easy to remove some of the

color. If you do, apply more of the original stain to that area, wipe the stain off quickly, and let it dry before continuing. If you can't get the color even, strip the wood and start over.

12 If you are using a finish that thins with lacquer thinner over the paste wood filler, follow one of two procedures to reduce pinholing and the chance of the lacquer thinner swelling the filler and causing it to push up out of the pores:

■ Apply a washcoat of shellac before the first coat of lacquer. Then apply several light coats of lacquer before applying heavy coats. The shellac will slow the

penetration of the lacquer thinner into the paste wood filler.

■ Spray several mist coats of lacquer before applying fully wet coats. The mist coats won't soak and swell the paste wood filler.

13 When you apply a finish on top of the filled wood, you may notice that there is still some pitting. This is due to shrinkage and to your having wiped some of the filler out of the pores when you wiped off the excess. It can't be helped. To get a perfectly mirror-flat surface, you will have to sand back the finish to complete the filling. (See "Filling Pores with the Finish" on p. 94.)

Using Water-Based Paste Wood Filler

The distinguishing characteristic of water-based paste wood filler is that it dries very quickly. If you apply the filler either straight from the can or thinned with water, you will have very little time to remove the excess. (You can increase your working time a little by adding a propylene-glycol retarder or a proprietary thinner supplied by some manufacturers.)

You can apply water-based filler the same as oil-based filler, over a stain and washcoat, or you can apply it directly to the wood and stain it after it has dried. Both methods are in common use. I prefer the first. The actual application is the same with each.

1 Add UTC- or acrylic-pigment colorant to the filler if necessary to get the color you want. Stir the filler, and keep it stirred while you're using it.

2 Use the filler straight from the container, or thin it with water or propylene glycol.

3 Apply a glob of filler to the surface and begin spreading it with a plastic spreader or squeegee (photos, right). As you spread the filler, press it into the pores. Then remove the excess quickly, before it dries. You can remove in any direction, but go back over the area immediately in the direction of the grain to line up any streaking you might leave. By applying the filler in this manner, you can cover a large surface very quickly, but it is still usually best to work in small sections at a time. If any filler

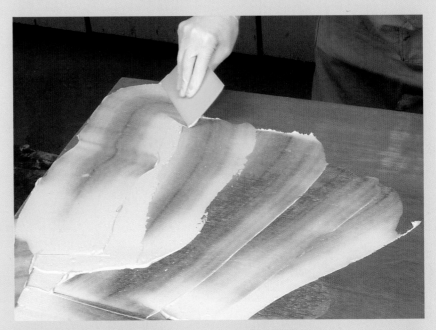

Because water-based paste wood filler dries very quickly, you have to remove the excess immediately. Use a plastic spreader to spread the filler and press it into the pores (top). Then, angling the spreader a little steeper and pressing a little harder, quickly remove the excess from the surface (bottom).

hardens on your spreader, remove it or it will scratch the surface.

4 Once you have spread the filler and removed as much of the excess

as you can, try to rub off more using burlap, rubbing across the grain. If there is considerable excess that you can't remove, wipe over with a water-dampened cloth to soften the filler. If this removes some of the filler from the pores, apply more filler.

5 Allow the filler to harden for an hour or two. It may take longer if you've added a retarder or if the weather is humid.

6 Use a medium-grit (150 to 220) sandpaper, backed by your hand or on a random-orbit sander, to sand off the filler that has hardened on the surface of the wood. The filler should powder like plaster. It's more risky to use a power sander if you have stained and washcoated the wood, because you might sand through. If you have used a neutral or colored filler, you need to sand off all the excess, or the wood will be muddied. Sand until you reach the wood or the washcoat. If you have used a transparent filler, you don't have to sand off all the excess. You just need to sand the surface level and smooth.

7 Clean off the dust and apply a second coat of filler, which will produce a more level surface, or continue with your finish coats. You can apply stain to the filled surface to add color.

8 When you apply a finish on top of the filled wood, you may notice that there is still some pitting. This is due to shrinkage and to your having wiped some of the filler out of the pores when you wiped off the excess. It can't be helped. To get a perfectly mirror-flat surface, you will have to sand back the finish to complete the filling. (See "Filling Pores with the Finish" on p. 94.)

keep the thickness even, the solvent will flash off evenly across the surface, offering an ideal moment to begin wiping off the excess. (It's important to let as much of the thinner as possible evaporate out of the filler, without it getting too hard, so there is less shrinkage back into the pores.) This is the way I prefer to apply oil-based paste wood filler, and it is the method used in the furniture industry and by most large shops.

Water-based paste wood fillers are fast drying, and this affects application procedures and the wait time before applying a finish. In fact, the shortened wait time is probably the primary benefit of using water-based fillers. There are also fewer problems during the application of a finish.

Instead of brushing or spraying the filler onto large flat surfaces and wiping off the excess with burlap or a cotton cloth as is common with oil-based fillers, it's usually better to apply a glob of un-thinned filler to the surface and spread it with a plastic spreader or squeegee. Spread, press the filler into the pores, and remove the excess immediately. You can then follow this with a burlap wipe, but the filler is usually too hard by then. (See "Using Water-Based Paste Wood Filler," left.)

Because the filler dries so fast, and because it sands so easily and takes stain so well, it's possible to apply the filler directly to the wood. Then remove as much of the excess as possible and sand off the rest after the filler dries. Once sanded smooth, you can apply a stain to color both the wood and the filler left in the pores. Because the various manufacturers' fillers accept stains differently, you should try your stain first on filled scrap to be sure it performs up to your expectations.

Photo 7-5: These four panels illustrate different looks obtained filling mahogany in different ways with different products. The same mahogany water-soluble dye stain was used on all four, and all four were cut from the same veneered sheet. Panel 1 (left): Lacquer washcoat over the stain, then a walnut-colored oil-based paste wood filler and topcoats of lacquer. Panel 2: Water-based washcoat over the stain, followed by a walnut-colored water-based paste-wood filler and topcoats of water-based finish. Panel 3: Water-based paste wood filler first and then the stain, topcoated with water-based finish. Panel 4: Shellac washcoat over the stain, followed by a transparent water-based paste wood filler and topcoats of water-based finish. I got the deepest and richest look from the oil-based paste wood filler and lacquer (panel 1). Among the water-based samples, transparent filler (panel 4) produced considerably more color and depth than "neutral" filler, either way I applied it (panels 2 and 3).

It's also possible to apply water-based filler over a stain and washcoat just as with oil-based fillers. I find that this method produces better results, but there are a great many finishers who apply the filler directly to the wood and stain afterwards. Try each on scrap panels to determine which method you prefer (Photo 7-5).

Just as with oil-based fillers, it's possible to soften and remove excess filler after is has hardened too much to wipe off. With water-based fillers, use a water-dampened cloth. If you remove too much filler from the pores, apply more filler.

Most of the water-based paste wood fillers on the market are "neutral," that is, they have a light tan or off-white color. Some have a colored pigment included, but usually not enough for dark or dark-stained woods. You have to add more pigment to these fillers or apply a stain after they have dried. There are a few fillers, however, that are transparent, and these produce a rich clarity equivalent to that achieved with oil-based fillers. They have another good quality as well. Because they are transparent, you don't have to sand off all the excess. You need to sand them only level and smooth. Then apply the finish of your choice.

CHAPTER 8

Introduction to Film Finishes

Finishes can be divided into two groups: penetrating and film. A better name for penetrating finishes would be "non-film-building" because all finishes penetrate, but "penetrating" is the name that is commonly used. Penetrating finishes contain straight oil and don't cure hard, so they become gummy if the excess isn't wiped off after each coat. (See Chapter 5: "Oil Finishes.") Film finishes cure hard so they can be built up to any thickness you want. There are five types of film finishes commonly used in woodworking. (See also "What's in a Name?" on p. 106.) You will find each of these discussed in a separate chapter:

- shellac
- lacquer
- varnish (including oil-based polyurethane, which is a type of varnish)
- two-part (catalyzed, two-part polyurethane, epoxy, etc.)
- water base

Film finishes protect better than penetrating finishes because of their thickness on the surface of the wood. The thicker the finish, the better it protects the wood from scratches, water, and water-vapor (humidity) exchange. There are practical limits to film thickness, of course, because if the finish is too thick, it may develop cracks due to internal stresses or expansion and contraction of the wood underneath. (To learn a way of measuring the thickness of a finish, see "Solids Content and Mil Thickness" on p. 108.)

Film finishes also offer more possibilities for decoration than penetrating finishes. You build a finish film the way you make a sandwich—in layers. The first

What's in a Name?

Some of the confusion surrounding film finishes exists because of an imprecision in the names used for the finishes. Shellac, lacquer, varnish, and water base are each identified by a number of different names:

- Shellac used to be called "spirit-varnish" (in contrast to oil-varnish), and it is sometimes still referred to by this name. Shellac is also identified as "lacquer" when referring to its lac bug origins or when the word lacquer is used to indicate any finish that cures by evaporation. For example, *padding lacquer* (see Chapter 19: "Repairing Finishes") is essentially shellac that has an oily solvent included so it can be used for French polishing.

- Lacquer is called varnish when the term "varnish" is used to indicate any finish that dries to a hard, glossy, transparent coating.

- Varnish is called "lacquer" when referring to Chinese or Japanese lacquer, which is actually a reactive-curing resin tapped from certain trees. Varnish used to be called lacquer when it was baked hard and used as a coating in food cans. (Now water base is used,

and called "lacquer" and "varnish.")

- Water base is often called "lacquer" or "varnish" for marketing reasons. This makes an entirely new type of finish seem familiar. Water base is also called "polyurethane" for the same reasons when some polyurethane resin is blended with the usual acrylic resin.

This interchangeability of names adds to the confusion about film finishes. When you hear or read that someone varnished their table, it could mean they applied either of the evaporating finishes (shellac or lacquer), a reactive finish (varnish or conversion varnish), or a coalescing finish (water base).

In this book I use the names most often associated with each of the finishes, the names likely to be used in paint stores. In the case of water-based finishes, I avoid calling them lacquer, varnish, or polyurethane, as is so often done by marketers, because this leads to confusion and does nothing to distinguish one water-based finish from another. All water-based finishes have far more in common with each other than with any of the finishes that have traditionally been identified by those names.

layer, or *coat*, of finish is called the *sealer* coat. It stops up, or *seals*, the pores of the wood. (See "Sealers and Sealing Wood" on p. 116.) Subsequent coats, called *topcoats*, increase the thickness of the film, add decorative color, and raise or lower the sheen if you choose.

You can incorporate decorative color into a film finish in several ways (Figure 8-1):

- You can add color by putting it in the finish—called *toning* if the coat covers the entire surface or *shading* if it covers only part of the surface.

- You can add color by putting it in between coats of finish—called *glazing*. (See Chapter 15: "Advanced Coloring Techniques.")

You can control the sheen of a finish by rubbing the last coat with abrasive compounds (see Chapter 16: "Finishing the Finish"), or by using a finish that includes a *flatting agent*. (See "Controlling Sheen with Flatting Agent" on p. 110.)

Making Sense of Finishes

One of the biggest problems woodworkers face with finishes is making sense of all the choices. You have to understand how finishes differ before you can choose intelligently among them. (See Chapter 14: "Choosing a Finish.")

At first, the key may seem to lie with the resins. All film finishes are made with resins, which are the hard part that is left after the finish has cured. Common resins used in wood finishes include alkyd, acrylic, melamine, and polyurethane. Polyurethane is the best-known resin and is widely understood to be very tough and durable. So it follows that any finish made with polyurethane should be tough and durable. This is true to a point, but consider the finishes that are sometimes made with polyurethane resin:

- oil-based polyurethane
- water-based polyurethane
- polyurethane lacquer
- two-part polyurethane

If you have used any two of these finishes, you know that they are very different. Oil-based polyurethane cures very slowly to a very protective and durable film. Water-based polyurethane dries much faster, raises the grain of the wood, and isn't anywhere near as impervious to liquids or as resistant to heat, solvents, or chemicals. Polyurethane lacquer dries very rapidly, so it has to be sprayed. It dries to a hard film that is more durable than water-based polyurethane and less durable than oil-based polyurethane. Two-part polyurethane also dries very rapidly and is so durable that it is very difficult to damage, repair, or strip.

NOTE
▼

Technically, "drying" and "curing" describe different ways a liquid converts to a solid. Drying refers to solvent evaporation. Evaporative finishes "dry" because they convert to a solid entirely by solvent evaporation. Curing refers to a chemical change. Reactive finishes "cure" because they convert to a solid by a chemical reaction brought about by oxygen or a catalyst. A coalescing finish (water base) converts by both drying and curing (drying between the droplets and curing—or pre-curing—within the droplets). When possible, I use the term that correctly describes the conversion to a solid. But there are many situations (as when talking about multiple finishes or water base) when it's not possible. For these I use "curing."

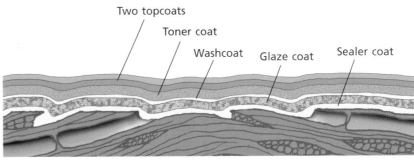

Figure 8-1: A film finish is built up in layers. The first layer is the sealer coat (a stain could be applied underneath). The last layer is composed of topcoats. You can add color in between the sealer coat and topcoats. If the color is in between layers of finish, it's called *glazing*. If the color is in the layers of finish and it covers the entire surface, it's called *toning*. If the color is in the layers of finish and you apply it to only part of the surface, it's called *shading*. Layers of color are usually separated by *washcoats*, which are thin coats of finish. A complex finish might include all of these layers.

The other resins are equally inadequate for explaining the key characteristics of the finishes in which they are included. Clearly, knowing something about the resin, or resins, used in a finish goes only part way toward understanding that finish. More useful is to classify film finishes by how they cure.

How Finishes Cure

All finishes cure in one of three ways: by evaporation of the solvents (these are called *evaporative* finishes); by a chemical reaction that occurs within the finish after the solvents have evaporated (these are called *reactive* finishes); or by a combination of the two: solvent evaporation and chemical reaction (these are called *coalescing* finishes). (See "Finishing Materials: How They Cure" on p. 112 and "Comparing Evaporative, Reactive, and Coalescing Finishes" on p. 115.)

There is a very easy way to picture how each of these types cures. Evaporative finishes, which include shellac and lacquer, are like spaghetti in a pot of water. Reactive finishes, which include varnish and two-part finishes, can be illustrated with Tinker Toys. Coalescing

> It's wise to strain film finishes before spraying or brushing. Even newly opened containers can be contaminated with dirt or with small dried or coagulated lumps of finish. Use a paint strainer, which is inexpensive and easy to use and is available at paint stores and from finish suppliers. Or use tightly woven cheesecloth.
>
> **TIP**

Solids Content and Mil Thickness

Most woodworkers and finishers express the thickness of a finish in "coats." For example, "I applied three coats." The problem with this method is that a coat of one type of finish applied by one person can vary greatly in thickness from a coat of another type of finish applied by someone else.

Different finishes vary in *solids content* (the amount of solid material, mostly resin, relative to the amount of thinner, which evaporates), and people differ in how much they thin a finish and in what they call a "coat." Some brush the finish out thin, while others lay it on thick. Some spray one pass and call it a coat, while others apply two fully wet layers, one right on top of the other, and call this a coat.

A much more accurate method of expressing film thickness is to measure the thickness of the coat just after application while it is still wet using a tool called a "wet-mil-thickness gauge," or "mil gauge," for short. (A mil is one/one-thousandth of an inch—.001.) Then calculate the dry film thickness by multiplying the wet mil thickness by the finish's solids content. (You must also

> **TIP**
> The appearance of a film can be used to estimate film thickness. A dry appearance is typically 2 mils or less. A level, wet appearance is about 4 mils. A wrinkled or wavy appearance is 6 mils or more.

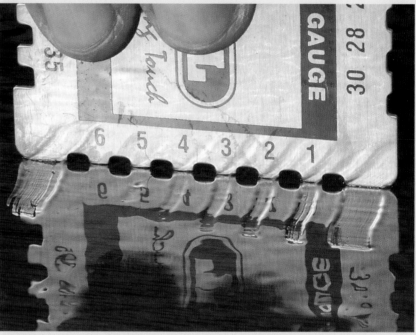

To measure the dry film thickness of one coat of finish, place a mil gauge on a wet finish just after brushing or spraying it. The highest-numbered tooth that marks the finish is the wet mil thickness. Then multiply this number by the volume solids content of the finish to determine the dry mil thickness. Be sure to take into account any thinner you have added. In this example I have applied the finish with a wet thickness of 5 mils. I dragged the mil gauge a little, so you could see the marks better. Dragging isn't necessary.

take into account any thinner you have added.)

To measure the wet mil thickness of a finish film, place the mil gauge on the finish as shown in the photo above just after you spray or brush it. (Do this on a piece of scrap wood.) The thickness of the film is equal to the highest-numbered mil tooth that leaves an impression in the finish.

Once you've determined the approximate wet mil thickness, you can calculate the dry film thickness of a typical coat of that finish as you apply it. To do so, find the percent solids by volume of the finish you're using. (See table on facing

page.) The manufacturer usually provides the percent solids by weight because it is weight that manufacturers use to measure how much of each ingredient to put into the mixing vat. Volume is about 20 percent less than weight, but to be more accurate, call the manufacturer or figure the volume from the MSDS sheet supplied for the product. (You may have to call the manufacturer for this also, but most now put MSDSs on their web sites.)

On the MSDS, find the "percent volatiles." This is everything in the finish that will evaporate. Subtract this from 100

Finish Type	Approximate % Solids by Volume
Shellac (1-lb. cut)	9
Shellac (2-lb. cut)	16
Shellac (3-lb. cut)	22
Lacquer	20
Varnish	30
Water Base	30
Pre-Catalyzed Lacquer	30
Post-Catalyzed Lacquer	35
Conversion Varnish	35
Two-Part Polyurethane	50
Polyester	90
Epoxy Resin	100
UV-Cured	100

to give you the solids content by volume. Everything that doesn't evaporate has to be solids.

Now take this figure and multiply it by the mil thickness of the wet coat. For example, to figure the mil thickness of one coat of post-catalyzed lacquer with 35 percent solids by volume, applied 4 mils thick, multiply 4 x .35 to get 1.4 mils. It will take three coats of this finish to obtain a total dry film thickness of about 4 mils. You usually want the total dry mil thickness of your finish to be between 2.5 mils, which looks thin on wood, and 5 mils.

Here is another example in which you add thinner. You must factor this in. Let's say you spray a 4-mil wet-film thickness of nitrocellulose lacquer with a volume solids content of 20 percent, thinned with 10 percent lacquer thinner. Multiply 4 x (.20 minus .02) to get .72 mils. It will take five to six coats to achieve a dry film thickness of 4 mils.

finishes, which consist of water-based finishes, resemble plastic soccer balls coated with solvent and pressed together. (See "Classifying Finishes" on p. 116.) Let's take each in turn.

Evaporative Finishes

The evaporative finishes are shellac and lacquer. They are composed of long, stringy molecules that resemble spaghetti on a microscopic scale. In a solvent, these molecules float around like spaghetti does in a pot of water. As the solvent evaporates, the molecules become entangled (just as spaghetti would in less water), and they become hard and solid when all the solvent (the water in spaghetti) is gone (Figure 8-2).

In solution

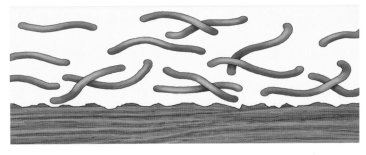

As a film

Back in solution

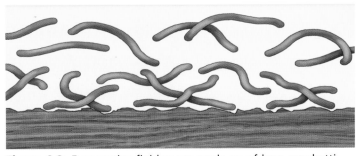

Figure 8-2: Evaporative finishes are made up of long spaghetti-like molecules that pack together and entangle when the solvent evaporates. When the solvent is reintroduced, the molecules separate, and the finish returns to liquid form.

Controlling Sheen with Flatting Agent

Flatting agent is the solid stuff, usually silica, that settles to the bottom of a can of satin or flat finish. When stirred into the finish and applied to wood, the flatting agent reduces the gloss by creating a micro-roughness on the surface that scatters light randomly. The more flatting agent added to the finish, the lower the sheen (photo right).

All film finishes, except shellac, are available with flatting agent included. The finishes are usually labeled semigloss, satin, eggshell, rubbed effect, matte, flat, dead flat, or something similar depending on how much flatting agent the manufacturer has added. Unfortunately, these terms are very loosely defined, so one brand of satin is not likely to produce the same sheen as another. A more exact numbering system, ranging from 1 to 100, is available (100 is perfect gloss), and a few manufacturers use it.

You can buy flatting agent (usually sold as "flatting paste") separately from some suppliers and create your own sheen by adding it to a finish. Or you can blend cans of different sheens of the same finish. You can also pour off some of the finish from a can in which the flatting agent has settled, giving you one portion of gloss and another of very flat. Then you can blend these to get the sheen you want.

Depending on the type of flatting agent used, the particles are totally transparent or nearly transparent within the film of finish. The sheen is created by the particles lying at the surface of the film. As the wet film shrinks during drying, it pulls taut over these particles,

A gloss finish reflects light and objects clearly (right). A flatted finish (satin, flat, etc.) breaks up light, and thus an image, due to the surface micro-roughness created by the flatting particles (left).

Flatting agent reduces gloss by scattering reflected light. As the finish dries, it shrinks and pulls taut over the flatting particles at the surface of the film. The microscopic bumps this creates scatters the light. The more flatting agent added, the more dense the bumps and the flatter the appearance. Most flatted finishes are totally transparent within the film. Some manufacturers use flatting agents that leave the film a little cloudy. You can test the transparency by applying a coat of gloss over two coats of satin and comparing it with two or three coats of gloss.

It's the topcoat that creates the sheen. Coats underneath have very little or no impact. To demonstrate, I finished the left half of this panel with two coats of satin finish and then applied a coat of gloss finish over just the left quarter. I finished the right half with two coats of gloss finish and then applied a coat of satin finish over just the right quarter. The first two coats had no impact on sheen where a third coat was applied.

creating the micro-roughness that produces the flatted effect (drawing at left). The change from wet gloss to flatted during application usually occurs within a short time and is very apparent if you are watching.

Because the flatted effect is created by a roughened surface and not by the particles that have cured deep within the film, it should be obvious that the last coat of finish applied establishes the sheen. If you apply two coats of satin and then one coat of gloss, the finish will appear glossy. Likewise, if you apply two coats of gloss and then one coat of satin, the finish will appear satin (photo below left). It should also be obvious that a flatted sheen can be made glossy simply by rubbing with fine abrasives. In fact, any abrading you do to the surface of a flatted finish will change the sheen in one direction or the other. Near the edges of well-used tabletops, for example, it's common to see a flatted finish rubbed glossy by wear.

Many flatted finishes appear to scratch more easily than gloss finishes. This is because of the relative ease with which coarse objects can level the micro-roughness. Some manufacturers use wax-coated flatting particles to resist this leveling, but I've never seen this information listed.

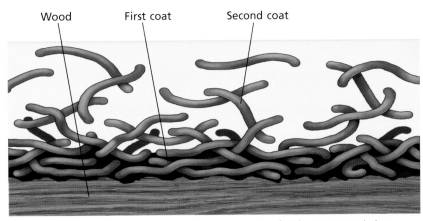

Wood   First coat   Second coat

Figure 8-3: When you apply a coat of evaporative finish over an existing dried coat, the solvent in the new coat partially dissolves the underlying coat, and the molecules of each entangle, making one thicker layer.

If you were to touch hardened spaghetti with some water on your finger, the spaghetti would become sticky. If you were to soak the hardened spaghetti in water, the strands would separate and return to the state of individual spaghetti floating in water. The same happens when you touch hardened lacquer with lacquer thinner or hardened shellac with alcohol, and the same happens when you soak dried lacquer with lacquer thinner or dried shellac with alcohol. The finish first softens and becomes sticky. Then it dissolves and goes back to its liquid state. (Wax is also an evaporative finish, but it never gets hard, so it can't be built up.) From this method of curing, we learn the following:

- The drying time of shellac and lacquer is entirely dependent upon how fast the solvents evaporate. If you want to speed up or slow down the drying, use a faster- or slower-evaporating solvent.
- When you apply one coat of an evaporative finish over another, the newly applied coat dissolves into the existing coat or coats, creating one thicker coat (Figure 8-3). You can't wipe off the new coat without making a mess. You can't even touch it before it dries

or you will leave a mark that may go all the way through to the wood.

■ You can spray coats of evaporative finish, one over the other, without waiting for each previous coat to dry. The only downside to this procedure is that you have to wait longer for the finish to dry all the way through, as the solvents at the bottom work their way out of the finish.

■ Because the stringy molecules are held together by little more than entanglement, they are easy to separate (damage) with abrasion, heat, solvents, and chemicals. On the positive side, this makes evaporative finishes easy to rub (abrade) to an even sheen, and possible to repair invisibly by

melting or dissolving more finish into the damage.

■ Due to the microscopic spaces created by the entangled finish molecules, tiny water molecules can find a path through to the wood, so evaporative finishes are not especially water-vapor resistant. (There is some evidence, however, that shellac may be an exception.)

Reactive Finishes

The reactive finishes are varnish and all two-part finishes. They are composed of small molecules that resemble the blocks in a set of Tinker Toys. In a can of finish these molecules are floating in a thinner. As the thinner evaporates, the molecules

Finishing Materials: How They Cure

Once you understand the three types of curing—evaporative, reactive, and coalescing—you gain much better control over almost all finishing products. Except for dyes and bleaches, all the products you use in finishing cure by one of these three methods. Generally it's easy to tell which type of curing you're dealing with from the solvents, thinners, and cleanup materials listed on the container.

Evaporative (solvents are alcohol, acetone, and lacquer thinner)	Reactive (thinners are mineral spirits and naphtha, often listed as "petroleum distillate")	Coalescing (solvent is glycol ether; thinner is water)
■ shellac	■ linseed oil and tung oil	■ water-based finishes
■ lacquer	■ oil/varnish blend	■ wiping stains that clean up with water
■ fast-drying stains with lacquer binder	■ wiping varnish	■ all-in-one stain, seal, and finish that cleans up with water
■ wood putty that thins with lacquer thinner or acetone	■ gel varnish	■ wood putty that cleans up with water
■ wax (solvent is mineral spirits or turpentine)	■ varnish (including polyurethane)	■ paste wood filler that cleans up with water
	■ wiping stains that thin with mineral spirits	■ glaze that cleans up with water
	■ all-in-one stain, seal, and finish that thins with mineral spirits	
	■ paste wood filler that thins with mineral spirits	
	■ glaze that thins with mineral spirits	
	■ two-part finishes (thinners vary)	

approach each other and connect either with the help of oxygen (in the case of varnish) or with the aid of a catalyst, activator, crosslinker, or hardener (in the case of two-part finishes). This connection is commonly referred to as *crosslinking* or *polymerization* and is represented by the sticks in the Tinker Toys (Figure 8-4).

A cured varnish or two-part finish resembles a gigantic Tinker-Toy network on a molecular scale. Touching the cured finish with the thinner for that finish (or with any solvent, for that matter) doesn't have any effect. Soaking the cured finish in solvent may blister it, but no solvent will dissolve it. (Linseed oil and tung oil are also reactive finishes, but they never get hard, so they can't be built up.) From this method of curing, we learn the following:

■ The curing time of varnish and two-part finishes is dependent upon the speed of the crosslinking, not on the speed of thinner evaporation. The evaporation usually has to be well along, however, before the cross-linking can begin.

■ Coats of reactive finish don't dissolve into each other. So you have to apply coats within days or weeks of each other for varnish, and within a much shorter time for two-part finishes, to get a good bond. Either this, or you have to scuff the existing finish, so the newly applied finish can bond mechanically by interlocking in the grooves (Figure 8-5). If you want to remove a bristle or some dust in a newly applied coat, you can do so without fear of damaging the finish below. You can even wash off this coat with thinner if you are quick. But if you sand or rub through one coat into the one below, a visible line will appear at the intersection (Photo 16-6 on p. 213).

In solution

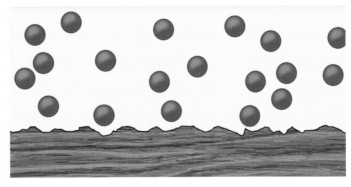

Cured

With thinner reapplied

Figure 8-4: Reactive finishes crosslink when they cure. The molecules of resin bond together chemically, resembling a Tinker Toy–like network on a molecular scale. Reintroduction of the thinner doesn't break these bonds apart.

First coat   Second coat

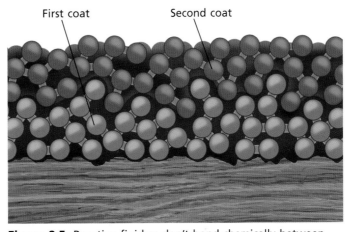

Figure 8-5: Reactive finishes don't bond chemically between coats once the underlying coat has fully cured. To get the two coats to bond, you have to make scratches in the underlying coat with sandpaper or steel wool, so the new coat can interlock mechanically.

In solution

Cured

With alcohol or lacquer thinner introduced (water won't do this)

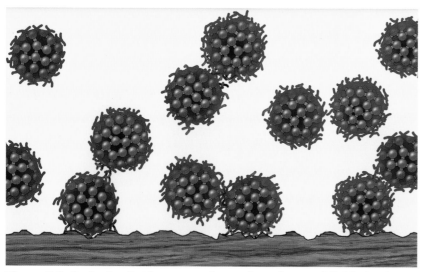

Figure 8-6: Coalescing finishes are made up of reactive-cured finish droplets that pack together as the water evaporates. The glycol-ether solvent then softens the outer surfaces of the droplets, causing them to become sticky. When the solvent evaporates, the droplets stick together and the film becomes hard. If a solvent, such as alcohol or lacquer thinner, is reintroduced to the cured finish, the droplets become sticky and gummy at first, then become liquefied.

- In contrast to evaporative finishes, each coat of reactive finish has to cure hard before the next coat can be applied. Otherwise, the existing coat may wrinkle.

- The crosslinked Tinker-Toy network creates a finish that is very scratch, heat, solvent, and chemical resistant. Coarse objects have to tear the molecules apart to cause a scratch. Very high heat is required to blister these finishes. It takes very strong solvents (on the order of methylene chloride) to remove these finishes. On the other hand, reactive finishes are difficult to rub to an even sheen and difficult to repair so the repair doesn't show.

- Because of the very tight network created by the crosslinked molecules, reactive finishes are exceptionally resistant to water-vapor penetration.

Coalescing Finishes

Water base is the only coalescing finish. It is composed of droplets (latexes) resembling microscopic soccer balls with plastic covers and solid insides. The insides are reactive finish that has been crosslinked. The droplets are suspended in water and a very slow evaporating solvent. The water evaporates first. The solvent then softens the outside of the droplets (as solvent would soften the outer skin on plastic soccer balls). The droplets become sticky and stick together when the solvent evaporates (Figure 8-6). White and yellow glues dry in the same way.

Bringing water in contact with a cured water-based finish doesn't cause any negative effect. But touching the finish with a strong solvent softens it and turns it gummy. The solvent separates the droplets, and they return to their sticky state. Some people try to group water-based finishes with evaporative finishes or with reactive finishes, but this leads to confusion. In fact, water-based finishes have some of the characteristics of each. These are the major ones:

■ Water-based finishes resemble evaporative finishes in drying characteristics. Drying is dependent on the speed of solvent evaporation. The drying rate of water base can be slowed by adding a slower-evaporating solvent. But once the finish has been made, the drying rate can't be speeded up except with heat (all finishes cure faster with heat).

■ Coats of finish have minimal dissolving effect on the coat below, just enough to create an adequate bond if coats are applied within days or weeks of each other (Figure 8-7). The dissolving is not enough to create one thicker layer as with evaporative finishes. If considerable time goes by between coats, the existing finish should be scuffed so the newly applied coat can bond mechanically by interlocking

Figure 8-7: When you apply a coat of coalescing finish over a recently applied coat, the small amount of solvent in the new coat softens the surface droplets in the existing coat, so the two coats stick together. There is not enough solvent in the new coat to soften the existing coat deeper than the surface.

Comparing Evaporative, Reactive, and Coalescing Finishes

The way a finish cures tells you a lot about that finish. Here is an overview of the three types.

Type of Finish	Evaporative (shellac and lacquer)	Reactive (varnish and two-part finish)	Coalescing (water base)
Curing is totally dependent upon the speed at which the solvent evaporates	Yes	No	Yes
Coats dissolve into each other	Yes	No	Partially
Can pile coats on top of each other without waiting for the previous to dry	Yes	No	No
Difficult to damage	No	Yes	Difficult to scratch but easy to damage with heat or solvents
Very water and water-vapor resistant	No	Yes	No

in the grooves. The longer you wait between coats, the more likely you will get a visible line at the intersection of the coats if you rub through one into the other.

- As a result of the coats not dissolving well into each other, each coat should be allowed to dry hard before applying the next coat. Coats should not be applied over partially dry coats, or problems may occur.
- The crosslinking within each droplet creates a surface that is very scratch resistant. But the evaporative-type joining of the droplets makes water-based finishes susceptible to damage from heat, solvents, and chemicals. The combination of evaporative and reactive curing characteristics makes water-based finishes easier to repair and rub to an even sheen than reactive finishes but more difficult than evaporative finishes.
- The crosslinked resin within each droplet is very resistant to water-vapor penetration, but the evaporative-type connections established between the droplets let water vapor through similar

Classifying Finishes

Group	Finish	Type of Cure
Film	Shellac	Evaporative
	Lacquer	Evaporative
	Varnish (including polyurethane)	Reactive
	Two-part finish (Catalyzed lacquer; Conversion varnish; Two-part polyurethane; Polyester; Epoxy; UV-cured)	Reactive
	Water base	Coalescing
Penetrating	Oil and oil/varnish blend	Reactive

Sealers and Sealing Wood

Many people think they have to use a special sealer to seal wood because the finish won't do it. This is not correct. The first coat of any finish seals the wood. It penetrates, cures, and stops up the wood's pores (figure at right). Liquids, including the next coat of finish, won't penetrate through the cured first coat. So *all finishes* can be sealers.

Separate "sealing" products exist to solve one of four problems:
- Make the first coat easier to sand.
- Reduce grain raising.
- "Seal off" oil, resin, wax, or odors in the wood.
- Lengthen the application window for some two-part finishes.

MAKE SANDING EASIER
Sanding the first coat of any finish is good practice because this coat is always a little rough. Sanding it smooth makes all additional coats go on more smoothly and produce a better end result. Varnish and lacquer are difficult to sand, however. So *sanding* sealers, which are varnish or lacquer with mineral soap (zinc stearate) added, are provided for these finishes. Mineral soap causes the varnish or lacquer to powder when sanded (photo upper right), reducing clogging in the sandpaper. (Note that sanding sealers are not provided for polyurethane, shellac, or pre-catalyzed lacquer, and rarely for water base, because these finishes are not as difficult to sand.)

Sanding sealers made for varnish and lacquer powder when you sand them. This reduces sandpaper clogging.

The first coat of any finish stops up the pores in wood, thus sealing them. You don't need a separate "sealer" to do this.

Sanding sealer is soft and crumbles if applied thick and then struck with a blunt object. This happens even under the topcoats, and the damage can be repaired only by filling with colored finish. (See Chapter 19: "Repairing Finishes.") Never apply more sanding sealer than needed for easy sanding without sanding through. In most cases, this means one coat.

MYTH

Sanding sealer provides a base for better finish adhesion.

FACT

The opposite is the case. The mineral soap in sanding sealer weakens the bond of the finish to the wood. This myth may be caused by confusing the role of a sanding sealer with that of a primer. Paints contain so much pigment that there's proportionally not enough binder to both glue the pigment particles together and create a good bond to porous wood. Primer is less pigmented, so it has a higher proportion of binder and therefore bonds well to the wood. Clear finishes are all binder. They bond perfectly well to wood by themselves.

Confusion about the role of sanding sealers is made worse by mislabeling and misleading marketing:

- Some sanding sealers are labeled "sealer," and this may lead you to believe that it *has* to be applied under the finish.
- Some finishes are marketed as "self-sealing," again leading you to believe that other finishes may need a separate sealer. (Self-sealing means simply that the finish is already easy enough to sand.)

Sanding sealers have a downside: They reduce durability. The mineral soap reduces water resistance and

Sealers and Sealing Wood (continued)

crumbles and turns white if struck hard, especially if the sanding sealer is applied thick (photo left). It's best to apply no more than one coat. In fact, it is even better not to use sanding sealer at all unless you are working on a large job. In this case, it is usually worth trading off some durability for much easier sanding. Think of sanding sealer as a tool for speeding production.

REDUCE GRAIN RAISING

Some water-based finishes are quite alkaline (you can smell the ammonia), and alkaline water raises grain worse than pH-neutral water. So manufacturers sometimes provide a more acidic water-based sealer to reduce grain raising. Without the alkali, however, the sealer is less durable, so you are sacrificing some durability if you use it.

Unfortunately, manufacturers often label this product "sanding sealer," but it isn't easier to sand. Just as with traditional sanding sealer, think of this product as a production tool.

CAUTION

▼

Polyurethane doesn't bond well to finishes that contain mineral soaps or to shellac that contains wax, so you shouldn't use a separate sanding sealer or wax-containing shellac under polyurethane.

SEAL OFF PROBLEMS IN THE WOOD

If you are refinishing furniture or woodwork, you may run into situations where there is oil (usually silicone oil from furniture polishes) or wax in the wood that causes problems such as fish eye, poor drying, or weak bonding. You may also come across wood with a strong odor from smoke or animal urine. For these situations, you can use shellac to seal off the problem. ("Sealing" has a slightly different meaning here. The word is usually combined with "off" or "in" and means to block off or "seal in" a problem in the wood or to separate one color step from another.)

In new-wood finishing, you may have to deal with resinous pine knots that cause drying and bonding problems. Shellac is an excellent sealer for sealing off this problem also.

Shellac is often touted as a great sealer for all situations and is now thought of more as a sealer than as a finish. This is unfortunate. There is no reason to use shellac under another finish unless there is something in the wood that may cause a problem. There is always some risk of blistering, wrinkling, or poor bonding whenever you apply one finish over another. You may also be weakening the protection and durability of the total finish if the finish you apply over the shellac is more protective and durable. If you do use shellac, it is best to use dewaxed shellac—

that is, shellac with its wax removed. You will usually get a better bond with it. (See Chapter 9: "Shellac.")

LENGTHEN THE APPLICATION WINDOW

Two-part catalyzed lacquers and conversion varnishes often have a very limited time within which all coats of finish have to be applied. (See Chapter 12: "Two-Part Finishes.") Incorporating filling, coloring, and glazing steps may cause you to extend past this limit. For these situations, you can use vinyl sealer to seal the wood and then apply washcoats of vinyl sealer in between the decorating steps. (See "Washcoats" on p. 64.) Finally, apply the two-part finish on top.

Vinyl sealer is nitrocellulose lacquer with vinyl resin added to improve water resistance and bonding properties. Many finishers use vinyl sealer to seal the wood even without the time considerations because vinyl sealer is less expensive than the finish itself and doesn't sacrifice water resistance.

The downside of vinyl sealer is that it is difficult to sand. To overcome this, some manufacturers add mineral soaps, the same as those added to sanding sealers. And just as with sanding sealers, these soaps reduce the water resistance of the total film. You have to make the choice: easier sanding or greater durability.

to evaporative finishes. (Latex paint, which is water-based finish with pigment added, is valued for its ability to "breathe"—that is, let water vapor through.)

Solvents and Thinners

When I was first learning finishing, I once asked my foreman how he knew which solvent to use with which finish. He just knew, he said; he didn't have an explanation. I've concluded he was on to something. There is no easy explanation. You just have to learn which solvent or thinner works with which finish. (See "Solvents and Thinners for Various Finishes," below.)

It does help to understand the difference between a solvent and a thinner, however. A solvent dissolves a cured finish; it turns a solid into a liquid. (See "Finish Compatibility" on p. 120.) A thinner just thins a liquid. One substance can be a solvent for one finish and a thinner for another, or both a solvent and thinner for the same finish. Here's how they sort out:

- Mineral spirits, naphtha, and turpentine are solvents for wax and thinners for wax, oil, and varnish. They dissolve solid wax, but they don't dissolve

NOTE

Information about the negative health effects associated with the use of solvents has increased in recent years. But it's the solvents in finishes that make them possible to apply, and it's the solvents you add to finishes that solve problems. Solvents are indispensable, even for water base. The trick to using solvents in a healthy manner is to protect yourself with good ventilation and an organic-vapor respirator mask, especially if you use solvents often.

Solvents and Thinners for Various Finishes

The words "solvent" and "thinner" are often used interchangeably, but they have different meanings. A solvent will dissolve a cured finish (or other solid material). A thinner won't necessarily; it thins a liquid solution. The same substance can often be both a solvent and a thinner for a finish—that is, it will dissolve the hardened finish, and it will also thin the liquid finish.

Substance	Solvent for	Thinner for
Mineral spirits Naphtha Turpentine	Wax	Wax Oil Varnish
Toluene Xylene	Wax (will break down water base and white and yellow glue)	Wax Oil Varnish Conversion varnish
Alcohol	Shellac Lacquer (partial)	Shellac Lacquer Water base
Lacquer thinner	Shellac Lacquer Water base	Lacquer Shellac (padding lacquer) Catalyzed lacquer
Glycol ether	Shellac Lacquer Water base	Water base
Water		Water base

cured oil or varnish. They also don't dissolve any other finish, so they are used in furniture polishes and cleaners. (See "Turpentine and Petroleum-Distillate Solvents" on p. 158.)

- Alcohol is a solvent and thinner for shellac and a weak solvent and partial thinner for lacquer and water base. Alcohol will damage lacquer and water

base but not actually dissolve them. Alcohol won't damage reactive finishes. (See "Alcohol" on p. 126.)

- Lacquer thinner is a solvent and thinner for lacquer and a thinner for catalyzed lacquer. It is also a solvent for shellac and water base. Lacquer thinner will soften and sometimes blister reactive finishes, but it won't

Finish Compatibility

With two important cautions, all finishes can be applied over all other cured finishes. The cautions are these:

- The surface of the finish you are coating over must be clean and dull.
- If the thinner in the finish you are applying is lacquer thinner, you should begin spraying with very thin coats, or you should apply a barrier coat.

There also is a third factor. A thick layer of one finish may shrink and expand differently than a thick layer of another finish. This may cause separation at some point in time. But if temperature variations are not extreme, separation may never occur. Rarely should you avoid coating over a finish for this reason.

CLEAN AND DULL
No rule in finishing is more important than this one: Any fully cured coating, whether clear finish or paint, must be clean and dull for a new coat to bond well. The surface has to be clean of grease, wax, and most any other foreign material, or the bond of the new finish will be weakened. The surface has to be dull, which indicates a

micro-roughness, or the new finish may not have anything to grip on to when bonding. (This type of bond is called a *mechanical* bond, in contrast to a *chemical* bond when two coats of the same finish are applied within a short time of each other and bond chemically.)

Because there are two types of dirt, water-soluble and solvent-soluble, there are two types of cleaners. For water-soluble dirt, wash with soap and water. For solvent-soluble dirt, wash with a petroleum-distillate solvent. (See "Turpentine and Petroleum-Distillate Solvents" on p. 158.) In most cases, you can clean both types of dirt with one solution: either household ammonia and water or trisodium phosphate (TSP) and water.

You can dull a surface by abrading with steel wool, sandpaper, or a synthetic abrasive pad (Scotch-Brite). Of course, abrading a finish also removes surface dirt, so you may be able to accomplish both ends in one step. Household ammonia and water and a solution of TSP usually dull in addition to clean, so you may accomplish both ends with one of these products also.

IMPACT OF THE THINNER
It's important to take into account the thinner in the finish you are applying. Many thinners are benign when brought into contact with a fully cured finish. But lacquer thinner and all the active solvents in lacquer thinner attack most finishes in some way, often blistering or wrinkling the finish if applied wet enough. (See "Lacquer Thinner" on p. 140.) If you apply a finish that thins with lacquer thinner over any fully cured finish, including old lacquer, you should follow one of two procedures, understanding that there is always some risk:

- Spray thin mist coats at first until you have established some build. Then spray a medium wet coat to dissolve the mist coats and create a smooth surface.
- Apply a barrier coat, almost always shellac, between the existing finish and the fresh coat. Even with a barrier coat, however, you shouldn't apply a fully wet coat of a finish thinned with lacquer thinner, because it might dissolve through. Brushing a finish that contains lacquer thinner is very risky, because you have to apply the finish wet.

dissolve them. (See "Lacquer Thinner" on p. 140.)

■ Glycol ether is a solvent and thinner for water base. It is also a weak solvent for shellac and a solvent and thinner for lacquer. Glycol ether can damage reactive finishes. (See "Glycol Ether" on p. 179.)

■ Water is a thinner for water base.

Keep in mind that each of these liquids is also a solvent for one of the dye stains. Water and glycol ether dissolve water-soluble dye. Alcohol dissolves alcohol-soluble dye. Mineral spirits, naphtha, turpentine, and lacquer thinner dissolve oil-soluble dye. (See Chapter 4: "Staining Wood.")

Identifying an Old Finish

You can take advantage of the ways different solvents react with different finishes to identify an old finish. Proceed as follows:

1 Apply a few drops of alcohol to an inconspicuous spot. If the finish becomes soft and sticky within seconds, it is shellac. If it doesn't, the finish is not shellac.

2 Apply a few drops of lacquer thinner. If the finish becomes soft and sticky within seconds, it is shellac, lacquer, or water base. You've already ruled out shellac, so the finish has to be one of the other two. Water base was rarely used before the 1990s, so age may give you a clue as to which of the two it is.

3 To distinguish more definitively between lacquer and water base, apply a few drops of toluene or xylene. If the finish becomes gummy, it's water base, not lacquer.

4 If none of these solvents affect the finish, it is a reactive finish. You don't know which one, but it rarely makes any difference.

The Future of Film Finishes

The trend in finishing since the late 1980s has been to reduce solvent emissions into the atmosphere. Two simultaneous tracks are being followed to accomplish this:

■ The solvent content in finishes is being reduced.

■ Spray guns using less air pressure to atomize finishes are replacing high-pressure spray guns.

Reducing Solvent Content

Due primarily to increasingly stricter air-pollution laws passed in California and various other states and localities, finish manufacturers are reducing the solvent content in their finishes. In addition, many factories and large shops are switching from lacquer to high-solids-content finishes, which contain less solvent, or to water-based finishes, which contain considerably less solvent. Some factories are beginning to use UV-cured finishes or powder coatings that contain no solvent. (See Chapter 12: "Two-Part Finishes" and Chapter 13: "Water Base.")

Local and state laws setting a maximum solvent content for various finishing products have led many manufacturers to state on their cans that the finish should not be thinned. This is unfortunate because it causes many finishers to get bad results applying finishes that are too thick. All finishes can be thinned, no matter what it says on the can. The only restrictions are the VOC laws in your area, and these are unlikely to apply unless you use a lot of finish.

To learn what might happen to finishes in the future, it's helpful to look at the South Coast Air Quality Management District (SCAQMD), which comprises the area around Los Angeles. This

MYTH

Some finishes should not be thinned.

FACT

All finishes can be thinned. The warnings against thinning that appear on some containers are made to comply with VOC laws in some parts of the country. Unless you use a lot of finish, you probably aren't subject to these laws.

district has passed the most stringent air quality laws in the country, and other localities often follow. As of this writing, SCAQMD is in the process of lowering the permissible VOC content in varnishes, lacquers, and many two-part finishes to a point where they can't be made. In other words, these finishes will become illegal to sell in the Los Angeles area. Water-based finishes and shellac will still be legal.

As explained elsewhere in this book, varnish, lacquer, and two-part finishes provide qualities not available with water base or shellac. To eliminate varnish, lacquer, and most two-part finishes is, in my opinion, misguided policy because it's not finishes that cause the bulk of pollution. In fact, it's estimated that less than 1 percent of pollution is caused by all coatings combined—including all paints used to coat houses, bridges, water towers, ships and so on. Eliminating varnish, lacquer, and two-part finishes is not likely to have much effect on reducing pollution caused primarily by industry and the internal combustion engine. But it will significantly reduce the quality and appearance of finishes applied to wooden objects.

Reducing Air Pressure

Also due to stricter air-pollution laws, several new atomizing technologies are replacing traditional high-pressure spray guns. The technology you are probably familiar with is high volume, low pressure (HVLP). Another technology called air-assisted airless or airmix is coming into greater use in professional shops and factories. Both reduce bounce-back and loss of solvent by producing a soft spray. (See Chapter 3: "Tools for Applying Finishes.")

CHAPTER 9

Shellac

Shellac is the most interesting of the wood finishes. It has a very long history. For the 100 years between the 1820s and 1920s, shellac was used on almost all the furniture and woodwork made in the United States and Europe. Then nitrocellulose lacquer became available and replaced shellac in the furniture industry in the United States. But shellac continued to be used extensively in Europe and by professional painters and amateur woodworkers in the United States until the middle of the century. By then spray guns had become more widely available, and painters finishing woodwork on site and the European furniture industry switched to lacquer.

The amateur market disappeared in steps.

- In the early 1960s, polyurethane became widely available and took some of the market. People wanted the better durability.
- In the late 1960s, varnish thinned with mineral spirits and marketed as tung oil took more of the market. (See "Wiping Varnish" on p. 155.)
- In the mid-1970s, Watco Danish Oil took a large part of the burgeoning amateur woodworking market. (See Chapter 5: "Oil Finishes.")

By the 1980s, hardly anyone was even mentioning shellac anymore as a wood finish. But shellac was to be given

In Brief

- **Pros & Cons**
- **What Is Shellac?**
- **Categories of Shellac**
- **Alcohol**
- **Shellac in Modern Use**
- **Brushing and Spraying Shellac**
- **French Polishing**
- **Common Problems Applying Shellac**
- **Padding Lacquer**

another chance with the amateur market. In the early 1990s, water-based finishes became available and the amateur woodworking community tried these finishes with the goal of replacing smelly and more polluting varnish and lacquer. But water-based finishes were more difficult to apply, and they didn't look as nice on the wood. Here was the opportunity for shellac to stake out some of this market.

By then, however, one company supplied almost all the shellac in the United States, and this company was repositioning shellac as a sealer. Though the company eventually saw the error of its ways, it still didn't defend shellac as a viable finish. Nor did it produce a satin version of shellac, which would be necessary if shellac were to have a chance. So the opportunity was lost.

Pros & Cons

PROS

- Bonds well over oil, wax, and resin and blocks odors
- Excellent barrier to silicone
- Denatured-alcohol solvent is less harmful to breathe and less smelly than most other solvents
- Dewaxed variety has excellent clarity and depth
- Amber variety adds warmth to dark and dark-stained woods
- Good rubbing properties

CONS

- Weak resistance to heat, water, solvents, and chemicals
- Only moderate resistance to wear
- Short shelf life

What Is Shellac?

Shellac is a natural resin secreted by insects, called lac bugs, which attach themselves to certain trees that grow in South Asia, primarily in India. (The word *lac* means "one hundred thousand," referring to the number of insects found on a single branch. Approximately 1.5 million bugs are required to make one pound of shellac.) The resin is scraped from the twigs and branches of the trees. It's then melted; strained to remove twigs, bug parts, and other foreign matter; and formed into large thin sheets that are broken up into flakes and shipped around the world.

You can buy shellac in this flake form and dissolve it yourself in denatured alcohol, or you can buy the shellac already dissolved and packaged in cans (Photos 9-1 and 9-2).

Categories of Shellac

Natural shellac resin is dark orange in color and contains about 5 percent wax. You can buy shellac with its color intact or bleached out, with its wax included or removed, and in liquid or solid-flake form.

Color of Shellac

Shellac sold in liquid form is either orange (called amber) or bleached (called clear). Flake shellac is sold in a variety of colors, ranging from "ruby red" to "blond," which has a slight yellow tint. You can use darker shellac on dark woods, or dark-stained woods, to add warmth. Clear shellac is better for light, or bleached, woods when you don't want the finish to add much color.

The orange color is the remainder of a red dye, which gave shellac its original value in the ancient world. The dye was separated from the resin and used to color cloth. Orange shellac is a natural

Photo 9-1: Many varieties of shellac are available in flake form. To turn the flakes into usable shellac, dissolve them in denatured alcohol. Shown here, from the left: blond (dewaxed), orange, button, garnet, ruby red (dewaxed).

Photo 9-2: One company supplies virtually all of the pre-mixed shellac in the United States. This company offers three varieties (from the left): SealCoat, amber, and clear. Amber and clear contain wax and have limited shelf lives. SealCoat is dewaxed and has an extended shelf life.

TIP

Shellac is available only in gloss sheen. To flatten the sheen, you have to rub the shellac with an abrasive, such as #0000 steel wool, or add a flatting agent. (See "Controlling Sheen with Flatting Agent" on p. 110.) You can buy flatting agent, sold as flatting paste, made especially for shellac at www.woodfinishingsupplies.com. Otherwise, add flatting agent made for lacquer.

Photo 9-3: Shellac contains about 5 percent wax unless it has been removed by the manufacturer. This wax will settle in the container.

dye *toner*. (See Chapter 15: "Advanced Coloring Techniques.") You can also add your own alcohol-soluble dye to make shellac any color you want. As long as you keep the color weak, you can usually brush the toner onto wood without causing streaks. Otherwise, it's better to spray it.

Wax in Shellac

Most shellac still contains its natural wax. This wax settles to the bottom of the container (Photo 9-3). When you stir a can of amber shellac, the lighter-colored wax rises to the top and causes the finish to appear cloudy. The wax makes clear shellac appear white, which accounts for its traditional name, "white" shellac.

The wax slightly reduces the transparency of the shellac on the wood. It also makes the shellac less water resistant, and it prevents good bonding when reactive and coalescing finishes (varnish, two-part finishes, and water base) are applied over shellac. You can

buy pre-mixed, dewaxed clear shellac as SealCoat, and you can buy a number of shades of dewaxed shellac in flake form. You can also dewax any shellac by letting the wax settle and then pouring or siphoning off the clear part (straining is less effective). The thinner the shellac, the faster the wax will settle. If you pour the dewaxed shellac off, do so very gently. The wax is easily stirred up. You can see what you're doing if you work from a glass jar.

Liquid and Flake Shellac

You can buy shellac as a liquid or as solid flakes that you dissolve into a liquid yourself.

Liquid shellac is sold in 2-, 3-, and 4-pound "cuts." *Cut* is the measuring term used to indicate how many pounds of shellac flakes are dissolved in one gallon of alcohol. The higher the cut number, the thicker the solution and the higher the solids content. For example, you are getting twice as much shellac in

Photos 9-4: To test shellac for freshness, drip some onto a nonporous surface such as glass and stand the glass vertical so the shellac runs down and off the bottom edge. After about 15 minutes, you should not be able to fingerprint the flat area in the center of the runoff.

a quart of 4-pound-cut solution than in a quart of 2-pound-cut solution. (See "Solids Content and Mil Thickness" on p. 108.)

Most of the shellac sold in paint stores is 3-pound cut—3 pounds of shellac to every gallon of alcohol. Seal-Coat is 2-pound cut. You can use the shellac right out of the can, or you can thin it as much as you want. Use denatured alcohol, sometimes sold as *shellac thinner,* for thinning. (See "Alcohol" at right.)

The problem with buying shellac in liquid form is that it is seldom fresh. Shellac has a *shelf life.* From the moment the shellac flakes are combined with alcohol, the resin begins losing some of its water resistance and ability to dry hard. For some time the drying is just slowed. Eventually, the shellac refuses to dry at all and remains gummy on the wood.

The process is very slow—you couldn't measure it day to day, and there's no clear point at which the shellac should no longer be used. The deterioration is accelerated by higher temperatures. If shellac is kept cool, it may still dry hard after a couple of years. But the drying will definitely take longer. It's a common rule among finishers never to use shellac that is more than six months old without checking it first. (SealCoat, marketed as a sealer, has a slightly longer shelf life, and it can be used as a finish, of course.)

To check shellac for freshness, pour a little onto a nonporous surface such as glass or plastic laminate. Then tilt the surface nearly vertical so the shellac runs down and off to provide a uniform thinness (Photos 9-4). After about 15 minutes you should not be able to fingerprint the flat area in the center of the runoff.

After each has been dissolved in alcohol, clear flake shellac has a shorter shelf life than orange flake shellac. The bleaching that's done to take the color out of the shellac causes it to deteriorate faster. You should be more diligent in checking clear shellac for its ability to dry hard. Unlike orange shellac, bleached shellac deteriorates in flake form as well as in liquid form. (This happens faster if the shellac is stored or shipped in very hot conditions.) You will have difficulty dissolving old bleached shellac flakes, and the solution may not dry hard. If you find out after you've applied the shellac that it doesn't dry

MYTH

You can fix a gummy shellac finish by applying a coat of fresh shellac (or another finish) on top.

FACT

Though this may give the appearance of correcting the problem, it will lead to greater problems later. The fresh coat will begin cracking much sooner because of the soft coat underneath. One of the oldest painter's rules is, "Never apply a hard coat over a soft one."

Alcohol

There are three types of commonly available alcohol:

- methanol (also called methyl or wood alcohol)
- ethanol (also called ethyl or grain alcohol)
- isopropanol (also called isopropyl or rubbing alcohol)

MYTH

Some alcohols dissolve shellac better than others.

FACT

All the lower (more volatile) alcohols—methyl, ethyl, propyl, and butyl—dissolve shellac totally. You can't do any better than that. The difference between these four alcohols is their evaporation rate. Methyl evaporates the fastest, butyl the slowest.

Any of these alcohols in near-pure form will dissolve shellac. But methanol is quite toxic, ethanol is very expensive because of liquor taxes, and isopropanol usually contains too much water to be a good solvent.

The best alcohol to use with shellac is ethanol that has been made poisonous so it can be sold without liquor taxes. It is sold as denatured alcohol or shellac thinner. Denatured alcohol has these advantages:

- It is inexpensive.
- It is not harmful unless you drink it or breathe excessive amounts.
- It evaporates a little more slowly than methanol, giving you more time to brush the shellac.

You can slow the drying of shellac by adding a little (usually 10 percent or less) propyl or butyl alcohol or lacquer retarder to the shellac. Lacquer retarder will add a disagreeable odor.

Photo 9-5: To make your own solution of 2-pound-cut shellac, add a ratio of 1 pint of alcohol to ¼ pound of shellac flakes.

hard, you'll have to remove it with alcohol or paint-and-varnish remover and begin all over again with fresh shellac.

To ensure maximum freshness and the best results on your work, dissolve your own shellac from solid shellac flakes and use the shellac within a few months. Here's how to do it:

1 Using a non-metal container, combine the correct proportions of shellac flakes and alcohol for the pound cut you want (Photo 9-5). I suggest you begin by making a 2-pound cut, adding a ratio of 1 pint of denatured alcohol to a quart jar containing ¼ pound of shellac flakes. This will give you the feel for how to do it. You can then try thicker solutions.

Photo 9-6: Stir periodically until the shellac is dissolved.

Photo 9-7: Once the shellac is dissolved, strain it into another jar to remove impurities and undissolved residue.

2 Stir the mixture often during the next couple of hours to keep the flakes from solidifying into a lump at the bottom of the jar (Photo 9-6).

3 Keep the jar covered when you're not stirring the shellac so moisture from the air isn't absorbed by the alcohol.

4 When the flakes are totally in solution, strain the shellac through a paint strainer or loose-weave cheesecloth into another quart jar. This will remove impurities (Photo 9-7).

5 Write the current date on the jar so you will know when the shellac was made.

6 If you want to dewax the shellac, let the wax settle (this could take weeks if the shellac is thick). Then pour or siphon off the dewaxed layer into another jar.

Shellac in Modern Use

Though shellac is still every bit as good a finish as it ever was, it has been largely relegated to a few niche uses:

- A finish for old antiques and a few modern reproductions
- A sealer to block off problems in the wood
- French polishing

Shellac as a Finish

Shellac was used as a finish on furniture and woodwork through most of the nineteenth century and into the twentieth. Contrary to common belief, however, shellac wasn't used often in the eighteenth century. Wax seems to have been the most common finish used on better furniture. But wax doesn't perform well as a finish, so most of the surviving eighteenth-century furniture was coated over with shellac in the nineteenth century. (Though shellac is compatible with wax and bonds well over it, it's still best to remove as much of the wax as possible before applying the shellac.)

As a result, there is a lot of antique furniture that either was, or is believed to have been, finished originally with shellac. Many people restoring antiques or making reproductions use shellac because they prefer to stay with what was used originally.

Shellac is a very user-friendly finish. It dries rapidly enough so dust problems are minimal but not so rapidly that brushing and spraying are difficult. (See "Brushing and Spraying Shellac" on p. 130 and "Common Problems Applying Shellac" on p. 133.) In addition, shellac doesn't smell bad to most people, and it's not harmful to breathe in moderate amounts. Typical of evaporative finishes, shellac is also easy to repair, rub out, and strip. Also typical of evaporative finishes, however, shellac is not especially durable. It scratches relatively easily, and heat, solvents, acids, and alkalis cause damage fairly easily. Like lacquer, it also blushes easily in humid weather. (See "Alcohol" on p. 127.)

Even though shellac can be damaged more easily than other film finishes, it's still durable enough for use on most wooden household objects. The damage you see on old furniture that was finished originally with shellac is more the result of the finish having aged than the finish itself. All finishes deteriorate and become more susceptible to damage as they age.

Shellac as a Sealer

Shellac finds its greatest use today as a sealer under another finish. (See "Sealers and Sealing Wood" on p. 116.) For sealing off problems in wood, shellac is

TIP To dissolve the shellac more quickly, pulverize the flakes into powder before adding the alcohol, or put the jar of flakes and alcohol into hot water, or both. Alcohol is flammable, so don't put the container of shellac and alcohol directly over a heat source!

MYTH You can protect shellac from water damage by applying a couple of coats of paste wax.

FACT Wax slows water penetration only if it is left thick (as on the ends of boards in lumber yards), or if it is applied to a perfectly smooth surface such as glass. Though it's possible to level and polish a shellac finish almost perfectly smooth, in practice you can't count on any protection from wax. First, it's rare that you have such a smooth surface. And second, once that surface has received even a little wear, minute gaps will develop in the wax that will allow water to pass through. (See Chapter 18: "Caring for the Finish.")

Brushing and Spraying Shellac

Shellac is an evaporative finish. (See Chapter 8: "Introduction to Film Finishes.") It dries entirely when its solvent, alcohol, evaporates, and it redissolves on contact with alcohol. These two characteristics govern how shellac should be applied.

1 Position your work so you have a light source reflecting off the surface. This way you can see what's happening by looking into the reflection.

2 For your first coat I suggest you use a 1-pound cut. It will be easy to brush or spray, and less likely than a thicker coat to clog the sandpaper. Thin any given amount of store-bought, 3-pound-cut shellac with 2 parts denatured alcohol to 1 part shellac, or dissolve your own 1-pound cut from flakes.

3 If you're brushing, use a good-quality natural- or synthetic-bristle brush ("badger"-style brushes are my favorite for shellac). On flat surfaces, spread the shellac quickly in long strokes with the grain. Shellac dries very quickly. Don't brush back and forth as much as you might with paint or varnish; you'll drag the partially dried shellac and create severe ridges. If you miss a place and the shellac has begun to dry, leave the gap until the next coat.

4 If you're using a spray gun, don't leave shellac in an aluminum cup for more than a few hours at a time. The acidic shellac will react with the metal and turn dark.

5 After at least two hours, sand the first coat lightly with 280-grit or finer sandpaper. Sand just enough to make the surface feel smooth.

6 Remove the sanding dust. (See "Cleaning Off the Dust" on p. 14.)

7 If you've never used shellac before, I suggest you use a 1½-pound cut for your topcoats. Thin any amount of store-bought, 3-pound-cut shellac 1:1 with denatured alcohol, or dissolve your own from flakes. A 1½-pound cut is easy to brush and usually easy to spray. It will also flow out more smoothly than shellac straight out of the can. (The thinner the shellac, the easier it is to brush or spray, but the more coats it will take to achieve a good build.) After you have some experience, you can try brushing or spraying thicker coats. (You probably won't be able to spray 3-pound-cut shellac without severe orange peel; shellac is difficult to atomize because of its cohesiveness.) Apply a coat and let it dry for at least two hours. Applying many thinned coats is better than applying fewer thick coats, because each coat dries more thoroughly before being covered over. Thick coats take longer to dry.

8 You can stop here or apply any number of additional coats to achieve the thickness you want. Allow at least two hours' drying time between coats. Don't brush excessively in any one area or you'll redissolve and pull up the undercoats. You don't need to sand between coats unless you want to remove dust nibs or smooth out flaws or brush marks. Each new coat of shellac dissolves into the previous one.

9 If you do sand between coats, small hard lumps of finish will probably collect on your sandpaper (Photo 16-3 on p. 208). To avoid this, sand with a lighter touch. You'll have less clogging (called *corning*) if you use stearated (dry-lubricated) sandpaper or wet/dry sandpaper lubricated with mineral spirits. Once the corns begin forming, change to fresh sandpaper, or you'll scratch the finish.

10 When you're satisfied with the thickness of the film, you can leave it as is, or you can finish it with sandpaper, steel wool, or rubbing compounds, or by French polishing. (See "French Polishing" on facing page and Chapter 16: "Finishing the Finish.")

> **TIP** If the shellac dries too fast to flow out evenly or to let bubbles pop out, slow the drying by adding denatured alcohol, propyl alcohol, butyl alcohol, or lacquer retarder.

> **TIP** You can take advantage of shellac's poor resistance to alkalis by using household ammonia, reduced with a little water, to clean a brush. Then wash the brush with soap and water and wrap it in paper or the sleeve it came in.

unparalleled. The problems include the following:

- oil (usually silicone oil from furniture polishes)
- resin (usually from pine knots)
- wax
- odors (usually from smoke or animal urine)

Notice, however, that the only situation common to new wood is pine knots, so it's rare that shellac would be needed on new wood. The rest of these problems are all associated with refinishing. Silicone is such a problem for refinishers, in fact, that many automatically apply a sealer coat of shellac to everything. (See "Fish Eye and Silicone Oil" on p. 146.) Unfortunately, shellac is being hyped as a sealer for all situations. and it's not. Virtually no one in the cabinet or furniture industry uses shellac as a sealer.

French Polishing

French polishing is a technique of applying shellac with a cloth pad to produce an almost perfectly flat, dust-free, gloss finish. It came into use early in the nineteenth century when the only alternative methods of applying a finish were to wipe on oil or wax or brush on spirit varnish or oil varnish. ("Spirit varnish" refers to an alcohol-soluble resin, of which shellac was one among several available. "Oil varnish" was similar to our current varnish, only made with natural resins instead of synthetic resins.)

Oil and wax gave little protection and produced a relatively dull sheen, so these finishes didn't reflect light well in the dimly lit buildings of the time. Spirit varnish and oil varnish were protective and shiny, but brushing them left brush marks, and there was no sandpaper available with which to level the surface.

Using the French-polishing technique to apply shellac was perfect for the popular high-style (Regency and Federal) furniture of the day.

Today, French polishing is probably used more to repair dull and lightly damaged finishes than to finish new wood. The technique for doing both is the same. (See Chapter 19: "Repairing Finishes.")

There are four steps in French polishing:

1. Make the French polishing pad. (See "Making a Rubbing Pad" on p. 22.)
2. Fill the pores.
3. Build the shellac with a pad.
4. Remove the oil.

Filling the Pores

If you want to create a mirror-flat surface on medium-to-large-pored woods, such as walnut and mahogany, you will need to fill the pores. On small-pored woods, such as cherry and maple, you can usually skip this step. The shellac itself will fill the pores during French polishing.

Filling the pores of today's common hardwoods by traditional French-polishing methods is much more time-consuming than it once was. Most hardwoods used today have larger pores than the hardwoods used on the finest furniture in the nineteenth century. Our Honduran mahogany, for example, is not nearly as dense as the Cuban mahogany available 150 years ago.

There are four methods you can use to fill the pores:

- with paste wood filler (See Chapter 7: "Filling Pores.")
- with the French-polishing method itself
- with pumice and wood dust
- with several thicker coats of shellac sanded back

MYTH

Shellac is the best sealer under all kinds of finishes.

FACT

Shellac is wonderful for "sealing off" oil, resin, wax, and odors in the wood. But except for pine and stripped wood, it's rare that you would have one of these problems. It is always best to stick with one finish for all your coats unless you have a good reason not to. Mixing finishes weakens bonds and can weaken protection and durability if the primary finish is more protective and durable. It's unwise to use shellac as a sealer unless you have a problem that needs to be sealed off. (See "Sealers and Sealing Wood" on p. 116.)

NOTE

There's a mystique about French polishing. Maybe it's the name. Maybe it's the claim that French polishing is the most beautiful finish ever developed. Maybe it's the exotic vocabulary that is often used to describe how to do it—"charge the rubber," "fad in," "spirit off." Whatever the reason, French polishing has been largely replaced by the modern method of rubbing finishes. It's now used mostly for renewing old and damaged finishes and for refinishing old, high-style antiques.

TIP

"Mind your edges; the middle will take care of itself." This is the mantra you should be whispering to yourself while French polishing, so you coat the surface evenly. Otherwise, you will almost surely apply more finish in the middle than around the edges.

MYTH

The outer cloth serves to control the discharge of shellac from the inner cloth.

FACT

The outer cloth is used to pull the pad tight and remove wrinkles. It has no effect on the discharge of shellac. When both cloths are wrapped tightly together, the wetness of the shellac penetrates as if there were one cloth.

Paste Wood Filler: Using paste wood filler is efficient, but it changes the look of the wood by highlighting the pores. For a traditional French-polish appearance, you should use one of the other methods.

The French-Polishing Method: Filling the pores simply by moving the shellac-loaded pad back and forth over the surface is fairly effective on small-pored woods such as maple or cherry, but it is a very inefficient method of filling pores on larger-pored mahogany and walnut. You should use one of the other methods on these woods. Even on small-pored woods, you will probably have to sand the finish back a few times to eliminate all the pitting.

Pumice and Wood Dust: A slightly faster method for larger-pored woods is to fill the pores with wood dust generated by abrading with pumice. Here are the steps:

1 Make a French-polishing pad and fill it with just enough denatured alcohol so it feels damp, but not so much that you can squeeze any alcohol out of it.

2 Sprinkle a small amount of pumice powder on the wood—about ¼ teaspoon dusted over a 1-square-foot area.

3 Moving in circles, rub the pumice over the wood with the pad. The wood dust this creates slowly fills the pores. Work in a small, 1-square-foot area at a time. Then move on until the entire surface is filled. If the wood feels smooth (indicating there is no more pumice on the surface) and the pores aren't totally filled, begin again with more pumice and more alcohol in the pad. If the outer cover of the pad wears through, readjust the cover to work an unused part. You can see

whether the pores are filled by looking at the wood in a raking light.

Use pumice sparingly. If you use too much, you'll begin to build ridges of pumice and wood dust. If this happens, try removing the ridges by putting more alcohol in your pad and rubbing with a clean part of your outer cover. If this doesn't work, you'll have to sand or scrape off the ridges.

Coats of Finish: The most efficient method of filling pores to create the traditional French-polish appearance is to brush or spray on several coats of shellac and sand the coats back until the shellac in the pores is level with the surface. This method is looked down upon by purists, but you (and they) will have difficulty seeing any difference. Most French polishers I've met use this method.

Building the Shellac

Here are the steps for building the shellac once the pores have been filled:

1 Begin with a clean pad. You can use one you've used before for French polishing, but you shouldn't use one you have used with pumice. Make the pad larger for large surfaces and smaller for small surfaces.

2 Pour enough 2-pound-cut shellac onto the pad so a little liquid seeps out when you press your thumb hard into the pad (Photo 9-8 on p. 134). If the outer cloth is so thick and tightly woven that the shellac runs off rather than soaks in, pull this cloth back and pour the shellac directly onto the inner cloth. (I prefer to use thin cotton cloths such as well-worn handkerchiefs.) To obtain maximum transparency, use blond, de-waxed shellac. A plastic container with a spout (as for mustard or ketchup) serves as a convenient dispenser.

Common Problems Applying Shellac

Most problems applying shellac can be avoided by thinning the shellac further with denatured alcohol and by moving more rapidly when you're brushing. (For problems specific to brushing and spraying, see "Common Brushing Problems" on p. 26 and "Common Spraying Problems" on p. 32.)

PROBLEM	CAUSE	SOLUTION
The shellac blushes during application. Part or all of the surface appears off-white in color.	There is too much moisture in the shellac. This could be caused by too much moisture in the air (high humidity), or too much water in the shellac or in the alcohol you are using to thin the shellac. If you suspect the shellac or the alcohol, don't use it anymore.	Try letting your project dry for a few hours. Often the blushing will disappear on its own.
		On a dry day, spray, brush, or wipe straight alcohol onto the shellacked surface. The alcohol will soften the shellac and the blushing will disappear.
		Rub the surface with sandpaper or steel wool to cut through the blush.
Pinholes appear in the dried shellac.	Air trapped in large pores has come up into the finish, creating bubbles that become pinholes when you sand them level.	Remove or sand back the finish and dust on several coats if you are spraying. If you are brushing, wipe on thin coats (similar to French polishing, but without oil) to seal the wood. Then spray or brush wet coats.
The shellac doesn't flow out well: It ridges if you're brushing or orange-peels if you're spraying.	The shellac is too thick for the weather conditions.	Sand out the problem, and thin your next coats of shellac with more alcohol.
	Your spray gun is not atomizing the shellac well enough.	Add more alcohol to the shellac, or increase the air pressure to your gun, or both.
Dust cures in the finish, leaving small dust nibs.	The air, work surface, finish, or your brush is dusty.	Sand out the dust nibs, and let the dust settle out of the air before applying another coat. Clean the work surface and brush, and strain the finish.
Occasional mark or ridge.	You damaged the surface by touching partially dried shellac with a brush, spray gun, or finger.	Sand out the damage and apply more coats. Or apply more coats and then sand the surface level.

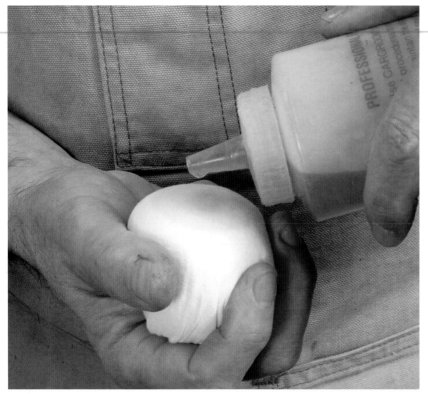

Photo 9-8: Pour just enough shellac and alcohol onto the pad so you can squeeze out a small amount of liquid by pressing your thumb hard into the pad. A plastic spouted container easily dispenses controlled amounts.

3 Tap the pad hard against the palm of your other hand to disperse the shellac.

4 Begin moving the pad on the bare wood or previously applied finish, using light pressure (Photo 9-9). You can move the pad in any pattern you want. If you are just beginning to do French polishing, I suggest you move in straight strokes with the grain, lifting the pad at the end of each stroke. Or move in large "S" patterns so the pad stays in contact with the surface and doesn't cross over previous strokes. The idea is to cover the surface evenly with several thin layers of shellac. (Shellac bonds perfectly to a shellac finish, fairly well to a lacquer finish, and sufficiently well to varnish if it has been cleaned and scuffed.)

5 Whenever the pad becomes dry, add more shellac and disperse it. After you have applied a couple of layers, you

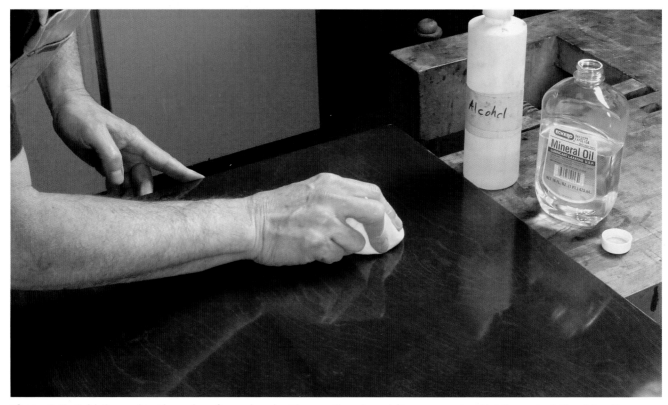

Photo 9-9: Hold the pad in the palm of your hand with your thumb and fingers pressing tightly against the sides. Never make an abrupt change of direction or stop moving your pad while it is touching the surface; your pad will leave a mark that you may have to sand out.

will feel your pad dragging a little. This is caused by it biting into the still "green" shellac underneath. Begin adding a couple of drops of mineral oil to the pad each time you add more shellac, and disperse the oil by tapping the pad hard against your other hand. (I find it easiest to remove the cap from a bottle of mineral oil and pour a little oil into it. Then I dip the tip of my finger into the oil and spread it onto the pad.) The oil will mask problems and will also trick you into thinking that you are finished when you aren't. Anytime you want to see where you are in the process, remove the oil from the surface by wiping with naphtha.

6 Now begin moving the pad fairly slowly in large circles or figure eights so it doesn't leave the surface (Figure 9-1). Lifting the pad off the surface means that you will have to set it back down, and this may leave a mark. Use a motion like an airplane landing and taking off when you have to contact or leave the surface. To get into inside corners and tight areas, remove the inner cloth and shape it into a point.

7 There are two tricks for achieving good results in French polishing, whether on new wood or an old finished surface:

Look for a vapor trail following the pad as soon as you start adding oil to it. The vapor trail is caused by the alcohol evaporating through the oil and tells you that you have the right mixture. You won't see the vapor trail if the pad is too wet or too dry. You will see only wetness, which means that your pad is too wet and is causing damage. Or you will see only streaking, which means that you are just moving the oil around. As you start padding after each reloading, the vapor trail should be up to a foot long. It should tighten as the pad dries until it trails by only an inch or two. Then reload.

Reduce the shellac-to-alcohol ratio until you're adding only alcohol to the pad. The goal is to eliminate all the marks, or "rag tracks," left by the cloth. Have one squeeze container with 2-pound-cut shellac and another with denatured alcohol. Once you have applied enough shellac to the surface to create an even gloss with no sanding scratches or other flaws showing through, begin blending the two liquids right on the pad. Pour on a little shellac. Then pour on a little alcohol. Add more alcohol and less shellac with every reloading. After each, disperse the mixture by tapping hard against your other hand, then add a finger dab of mineral oil and disperse it. After you have been rubbing an area for a while, you won't need as much oil. Enough will already be on the surface.

8 Any time you cause a problem in the finish (rag tracks too pronounced, a mark because you stopped moving the pad, whatever), sand out the damage using the finest-grit sandpaper that will remove it efficiently, usually 600- or 1000-grit. Then resume French polishing.

9 Keep in mind that the most common mistake beginners make is continuing to work a surface even though it has softened to the point that damage is being caused. If the rag tracks seem to be getting worse, stop for an hour or so and let the surface harden.

10 You're finished when the surface has an even glossy sheen after you have removed the oil. Remember, oil masks problems, so you may think you're finished when you're not.

Non-crossover or "S" pattern

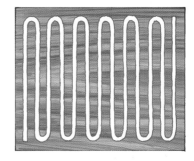

Circular

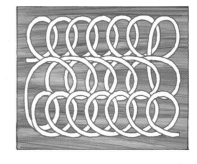

Figure-eight

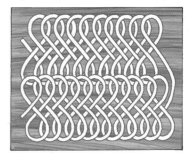

Figure 9-1: You can use any pattern you want to apply the shellac to the wood. Each time you replenish your pad, begin with non-crossover strokes, just in case you've gotten your pad a little too wet. Once you begin crossing over, move in sequences of circles and figure-eights so you apply an even thickness to all parts.

TIP

The trick to applying padding lacquer is to rub the pad continuously over a given area until the pad is totally dry and all the streaking has disappeared. This is why it's better to use a freshly made pad each time you pad a surface. Previously used pads will take much longer to dry out. You may even want to change to a new pad in the middle of a job if the surface is large and your pad becomes too wet.

NOTE
▼

You don't have to use oil to do French polishing, and many experienced French polishers don't use it. But using oil can be a great help for mastering the French polishing technique because the oil helps you see what you are doing.

Removing the Oil

The oil is necessary when applying the shellac to keep the pad from sticking to the surface and damaging it. The oil is also helpful for creating the vapor trail that tells you that you have loaded your pad correctly. But the oil is smeary and has to be removed.

Traditionally, the oil is removed with alcohol. This method continues to be repeated in books and articles on French polishing. You put a few drops of alcohol on a freshly made pad and wipe the pad over the surface. The alcohol picks up the oil. The problem with this method is that if you have too much alcohol on the pad, or even at one spot on the pad, you will damage the shellac and ruin the even shine you worked so hard to get. It's at this point that most people have trouble with French polishing. It's very difficult to avoid causing damage.

There's no longer any need to take that risk. You can use naphtha to remove all the oil without any chance of damaging the shellac. Just dampen a cloth and wipe it over the surface—as you would do to remove oil from any surface. There's probably no better example in finishing of how antiquated methods persist because of a mythology that the old masters knew best. The old masters didn't have naphtha, or they surely would have used it. (Mineral spirits will work too, but mineral spirits will take longer to evaporate from the surface.)

Removing the oil with naphtha is more effective than removing it with alcohol. You take off all the oil, and this may leave the surface appearing drier and less rich. You can replace the richness the same way you would on any finished surface: by applying some paste wax or furniture polish.

Padding Lacquer

You can use padding lacquer instead of shellac to do French polishing. Padding lacquer is primarily shellac dissolved in lacquer-thinner solvents instead of alcohol. It produces the same results as shellac, but you apply it a little differently (Photo 19-6 on p. 266). It's best to begin with a new rubbing pad that is totally dry.

To pad a large surface, pour 1 or 2 teaspoons of padding lacquer onto the pad to make it damp—damper than for shellac in French polishing. Tap the pad against your palm to disperse the liquid. (For a small surface that you are repairing, use a small rubbing pad and much less padding lacquer.)

Work in small (3- or 4-square-foot) areas at a time. Complete each area before moving on. Then overlap.

Increase your pressure as you proceed. You will notice that your pad is causing streaks and you will want to add more padding lacquer to your pad. *Don't do it!* This is the biggest difference between French polishing and applying padding lacquer. With padding lacquer you should continue burnishing the surface until your pad becomes totally dry and the streaking disappears. Then you are finished. The oily solvent included in the padding lacquer by the manufacturer will evaporate on its own.

The biggest downside to using padding lacquer is the stronger and more smelly solvents that are included. They can make you feel lightheaded, and they can temporarily affect your nervous system. So work in an area with good cross ventilation, or wear an organic-vapor respirator mask. The solvents will also remove the oily fat from your skin. If your hands are sensitive, wear gloves to protect them.

CHAPTER 10

Lacquer

When lacquer became available in the 1920s, it was widely believed to be the ultimate finish. Being an evaporative finish, it had all the easy application and repair qualities of shellac, but it was more resistant to water, heat, alcohol, acids, and alkalis. In addition, it was a synthetic, so its characteristics could be varied to meet different needs, and its supply didn't depend on exotic natural materials. To top it off, the thinner used with lacquer—lacquer thinner—could be varied in strength and evaporation rate, making it enormously more versatile than alcohol, the thinner used with shellac. (See "Lacquer Thinner" on p. 140.) Indeed, the belief

in lacquer's superiority has proved prophetic. Lacquer is still the most widely used furniture finish.

Most lacquers are based on nitrocellulose, which is made by treating the cellulose fibers in cotton and wood with nitric and sulphuric acids. The nitrocellulose is the binder (similar to the oil in varnish) and gives the finish its fast-drying properties. By itself, however, nitrocellulose has poor build, is not very flexible, and doesn't bond well. So a resin is added to improve these qualities, and oily chemicals, called *plasticizers,* are added to further improve flexibility. Manufacturers vary the amounts and types of resins and plasticizers to pro-

In Brief

- **Nitrocellulose Lacquer Variations**
- **Pros & Cons**
- **Advantages of Lacquer**
- **Lacquer Thinner**
- **Comparing the Solvents in Lacquer Thinner**
- **Crackle Lacquer**
- **Common Problems Applying Lacquer**
- **Fish Eye and Silicone**
- **Spraying Lacquer**
- **Lacquer's Problems**

CAUTION

A lacquer finish can be damaged by extended contact with plastic materials, such as pads for tabletops and cushions for lamps and sculptures. The oily plasticizers in the plastic and in the lacquer migrate into each other, causing both to soften and stick together. You should not leave plastic in contact with lacquer for more than a few days at a time.

duce lacquers that dry with varying degrees of elasticity, color, and resistance to water, solvents, heat, acids, and alkalis. (See "Nitrocellulose Lacquer Variations," below.) Generally, the more elastic, colorless, and resistant the lacquer is, the more it costs. Unfortunately, only a few manufacturers provide more information than the price, which is not always an accurate indicator.

The term *lacquer* is used in a broader sense than to refer only to lacquers that contain nitrocellulose. (See "What's in a Name" on p. 106.) There's no nitrocellulose, for instance, in acrylic lacquer. This lacquer is applied to many surfaces, but not often to wood because of its high cost. By combining acrylic resin with cellulose-acetate-butyrate (CAB), a resin closely related to nitrocellulose, the principal quality of acrylic lacquer, its non-yellowing, can be captured at a lower cost.

CAB-acrylic lacquers are usually identified as CAB-acrylic, but sometimes as CAB or, very confusingly, acrylic. They are also called water-white. (Water-white can also refer to acrylic-modified nitrocellulose lacquer, which is not entirely non-yellowing.) The main trade-off for the non-yellowing characteristic of CAB-acrylic is reduced water resistance.

Nitrocellulose Lacquer Variations

The nitrocellulose in nitrocellulose lacquer is responsible for the fast-drying properties of the finish. But by itself nitrocellulose has poor build, is not very flexible, and doesn't bond well. So resins are added to modify and improve these qualities. Following is a list of the most commonly used resins and the qualities each provides. More than one resin can be included in any given lacquer.

RESIN	CHARACTERISTICS	SOLD AS
Alkyd	Adds a slight orange coloring, has good flexibility, and provides good protection and durability.	Nitrocellulose lacquer
Maleic	Adds a noticeable orange coloring, especially in the can. Hardness makes it easier to rub out but can make the lacquer too brittle if plasticizers aren't also added. Provides less protection and durability than alkyd resin.	Nitrocellulose lacquer
Acrylic	Most valuable for being colorless and not yellowing over time, although the nitrocellulose adds a slight yellow color. (For a totally colorless lacquer use CAB-acrylic, which doesn't contain nitrocellulose.) Provides less protection and durability than alkyd resin.	Acrylic-modified lacquer; Water-white lacquer
Urethane	Substantially increases protection and durability. Very little yellowing.	Polyurethane lacquer
Vinyl	Adds exceptional water resistance and bonding properties, but too soft to be used as a finish.	Vinyl sealer (See "Sealers and Sealing Wood" on p. 116.)
Amino (Melamine formaldehyde and Urea formaldehyde)	Substantially increases protection and durability. Very little yellowing.	Pre- and post-catalyzed lacquer (See Chapter 12: "Two-Part Finishes.")

Photo 10-1: Most lacquers dry too fast to be brushed. They are designed to be sprayed. But lacquers made with slower-evaporating solvents can be brushed successfully. They can also be sprayed.

Pros & Cons

PROS

- Very fast drying
- With the addition of slower- or faster-evaporating thinners, can be applied in all types of weather
- Much reduced runs and sags when spraying
- Excellent clarity and depth
- Excellent rubbing properties

CONS

- High solvent content (solvent is toxic, flammable, and air-polluting)
- Only moderate heat, wear, solvent, acid, and alkali resistance
- Only moderate water and water-vapor resistance

Two additional types of lacquer should be mentioned: crackle lacquer (see "Crackle Lacquer" on p. 142) and brushing lacquer. Brushing lacquer can be any of the lacquers included in "Nitrocellulose Lacquer Variations" on the facing page, but it is usually an alkyd-modified lacquer. Brushing lacquer dries more slowly than other lacquers, a characteristic achieved by using slower evaporating solvents in manufacturing (Photo 10-1).

Advantages of Lacquer

The principal characteristic that makes all the varieties of lacquer different from every film finish except shellac is evaporative drying. All that is necessary for lacquer to become hard is for the solvents to evaporate, and evaporation is controlled by which solvents are used (both in the finish itself and in the

MYTH

The best finish for wood is acrylic lacquer used for automobiles, because acrylic lacquer is harder than nitrocellulose lacquer.

FACT

Acrylic lacquers made for use on automobiles are harder, but they usually aren't flexible enough for wood. They don't have to be, because they are intended for a substrate that moves considerably less than wood. If you use an acrylic lacquer not specially formulated for wood, you risk cracking due to wood movement, especially at joints.

Lacquer Thinner

When you use a lacquer thinner with too little active solvent to thin lacquer, you get white cottonlike flecks in your sprayed finish. This is called "cotton blush." Always use lacquer thinner designed to thin lacquer. Avoid using cleanup lacquer thinner to thin lacquer.

Lacquer thinner is unique among finish solvents because it's made up of a number of individual solvents blended together in many combinations. It's not important that you know the names of all these solvents, but it is helpful to understand that there are three categories of solvents used:

- Active solvents (ketones, esters, and glycol ethers) dissolve lacquer all by themselves.
- Latent solvents (alcohols) dissolve lacquer in combination with active solvents but not well by themselves.
- Diluting solvents (fast-evaporating petroleum distillates, such as toluene, xylene, and some naphthas) do not dissolve lacquer at all but mix with solvents that do.

The first two categories might make up less than 50 percent of a lacquer thinner. The third category serves only to dilute the mixture. Solvents in this group evaporate quickly and reduce the cost. (It doesn't take much solvent to separate the stringy, spaghetti-like lacquer molecules, but it takes a lot of solvent to separate them enough so the lacquer is thin enough to spray.) Inexpensive "cleanup" lacquer thinners have too high a percentage of diluting solvent, so they don't put the lacquer into solution. The lacquer coagulates in the cup or pot and shows up as white cottonlike flecks on the surface you are spraying. This is called *cotton blush*. Always use lacquer thinner designed to thin lacquer.

If the lacquer thinner is designed properly, the diluting solvent evaporates very quickly, part of it while the spray is traveling from the spray gun to the wood and the rest soon thereafter. The finish thickens rapidly so that sagging doesn't occur unless a lot of lacquer is sprayed onto one area. Some of the dissolving solvents then evaporate as the lacquer is leveling, and a few "tail" solvents (those dissolving solvents that evaporate most slowly) remain for a few minutes to allow for more leveling. This progression of solvent evaporation gives lacquer one of its most appreciated qualities, that of significantly reduced runs and sags on vertical surfaces.

The active solvents control the speed at which the lacquer dries. Slower-evaporating active solvents are used to make brushing lacquer and lacquer retarder. Lacquer retarder can be used to eliminate blushing and dry spray, and to improve flow out and leveling. On the other hand, lacquer retarder lengthens the time it takes for the lacquer to dry hard.

Faster-evaporating active solvents are used to make fast, or "hot," lacquer thinner. This thinner can be used to speed drying in cold temperatures. Fast lacquer thinners are available at auto-body supply stores. I don't know of any wood-finish manufacturer that supplies these.

It's rare that you would use only lacquer retarder or fast lacquer thinner to thin lacquer. In most cases, adding just a little retarder or fast thinner in place of some of the standard thinner solves the problem. Unfortunately, you have to learn the amounts to add by trial and error. Manufacturers provide no help.

Even the terms "standard" lacquer thinner, lacquer "retarder," and "fast" lacquer thinner are just generalizations. Different manufacturers provide these products with very different evaporation rates. Fortunately, you don't have to be exact in your mixes. Wide variations will work. But be conscious that if you change brands of any type of lacquer thinner, the evaporation rates could be significantly different. Although you may not want to get into lacquer thinner in this detail, I am providing a chart of the common active solvents used in lacquer thinners and their relative evaporation rates. (See "Comparing the Solvents in Lacquer Thinner" on the facing page.) You can compare the solvents listed on cans of lacquer thinner or on material safety data sheets (MSDS) to get an approximation of the relative evaporation rate of the thinner.

thinner added to the finish). Beyond this, the reasons for the popularity of lacquer in the furniture manufacturing industry, among professional finishers and refinishers, and among amateurs with spray guns include the following:

- possibility of invisible repair
- reduced runs and sags on vertical surfaces
- ease of achieving a dust-free, blush-free, and overspray-free finish in all types of weather
- ease of use in combination with stains, glazes, paste wood fillers, and toners for a wide range of decorative effects
- superior depth and beauty
- superior rubbing qualities
- relative ease of stripping

Invisible Repair

In the furniture industry and in shops that make and refinish furniture and cabinets, the ability to repair damage to a finish is very important. There is a high probability that damage will occur somewhere between the finish room and the object's final destination. Of all film

TIP

It's not necessary to clean your spray gun on a daily basis if all you are spraying is lacquer. In fact, you can leave lacquer in the cup for many days without problems. The lacquer redissolves and cleans itself.

Comparing the Solvents in Lacquer Thinner

Because temperature affects evaporation rates, the solvents used in lacquer thinner are compared using a relative rather than an absolute scale. The solvent *butyl acetate* is used as the standard to which the other solvents are compared.

In this table, which lists the most common solvents used in lacquer thinner, butyl acetate is assigned the value of 1. So acetone, with a value of 5.7, evaporates 5.7 times faster than butyl acetate, and butyl Cellosolve, with a value of .08, takes 12 times longer than butyl acetate to evaporate.

By comparing the solvents listed in this table with those on the material safety data sheets (MSDS) or cans of different lacquer thinners, you can get an idea of the relative evaporation rates of these thinners.

Notice that acetone, which is often recommended for use with lacquer thinner, could easily be responsible for creating dry spray, and that butyl Cellosolve, often used by itself as a retarder, could significantly slow the drying of a finish.

Relative Evaporation Rate	Active Solvent*	*Ketones have the suffix "–one"; Esters have the suffix "–ate"; Glycol ethers end in "ether."
5.7	Acetone	
4.1	Ethyl acetate	
3.8	Methyl ethyl ketone (MEK)	
3.0	Isopropyl acetate	
2.3	Methyl n-propyl ketone	
2.3	Propyl acetate	
1.6	Methyl isobutyl ketone (MIBK)	
1.4	Isobutyl acetate	
1.0	**Butyl acetate**	
.7	Propylene glycol methyl ether (Eastman PM)	
.5	Methyl isoamyl ketone (MIAK)	
.5	Methyl amyl acetate	
.4	Propylene glycol methyl ether acetate (Eastman PM acetate)	
.4	Amyl acetate	
.4	Methyl amyl ketone (MAK)	
.4	Isobutyl isobutyrate (IBIB)	
.3	Cyclohexanone	
.2	Diisobutyl ketone	
.2	Ethylene glycol propyl ether (Eastman EP)	
.12	Ethyl 3-ethoxypropionate (EEP)	
.08	Propylene glycol butyl ether	
.08	Ethylene glycol butyl ether (Butyl Cellosolve, Eastman EB)	

Crackle Lacquer

Crackle lacquer is a lacquer-based product that is used to imitate the alligator skin–like cracking that occurs in very old paints and finishes. Crackle lacquer is based on a very simple concept—include so much pigment in the finish that there is not enough finish, or binder, to glue all the pigment particles together. As the finish dries and shrinks, it cracks.

The pigment most often used in crackle lacquer is flatting agent (silica), the same stuff that settles to the bottom of cans of satin and flat lacquer and makes them appear satin or flat when they dry. (See "Controlling Sheen with Flatting Agent" on p. 110.) You can make your own crackle lacquer by adding flatting agent, often sold as "flatting paste," to lacquer.

APPLYING CRACKLE LACQUER

Crackle lacquer is always applied by spraying it over a sealed surface, not directly onto the wood. The coating used to seal the surface can be clear or colored and is commonly called a *base coat* in this context because the cracks in the crackle coat open up to expose it to view.

The most basic crackle finish consists of a base coat followed by a coat of crackle lacquer (the *crackle* coat) and a clear lacquer topcoat. The base coat should be gloss, or a clear gloss coat should be applied over the base coat so there's less resistance to the crackle coat shrinking and developing cracks. The topcoat of lacquer is needed to dissolve into and strengthen the crackle coat, which is naturally fragile. The topcoat also affords some protection of its own.

In most cases, the base coat is one color and the crackle coat another, but the base coat can be clear and the crackle coat colored, or the crackle coat can be clear and the base coat colored. To imitate an alligatored clear finish, both coats would be clear. Any color combination is legitimate. You can even apply a colored glaze over the crackle coat to highlight the cracks. Creating an appealing look is limited only by your imagination. The topcoat is usually acrylic-modified lacquer or CAB-acrylic lacquer to reduce the amount of yellowing, and satin or flat sheens are usually preferred to better imitate the sheen of aged finishes.

CONTROLLING THE CRACKLE

The real trick in applying crackle lacquer is learning to control the size of the cracks and the "islands" in between. You do this by varying the thickness of the crackle coat and the length of time it takes for that coat to dry.

Thicker crackle coats develop larger islands and cracks, and thinner coats produce smaller islands and cracks. Slower drying results in larger islands and cracks, while faster drying creates smaller islands and cracks. To fix this in your mind, think of mud. As a rain-soaked dirt road dries, the cracks that develop are large and widely spaced because the mud is thick, whereas the thin layer of mud that seeps onto a sidewalk from under grass dries with tightly spaced, narrow cracks.

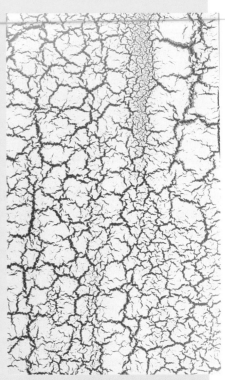

A decorative alternative, crackle lacquer can be used to imitate the alligator-skin appearance of many old paints and finishes. The finish consists of a base coat, a crackle coat, and a clear topcoat.

Moreover, mud located in a crawl space under a house develops even larger cracks than mud on a road because the mud under the house dries so much more slowly.

To control the thickness of the crackle lacquer, move your spray gun faster or slower, or hold the gun closer to or farther away from the surface. To achieve a more realistic aged effect, vary the speeds and distances so the crackle varies. To control the drying of the crackle lacquer, add lacquer retarder to slow it down and fast lacquer thinner or acetone to speed it up. Of course, adding any thinner reduces the thickness of the coat, which also affects the size of the cracking.

finishes, only shellac is as easy to repair as invisibly as lacquer. Invisible repairs are possible because more finish, in liquid or solid form, can be dissolved or melted into the damage. (See Chapter 19: "Repairing Finishes.")

Reduced Runs and Sags

Because of the unique characteristics of lacquer thinner, finishes thinned with lacquer thinner can be sprayed onto vertical surfaces with much less risk of runs and sags than can other finishes. This provides lacquer with an enormous advantage that is not often mentioned or considered when comparing finishes. (See "Lacquer Thinner" on p. 140.)

More Problem-Free Application

The unique characteristics of lacquer thinner also make it possible to get dust-free, blush-free, and overspray-free results with lacquer and some catalyzed finishes in widely varying weather conditions. Lacquer retarder can be used to eliminate blushing on humid days (Photo 10-2). It can also be used on hot, dry days to eliminate overspray settling back on the surface and giving it a sandy feel, and it can be used for the same purpose when spraying inside corners or the insides of cabinets or drawers. (See "Common Spraying Problems" on p. 32.) Fast lacquer thinner can be used in cold weather to speed drying so dust doesn't have time to settle and become embedded in the lacquer. No other thinner provides so much control.

Use in Decoration

Lacquer is the easiest finish to use for achieving sophisticated multistep decoration, including pore filling, glazing, and toning. There are no thickness limitations and no time limit involved for getting all coats applied. Good bonding

Photo 10-2: Blushing is the appearance of a whitish haze in the lacquer right after application. It is caused by moisture in the air condensing and taking the the lacquer out of solution near the surface. See "Common Problems Applying Lacquer" on p. 144 for ways to avoid this problem.

is achieved between coats even with layers of coloring in between. And the lacquer can be thinned infinitely to reduce the build during the coloring steps. (See Chapter 15: "Advanced Coloring Techniques.")

Depth and Beauty

Along with dewaxed clear shellac and varnish, lacquer stands out for the depth, clarity, and beauty it brings out in wood, especially in quality hardwoods such as mahogany, walnut, and cherry. In comparison, other finishes tend to cloud the wood a little, though you may have to place the examples side by side to see the difference.

Rubbing Qualities

Lacquer is the easiest of all finishes to rub to an even sheen. First, there is no crosslinking in a lacquer finish, so it scratches easily and evenly with abrasives.

> Warming lacquer reduces its viscosity and makes it level better. Warm the lacquer by putting the can or spray-gun cup in a pot of hot water. A lower viscosity means that less thinner needs to be added. **TIP**

Second, the coats dissolve together creating one thicker layer, so sanding through from one layer into the one below isn't possible. You don't have to worry about "ghosting" with a lacquer finish. (See Chapter 16: "Finishing the Finish.") The highest-quality and most expensive furniture produced by the furniture industry is usually finished with a rubbed nitrocellulose lacquer. Consumers will pay more for appearance than for protection and durability.

Common Problems Applying Lacquer

Lacquer is a very forgiving finish. Problems are easier to repair than with most other finishes. But they're not easy when you don't understand why they occurred. The most common problems are runs and sags, orange peel, and dry spray. (See "Common Spraying Problems" on p. 32.)

PROBLEM	CAUSE	SOLUTION
Blushing: The lacquer develops a white haze right after you apply it.	The rapid evaporation of the lacquer thinner cools the surface so fast that humidity from the air is drawn into the film. This takes the lacquer out of solution so it appears white. (The water doesn't get trapped in the finish as is so often claimed.) Blushing usually occurs during warm, humid weather.	Thin the lacquer with a slower-evaporating thinner (lacquer retarder) to give the moisture more time to escape before the lacquer dries.
		Warm the lacquer by putting the can or the spray-gun cup in a pot of hot water. The warmer sprayed lacquer will take longer to cool, thus reducing the tendency to blush. (Warming the lacquer will also make the finish level better.)
		If the blushing has already dried in the lacquer, allow a few hours or overnight for the lacquer to continue drying. The blushing may disappear. Or, spray a light coat of lacquer retarder to put the lacquer back into solution and then dry clear. Or, remove the blushing (usually right at the surface) by abrading the surface with fine steel wool.
Cotton blush: The sprayed lacquer looks like small dusted pieces of white cotton.	The lacquer thinner used to thin the lacquer wasn't strong enough to fully dissolve the lacquer. (See "Lacquer Thinner" on p. 140.)	Remove the whiteness by sanding or washing with lacquer thinner. Then spray on more lacquer, thinning with a proper lacquer thinner rather than one used for cleanup.

Ease of Stripping

Lacquer and shellac are the only film finishes that can be "washed" off of wood. No abrasives, scraping tools, or strong solvents or chemicals, such as lye or ammonia, are needed. Stripping other finishes, especially on pieces with decorative carvings, turnings, and moldings, will likely damage the wood. This is why it is so important to use an evaporative finish when refinishing elaborate or valuable antique furniture.

PROBLEM	CAUSE	SOLUTION
Fish eyes: Small craters develop in the wet film.	The wood has been contaminated with silicone from a furniture polish, lubricant, or body lotion.	See "Fish Eye and Silicone" on p. 146.
Pinholes: Small bubbles develop over large pores and become tiny holes when you sand them level.	Air trapped in large pores has broken through the film, sometimes because the wood is warmer than the finish.	Pinholes are difficult to repair, though you can try sanding the finish back and dusting on a few coats of lacquer before applying a wet coat. Otherwise, strip off the lacquer, and begin again by dusting on several coats followed by wetter coats.
Press marks or printing: These occur when the finish is still soft.	The lacquer hasn't fully hardened, because of temperature, solvent, or coat thickness.	The most common cause is low ambient temperatures, as the finish takes longer to harden when it's cold. Warm the finish room, or add some fast lacquer thinner to speed up the drying.
		You may have added lacquer retarder to solve a blushing or overspray problem. The finish will remain softer for a longer time. Add less retarder or give the finish longer to harden fully.
		The thicker the film, the longer it will take to harden all the way through. Apply thinner coats or give the finish longer to harden completely.

Fish Eye and Silicone

One of the most frustrating problems you will encounter in finishing and refinishing is *fish eye*. Fish eye usually appears as circular, moonlike craters in the finish immediately after you apply it (as shown in the photo on the facing page). It sometimes appears as random ridges, and when it takes this form, it is called *crawling*.

Though fish eye can occur when using any film finish, I'm including it here because it is usually associated with lacquer. (Fish eye doesn't show up in oil finishes because the excess is wiped off.)

Fish eye is caused by silicone contamination in the wood. Silicone has a very low surface tension, and finishes having a higher surface tension don't flow over it. It's the same phenomenon you see when you put water on a car that has just been waxed. On a car the water beads up because the wax is everywhere. On wood the finish usually craters or ridges around the spots where the silicone has gotten into the pores.

Silicone is an oil used in some lubricants, furniture polishes, and body lotions. The usual cause of fish eye is the silicone in some furniture polishes. (See Chapter 18: "Caring for the Finish.") The silicone gets through cracks in the finish and into the wood.

Once silicone has gotten into wood, it is very difficult to remove—the same as with any oil. Silicone may cause fish eye in your first coat of finish, or it may get worked into the first coat and not

cause problems until the second or third coat. Silicone contamination can vary from a mild case that can be easily corrected to a severe case that is very difficult to correct. It can also be spotty on the wood, showing up in some places and not in others.

If you suspect silicone contamination, take one or more of the following measures to prevent fish eye.

- Remove the silicone from the wood.
- Seal the silicone in the wood.
- Lower the surface tension of your finish.
- Spray four of five mist coats of lacquer.

If fish eye occurs after you have applied a finish, you can try sanding the ridges level and then using one of the above methods to avoid the problem with the next coat. Usually, it is best to quickly wash off the still-green finish using

lacquer thinner and begin again using one or more of these methods.

REMOVE THE SILICONE FROM THE WOOD

You can wash silicone from the wood in the same way you would wash any oil from wood: using a petroleum-distillate solvent, ammonia and water, or a solution of TSP (tri-sodium phosphate) and water. With petroleum-distillate solvent, flood the surface and dry off the excess several times, turning the cloth as you wipe. (See "Turpentine and Petroleum-Distillate Solvents" on p. 158.) Each time you do this, you will thin the oil and remove some of it. The other cleaners will break down the oil, but water will raise the grain of the wood, so you will have to sand it smooth. If the ammonia or TSP darkens the wood, wash it with oxalic acid to restore the color. (See "Using Oxalic Acid" on p. 286.)

SEAL THE SILICONE IN THE WOOD

Use shellac to seal the silicone in the wood. (See Chapter 9: "Shellac.") This will work in all

Fish eye is a common problem when refinishing old furniture with lacquer. The defect looks like moon craters.

but the most severe cases. It's best to spray the shellac. Be careful not to sand through the shellac when sanding it smooth, and don't apply a heavy wet coat of lacquer on top of the shellac, or the lacquer might break through.

LOWER THE SURFACE TENSION OF THE FINISH

Add silicone to your finish to lower its surface tension so it will flow over the silicone in the wood. Once you have added silicone to one coat of finish, you must add it to each additional coat. You can brush or spray each coat.

Silicone intended for this purpose is sold under a number of trade names, including Fish Eye Eliminator, Fish Eye Flow Out, Sil Flo, and Smoothie. The amount to add can range from a few drops per quart of finish to an eyedropper full, depending on the brand and the extent of the contamination you're correcting. The greater the contamination, the more silicone you will need to add. Try following the directions on the container of silicone, and add more if it doesn't work. I typically add an eyedropper full every time. Don't overdo it, though, or you may cause cloudiness in the finish.

Adding silicone to the finish raises its gloss a little and makes it slicker so it doesn't scratch as easily. Some finishers add silicone to all their finishes to achieve these qualities.

With lacquer you can add the silicone directly and then stir. With varnish it's best to thin the silicone in a little mineral spirits before adding it. With water base you will need to use a special emulsified silicone, available from finish suppliers.

Keep in mind that adding silicone to your finish will contaminate your spray gun or brush, requiring that you clean it extra well to remove all the oil. And if you're spraying without adequate exhaust, overspray may also contaminate any finished or unfinished wood in the area.

DUST ON FOUR OR FIVE COATS OF LACQUER

If you are spraying lacquer, you can dust on coats until you create a build. Then spray one coat just wet enough to dissolve all the dusted coats, but not enough to get into the wood and cause the finish to fish-eye. As you can imagine, it takes practice to get this just right, so this is not the best solution. But I know it works, because I used it for a number of years until someone told me about shellac and adding silicone to the finish.

You are not limited to just one of the above methods for eliminating fish eye. You can employ several together. All refinishers do some cleaning automatically as part of the stripping process. In addition, many refinishers make it a practice to seal all their work with shellac, and many others add silicone regularly to their finish even when they've had no indication of a problem. Some do all of these.

Spraying Lacquer

Lacquer dries rapidly, so it is usually sprayed. Here's how to do it:

1 Arrange your work so you can see what's happening in reflected light.

2 Decide whether you want to use sanding sealer, vinyl sealer, shellac, or the lacquer itself as a sealer. (See "Sealers and Sealing Wood" on p. 116.)

3 Spray the first coat on the wood. (See "Using Spray Guns" on p. 38.)

4 Allow the first coat to dry thoroughly, then sand it lightly

Spray edges first on large, flat surfaces (above). Spray less noticeable parts first on complex objects (below). Spray prominent surfaces last.

TIP

It isn't necessary to let lacquer dry completely between coats. In fact, many finishers like to apply a thin "tack" coat to soften the existing lacquer and then come right back over with a full coat. I often apply two full coats, one right after the other. It doesn't make any difference in the final result, so it's really just a matter of personal preference.

with 280-grit or finer sandpaper to remove roughness.

5 Remove the sanding dust with compressed air, vacuum, brush, or a tack cloth. Because the next coat of lacquer will redissolve any remaining lacquer sanding dust, it isn't essential to remove all of it.

6 Apply the next coat of lacquer.

7 Allow it to dry, and sand it lightly with stearated (dry-lubricated) sandpaper if there are dust nibs or other flaws you want to remove. Otherwise, it's not necessary to sand.

8 Build the lacquer until you are satisfied. If you aren't trying to fill the pores, three or four coats are usually adequate. But it will depend on how much you thin the lacquer and how thickly you apply each coat. (See "Solids Content and Mil Thickness" on p. 108.)

9 You can leave the lacquer as is, or you can finish it off with sandpaper, steel wool, or rubbing compounds. (See Chapter 16: "Finishing the Finish.")

Lacquer's Problems

No finish is perfect, and lacquer has several significant problems. These include the following:

- reduced protection and durability
- slow build
- tendency to blush in humid weather
- susceptibility to fish-eyeing, or cratering, from silicone contamination
- the inclusion of toxic, polluting, and flammable solvents

Reduced Protection and Durability

In an age when many people want their finishes to hold up to almost any abuse, lacquer falls short compared to most other finishes. As an evaporative finish, lacquer can be damaged by water, wear, heat, solvents, acids, and alkalis easier than all film-building reactive finishes and easier than many water-based finishes. Only shellac among the film finishes is less protective and durable than lacquer.

Slow Build

Because the molecules in lacquer are very long and stringy, lacquer requires a lot of solvent to spread them apart enough for spraying or brushing. (Think of how much water would be required in a pot of spaghetti to keep the individual strands from contacting one another while the spaghetti is poured into the sink. See Chapter 8: "Introduction to Film Finishes.") High solvent content means reduced build per coat. The result is that it takes more coats of lacquer to achieve the same film thickness that can be accomplished with fewer coats of other finishes.

Blushing

Probably the most common problem specific to the application of lacquer is *blushing*. This is the appearance of a

NOTE

Though lacquer is not as protective or durable as most other finishes, it's important to emphasize that lacquer is protective and durable enough for most situations. It's most likely that all the furniture you grew up with and most of the furniture you live with now was finished with lacquer.

NOTE

▼

Finishers love lacquer for its forgiving qualities and its beauty as a finish and versatility in creating different effects. But the solvents in lacquer are noxious and irritating, and this has caused many finishers to switch to less forgiving and less versatile water base.

milky-white haze in the film right after spraying (Photo 10-2). Blushing occurs in humid weather and is caused by moisture condensing on the lacquer and taking it out of solution. For methods of countering blushing, see "Common Problems Applying Lacquer" on p. 144.

Fish Eye

"Fish eye" is the name used to describe moonlike craters that can appear in a finish just after application. The craters are caused by silicone in the wood and occur easily in lacquer. The usual culprits are furniture polishes, spray lubricants, and body lotions. Most fish-eye problems occur in refinishing, but silicone contamination can be a problem in new-wood finishing also. If this is your situation, you should try to eliminate the source of the contamination so you don't have to deal with the problem on a constant basis. In a refinishing shop, silicone contamination can't be eliminated because it comes with the furniture being refinished. Though a serious problem if you don't understand it or know how to correct it, fish eye can be controlled. (See "Fish Eye and Silicone" on p. 146.)

Toxic, Polluting, and Flammable Solvents

The solvents used in lacquer thinner are toxic to breathe, polluting to the atmosphere, and highly flammable. To make matters worse, a high percentage of thinner is required to make the lacquer thin enough to spray or brush.

Despite lacquer's many advantages (listed on p. 141), many professional finishers switch to water-based finishes to get away from the noxious solvent odors. Even expensive spray booths and quality respirator masks aren't fully effective in protecting finishers in smaller shops, because the solvents continue to evaporate out of the finish for a considerable time after the finish is applied. (Factories run the objects through an oven to speed the drying.)

Beyond the health issues, many localities and some entire states are restricting the use of lacquer, or at least the amount of solvent that can be added to lacquer, in order to reduce air pollution. Manufacturers are trying to reduce bad solvents in two ways. One is to use nitrocellulose with a lower molecular weight (shorter spaghetti strands). It takes less thinner to put smaller molecules into solution. The problem with this approach is that it weakens the durability of the film. The other method manufacturers are using is to substitute acetone for some of the other solvents in lacquer thinner. Acetone is not listed by the government as an air pollutant, so there are no restrictions on its use. The problem with this solution is that acetone increases the cost, and it evaporates very rapidly. Blushing, orange peel, and dry spray become more prevalent.

CHAPTER 11

Varnish

Varnish (including polyurethane varnish) is the most protective and durable of the commonly available finishes. It forms a good barrier against water penetration and water-vapor exchange, and it resists heat, wear, solvents, acids, and alkalis. In addition, varnish is inexpensive and it builds fast. It has all the good qualities you probably want in a finish, except one: It's the most difficult of all finishes to apply with good results.

Varnish is made by cooking a curing or modified semi-curing oil with a resin. Driers are added to speed the curing. Traditionally, the oil used was linseed oil, because it was the best oil available. In the late nineteenth century, tung oil was introduced into the Western world from China and began to be used in some piano and furniture varnishes and in spar varnishes meant for outdoor use. By the mid-twentieth century, chemists had learned how to modify semi-curing oils, such as soybean (soya) oil and safflower oil, so they would cure better. These oils are cheaper, and they yellow (actually "orange") less than linseed oil and tung oil, so they are now the primary oils used in varnish. (All varnishes yellow over time.)

Traditional resins were fossilized sap from various species of pine trees. The best pine-tree resins were imported. (American pine-tree resin is too soft to

Photo 11-1: Examples of some natural resins used in varnish. From left, copal, amber, and rosin.

make good varnish.) The resins came from eastern Asia, New Zealand, Africa, and northern Europe. The best resins were copals, such as kauri, congo, and manila. Amber was also used. Amber is the fossilized sap from an extinct pine that once grew in northern Europe. You often see amber in gift stores, sold for making into necklaces and jewelry. Natural resins are rarely used anymore to make varnish (Photo 11-1).

Early in the twentieth century chemists began developing synthetic resins, which were more consistent in quality and availability. The first to be developed was *phenolic* resin (a combination of phenol and formaldehyde). Originally it was used as a plastic and, in fact, saw widespread use in early radio cases. To use phenolic resin for finishing, chemists developed a way of making the resin into liquid by cooking it with oil. The liquid resin/oil combination changes to a solid when exposed to oxygen in the air. This process is called *oxidation*. Phenolic resin, the first synthetic varnish resin, is rarely used in varnish anymore, largely because it yellows so much.

The next was *alkyd* resin, a type of polyester, developed in the 1920s. The name "alkyd" is a contraction of the names of the two main ingredients used to make the resin—alcohol and acid. Alkyd resin is also cooked with oil to

make varnish. It is cheaper than phenolic resin and has become a workhorse in the finish industry. It's not only the most common resin used in varnish, it's also used in lacquer, catalyzed finishes, some water-based products, and oil-based paint.

The last of the three main varnish resins is *polyurethane*. It was developed in the 1930s and is commonly used as a plastic. Polyurethane is very tough. There are several varieties of polyurethane finish. Pure polyurethane finishes come in two parts, or they cure with heat or by absorbing moisture. (See Chapter 12: "Two-Part Finishes.") The polyurethane you most often see in paint stores is actually an alkyd varnish modified with polyurethane resin, a *uralkyd*. Since the base of the finish is alkyd varnish, it applies and cures like alkyd varnish. This type of varnish has become the most popular of the three varnish types because it is the most scratch-resistant.

Varnish made from oil and resin alone doesn't cure fast enough to be useful as a finish, so metallic driers are added to speed the curing. The driers act as a catalyst, accelerating oxidation. Originally, lead was used as a drier because it was available and it worked well. Other metallic driers have since been developed. When the use of lead as a drier was outlawed in the 1970s because it causes health problems, these other driers were substituted. They include salts of cobalt, manganese, and zinc. These driers are all approved by the Food and Drug Administration (FDA) for use in oil, varnish, and paint. They are not known to cause any health problems as long as the oil, varnish, or paint is formulated so that it cures thoroughly. With a few rare exceptions for specialty products, lead is no longer used. (See "The Food-Safe Myth" on p. 76.)

You can buy a prepared mix of driers and add them to oil, varnish, or oil-based paint to speed the curing. The mix is in liquid form and is usually sold as *japan drier*. Adding your own japan drier to varnish is risky. First, the combination of driers in the pre-packaged can may not be optimal for the finish you're using. Second, adding driers to the finish will not only speed the curing, it will make the film more brittle and promote cracking. Add only a few drops at a time, and proceed cautiously until you get a feel for the effect the driers have.

The Mix of Oil and Resin

Whichever oils and resins are used in making a varnish, the greatest difference is made by the ratio of oil to resin. The more oil, the softer and more flexible the resulting cured-varnish film. The less oil, the harder and more brittle the resulting cured-varnish film.

Varnish made with a high percentage of oil is called *long-oil varnish*. It is commonly sold as "spar" or "marine" varnish and is intended for outdoor use, where more flexibility is needed to accommodate greater wood movement. Varnish made with a low percentage of oil is called *short-oil* or *medium-oil varnish*. It is meant to be used indoors, where extreme wood movement is not a problem and a harder finish is usually desired.

In the labeling as commonly practiced, spar and marine (or "boat") varnish are quite different. Both are long-oil varnishes, of course, meaning that they are made with a higher-than-normal percentage of oil, but the term "spar" simply indicates a long-oil varnish while the term "marine" indicates a spar

varnish with UV absorbers included. UV absorbers resist damage from UV light. (See "UV Protection" on p. 280.)

A lesser but still significant difference results from which oils and which resins are used to make a varnish. (It also makes a difference which driers are used, but only in the speed and thoroughness of the curing, not in the physical properties of the cured film.) Here is how resins and oils affect the characteristics of varnish:

- Phenolic resin cures tough and flexible. It also yellows significantly (as seen in the old radio cases). Phenolic resin is often combined with tung oil to make spar varnish for use outdoors, and it was once combined with tung oil to make rubbing varnish for use on rubbed tabletops and pianos.

- Alkyd resin is not as tough as phenolic resin, but it is adequate for most situations, and it is cheaper and doesn't yellow as much. Alkyd is therefore the most common resin used in varnish. Because of the reduced yellowing of the resin, alkyd varnish is usually made with modified soybean oil because this oil doesn't yellow much either.

- Polyurethane resin is the toughest of the three varnish resins and is commonly combined with alkyd to make a one-part polyurethane finish. Most of these finishes are made with modified soybean oil for reduced yellowing. Polyurethane varnish has three shortcomings: It has a slightly cloudy appearance when applied thick (one reason for its being singled out as a "plastic"); it doesn't bond well with most other finishes, nor do most other finishes bond well with it; it doesn't even bond well to itself after it has cured thoroughly. Always scuff old polyurethane with sandpaper or steel wool before recoating. Finally, it doesn't hold up well in sunlight. UV

Photo 11-2: All of these products are varnish. They thin with mineral spirits and cure hard. Salad Bowl Finish, Seal-a-Cell, Wood Conditioner, Waterlox, and Formby's are sold in thinned form. Polyurethane and Varathane are made with polyurethane resin rather than alkyd resin. Interlux Schooner and Spar Varnish are made with a higher percentage of oil so they are flexible. Interlux Schooner contains enough UV absorber to hold up well in sunlight.

rays destroy its bond to the wood and cause it to peel. A lot of UV absorbers have to be added by the manufacturer to make a polyurethane that performs well in direct sunlight. (For a guide to the various varnishes, see "Identifying Varnish Types" on facing page.)

Characteristics of Varnish

Beyond the color variations, varnish has six primary characteristics, each of which is related to its reactive curing. (See "Reactive Finishes on p. 112.")

- *Excellent resistance to water and water-vapor exchange:* The crosslinked molecular network reduces the size of spaces for water or water vapor to pass through.
- *Excellent resistance to heat, wear, solvents, acids, and alkalis:* Due to the crosslinking of the resin molecules, varnish is an exceptionally durable finish. The molecules are hard to

break apart, so it takes high heat, sharp force, or strong solvents or chemicals to cause damage.

- *Long curing time:* Slow oxidation allows you plenty of time to brush varnish without it getting tacky and dragging. But this also leads to dust problems. Any dust that settles on the surface while the varnish is still wet or tacky will stick, detracting from the finished object.
- *Difficulty in repairing and stripping:* This is the flip side of good solvent, heat, and chemical resistance.
- *Difficulty in rubbing to an even sheen:* This is the flip side of good wear resistance.
- *Skinning over in the can:* Because varnish cures by absorbing oxygen, any air left in a can of varnish will begin to cure the varnish. If there is enough air, the varnish will skin over. (If the varnish hasn't begun to gel under the skin, it is still good. Remove the skin and strain the remaining varnish into a smaller container, such as a glass jar or a collapsible plastic container, so little or no air remains to cause skinning. Label the container. You can also replace the air in the container with an inert gas contained in a product such as "Bloxygen.")

Applying Varnish

Varnish takes a long time to cure: an hour or more to cure enough for dust not to stick to it, and at least overnight to cure enough to apply another coat. For these reasons varnish is seldom used in factories or by professional finishers. It is mostly used by amateurs who don't own spray equipment (Photo 11-2). (See also "Brushing Varnish" on p. 156.)

Varnish is a joy to brush and miserable to spray. It brushes easily because there is plenty of time to spread it out evenly on the wood. It's troublesome to spray because small particles of uncured varnish float around in the air and settle on you (and everything else), making your skin sticky. (Nevertheless, I know some people who spray varnish.)

It takes very few coats of full-strength varnish to build a significant thickness of film. Varnish has a high-solids content. (See "Solids Content and Mil Thickness" on p. 108.) Two coats of varnish after the first "sealer" coat are almost always enough. (See "Sealers and Sealing Wood" on p. 116.)

The weather affects the speed at which varnish cures. Cold and damp weather slows the curing significantly. Don't apply varnish in temperatures below 60 degrees Fahrenheit: It may take days to cure. Hot weather speeds the curing. The thinner evaporates more quickly, and the varnish reacts more quickly with oxygen. You may find it difficult to brush varnish on a large surface if the temperature is 90 degrees or higher. Brush marks may not have time to level out, and air bubbles may not have time to pop out before the varnish cures. (See the table "Common Problems Using Varnish" on p. 160.)

There's nothing you can do to speed up the curing on cold or damp days except raise the temperature in the area in which you're working. You can slow the curing somewhat on hot days, however, by adding 5 to 10 percent mineral spirits (paint thinner) to the varnish. (See "Turpentine and Petroleum-Distillate Solvents" on p. 158.)

Adding a little mineral spirits to varnish makes it spread more easily and flow out more smoothly, in addition to giving air bubbles more time to pop out of the finish. Many finishers make it a practice to thin each coat. The downside, of course, is reduced build, so you may have to apply more coats.

Identifying Varnish Types

Unless a varnish contains polyurethane, manufacturers seldom tell you the type. Here are some clues that will help you determine this.

CLUE	THE VARNISH IS PROBABLY
No identification on the can.	Alkyd
The varnish is light in color.	Alkyd/soybean oil
The varnish is amber-colored.	Alkyd/linseed oil or phenolic/tung oil

Wiping Varnish

"Wiping varnish" is a term I coined in an article in *Woodwork* magazine in 1990. The term describes a popular, easy-to-use finish made by thinning varnish about half with mineral spirits, but there aren't any products on the market labeled "wiping varnish." (See "Wiping Varnish Sold as Oil" on p. 78.) Thinning the varnish makes it easy to wipe (rather than brush) on wood—thus the name. The purpose of the name was to distinguish thinned varnish from the misleading and uninformative labeling that was, and still is, prevalent. Most wiping varnishes are labeled "Tung Oil," "Tung Oil Finish," or "Tung Oil Varnish." Some are labeled "Salad Bowl Finish" and others use a proprietary name such as Waterlox, Seal-a-Cell, ProFin, or Val-Oil.

Because they are varnish (sometimes polyurethane varnish), all of these finishes provide excellent protection and durability if enough coats are applied to achieve a build on the wood. The problem is the labeling. It compromises our ability to communicate, and it causes many to experience failures in their finishing. If someone tells you that he or she used tung oil on a project, you don't know if it really was tung oil or if it was

MYTH
You can prevent air bubbles by not shaking or stirring the can of varnish and by brushing very slowly and smoothly.

FACT
You can't keep air bubbles from occurring in varnish if you brush it. The trick is getting the bubbles to pop out of the film before it skins over. If the bubbles don't pop out on their own, thin the varnish with 5 to 10 percent mineral spirits. The mineral spirits will slow the curing enough to allow them to pop out. If you still have problems, change brands of varnish. Some brands bubble a lot less than others.

Brushing Varnish

Varnish can be applied by brushing, spraying, or even wiping, as is done with wiping varnish and gel varnish. But it's usually brushed. The key to getting good results with varnish is cleanliness—even more so than with other finishes, because varnish takes so long to cure. Here are some suggestions:

- Don't do your sanding and dusting in the same room where you are about to apply the varnish.
- Wet-mop the floor so you don't kick up dust when you walk around.
- Put clean paper under your work.
- Strain the varnish if it is dirty or has formed a skin.
- Be sure your brush is clean. Hit it against your hand to shake out any loose bristles.

TIP A tack cloth is cheesecloth made sticky with a varnishlike substance. You can buy one (which I think is the best idea), or you can make your own. To make one, wet a piece of cheesecloth with mineral spirits. Wring out the cheesecloth, and apply a few drops of varnish. Work the varnish into the cheesecloth. The cheesecloth should be sticky enough to pick up dust but not so sticky as to leave a residue when you wipe it over the wood. Store the tack cloth in an airtight coffee can or Ziplock-type bag to keep it from hardening.

- Be sure the wood's surface is clean. Wipe it with a tack cloth or your hand just before you start applying the varnish.
- If the object isn't too large, make a cover to put over it or slide it under something that will block dust from landing.

With cleanliness foremost in mind, here are the steps for brushing varnish:

1 Arrange your work so you can see what's happening in a reflected light source.

2 Decide whether you want to use a varnish sanding sealer or varnish thinned half with mineral spirits (paint thinner) for the first coat. (See "Sealers and Sealing Wood" on p. 116.)

3 Pour enough sanding sealer or varnish to do the job into another container (a jar or coffee can) and work out of that container. This way you won't transfer dust or dirt back into your original supply.

4 Brush on the first coat. Brush with the grain, except on three-dimensional surfaces such as turnings, and don't leave puddles or runs. (See "Using Brushes" on p. 25.)

5 Allow the varnish to cure overnight.

6 Sand the surface lightly with the grain using 280-grit or finer sandpaper. Stearated (dry-lubricated) sandpaper works best. Sand outside your finish room, or sand several

MYTH You should thin your first coat of varnish half with mineral spirits to get a better bond to the wood.

FACT Varnish bonds well to wood whatever the varnish thickness. The reason to thin your first coat is so the film will be thinner and cure harder faster, making it easier to sand sooner. Thinning also causes a finish to penetrate faster, but it will penetrate anyway if it stays liquid long enough. The real advantage to thinning is harder, faster curing.

hours before you intend to apply the next coat of varnish, so dust in the room will have time to settle.

7 Remove the sanding dust with a vacuum or tack cloth. Finish off with a tack cloth or your hand.

8 Working from a separate container, apply the next coat of varnish full strength or thinned with 5 to 10 percent mineral spirits to reduce bubbling.

9 Coat one part at a time. When each part is coated, remove any excess varnish by *tipping off*. Here's how: Hold your brush almost vertical and brush very lightly with the grain. If you are picking up excess varnish, wipe the brush over the clean lip of a jar or onto another clean surface to remove the excess.

TIP Brushing parts in a horizontal position reduces runs and sags. If possible, reposition a piece so the surface you're finishing is horizontal. Brush the most important parts, such as the top and drawer fronts, or chair seat and chair back, last.

10 Allow the varnish to cure overnight in a warm room.

11 Sand the surface lightly with 320-grit or finer stearated sandpaper. You can substitute #000 or #0000 steel wool or a gray synthetic-abrasive pad (Scotch-Brite). Neither will clog like sandpaper does, but they aren't as effective at cutting off dust nibs.

12 If you're trying to achieve a perfect or near-perfect flat surface, sand out the brush marks after the next-to-last coat. On flat surfaces use a cork, felt, or rubber block to back your sandpaper. Use 320- or 400-grit wet/dry sandpaper lubricated with soap and water or mineral spirits. The last coat will then level better.

13 Decide what sheen you want. You can use gloss and rub it after it has cured, or you can use a flatted varnish. (See "Controlling Sheen with Flatting Agent" on p. 110.) Gloss varnish seldom looks good without rubbing; satin and flat look fine without rubbing.

14 Clean off the sanding dust and brush on the last coat. If you have sanded the next-to-last coat, the last will level fairly well, leaving you with less to do to make the surface

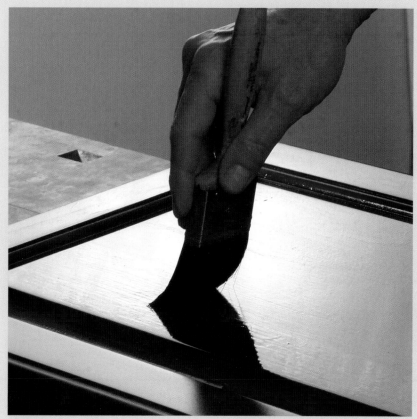

Varnish is the easiest of all finishes to brush because it cures so slowly. But slow drying makes good results elusive because it is difficult to avoid dust and runs.

perfectly flat. Alternatively, you can thin the varnish with 25 to 50 percent mineral spirits, making a wiping varnish (see "Wiping Varnish" on p. 155) and brush it on. Because the varnish is thinned, it will level better and dry faster, reducing dust nibs. Another alternative is to apply a gel varnish over this next-to-last coat. This will also reduce brush marks and dust nibs (see "Gel Varnish" on p. 162.)

15 When you're satisfied with the thickness of the finish, you can leave it as is, or you can finish it with sandpaper, steel wool, or rubbing compounds. (See Chapter 16: "Finishing the Finish.")

MYTH Thinning varnish with naphtha will make it cure faster.

FACT Using naphtha instead of mineral spirits will just shorten the time until the varnish becomes tacky. Curing is brought about by a reaction with oxygen in the air, and has nothing to do with the thinner used.

thinned varnish—two very different finishes (Photo 5-3 on p. 78). For that matter, it could have been an oil/varnish blend. (See Chapter 5: "Oil Finishes.")

You can, of course, make your own wiping varnish and have much more control of the viscosity—and thus the potential build. Simply add mineral spirits to any varnish. Begin with as little as 25 percent mineral spirits and increase the amount until you are happy with the way the finish applies. (There

Turpentine and Petroleum-Distillate Solvents

Common solvents for wax, and common thinners for oil and varnish, are derived from two sources: pine sap and crude-oil petroleum. Distilled pine sap, called *turpentine*, was used before petroleum solvents were introduced around the turn of the twentieth century. The best-quality turpentine is steam-distilled from the sap of the living tree and is usually called *gum turpentine*. A lesser quality is steam-distilled from extracts of the dead tree or the stump and is usually called *wood turpentine*. Both types are available but have fallen out of favor because of higher cost and stronger odor than petroleum

NOTE
▼

Turpentine and naphtha are fairly close in solvent strength (turpentine is more oily). Mineral spirits is considerably weaker, and odorless mineral spirits is weaker still. Solvent strength is seldom important in thinning oils and varnishes, but using a stronger solvent can be helpful when removing partially cured oil or varnish, or a product made with oil or varnish, from the surface. It can also be helpful in removing wax.

solvents. Some painters still prefer to use turpentine, however, because they like the "feel" it gives to the paint while brushing.

Petroleum is the source of most of the solvents and thinners used in finishing. Those derived directly from petroleum are called *petroleum distillates*, because they are obtained by distillation. They include mineral spirits, naphtha, kerosene, benzene, toluene, and xylene. (These solvents are known generically as *hydrocarbons*, because they are made up of hydrogen and carbon.)

The petroleum is heated until gases form. The gases are drawn off and allowed to cool back into liquid form, different substances condensing at different temperatures. For example, at relatively low temperatures heptane and octane are distilled to be made into gasoline. At higher temperatures naphtha, usually sold as Varnish Maker's and Painter's Naphtha (VM&P Naphtha), is derived. This is followed by mineral spirits and then kerosene. Mineral oil (also called paraffin oil) can be distilled at even higher temperatures, and paraffin wax (used to seal jelly jars) at still higher temperatures. Each of these distillations is called a petroleum *fraction*. The lower-temperature

Benzene, which is carcinogenic, is often confused with benzine, which is another name for naphtha. **TIP** It will help you to remember which is which if you associate benz**i**ne with the word al**i**ve and benz**e**ne with the word d**e**ad.

fractions are far more volatile (and therefore flammable) than the higher-temperature fractions.

The relationship between the fractions is important because it helps you understand these solvents so you know when to use each. (See diagram on facing page.)

VM&P naphtha (also called benzine) is distilled at a lower temperature than mineral spirits. Therefore, at any given temperature naphtha will evaporate faster than mineral spirits. Kerosene barely evaporates, and mineral oil doesn't evaporate.

The faster the solvent evaporates, the less oily it is. The slower it evaporates, the more oily it is. Naphtha is less oily than mineral spirits, which is less oily than kerosene. Mineral oil *is* oil. Finally, at higher temperatures, the distillate is no longer a liquid at room temperature, it's a wax.

is seldom a reason to thin the varnish as much as manufacturers do.) Apply the finish as you would an oil finish—wipe it on the wood, then wipe off all the excess. Or apply it as you would full-strength varnish—by brushing and leaving it to cure. Because it is so thin, wiping varnish will level well, leaving you with a brush-mark-free finish. You can also wipe off some, but not all, of the wiping varnish, leaving a very thin film, or you can let the varnish set up a

You use naphtha when you want a solvent that evaporates relatively fast or is non-oily. Naphtha is best for degreasing. You use mineral spirits when you want a slower-evaporating solvent and you don't mind the oiliness. Mineral spirits is good for thinning oil finishes and varnish. Kerosene is not used in finishing; it evaporates very slowly or not at all, and it is very oily. All fractions of petroleum distillate can be mixed together.

Benzene, toluene, and xylene are the strong and smelly parts of naphtha and mineral spirits. Refineries remove these parts, and odorless mineral spirits is left. Odorless mineral spirits is not as strong a solvent as mineral spirits, but it is strong enough to be a substitute in most situations.

Benzene (also called benzol) was once used as a thinner and paint stripper, and you still see it recommended now and then for these purposes in books and magazine articles. But benzene is carcinogenic, and it was removed from the consumer market in the early 1970s. Mineral spirits and naphtha contain only a trace of benzene.

Toluene (also called toluol) is used as a diluting solvent in lacquer thinner. (See "Lacquer Thinner" on p. 140.) Xylene (also called xylol) evaporates more slowly than toluene. It is used as a thinner in conversion varnish and is sometimes

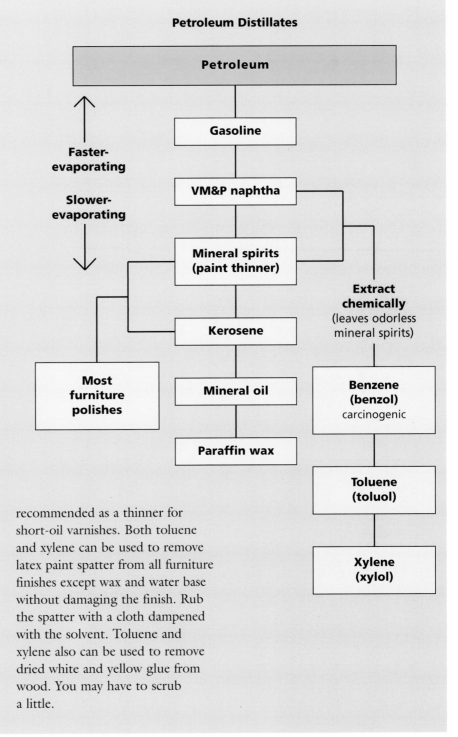

Petroleum Distillates

recommended as a thinner for short-oil varnishes. Both toluene and xylene can be used to remove latex paint spatter from all furniture finishes except wax and water base without damaging the finish. Rub the spatter with a cloth dampened with the solvent. Toluene and xylene also can be used to remove dried white and yellow glue from wood. You may have to scrub a little.

Common Problems Applying Varnish

Varnish brushes easily, but it is nevertheless difficult to get a good-looking finished result. Many things can go wrong. Here are the most common problems, their causes, and solutions. (See also "Common Brushing Problems" on p. 26.)

	PROBLEM	CAUSE	SOLUTION
	Dust nibs cure in the varnish.	Dust settles on the uncured varnish and sticks to it. Dust nibs are worse in varnish than in any other finish, because varnish cures the slowest.	Sand the surface level and rub it to a desired sheen using steel wool or rubbing compounds. (See Chapter 16: "Finishing the Finish.") For suggestions on cleanliness, see "Brushing Varnish" on p. 156.
	Brush marks cure in the finish.	You have applied the varnish full strength. There is no way to eliminate brush marks when brushing full-strength varnish.	Sand the surface level and rub it to a desired sheen after the varnish has fully cured. (See Chapter 16: "Finishing the Finish.")
			Reduce the brush marks during application by thinning the varnish. The more you thin it, the less pronounced the brush marks.
	Runs and sags develop in the varnish as you are applying it.	You have applied too thick a coat on a vertical surface.	Watch the surface in a reflected light as you are applying the varnish. If you see any runs or sags developing, remove some of the finish with your brush. Apply the excess to another part or remove it from the brush by dragging it over the clean edge of a jar.
	The varnish fish-eyes or crawls into ridges.	The wood has been contaminated with silicone from a furniture polish, lubricant, or body lotion.	Before the varnish cures, remove it with a cloth soaked with naphtha or mineral spirits. If you're too late, strip off the varnish and begin again. To prevent it happening again, see "Fish Eye and Silicone" on p. 146.

	PROBLEM	CAUSE	SOLUTION
	Air bubbles appear in the varnish as you apply it and don't pop out before the varnish cures—even after you have tipped off the varnish.	The bubbles are the result of turbulence caused by the brush gliding over the surface.	Sand the surface smooth and add 5% to 10% mineral spirits to the next coat. The mineral spirits will produce a thinner coat and will slow the curing enough for the air bubbles to pop out.
			Sand the surface smooth and work in a cooler room. The bubbles will have more time to pop out on their own.
	The varnish doesn't cure; it remains tacky.	The air is too cold.	Warm the room or wait for a warmer day. The ideal temperature is between 70°F and 80°F.
		There is uncured oil in the wood. Many people make the mistake of thinking a coat of linseed oil under the varnish helps things.	Warm the surface and allow more time for the varnish to harden. If it still doesn't, strip it and the oil off the wood and start over. If you apply linseed oil first, give it several days in a warm room to cure before applying the varnish.
		The wood is an oily wood such as teak, rosewood, cocobolo, or ebony. The oils in these woods retard the curing of varnish.	Warm the surface and allow more time for the varnish to harden. If it doesn't, strip the varnish off the wood and wash the wood with a non-oily solvent, such as naphtha, acetone, or lacquer thinner, just before reapplying the varnish.
	A topcoat of varnish wrinkles.	The coat was applied over another coat that hadn't cured sufficiently.	Strip and start over. Allow more time for each coat to cure. Remember that varnish cures much more slowly in cool temperatures.

TIP To achieve a build with full-strength varnish while minimizing dust and brush marks, build the thickness you want by brushing the varnish. Then sand the surface level, up to 400-grit. Finally, apply one coat of wiping varnish or gel varnish and wipe off most of the excess. This will leave a layer so thin that it will cure very fast, leaving little chance for dust to stick.

little and then rub it to remove some and burnish what remains.

Gel Varnish

Gel varnish is the same as a gel stain without the pigment. Said another way, gel varnish is thickened wiping varnish—without as much thinner or odor. It's designed to be wiped on and then wiped off of wood. Most gel varnishes produce a satin sheen, and this distinguishes them from wiping varnishes, which usually produce gloss.

Unlike wiping varnish, gel varnishes are correctly labeled. Like wiping varnish, gel varnishes are very easy to apply, and they produce excellent results. These finishes provide people without spray guns with the possibility of achieving near flawless finishes that are, at the same time, quite protective and durable.

Apply gel varnish using a cloth. Because the finish dries fairly rapidly, wipe off the excess quickly after application. If you don't get the excess wiped off before it begins to set up, remove it quickly by wiping with naphtha or mineral spirits. Then begin again, working faster or on a smaller area. Sand after each coat if you need to remove dust or other flaws. Apply three or four coats, or as many as you need to be satisfied with the appearance.

The Future of Varnish

Some localities are restricting solvent content below that which has been normal for varnishes. To comply with the restrictions, manufacturers produce thicker varnishes, use smaller molecular-weight resin, or substitute non-evaporating oil for some of the thinner.

Thicker varnishes are more difficult to apply and leave more pronounced brush marks. To comply with VOC laws, the manufacturer may warn against thinning the varnish. There is no physical problem with thinning it, however. Doing so simply makes the varnish non-compliant with the VOC laws.

Resins that have a smaller molecular weight may cause the varnish to cure more slowly and be less protective and durable. To some extent, manufacturers can compensate with a better mix of driers, but not all do so. Unfortunately, you may not know that you have bought one of these varnishes unless you notice the difference or the manufacturer gives you some clue on the label. Some manufacturers make their varnishes comply with the strictest local VOC laws in the country and then sell that varnish everywhere.

Adding a non-evaporating oil to varnish has the obvious effect of producing a varnish that takes longer to cure and doesn't cure as hard. (See "Oil/Varnish Blend" on p. 79.) Again, the manufacturer may not give you any clue on the label. You will have to notice the difference.

For at least the foreseeable future, you need to be more discriminating in the brand of varnish (or polyurethane) you use. If the varnish you are using doesn't dry or harden properly, and the cause is not the temperature or oil in the wood, try another brand. In the meantime, let's hope that governments and bureaucracies come to their senses and devote their energies to those segments of the economy that are truly responsible for the bulk of our pollution.

Two-Part Finishes

In the last several decades, two broad trends have been evident in wood finishes. You are surely aware of one of them—the trend toward water-based finishes. (See Chapter 13: "Water-Based Finishes.") The other is the trend toward high-solids, high-performance finishes. These are often referred to as "two-part," "two-component," or "2k" finishes because they are composed of two parts that, once mixed, cure by reacting together to form an exceptionally hard, durable film.

Water base and two-part have one thing in common. They both contain less solvent than most other finishes, so they go a long way toward satisfying the increasingly stringent VOC laws aimed at reducing solvent emissions into the atmosphere. The two haven't been equally received by users of finishes, however. While water base has met with a lot of resistance because of the problems caused by the water content, two-part finishes have made major headway, largely because they satisfy the public's desire for a finish nearly as durable as plastic laminate. Two-part finishes are now widely used in the office-furniture and kitchen-cabinet industries, and also in many smaller professional shops. (See "KCMA Testing Standards" on p. 164.)

The best-known and most widely used two-part finishes are the following:

- Catalyzed finishes (conversion varnish, post-catalyzed lacquer, and pre-catalyzed lacquer)
- Two-part polyurethane
- Crosslinking water-based finish
- Epoxy resin
- Polyester
- Ultraviolet-cured (UV) finishes
- Powder coatings

Except for epoxy resin, all of these finishes are used almost exclusively by professionals in furniture factories and

KCMA Testing Standards

You may have heard of the Kitchen Cabinet Manufacturer's Association (KCMA) Testing Standards. These standards are often used, especially by architects, to ensure that kitchen cabinets and other wooden objects are finished adequately with a finish that is protective and durable enough to hold up well in use. All two-part finishes meet KCMA standards, but it's not just the adequacy of the finish that is considered; it's also how the finish is applied. The most durable finish can be applied too thin or in conditions not conducive to proper curing and fail the tests. To find out if the finish you are using and your method of application meet the standards, finish a sample object in your normal manner and then subject the object (or four separate objects) to these four tests.

TEST NAME	DESCRIPTION OF TEST
Heat and Humidity Test	Place the finished object in a hotbox at 120 degrees Fahrenheit and 70 percent humidity for 24 hours. To pass, the finish must show no damage.
Hot-and-Cold Cycles Test (Cold-Check Test)[1]	Place the finished object in a hotbox at 120 degrees Fahrenheit and 70 percent humidity for one hour. Remove the object and allow it to adjust to room temperature and humidity. Then place the object in a cold box at –5 degrees Fahrenheit for one hour. Repeat the cycle 5 times. To pass, the finish must show no sign of blistering, cold check (cracking across the grain), or discoloration.
Household Chemicals Test	Subject the finish to mustard for one hour and lemon juice, orange juice, grapefruit juice, vinegar, tomato catsup, coffee, olive oil, and 100-proof alcohol for 24 hours. To pass, the finish must not be stained, discolored, or whitened to the degree that ordinary polishing doesn't remove the damage. Also there must be no blistering, checks, or other film failure.
Detergent Edge-Soak Test[2]	Submerge the edge of a finished board or cabinet door in detergent and water (a standardized formula is used in industry) for 24 hours. To pass, there must be no delamination or swelling and no appreciable discoloration, blistering, checking, whitening, or other film failure.

1. *Failure is usually the result of applying the finish too thick.*
2. *Failure is usually the result of applying the finish too thin.*

cabinet, woodworking, and refinish shops. Crosslinking water-based finish is also used by many floor finishers. Epoxy resin is the very thick finish you sometimes see on restaurant tables and bar tops. It is easy to use and is especially popular with amateurs for creating totally embedded montages of photos or other fairly flat items.

Also, with the exception of epoxy resin, two-part finishes are rarely available at stores catering to the general public. You have to go to distributors or suppliers to the professional finishing, refinishing, and woodworking trades to find them.

I'm going to discuss the first four of these finishes. The other three—polyester, UV-cured, and powder—are beyond the scope of this book. Polyester is a difficult and hazardous finish to use. UV-cured and powder coatings require very expensive application and drying equipment. They are, however, 100 percent solids, so they are becoming increasingly popular in the furniture industry because there are no solvent emissions.

Catalyzed Finishes

Catalyzed finishes have been available since the 1950s and were widely used in Europe well before they became popular in the United States. Now these finishes are used in this country on most office and institutional furniture and on manufactured kitchen and bathroom cabinets. The finishes dry rapidly and provide protection and durability that is generally better than oil-based polyurethane. Of all the two-part finishes, catalyzed finishes are by far the most widely used.

All catalyzed finishes are made with alkyd and amino resins. The amino resins include melamine formaldehyde and urea formaldehyde. You may be familiar with melamine in the context of plastic laminate, and with urea in the context of urea- or plastic-resin glue. If you are, you recognize that these resins are very resistant to all types of damage.

When an acid catalyst is added to these resin combinations, they cure to a hard film. The three classes of catalyzed finishes break down as follows:

- *Conversion varnish* (also called "catalyzed varnish") has the acid catalyst packaged separately and is the most protective and durable of the three. It thins with xylene, toluene, or a similar proprietary blend from the manufacturer. The *shelf life*, or amount of time before the finish goes bad in the can, is many years—as long as the two parts aren't combined. After they are combined, the *pot life* is usually 6 to 24 hours depending on the particular product.

- *Post-catalyzed lacquer* ("post-cat") is conversion varnish with some nitrocellulose lacquer added and an acid catalyst packaged separately. The nitrocellulose speeds the initial drying and makes the finish somewhat easier to repair and strip, but it weakens the resulting film a little. Because of the included nitrocellulose, post-cat thins with lacquer thinner. Note that lacquer thinner contains toluene or xylene. (See "Lacquer Thinner" on p. 140.) Otherwise, post-cat is like conversion varnish.

- *Pre-catalyzed lacquer* ("pre-cat") is the same as post-cat, but the acid catalyst (a weaker acid) is added by the manufacturer so the finish can be packaged in a single container. The weaker acid gives the finish a shelf life of a year or so depending on the manufacturer, after which the material may

Pros & Cons

PROS

- Excellent heat, wear, solvent, acid, and alkali resistance
- Excellent water and water-vapor resistance
- Very fast curing
- Reduced solvent emissions compared with most finishes

CONS

- Hazardous chemicals and fumes
- Often difficult to incorporate decorative coloring steps
- Very difficult to produce invisible repairs
- Very difficult to strip

thicken, lose durability, or have an increased tendency to *cold check*, (crack when exposed to cold temperatures). Pre-cat thins with lacquer thinner and has application characteristics very similar to nitrocellulose lacquer. (See Chapter 10: "Lacquer.") Pre-cat is considerably more protective and durable than nitrocellulose lacquer, but it is less so than post-catalyzed lacquer.

Some manufacturers add the acid catalyst just before shipping or delivery to create a short shelf-life product that is close to post-catalyzed lacquer in protection and durability but doesn't require further mixing. It is popular with finishers who want the most durable finish possible without having to fuss with mixing.

The use of the words "varnish" and "lacquer" in these names has some legitimacy. Conversion varnish cures entirely by crosslinking, so it is a pure reactive finish just like varnish. Post- and pre-catalyzed lacquers have some nitrocellulose lacquer included, so they are hybrid reactive/evaporative finishes. (See Chapter 8: "Introduction to Film Finishes.")

Conversion varnish is usually limited to simple, nondecorative use because, compared with nitrocellulose lacquer, it is difficult to rub evenly, it doesn't bring out as much richness or depth in the wood, it is much more difficult to repair, and it presents difficulties when coloring steps are included. Post-catalyzed lacquer is a little more versatile in all categories. Pre-catalyzed lacquer is most like nitrocellulose lacquer and is often substituted for it. If you haven't used any of these finishes, I recommend you begin with pre-cat and see if that gives you the performance characteristics you are looking for. Then advance to the more difficult-to-use finishes if you need the durability.

Applying Catalyzed Finishes

Catalyzed finishes dry fast, so they are almost always applied with a spray gun. The method of spraying is just like spraying lacquer. (See "Spraying Lacquer" on p. 148.) But there are a number of very important differences related to the finish itself. These differences apply especially to conversion varnish and post-catalyzed lacquer.

- Being high in solids, catalyzed finishes don't bond well to wood that is sanded too fine. You shouldn't sand past 220-grit, especially on tight-grained woods such as maple and cherry.

- The acid in the finish can cause a color shift in some stains, especially in non-grain-raising (NGR) stains. You should try your stain and finish together on scrap wood before committing an important project to them. To prevent an anticipated color shift, seal the wood and stain with vinyl sealer. (See "Sealers and Sealing Wood" on p. 116.)

- The acid catalyst has to be added in the exact proportions instructed by the manufacturer (usually between 3 and 10 percent catalyst). If you add too little, the finish won't cure properly. If you add too much, the film will crack prematurely and you may get *acid bloom*, an oily residue that seeps from the cured finish and keeps coming back each time you wipe it off (Photo 12-1).

- Though manufacturers are reducing the amount of formaldehyde in them, catalyzed finishes still contain a small amount of this toxic substance. You should protect yourself by working in an efficient spray booth or wearing an organic-vapor respirator.

- The pot life of catalyzed finishes is fairly short, so you should clean your equipment often. If you leave the finish in your gun, hose, or pressure pot for several days, you might ruin them. You won't be able to clean out the cured finish.

■ For a sealer coat, you are limited to vinyl sealer, catalyzed sealer, or the finish itself. Applying a catalyzed finish over another finish or sanding sealer might lead to poor bonding or wrinkling. The wrinkling usually occurs when you apply the second coat of catalyzed finish, not the first. A stain, filler, or glaze left too heavy can also cause this problem.

■ You are usually limited in the amount of time you have for getting all the coats applied. The time limit varies among manufacturers, but it seldom exceeds a day or two. If you need longer to complete your decorative steps, layer them between washcoats of vinyl sealer. (See "Washcoats" on p. 64.)

■ You are also limited in film thickness. Applying more than 5 dry mils (approximately three coats) of conversion varnish or post-catalyzed lacquer will likely lead to cracking, which might not show up for several months. Precatalyzed lacquer is more forgiving, but you should still avoid thick builds. (See "Solids Content and Mil Thickness" on p. 108.)

■ The temperature during application and for at least 6 hours afterwards should be kept above 65 degrees Fahrenheit. Otherwise, the finish may not cure properly.

Two-Part Polyurethane

In contrast to the "polyurethane" you find in home centers, which is made from a blend of polyurethane resin and alkyd resin, the resin in two-part poly-

Photo 12-1: It's critical that you mix two-part finishes in the exact right proportions. Otherwise, the finish might not cure properly. Because catalyzed finishes often call for only 10 percent or less of the catalyst part, it's even more important that the proportions be correct. Being off just a percentage or two makes a bigger difference than with finishes that are mixed two-thirds/ one-third or half and half.

urethane is 100 percent polyurethane, so it is much more protective and durable. It is also more difficult to use.

Two-part polyurethane has been used in the United States for many years to coat steel. But it has only recently come into use as a high-solids, high-performance wood finish. There are two types:

■ *Aromatic* is less expensive, but it yellows more and has a shorter pot life.

■ *Aliphatic* costs more, but it is completely non-yellowing and more resistant to UV light, and it has a longer pot life.

In practice, the two types are often blended when sold for interior use on wood, because UV resistance is not so critical and cost often is.

Two-part polyurethane is even more protective and durable than conversion varnish, but this comes at a price. Not only are repairing and stripping more difficult (abrading is often the only way to remove one of these finishes), the pot life is also considerably shorter than for conversion varnish—often as short as 4 hours. Two-part polyurethane is therefore not very user-friendly unless you have a production line where the finishing never stops.

On the other hand, the mixing of the two parts is less critical than it is with conversion varnish because the ratio is 2 parts urethane to 1 part isocyanate. So you can be off by a few percent without any noticeable effect. Also, there is almost no practical limit to the build you can get using two-part polyurethane without the finish cracking, and recoating can be done at any time without fear of wrinkling the previous coat.

Just as with catalyzed finishes, you need to protect yourself when using two-part polyurethane because of the isocyanates that are included. You should work in an efficient spray booth and wear an appropriate respirator.

Crosslinking Water Base

The growing emphasis on reducing solvent emissions while still producing a film that is exceptionally protective and durable has naturally led to an effort to make water-based finishes more protective and durable. This is being achieved by adding "crosslinkers" or "hardeners" to water-based finishes. These additives cause the resins to crosslink from droplet to droplet, making the finish totally reactive rather than a combination of reactive and evaporative, as is the case with non-crosslinking water-based finishes. The result is a finish that is more protective and durable but still considerably

less so than conversion varnish or two-part polyurethane.

Unfortunately, the crosslinker most commonly used is aziridine, which is a fairly toxic chemical. The use of this chemical adds a safety consideration that is more critical than those at issue with non-crosslinking water base. You should protect your hands and eyes when mixing the two parts, and you should work in an area with good ventilation.

Some one-part water-based finishes have a *self*-crosslinking mechanism built in, sort of the equivalent of pre-catalyzed lacquer. But I don't know of any standard method manufacturers use to identify this product. In fact, there doesn't seem to be any label distinction between non-crosslinking (common) and self-crosslinking water-based finishes. A two-part finish is easily recognizable, of course, because there are two parts.

Whether two-part or self-crosslinking, application methods are the same as for non-crosslinking water-based finishes. (See "Brushing and Spraying Water-Based Finishes" on p. 176.) Unfortunately, all the problems associated with water being included in the finish are also the same. (See "Water Content" on p. 177.)

Epoxy Resin

Epoxy resin is very thick, so it is commonly applied by pouring rather than brushing or spraying. This distinguishes epoxy resin from all the other finishes discussed in this book. Because of its thickness and its internal two-part curing, very thick layers can be applied (up to $1/16$ inch each), achieving an exceptionally effective barrier against moisture-vapor exchange. Uses for epoxy resin include encasing slabs cut from trees and small boards glued to plywood or MDF in parquetry designs. Wood

TIP Use a "two-cup" method with epoxy finishes to avoid getting poorly mixed finish into the blend that won't harden. After thoroughly mixing the two parts in one bucket, pour the contents into another bucket without scraping the sides or bottom. Stir the resin and hardener for a few seconds. This should thoroughly mix the two parts.

Photo 12-2: Pour equal parts of two-part epoxy (resin and hardener) into a plastic or unwaxed paper container.

Photo 12-3: Working quickly, thoroughly mix the two parts, folding into the center.

movement leading to splitting and separation can be totally prevented. Other applications include restaurant tables and bar tops, and embedding montages of photos, newspaper articles, or other relatively flat objects.

To apply epoxy resin, begin by mixing the two parts in a disposable, unwaxed paper or plastic bucket (Photo 12-2). Stir equal parts (or follow manufacturer's directions) for several minutes using a "folding-into-the-center" motion (Photo 12-3). Scrape the bottom as well as the sides occasionally and clean the stirring stick over the edge so that the mixture gets blended thoroughly to an even consistency and transparency. Work quickly because you usually have only 10 or 15 minutes before the epoxy begins to set up.

Photo 12-4: Pour the mixture onto the surface liberally. You can let it run over the edges, shaping them with a disposable brush, or create a dam at the edges using masking tape.

When the epoxy is mixed, pour it onto a horizontal surface and spread it with a plastic spreader so that the layer is evenly thick (Photo 12-4 on p. 169 and Photo 12-5). Remove bubbles in the finish by blowing on them with your breath or a blow dryer. Use a disposable brush to smooth out the epoxy as it runs over the edges, or create a dam at the edges using masking tape. Clean up with acetone before the epoxy hardens. Here are some variations you may want to consider:

- If you want to seal the underside of your panel, do so before applying the epoxy resin to the top.
- If you want to embed some objects, brush on a thin first coat of epoxy resin and lay the objects onto the surface while it is still sticky. (You can also use a thin first coat to reduce the number of bubbles in the finish, especially on large-pored woods.)
- If the surface will receive a lot of wear, apply several coats, waiting 2 or 3 hours between each (or follow manufacturer's instructions).
- If you want to reduce scratching to the surface, sand it lightly with fine sandpaper and apply a coat of polyurethane varnish. It is more scratch resistant than epoxy resin.

Photo 12-5: Spread the epoxy using a plastic spreader. You don't need to create a perfectly smooth surface. The epoxy is self leveling.

CHAPTER 13

Water-Based
Finishes

The technology for making water-based finishes has existed for more than half a century. It's the same technology that's used in making latex paint and white and yellow glues. Until recently, there was no demand for water-based finishes because they are more expensive than other finishes to produce, and they are more difficult to use. Now, however, with society's growing concern over air pollution, demand has been created. Local and state governments have changed the marketplace by passing increasingly stringent laws limiting the amount of solvent (volatile organic compounds, or VOCs) a container of finish or paint can contain or a user can exhaust into the atmosphere.

If the trend continues, you may someday find localities where high-solvent-content finishes such as nitrocellulose lacquer are no longer used or available. But this hasn't happened yet (and it may never happen), so even though you might hear rumors that solvent-based finishes are going to disappear, this isn't likely to happen anytime soon. We still need to deal with water-based finish as one among several finish choices, not the only choice.

In Brief

- **What Is Water-Based Finish?**
- **Pros & Cons**
- **Characteristics of Water Base**
- **Common Problems Applying Water Base**
- **Brushing and Spraying Water-Based Finishes**
- **Glycol Ether**
- **Is Water Base for You?**

Photo 13-1: Water base stands out among all finishes for its lack of color. The contrast is easy to see in these examples. On the left is water base and nitrocellulose lacquer on walnut. On the right is water base and varnish on maple.

What Is Water-Based Finish?

What is commonly called water-based finish, or *water base,* or *waterborne,* is really a solvent-based finish made with acrylic and polyurethane resins that are dispersed in water—*borne* in water, if you will. Calling the finish water base distinguishes it from solvent-based finishes—shellac, lacquer, and varnish—which don't use water. A true water-based finish would be impractical for use on household objects, because it would redissolve in water.

To make water-based finishes, the acrylic and polyurethane resins are manufactured in tiny droplets, also known as *latexes,* and then dispersed in water. A solvent that evaporates slower than water, usually glycol ether, is added. (See "Glycol Ether" on p. 179.) After the water evaporates, the tiny droplets of

finish come together (coalesce), and the solvent makes them sticky. As the solvent evaporates, the droplets stick together and harden, creating a continuous film. (See "Coalescing Finishes" on p. 114.) Once cured, water has no damaging effect on water-based finishes, but most solvents do. They dissolve the bond between the droplets, making the finish sticky and gummy—similar to the way it was just before the glycol ether solvent evaporated during initial curing.

Some water-based finishes are provided with a separate "crosslinker" or "hardener" that you can add to the finish to make it more protective and durable. These "two-part" finishes are usually available only through distributors to the floor-finishing and professional woodworking trades or through mail order. Other water-based finishes have the second, or crosslinking, technology built in. Unfortunately, there is no standard industry labeling to identify either of these variations. They are usually labeled the same as one-part finishes. (See Chapter 12: "Two-Part Finishes.")

Causing even more confusion, water-based finishes are sometimes labeled "lacquer," "varnish," or "polyurethane," with no indication in the names that they are different from traditional, solvent-based lacquer, varnish, or polyurethane finishes. Manufacturers do this to make water base seem familiar so you will buy it. Naturally, this improper labeling leads to a good deal of frustration among the unsuspecting. All water-based finishes, no matter how they are labeled or which resins are included, have far more in common with each other than they have with tra-

ditional lacquer, varnish, or polyurethane. (See "What's in a Name?" on p. 106.) Look for the thinning or cleanup liquid listed on the can. If it's water, then the finish is water base. (See "Brushing and Spraying Water-Based Finishes" on p. 176.)

Characteristics of Water Base

As mentioned, the protective and durability qualities of water-based finishes can vary depending on whether or not a crosslinker or hardener is added or built in. Most of the water-based finishes you buy in paint stores and home centers do not involve an additive. So these finishes are considerably less water, water-vapor, scratch, solvent, heat, acid, and alkali resistant than oil-based varnish. On the other hand, they are usually as resistant, or slightly more resistant, than nitrocellulose lacquer. (See "Comparing Finishes" on p. 187.)

All water-based finishes, whether crosslinking or not, have three characteristics in common:

- They contain less solvent than most other finishes.
- The cured finish is virtually colorless.
- They contain water, and they clean up with water.

Solvent Content

Water-based finishes contain much less solvent than solvent-based finishes, though the solvent content can still be as much as 20 percent of the total volume. Thus there is less solvent to evaporate into the atmosphere and cause pollution, to fuel a fire, and to breathe. Though reducing air pollution is the rationale for the existence of water-based finishes and the motivation for industry and large cabinet- and

Pros & Cons

PROS

- Minimal solvent fumes
- Not a fire hazard
- Easy brush cleanup
- Nonyellowing
- Very scuff-resistant

CONS

- Produces bland, washed-out appearance on dark and dark-stained woods
- Very weather sensitive during application
- Raises the grain of the wood
- Only moderate heat, solvent, acid, alkali, water, and water-vapor resistance (about the same as nitrocellulose lacquer)
- All decoration steps are more difficult than with solvent-based finishes

MYTH

Water-based finishes are nearly pollution free.

FACT

It is usually the reduced solvent content that is being referred to in such a claim. In fact, water-based finishes contain up to 20 percent solvent, so they still pollute the air. Moreover, they pollute water and landfills much more than solvent-based finishes. It's common to wash loaded brushes in sinks and throw excess finish down the drain when the finish is water base, and water-based finishes are often packaged in plastic containers that don't biodegrade. Neither do Scotch-Brite or the other synthetic pads used with water base. So water-based finishes are far from being pollution free.

FACT

Water-based finishes are safer to use than most other finishes, but they are not totally safe. If you've ever painted with latex paint (essentially water-based finish with pigment added) in a closed room, you've surely experienced a little dizziness caused by the paint fumes. You should protect yourself with good airflow and possibly a respirator mask when using water base just as you do when using other finishes.

NOTE
▼
Most water-based finishes appear white in the can. The color is the usual consequence of emulsifying solvent-based materials in water. Other examples are cosmetics and many furniture polishes. The whiteness disappears as the finish cures, as long as it is not too thick.

furniture-making shops to use these finishes, reduced fire and health hazards are probably of more immediate benefit to you if you are an amateur or small-shop owner. Water-based finishes don't contain enough solvent to burn in their liquid state, and the solvent they do contain has considerably less odor and is less noxious to breathe than mineral spirits or lacquer thinner.

Professional finishers who have switched from lacquer to water base always cite reduced odor and irritation as the principal benefits. Floor finishers, who can't always ventilate their work locations, also appreciate this quality. You will often see water base marketed as a floor finish for this reason.

Color in Water Base

You may not realize the amount of color other finishes add to wood until you see a piece of wood finished with water base (Photo 13-1 on p. 172). Water base is colorless, or very nearly so. On some surfaces, such as light-colored and pickled (white-stained) woods, a colorless finish can be quite attractive and even desirable. (See "Pickling" on p. 200.) But the lack of color causes darker woods such as walnut, cherry, and mahogany to look somewhat washed out and lifeless. There are three ways to overcome this problem:

- Stain the wood before applying the finish.
- Use another finish to seal the wood under the water base.
- Add a yellow-orange dye to the finish to imitate the color of other finishes. Some manufacturers already do this, but this means that you need to be especially careful about the water-based finish you are using. You probably won't want a tinted finish on pickled wood.

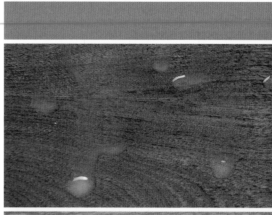

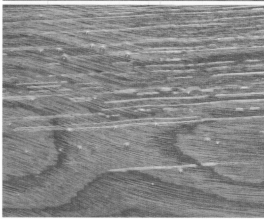

Common Problems Applying Water Base

Most problems applying water-based finish can be avoided by keeping coats thin and by not applying the finish in cold, hot, or humid weather. (For problems specific to brushing and spraying, see "Common Brushing Problems" on p. 26 and "Common Spraying Problems" on p. 32.)

PROBLEM	CAUSE	SOLUTION
Runs and sags appear opaque with an off-white color.	Water-based finishes often lose transparency in thick layers.	When the run or sag has thoroughly cured, scrape or sand it off smooth. Then apply another coat.
The finish bubbles or foams, and the bubbles cure in the finish.	You are stirring up bubbles with your brush.	Use a lighter touch; apply the finish as thinly as possible. If bubbling persists, thin the finish with 10 to 20 percent distilled water or a manufacturer's solvent (usually propylene glycol).
	The finish is not designed for brushing.	Change to another brand that is designed for brushing.
The finish takes too long to cure, allowing dust to settle.	The weather is too humid.	Wait until a drier day, or arrange an airflow over the work. This could introduce dust into the finish, however.
The cured finish peels away from the wood in sheets.	A substance on the wood—most likely an oil-based stain, paste wood filler, or glaze that wasn't fully cured—prevented the finish from bonding well.	Strip the finish, sand the wood, and avoid using any oil-containing stains or other products unless you give them ample time to cure. Or seal them in with a solvent-based washcoat—for example, dewaxed shellac.
The finish crawls up into ridges right after you apply it.	You are applying the finish too thick.	Allow time for the finish to cure. It usually levels out. If it doesn't, sand it level and apply another, thinner coat.
	There is silicone or other oil in the wood.	Remove the finish by washing it off with wet rags if you are quick enough, or with lacquer thinner or paint stripper. Wash the wood thoroughly with lacquer thinner and allow the wood to dry. Apply a washcoat of dewaxed shellac. Then proceed with coats of water base. For more on this problem, see "Fish Eye and Silicone" on p. 146.

Brushing and Spraying Water-Based Finishes

Water-based finishes are more difficult than varnish to brush, and more difficult than either shellac or lacquer to spray. Here are the steps for applying water base.

1 Arrange your work so you can see what's happening in reflected light.

2 Decide whether you want to dewhisker the wood before applying the finish. (See "Dewhiskering" on p. 14.) Dewhiskering will eliminate most of the raised grain, so the first coat of finish won't raise the grain much again.

If you choose not to dewhisker, you can "bury" the raised grain simply by sanding the first coat smooth after it has hardened. This is the most widely used practice.

3 If there is any evidence that the water base is beginning to skin over in the can, strain the finish through a paint strainer or nylon hose. It's a good idea to do this even when you don't see any evidence of skinning

over. There are often small clumps of cured finish that will show up in the cured film. Be sure to stir the finish if it includes a flatting agent.

4 If you're brushing, pour enough finish for the job into a wide-mouth plastic or glass container, so you won't contaminate your finish if you pick up dirt on your brush.

5 You can thin the finish with 10 to 20 percent water to make it spray or brush easier, but it is best to avoid doing this.

6 Brush (using a foam brush, paint pad, or good-quality synthetic-bristle brush) or spray a thin coat of water-based finish on the wood. (See "Using Brushes" on p. 25 and "Using Spray Guns" on p. 38.) It's very important to keep the coats thin, especially if you are spraying. At first the finish may have severe orange peel. But if the coat is thin, it will flatten as it dries. Keeping coats thin also reduces the tendency to run and sag on vertical surfaces.

7 Allow the finish to cure. An hour or two is usually enough, depending on temperature and humidity. Then sand the finish smooth with 220-grit or finer sandpaper. Even if you have dewhiskered the wood, there will still be some grain raising. As with any finish, you'll find that the raised grain is easiest to remove if the first coat is thin, if you allow it to harden well, and if you use stearated (dry-lubricated) sandpaper.

8 Remove the dust with a brush, a vacuum, compressed air, or a water-

> **MYTH**
>
> Sanding the wood to a very fine grit (usually 320-grit or finer) is the way to avoid raised grain.
>
> **FACT**
>
> Grain is raised by water swelling the wood fibers, no matter how finely they have been sanded. More importantly, sanding through all the grits up to 320 is a lot more work than either dewhiskering or burying the raised grain and then sanding it level.

> **MYTH**
>
> Sanding between coats of water base with a stearated (dry-lubricated) sandpaper will result in fish eye. (See "Fish Eye and Silicone" on p. 146.)
>
> **FACT**
>
> Not so. The lubricant in stearated sandpaper has no effect on the next coat. Nevertheless, you should always remove the dust after sanding between coats.

dampened cloth. Don't use a tack cloth: The oily residue will interfere with the next coat.

9 Apply a second thin coat of finish. If you're brushing, work fast. Water base gums up rapidly, especially if the weather is warm and dry. Avoid overworking the finish or you will create foam. If this happens, dry off the brush with a clean cloth, remove the foam with the tip of the brush, and smooth out the finish.

10 Apply as many additional coats of finish as you want, sanding between coats only if you want to remove dust nibs or flaws. Water base has a high solids content, so it builds quickly. Two or three coats are usually adequate, unless you intend to use the finish to fill the pores. (See "Filling Pores with the Finish" on p. 94.)

11 When you're satisfied with the thickness of the film, you can leave it as is, or you can finish it off with sandpaper, synthetic abrasive pads, or rubbing compounds. (See Chapter 16: "Finishing the Finish.")

Water Content

Water is the ingredient that fundamentally separates water base from all the other finishes. Though using a water-containing product can seem attractive because it is easier to clean from brushes, it is the water that is responsible for almost all the application problems. (See "Common Problems Applying Water Base" on p. 175.) These problems include the following:

- grain raising
- drying time (slower than lacquer; faster than varnish)
- foaming
- poor leveling
- increased difficulty applying decoration (stains, glazes, paste wood fillers, and toners)
- weather sensitivity
- increased runs and sags
- rust

Here are ways of dealing with each of these problems.

Grain Raising. Grain raising is the most difficult problem. If a stain or finish contains water, it raises the grain of the wood. Some water-based products raise the grain less than others, but they all do, so you have to deal with it. Here are four methods:

- Dewhisker the wood before applying the water-based stain or finish. (See "Dewhiskering" on p. 14.) This method significantly increases the amount of work involved in preparing the surface.
- Reduce the depth the stain or finish penetrates. Do this by spraying the stain or first coat of finish in light mist coats so it flashes dry quickly, or by using a thicker stain or finish. (See "Thickness" on p. 55.) You risk less color definition and a weaker bond to the wood with this method.

- "Bury" the raised grain under the first coat of finish, then sand it smooth. For example, if the stain raises the grain, just leave it and apply the sealer coat. Then sand the sealer smooth. Many professional finishers use this method.
- Use a hybrid system. Apply an oil- or lacquer-based stain and a solvent-based sealer. Then apply coats of water base on top. Be aware that the solvent-based stain and sealer may add some yellow coloring. This method is widely used in industry.

Drying Time. Water-based finishes dry more slowly than lacquer and more quickly than varnish. So compared to lacquer, water-based finishes collect more dust and have a much greater tendency to run and sag on vertical surfaces. Compared to varnish, water-based finishes are more difficult to brush onto large surfaces.

The only way to speed the drying is with heat or air movement. Factories pass finished objects through ovens to speed the curing. You can create air movement easily using a fan, but it's difficult to do so without also stirring up dust. You can slow the drying by adding a retarder. Some manufacturers supply

NOTE

Some water-based finishes bond well over some oil-based stains before the stain has cured, but there is no way of knowing for sure without trying it. The variables are the particular resins and solvents used in the finish and how much oil is in the stain. To test the bonding, apply the stain and finish to scrap wood. After drying for a few days, score the finish with a razor in a crosshatch pattern. Make the cuts about $1/16$ inch apart and about 1 inch long. Then press some masking tape over the cuts and pull it up quickly. If the finish has bonded well, the scored lines will remain clean and little or no finish will come off on the tape.

a retarder, or *flow additive,* which is usually propylene glycol. But it is rarely available at home centers or paint stores. (Antifreeze is ethylene glycol, and it will work, but it always contains a dye colorant, usually an inappropriate color for wood, such as blue or green.)

Foaming. Foaming isn't as great a problem as it once was. You might have heard that water-based finishes are better now than they were when they first came out. One of the improvements is reduced foaming. But you can still cause foaming if you overwork the finish with a brush. If you can't keep the finish from foaming, switch to another brand.

Poor Leveling. Another improvement manufacturers have made to water-based finishes is better leveling. But the leveling doesn't occur right away. The finish tends to orange-peel badly when you spray it and show brush marks badly when you brush it, but it usually levels out well as it cures (Photos 13-2).

Difficulty Applying Decoration. All decorative steps are more difficult using water base than they are using solvent-based finishes. This includes staining, glazing, paste wood filling, and toning. Water-based stains, glazes, and paste wood fillers dry too fast for relaxed application on large surfaces. You can slow the drying by adding a retarder (propylene glycol), but this also thins the product, and it adds solvent, the ingredient that you were probably trying to avoid when you chose this finish in the first place. (See "Using Water-Based Paste Wood Filler" on p. 102.) You can also use a hybrid system—apply solvent-based products and seal or washcoat between steps and over all steps before applying the water base. Of course, this also involves the use of solvents.

Toning is a problem because you can't thin a water-based finish with much water or it will bead up on the surface, like water on wax. So the toner will probably be thick and add a lot of

Photos 13-2: Water base initially orange peels badly when you spray it (left). You may be tempted to spray more finish on top, thinking you have not applied enough. Don't do it. Water base levels out as it cures (right).

build, which you may not want. (See "Toning" on p. 199.) You can spray a stain instead, but you won't have nearly as much control of the color or color intensity as you have when you make your own toner.

Weather Sensitivity. Water-based finishes are very weather sensitive, and solvents for dealing with the weather variations aren't widely available. Even if they were, using them would defeat the primary benefit of the finish—reduced solvent content.

Factories and large shops control the temperature and humidity of their buildings to avoid problems. If you are a small-shop professional or amateur, you probably can't do this. Manufacturers of water-based finishes sold to small shops and amateurs try to hit a happy medium with regard to the finish's ability to perform well in different weather conditions. If you live in a very dry or wet area of the country, or if you are trying to apply the finish in cold or hot temperatures, you may experience flow-out or foaming problems. Try to get better control of the temperature and humidity in your shop, wait for a better day, or switch to a different brand and see if it works better in your conditions.

Increased Runs and Sags. The only ways to keep water-based finish from running and sagging are to apply thinner coats or to thicken the finish. (Note that thick latex wall paint is very run-resistant.) The problem with thickening the finish is that it then doesn't level as well. So it's even more important that you watch the finish in a reflected light during application and brush out any developing runs or sags.

(The ease with which water-based finishes run and sag is one of the most distinguishing differences between these

Glycol Ether

You are surely not as familiar with glycol ether solvents as you are with mineral spirits, alcohol, and lacquer thinner. Glycol ether solvents are seldom available in paint stores, and they are not often mentioned in books and magazine articles about finishing.

Glycol ether is the "family name" for a number of solvents, much like the term *petroleum distillate*. Glycol ether solvents are made by reacting alcohols with ethylene oxide or propylene oxide. Examples of glycol ethers are ethylene glycol monobutyl ether (butyl Cellosolve) and propylene glycol monomethyl ether. (Now you understand why they are often referred to by their family name.) The individual solvents differ in strength and evaporation rate.

Glycol ether solvents are special because they are compatible with water and a number of solvents, and they evaporate very slowly, soften most resins, and dissolve lacquer. This makes them useful for water-based finishes, where the solvent has to evaporate more slowly than the water and then make the resins sticky, and for use in lacquer retarders. Glycol ethers also dissolve NGR dyes, which can then be thinned with a number of liquids, including alcohol, water, acetone, and lacquer thinner.

There are two large classes of glycol ethers—ethylene and propylene. The ethylene group has been dominant for the last half century. But this group is more toxic than the propylene group. So propylene glycol ethers are now seeing wider use. If you do have access to glycol ethers through a finish manufacturer or a chemical-supply house, you should use the propylene group, especially if you don't have good exhaust in your shop.

finishes and lacquer. For an explanation, see "Lacquer Thinner" on p. 140.)

Rust. You have to avoid all contact with metal when using water-based finishes, or the resulting rust may cause dark marks in your finish that you won't be able to remove short of stripping and starting over. Follow these practices:

- Avoid using steel wool at any point in the finishing process until all the coats have been applied.

- Avoid spray guns with ferrous-metal parts. (Aluminum cups are all right.)
- Seal any metal parts that you are finishing with a solvent-based finish before applying water base.
- Strain the finish you take from any can that has begun to rust around the lip. The rust is caused by the can's coating having been scratched off by removing and reattaching the lid.

Is Water Base for You?

Compared with other finishes, water base is an immature finish. It is going through a lot of changes, with much research being devoted to improvements, especially to overcoming the problems caused by water. With rare exceptions, it's the manufacturers of the raw materials who are making the improvements, not the manufacturers of the finishes. So it's important to note that all finish manufacturers have access to all improvements and choose whether or not to incorporate them in their products based on cost and perceived markets. The result is that there are significant differences among brands, but there aren't any secrets, as is so often claimed. More than with any other finish, you'll find that some brands of water base work better for you than others.

As of this writing, only a small percentage of factories, shops, and amateurs are using water-based finishes, though you might be led to believe otherwise if you read the woodworking press. Cabinet and furniture factories use water base primarily to comply with local air-pollution laws. Small-shop professionals use water base primarily to avoid the noxious lacquer-thinner fumes. Homeowners use water base for the low odor and easy brush cleanup. Some amateur woodworkers with spray guns use water base for the same reason small shops do. Woodworkers without spray guns seem to continue to prefer the ease of use and rich coloring offered by oil/varnish blends, wiping varnish, and gel varnish, and the durability and rich coloring offered by wiping varnish, gel varnish, and polyurethane varnish. I've seen very little movement to water base by this group.

CHAPTER 14

Choosing a Finish

One of the most common questions you hear in any discussion about finishing is, "What finish do you use?" The question presumes there is a "best" finish—one that should be used in all situations. Unfortunately, there is no *best* finish. There are only more or less appropriate finishes for given situations, depending on the qualities you're looking for. (See "Comparing Finishes" on p. 187.) When you're choosing a finish for any given project, you should take each of these qualities into account:

- appearance
- protection
- durability
- ease of application
- safety
- reversibility
- ease of rubbing

Appearance

You have three choices when picking a finish for its appearance: potential film build, clarity, and color. (A fourth choice, sheen, is not dependent upon the finish you choose, but upon whether or not flatting agent—gloss-reducing solid particles—has been added. See "Controlling Sheen with Flatting Agent" on p. 110.)

Film Build

The film build, or thickness of a finish on wood, greatly affects the wood's appearance. Wax and finishes that contain straight oil (linseed oil, tung oil, and oil/varnish blend) don't cure hard, so they have to be kept very thin on the wood. They produce a "natural" or "close-to-the-wood" look, in which the pores of the wood are left looking open and are sharply defined (even though they are sealed). Film finishes (shellac, lacquer, varnish, two-part, and water base) can be built up on the wood. But they can also be applied thin to look like oil or wax finishes. Imported Scandinavian teak furniture, for instance, is finished with very thin coats of conversion varnish, not oil, as is commonly believed.

Consequently, you can use any finish if you want a thin, close-to-the-wood look, but if you want a build, you must use a film finish (Photos 14-1, 14-2, and 14-3). A built-up film finish can look cheap if it rounds over into the pores of open-pored woods such as oak and mahogany. Or it can look very refined, giving the wood the appearance of great depth, if the pores are filled level to the surface and the finish is rubbed and polished to an even sheen. (See Chapter 7: "Filling the Pores.")

Clarity

The clarity of a particular finish may be important to your choice, though it's often hard to see a difference unless you compare two finished panels next to one another. Dewaxed shellac, lacquer, and alkyd varnish are the most transparent finishes, giving the wood the appearance of greatest depth. Wax-containing shellac, oil-based polyurethane, water base, and most two-part finishes are the least transparent finishes. In extreme situations, these finishes can appear somewhat cloudy.

Color

All finishes except wax and water base impart some degree of warmth to the color of wood. Wax adds no color, just sheen. Water base cools the color. Lacquer and most two-part finishes add some degree of yellowing. Any finish containing oil, including varnish, adds some color and yellows (actually "oranges") noticeably with age. Blond and clear shellac add about the same degree of color as lacquer does. But orange shellac adds an orange color (Photo 14-4 on p. 185). Yellowing is not generally a problem on dark or dark-stained woods. In fact, it's usually a plus: It makes the wood appear warmer. But yellowing can be objectionable on very light woods and over a white stain used to pickle wood. (See "Pickling" on p. 200.)

Protection

A finish protects the wood and glue joints by slowing the penetration of water and the exchange of water vapor. Resistance to water penetration is important when choosing a finish for tabletops. Resistance to water-vapor exchange is one of the most important functions a finish performs on any wood object. Excessive water-vapor exchange between the wood and the atmosphere causes joint failure and veneer separation. (See Chapter 1: "Why Finish Wood, Anyway?")

Resistance to water and water vapor depends as much on the thickness of the finish as it does on the type of finish. The two primary varnishes—alkyd and polyurethane—are nearly impermeable to water and water vapor when built up to a thick film, but they lose most of their resistance when applied thin in the form of a wiping varnish. Wax, which offers virtually no resistance to water and water-vapor penetration when used as a rubbed-out finish, is one of the best protective coatings when brushed thick on the ends of recently milled boards. It follows that all finishes containing straight oil offer very little protection against water and water vapor because they also are very thin.

Among the film finishes, the best water and water-vapor protection is provided by reactive finishes. Shellac also provides good water-vapor resistance, but it is the least water-resistant finish. The least water vapor–resistant finishes are lacquer and water base.

Durability

Finish durability divides almost exactly between crosslinking finishes and non-crosslinking finishes. (See Chapter 8: "Introduction to Film Finishes.") Crosslinking finishes (varnish and two-part finish) are far more durable than non-crosslinking finishes (shellac and lacquer). Oil and oil/varnish blends, though crosslinking, cure too soft. Water base crosslinks within the droplets, but the evaporative bonds between the droplets are weak. There are two different concerns when considering finish durability:

- scratch and wear resistance
- solvent, acid, alkali, and heat resistance

Photos 14-1, 14-2, 14-3: You can make wood look very different by how you build the finish. The mahogany and walnut tabletop (top) has many coats of wiping varnish sanded back; it leaves the pores partially filled and the wood with a natural look. The mahogany-veneered drawer (center) has its pores filled and the wood French polished to a high gloss; it produces a refined look and the appearance of depth in the wood. The oak tabletop (bottom) has a thickly applied finish that is rounded over in the pores; it makes the wood look cheap.

Scratch and Wear Resistance

This quality is the most touted, and it has become one of the most sought-after qualities in a finish. The most wear-resistant finishes are two-part finishes, oil-based polyurethane, and water-based polyurethane. (Though water-based polyurethane doesn't cure by crosslinking, the droplets are composed entirely of crosslinked resins.) The least wear-resistant are wax and oil-containing finishes. Alkyd varnish and water-based acrylic are considerably more wear-resistant than shellac or lacquer. Wear resistance can be an important consideration on floors and tabletops.

Solvent, Acid, Alkali, and Heat Resistance

These four properties tend to go together. A finish easily damaged by solvents is also easily damaged by acids, alkalis, and heat. Wax, shellac, lacquer, and water base are all susceptible to solvent, acid, alkali, and heat damage. Varnish and two-part finishes are very resistant to solvents, acids, alkalis, and heat. Oil-containing finishes are in between. Oil, though it crosslinks when it cures, breaks down more easily than varnish and two-part finishes. Resistance to solvents, acids, alkalis, and heat can be an important factor when choosing a finish for countertops and tabletops.

Ease of Application

The ease with which you can apply a finish depends on two factors:
- availability of spray equipment
- speed at which the finish dries

Spray Equipment

With spray equipment, all finishes are easier to apply. (Even wax is supplied by some companies in sprayable consistency.) Without spray equipment, oil, oil/varnish blend, wiping varnish, and gel varnish are the easiest to apply.

The ease with which fast-drying shellac, lacquer, water base, and two-part finishes can be applied with spray equipment is so significant that most professional finishers never even consider using any other finish. The various characteristics of these four finishes provide almost every individual quality a finisher might want.

Speed of Curing

Unless you wipe off all the excess finish, finishes that cure slowly cause problems no matter how you apply them, because dust has time to settle and become embedded in the finish. On the other hand, finishes that cure rapidly are difficult to apply with a brush, because one brushstroke may already be tacky by the time your next brushstroke overlaps it. As a result, you drag the finish.

The comparative ease with which oil, oil/varnish blend, wiping varnish, and gel varnish can be applied is so significant for those without spray equipment that they are often reluctant to try other finishes.

Safety

There are three issues of safety:
- safety to you, the finisher, during application
- safety to the environment during application
- safety to the ultimate consumer if food or someone's mouth will come in contact with the finish

Safety to You

All finishes except water base are combustible or flammable, so don't use them near flames or a source of possible sparks.

With the exception of straight oils, all finishes, including water base, contain

Photo 14-4: Most finishes impart color to wood, some more color than others. From the left are wax, water base, nitrocellulose lacquer, polyurethane varnish, and orange shellac, all on walnut.

solvents that can be damaging to your health, and many finishes have odors that you may find unpleasant. No matter which finish you use, you should ensure good cross-ventilation in your work area so you always breathe relatively clean air. Organic-vapor respirator masks can be an aid when you're forced to work in an enclosed area, but respirator masks lose their effectiveness over time, thereby leading to a false sense of security. If you can smell the solvent fumes with your respirator mask on, either you have a leak or the cartridges are worn out and should be replaced. The only truly reliable respirator masks are those that provide an outside source of air. (Nuisance particle masks provide no protection against solvent fumes.)

The finishes that cause the least problems for your health are boiled linseed oil, tung oil, water base, and shellac. Linseed oil and tung oil contain no solvents. Water base contains very little solvent. And denatured alcohol, the solvent for shellac, is relatively safe unless you drink it or breathe it in excessive amounts.

Safety to the Environment

All solvents evaporate into the atmosphere. Some have been shown to be factors in causing air pollution. As a result, many states and localities have passed laws aimed at limiting the amount of solvent or thinner that can be contained in a finish. These laws are aimed at large users, rarely at amateurs or small-scale professionals, and are the primary impetus for the substitution of water-based finishes for solvent-based finishes in factories and large shops. Reducing solvent exhaust is also responsible for the introduction of HVLP spray technology.

Of the common solvents used in finishes, petroleum distillates and lacquer thinner—used in most varnishes and in lacquer, respectively—cause the greatest problems. Alcohol (shellac's solvent) and glycol ether (used in water base) also cause pollution. But shellac seems to be off the enforcers' radar screen, and water

Disposing of Solvent Waste

Responsible solvent-waste disposal for amateurs and small professional shops can be a real problem.

Sealing the solvents in an old paint can and throwing it in the trash to be hauled to the dump is not a good idea and is illegal in most places. Together with everyone else's dirty solvents, they will seep into the ground and poison your town's groundwater supply. Pouring the solvents down the drain or onto some unwanted weeds will do the same and is also usually illegal.

Originators of solvent waste fall into two categories: large generators and small generators. Large generators include large shops or factories that do a lot of finishing, and furniture stripping shops. Small generators include amateurs and most small professional shops.

Large generators have two choices for getting rid of solvent waste: recycle the solvents or hire a solvent-waste disposal company to haul it off.

To recycle solvents, you use a *recycler*, which operates like a still. The waste is boiled within a closed container, and the gases are condensed back into pure solvent. The solid remainder can often then be thrown in the trash. Recyclers are available in sizes as small as two gallons, but even these are quite expensive. If you do a lot of spraying or stripping, however, a recycler will quickly pay for itself in what you will save, not having your waste hauled off.

Without a recycler, you will be required to hire someone with a special license to haul your solvents to a toxic-waste site. This could also be quite expensive, and you may be responsible for any damage your solvents cause...forever!

Small generators don't have many choices either. Here are some suggestions:

- Recycle your solvents. Keep your mineral spirits, lacquer thinner, or whatever, in separate cans. Let the solid material, if there is any, settle to the bottom. Pour off the solvent, and use it again for cleaning.
- Try to get a local user of solvents, such as a large furniture or auto-body refinish shop, to take your solvent waste and put it with theirs to be hauled off—for a price, of course. If you have some connections, you may be able to make a deal.
- Store the dirty solvents until your town or county has a periodic hazardous-waste collection day.
- Finally, if all else fails, you have two choices. You can let all the solvent evaporate from a can you leave open in your shop (unless pets or children have access), or you can pour the solvent out on concrete on a sunny day or spray it into the air (unless these are clearly illegal in your area). If this solution bothers you, you may console yourself by remembering that doing this is no different in terms of causing pollution than letting the solvent evaporate from a finish you have just applied.

base contains less than 20 percent solvent. (See "Disposing of Solvent Waste" at left.)

Safety to the Consumer

The safety of finishes for food or mouth contact is a non-issue, kept alive by certain woodworking magazines and implied by some manufacturers who label their wiping varnishes "Salad-Bowl Finish." In fact, all clear finishes are safe for contact with food or with someone's mouth once the finish is fully cured. The rule of thumb is 30 days, but it can be less if the finish cures in warm conditions. (See "The Food-Safe Myth" on p. 76.)

Reversibility

Reversibility refers to the ease of repair and ease of removal of a finish. Reversibility is the opposite of solvent and heat resistance. The finishes that are most easily repaired or removed—shellac and lacquer—are also the least solvent- and heat-resistant. (See Chapter 19: "Repairing Finishes.") Thus, your choice of using a reversible finish for its ease of repairing and removing must be weighed against your need for a solvent- and heat-resistant finish.

Oil finishes are also considered easy to repair and remove, but this isn't because of their reversibility. They are easy to repair because they are so thin. Simply wiping more oil over the finish colors in raw areas and scratches, and because there's no film thickness, the damage disappears to the eye. The thinness of oil finishes also makes them easy to remove.

Rubbing Qualities

There are two qualities in finishes that make them easier to rub to an even sheen: the hardness of the cured finish, and the ability of finish coats to dissolve together to form a single layer. Both of these properties are a function of the way the finish cures.

Hardness

Some finishes are hard, others are tough. You need to distinguish between the two. To understand hardness, think of slate, which is brittle and easily scratched. Shellac and lacquer dry hard. For toughness, think of an automobile tire, which is difficult to scratch. Varnish, two-part finishes, and water-based fin-ishes cure tough. Because rubbing fin-ishes means scratching them with abra-sives to get the sheen you want, hard finishes rub out well; tough finishes are difficult to rub to an even sheen.

Of course, all finishes can be rubbed with steel wool or abrasive compounds. Some finishes are just easier than others to rub to an even sheen.

Coats Dissolve Together

When you rub a finish, you cut some of it away. If you cut enough away to pen-etrate through the topmost coat in

Comparing Finishes

	Wax	Oil-Containing Finishes	Shellac	Lacquer	Varnish	Two-Part Finishes	Water Base
APPEARANCE							
Film build	0 to 1	0 to 1	1 to 5	1 to 5	1 to 5	1 to 5	1 to 5
Clarity	4	4	3 to 5	5	4 to 5	4	3 to 4
Non-yellowing	5	1 to 2	1 to 4	3 to 4	1 to 2	4	5
PROTECTION							
Water resistance	0 to 1	0 to 2	2	3	4 to 5	5	3
Water-vapor resistance	0 to 1	0 to 1	5	3	4 to 5	5	3
DURABILITY							
Wear resistance	0	0	3	3	4 to 5	5	4
Solvent and chemical resistance	0	3	1	2	4 to 5	5	2
Heat resistance	0	3	1	2	4 to 5	5	2
APPLICATION EASE							
Brush or cloth	3	5	3	1 to 3	5	1	3
Spray	3	5	4	5	4	4	4
Dust problems	5	5	4	4	0	4	3
SAFETY							
Health	5	3 to 4	4	2	3	0	4
Environment	4 to 5	1-5	4	0	1	0	4
Safety for food contact	*	*	*	*	*	*	*
REVERSIBILITY							
Repairing	5	5	4	4	1 to 2	0	3
Stripping	4	3	5	5	2 to 3	0	4
RUBBING QUALITIES	N/A	N/A	4	5	3	3	3

Legend: 0 = very poor; 5 = best   *All finishes are safe for food contact once they have fully cured.*

Guide to Choosing a Finish

Though you can spray, brush, or wipe any finish, faster-drying finishes lend themselves better to spraying, and slower drying finishes are easier to brush or wipe. You can make choosing a finish easier by first deciding whether or not you are going to use a spray gun. Doing this reduces the number of finishes you have to choose between.

TOOL YOU INTEND TO USE	BROAD FINISH CHOICES	CURING CATEGORY	SPECIFIC FINISH CHOICES	DESCRIPTION OF FINISH
Spray Gun	Shellac	Evaporative	Clear	Adds a slight yellow tint.
			Amber (orange)	Adds a significant orange coloring.
			With natural wax	Cloudy in the can but not on the wood.
			Dewaxed	Better if you are applying another finish over it.
			Pre-dissolved	More convenient.
			Dissolve your own from flakes	Will be fresher and perform better.
	Lacquer	Evaporative	Nitrocellulose	Almost any lacquer labeled just "lacquer." Adds a slight orange tint to wood.
			Acrylic-modified lacquer	Adds a slight yellow tint to wood.
			CAB-acrylic	Water white. Adds no coloring to wood.
	Two-part finish	Reactive	Pre-catalyzed lacquer	The catalyst is already added.
			Post-catalyzed lacquer	Have to add the catalyst yourself. More protective and durable than pre-catalyzed lacquer.
			Conversion varnish	Have to add the catalyst yourself. More protective and durable than post-catalyzed lacquer.
			Two-part Polyurethane	More durable and easier to work with than conversion varnish.
			Polyester	Very durable, but very difficult to use.
			Powder	Requires expensive special equipment.
			UV-cured	Requires expensive special equipment.
			(Epoxy resin)	A pour-on finish. Can build very thick.
	Water base	Coalescing	Acrylic	Almost any can of water-based finish not labeled "polyurethane." Adds no coloring to wood but does darken it a little.
			Acrylic/ polyurethane	More durable than acrylic. Adds a tiny bit of yellowing to the wood.

TOOL YOU INTEND TO USE	BROAD FINISH CHOICES	CURING CATEGORY	SPECIFIC FINISH CHOICES	DESCRIPTION OF FINISH
Brush or Rag	Oil	Penetrating: Doesn't cure hard	Boiled linseed oil	Yellows significantly. Takes overnight to cure when excess is wiped off.
			Tung oil	Slower curing, less yellowing, and more water resistant than linseed oil.
			Oil/varnish blend	More protective and durable than either boiled linseed oil or tung oil.
	Shellac	Evaporative	Clear	Adds a slight yellow tint.
			Amber (orange)	Adds a significant orange coloring.
			With natural wax	Cloudy in the can but not on the wood.
			Dewaxed	Better if you are applying another finish over it. Better for French polishing.
			Pre-dissolved	More convenient.
			Dissolve your own from flakes	Will be fresher and perform better.
	Brushing lacquer	Evaporative	Only one choice	Dries slowly enough to be brushed. Has a strong odor.
	Varnish	Reactive	Alkyd	Almost any can that is labeled just "Varnish."
			Polyurethane	More protective and durable than other varnishes.
			Spar	More flexible for outdoor use.
			Marine	Spar varnish with UV-resistant additives.
			Wiping	Any varnish thinned enough to be easily wiped.
			Gel	Varnish thickened for easy wiping.
	Water Base	Coalescing	Acrylic	Almost any water-based finish not labeled "polyurethane." Adds no coloring to wood but does darken it a little.
			Acrylic/ polyurethane	More durable than acrylic. Adds a tiny bit of yellowing to the wood.

places, you may leave a visible outline of the cut-through. You can't cut through a layer of an evaporative finish such as shellac or lacquer because they dissolve into one another. But you can cut through layers of reactive finishes such as varnish and two-part finishes, and you can cut through layers of water-based finishes, depending on how the finish is formulated and how quickly you apply one coat after another.

How to Choose

So how can you use this information in choosing a finish? Once again, it should be clear that there is no *best* finish. All finishes have certain positive qualities and certain shortcomings. Which finish you choose depends on which qualities you want most in the finish.

In choosing a finish, the first question you should ask yourself is, "Am I happy with the finish I'm using?" Every finish takes some getting used to, so there is no point in changing if the finish you are already using is fulfilling your needs. But you may be wondering if there is a better choice. Here is a four-step approach for choosing a finish.

1 Eliminate wax as a choice. Wax has very few uses as a finish, mostly for decorative objects that won't be handled much. This leaves only six finish types to choose among: oil, shellac, lacquer, varnish, two-part finish, and water base.

2 Decide if you will be using a spray gun. A spray gun makes it possible to apply fast-drying finishes to large surfaces. If you will be using a spray gun, you can eliminate two of the six finishes: oil and varnish. Though these can both be sprayed, you can achieve the look of oil with any finish by spraying just one or two thin

(meaning "thinned") coats, and you can achieve the durability of varnish, including polyurethane, by spraying a two-part finish. Why would you want to deal with the additional dust problems associated with varnish?

If you won't be using a spray gun, you can eliminate two-part finishes. They dry too fast to apply with a brush, and you can get equivalent durability with polyurethane. You can also eliminate regular lacquer because it dries too fast to be brushed easily. But brushing lacquer (using slower evaporating solvents) is available for brushing.

3 Now you have just four or five finishes to choose among. Look at "Comparing Finishes" on p. 187 and choose the finish type that gives you the most qualities you are looking for. You may have one overriding quality you need: maximum durability, no yellowing, minimal solvent odor, reparability, and so on. This will make your choice easier.

4 Now that you have chosen the type of finish you want to use, look at the chapter on that type. In all cases, there are variations. For example, if you decided on oil, you still have a choice among boiled linseed oil, tung oil, and an oil/varnish blend. If you decided on varnish, you still have the choice among alkyd varnish, polyurethane varnish, and marine varnish. If you decided on lacquer, you still have the choice among nitrocellulose lacquer, acrylic-modified nitrocellulose lacquer, and CAB-acrylic lacquer. The differences within each finish type are minimal compared to the differences among types, but they still may be significant enough to be important for your needs. (See "Guide to Choosing a Finish" on p. 188.)

Advanced
Coloring
Techniques

This chapter takes the decoration of wood beyond simple staining and pore filling to the advanced steps of adding color within a finish. Adding color this way isn't all that hard to do. It just comes later to the repertoire of most woodworkers and finishers.

Almost all factory-made furniture and most manufactured cabinets have some color added in the finish. Much of the higher style furniture sold in mid- and high-end furniture stores is finished with fifteen or more steps—many of them color steps. This means that most of the color you see in this furniture is in the finish, not in the wood. If you have ever stripped any of this furniture,

you may have been surprised to find that the boards underneath not only don't match in color, they are an entirely different color, usually almost white.

Adding color within the finish became popular in the furniture industry beginning in the 1920s when lacquer and spray guns replaced shellac and brushes as the finish and application tools of choice. Lacquer is especially user-friendly for adding color within the finish because it dries fast, can be thinned with any amount of thinner, and dissolves into previously applied coats— even through layers of color. Spray guns are almost essential to this type of finishing because they don't disturb the

Factory Finishing

The finishes used in factories on high-end furniture can sometimes include fifteen or more steps. Most of these steps are discussed in this chapter or elsewhere in this book. The finish most often used is lacquer, and factories pass the furniture through ovens between steps to speed the drying. Here is an overview.

UNIFORMING

Mass production rarely allows time to choose boards for color. Instead, boards are put together randomly, and it is left to the finisher to blend the color variations. There are a number of ways of doing this, including bleaching all the natural color out of the wood so the coloring can begin from a uniform base, sizing, equalizing the color, sap staining, and pre-staining. (See Chapter 4: "Staining Wood.")

- *Bleaching* is usually done with two-part bleach followed by an acid-wash neutralizer.
- *Sizing* is the same as washcoating—spraying, wiping, or brushing a highly thinned finish or PVA glue onto the wood.
- *Equalizing* and *sap staining* refer to the same procedure, that of spraying a non-grain-raising (NGR) dye onto lighter areas such as sapwood to blend the overall coloring.
- *Pre-staining* involves staining the entire surface, which has the effect of pulling the colors together somewhat—especially when the staining follows an equalizing step. When done this way, an oil-based stain containing

Factory-applied furniture finishes can include fifteen or more steps, many of which add color. Sometimes the coloring merely changes the appearance of the wood. Other times the coloring totally obscures the wood, as in this case, which includes an added crackle effect on the tabletop and the look of molded plaster (a stylistic substitute for carved wood) on the apron.

pigment or pigment and dye is most often used. Sometimes, the term "pre-staining" refers to equalizing or sap staining.

WASHCOATING AND SEALING

If the pores of open-pored woods such as mahogany, walnut, and pecan are to be filled, a washcoat is applied first.

On tight-grained woods such as maple and cherry and on open-pored woods that aren't being filled the wood is sealed, usually with a sanding sealer for easy sanding. This coat is then sanded to remove nibs, raised grain, and other minor flaws.

FILLING

Paste wood fillers are used to produce a smooth, nonporous surface and accentuate the grain. They are commonly thinned to a watery consistency and sprayed. The thinner is allowed to evaporate so the filler dulls, and then the filler is wiped, either across the grain or in

circles, to push it deeper into the pores and to remove the excess. Large-pored woods are usually filled a second time.

The filling step is followed by a sanding sealer, which is sanded smooth.

ADDITIONAL COLORING STEPS

Following the sanding sealer, additional coloring steps, including glazing, toning, shading, highlighting, striking-out, dry-brushing, pad-staining and distressing, can be added to create various effects. When more than one of these steps is added, a washcoat is often applied in between to separate them.

- *Glazing* consists of applying a thickened colorant and then manipulating it in some way. (See "Applying Glaze" on p. 195.)
- *Toning* and *shading* are the adjustment of color using a very thin colored finish. (See "Toning" on p. 199.)

- *Highlighting* and *striking-out* are the process of removing glaze in selected areas to highlight characteristics such as cathedral grain, knots, moldings, and wear. This step can be done while the glaze is still wet or after it has dried, and the tools used are brushes, rags, steel wool, sandpaper, and synthetic abrasive pads.
- *Dry brushing* is done with a very thick colorant applied almost dry using the tip of a brush (Photo 15-6 on p. 196).
- *Pad-staining* is a color-enhancing or blending step done with alcohol-soluble or NGR dye thinned with some water so the dye doesn't "bite" as much. This makes control easier. This step is similar to toning or shading in the effects it can produce, but it's done by hand rather than with a spray gun.
- *Distressing* usually consists of spattering, dry brushing, or cowtailing. (See "Antiquing Wood" on p. 198.)

TOPCOATING AND RUBBING

After all the coloring steps are completed, one or more transparent topcoats are applied.

Then the finish is rubbed, which usually begins with a leveling step using sandpaper and is followed by polishing with various grades of abrasive pads and rubbing compounds to produce the desired sheen. In-line, dual-pad rubbing machines powered by compressed air are almost always used for both the leveling and polishing steps. (See Chapter 16: "Finishing the Finish.")

surface as brushes do. It is difficult not to drag and smear a previous coloring step using a brush.

Of course, you don't have to actually apply one of these complex finishes to do good woodworking or finishing. The great advantage you have over factories is that you can choose your boards for color compatibility and consistency so the wood itself provides the color composition or decorative effect. Factories take the boards randomly as they come off the saw and have to make them match in color during the finishing phase. So, the use of the term "advanced" in the chapter title isn't meant to indicate that you have to master the skills introduced here to be a good finisher, only to say that there are additional techniques available if you should want to learn them. (See "Factory Finishing," at left.)

There are two primary techniques you need to understand to be able to apply a multistep finish: glazing and toning. Most of the coloring you see within finishes is made with one or both of these procedures. Antiquing and pick-

Photo 15-1: A glaze is a stain that is thick enough to stay where you put it, even on a vertical surface. A gel stain, for example, makes a good glaze.

ling are two examples. (See "Antiquing Wood" on p. 198, "Pickling" on p. 200, and "Common Glazing and Toning Problems" on p. 203.)

Glazing

Glazing is the application and then manipulation of a colorant over a sealed surface. The colorant can be common wiping stain, oil, japan colors, or universal tinting colorant (UTC), or it can be a specially made product called *glaze*. A glaze is simply a stain that is thick enough to stay where you put it, even on a vertical surface. Gel stain, for example, makes a good glaze (Photo 15-1 on p. 193).

Note that it's the position of the colorant in the order of finishing steps—over at least one coat of finish, but under a topcoat to protect the colorant from damage—that defines glazing (Figure 15-1). You don't have to be using a glaze to be glazing. On the other hand, applying glaze directly to bare wood is staining, not glazing.

Though it is easy to do, glazing is the most sophisticated decorating technique in finishing because it can be used to create so many effects. Glazing is also very forgiving. You can actually practice on the wood you are finishing, and if you make a mistake or don't like the results you're getting, you can remove the glaze and start over without damaging the finish. The skill involved in glazing

is knowing the look you want to create (having an artistic sense), and maintaining consistency when glazing multiple objects—for example, all the doors on a set of cabinets.

Types of Glaze

There are two types of glaze: oil-based and water-based. Oil-based glaze gives a deeper, richer appearance and is easier to control because of the longer working time. You can remove oil-based glaze for up to an hour or longer by wiping with mineral spirits or naphtha, neither of which will damage any paint or finish.

Water-based glaze is more difficult to work with because it dries rapidly. But it has less solvent smell, so it is less irritating to be around. Once you have applied a water-based glaze, you have only a few minutes to remove it using water before it dries too hard.

Oil-based glaze is best for cabinets and furniture when the finish is lacquer, varnish, or shellac and you are applying the glaze in a shop with good ventilation. Water-based glaze is best for faux-finishing large surfaces such as panels and walls in buildings with little air movement, and for glazing furniture and woodwork when you're topcoating with a water-based finish. To use a water-based finish successfully over an oil-based glaze, you have to let the glaze cure completely, which may take many days depending on the temperature and humidity. Or you have to use a barrier coat of another finish, typically shellac, which introduces a yellow tint that you may not want.

Brands of glaze vary in thickness and drying time. You can slow the drying of an oil-based glaze by adding boiled linseed oil. Add a teaspoon to a quart and test it before adding more. Add a few drops of japan drier to speed

> **CAUTION**
>
> ▼
>
> Because there's no build with oil and wax finishes, you can't glaze successfully between coats of these finishes. You must use one of the film-building finishes. It is possible to glaze between coats of wiping varnish, but only if you leave the excess finish to dry. You can't wipe off the excess.

Sealer coat   Glaze coat   Topcoat

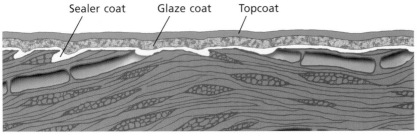

Figure 15-1: Glazing is the application of a colorant between coats of finish—that is, over at least one coat that has sealed the wood, and under one or more additional coats.

Photo 15-2: Glaze can be used to adjust a color without significantly obscuring the wood. In this example, unfinished mahogany (left panel) has been stained with a dye stain (second panel from left), then washcoated, filled with paste wood filler, and washcoated again to separate the filler from the glaze (third panel from left). Finally, it was glazed (right) to adjust the color by brushing the glaze out thin before it dried.

the drying. Slow the drying of water-based glaze by adding 5 to 10 percent propylene glycol. Speed the drying of both types by warming the air in the room. If you need to thin a glaze to lighten its color, it's best to use clear glaze base (neutral glaze) so you don't lose the run-resistant quality of the glaze.

Some manufacturers provide glazes in a range of colors. Others provide only a clear glaze base (neutral) to which you can add pigment. Use oil and japan colors with oil-based glaze; use universal tinting colorants (UTCs) with water-based glaze. Dark browns and whites (for pickling) are the colors most often used on furniture and cabinets.

Applying Glaze

Glazing is always done over a sealed surface. You can use any finish, sealer, or washcoat as long as it is thick enough so the glaze can't get through to the wood. (See "Sealers and Sealing Wood" on p. 116, and "Washcoats" on p. 64.) You can stain the wood and fill the pores under the glaze. It's best to do your glazing as close as possible to the wood, however, so you can apply enough finish on top to protect the colorant from scratches and wear without getting the finish thicker than you want.

If the sealed surface is smooth, sand or steel wool it lightly to create scratches so that some of the glaze color will be retained after wiping. (This is not always necessary, depending on how you intend to manipulate the glaze. For example, it's not necessary in recesses, which are usually a little rough.)

Wipe, brush, or spray the glaze onto the sealed surface to a thickness that will allow you to achieve the results you want.

TIP

As long as you are using a spray gun and lacquer as your finish, you can coat over oil-based glaze very soon after application. You don't have to wait overnight for it to cure. The trick is to mist some thinned lacquer onto the glaze after the thinner in the glaze has evaporated (the glaze turns dull), but before the oil or varnish binder becomes tacky. Unless the glaze is thick, in which case this trick might not work, the lacquer incorporates the glaze and bonds to the coat underneath. Let the mist coat dry, and then proceed with your finishing.

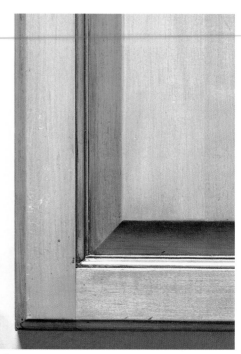

Photo 15-3: Glazing can be used to add depth or the appearance of dirt accumulation (as on antiques) to three-dimensional surfaces such as turnings. Simply wipe the glaze off the high areas, leaving it in the recesses.

Photo 15-4: Glazing is an effective technique for accentuating the three-dimensional structure of raised-panel cabinet doors. This door was stained and sealed before the glaze was applied to the entire surface and wiped off the raised areas. The glaze was then brushed out evenly in the recesses.

Photo 15-5: Some mass-produced furniture has hundreds of small brown or black dots scattered randomly in the finish. Factories use special spatter spray guns to create this "flyspeck" effect. You can imitate this by using a toothbrush to flip glaze onto the surface with your finger. I like to use India ink as the glaze because it flattens well and dries fast.

Photo 15-6: Instead of applying glaze and then wiping some off, you can use a technique called "dry brushing." Spread some glaze or japan color, which is also thick, onto cardboard or posterboard. Dip your brush into the colorant and remove almost all the excess by brushing onto paper or scrap wood. Then brush lightly over the surface to be highlighted.

Allow the thinner in the glaze to evaporate enough so the glaze dulls. It should still be moist. If it gets too hard to manipulate, wash it off with mineral spirits, naphtha, or water (for water-based glaze), or finish your manipulation by scrubbing with steel wool or an abrasive pad.

Following are seven effects you can achieve by manipulating the glaze. Pay attention to mass-produced furniture, and you will notice many more.

- Adjust a color without significantly obscuring the wood, even if it has already been stained and filled (Photo 15-2 on p. 195).

- Add depth or the appearance of dirt accumulation (making a new piece look old) to three-dimensional surfaces such as turnings (Photo 15-3).

- Accentuate the structural detailing of molded woodwork, such as frame-and-panel doors and interior trim (Photo 15-4).

- Some mass-produced furniture has hundreds of small brown or black dots scattered randomly in the finish. Factories use special spatter spray guns to create this "flyspeck" effect. You can imitate this by using a toothbrush to flip glaze onto the surface with your finger (Photo 15-5).

- Instead of applying glaze and then wiping some off, you can drag a "dry brush" over a surface, allowing color to be left behind (Photo 15-6).

- Adding character to a painted surface with glaze is a common antiquing technique (Photo 15-7). But it can also be used to produce creative new effects. As with all glazing techniques, you can add and remove material until you get the look you want.

- Using a commonly available graining tool, you can create the appearance of a heavy-grained wood, such as oak, on plain-figured woods (Photo 15-8).

Photo 15-7: Glaze is particularly effective at creating an antique appearance when brushed out thin over a painted surface. Continue brushing and removing excess glaze until you get the look you want.

Photo 15-8: By using this simple graining tool, which is like a curved rubber stamp that you simultaneously rock and drag over the still-wet glaze, you can create the appearance of a heavy-grained wood such as oak.

Antiquing Wood

Old furniture looks different than new furniture, even if the old furniture has been well cared for. The difference is caused, primarily, by color change (due to light and oxidation), wear, and dirt accumulation as the furniture has aged. Imitating the look of oldness in newly made furniture or cabinets, or newly made parts that you are attaching to old furniture, is called *antiquing*. To antique wood, you must approximate the color change, wear, and dirt accumulation artificially. Usually, you will want to apply a satin or flat topcoat.

Antiquing can be done either on the wood or in the finish. There is no step-by-step right way to do antiquing. It all depends on the look you are trying to imitate. Creating a realistic-looking antiqued finish is easier if you have a real antique to look at and imitate.

COLOR CHANGE

The best way to approximate color change is with stains, bleaches, and toners. Dye stains usually work better than pigment stains, because dye stains color wood more evenly and naturally. Toners can also be used to color wood evenly and are more effective than any stain if you don't want to highlight the pores at all. Think of the very even coloring of old cherry, maple, and mahogany, for example. Factories commonly use toners to recreate these looks.

Some woods, such as walnut, lighten with age. Other woods lighten because they have been

Marks imitating scratches are often applied between coats of finish and referred to as "cowtailing." You can use an artist's brush, grease pencil, or a Blendal stick (from Mohawk), as I'm using here to apply these marks.

The process of creating an antique look in a finish can sometimes be quite elaborate. In this factory finish, cowtails, flyspecks, and even a fake grain have been added to curly maple without totally obscuring the curls.

bleached by the sun. New wood can be lightened artificially with two-part bleach. (See "Bleaching Wood" on p. 50.) Then stain or tone the wood back to the color you want.

WEAR

Distressing is most often thought of as beating furniture with chains

or other metal objects. Beating furniture is one way to fake wear in furniture. But wear can take many forms, and the trick to making wear look convincing is to make it look natural.

Chains tend to make nearly identical marks. Dings and gouges made over 100 years of natural wear, however, would not look at all identical. They would take many shapes. Moreover, natural wear is not just dings but wood actually worn away on parts such as chair rungs and edges of tabletops. This type of wear can be better imitated using rasps, sandpaper, and wire brushes. The best way to determine the type of wear to add to new furniture is to look at old furniture and notice how it has been dinged and worn. Then choose the tools or objects that will most closely create the same effects. Most importantly, don't make the same marks all over.

The look of wear and age can also be created in the finish. A common technique is called *cowtailing*, using an artist's brush or special crayon to paint or mark the surface with small curved lines (top photo, left). Cowtailing can be combined with spatter, or *flyspecking* (Photo 15-5 on p. 196 and the bottom photo at left), to simulate the patina of age and use.

DIRT

Old furniture often looks as if dirt has accumulated in recesses such as those on turnings and moldings. In some cases what has actually happened is that much of the finish has been worn away from the high-contact areas by repeated rubbing, either from use or from a polishing cloth. The effect is the same, however. The recesses are darker. Use glazing techniques to imitate this look. (See Photo 15-3 on p. 196 and Photo 1-5 on p. 5.)

Dry brushing is another technique used to imitate dirt accumulation. Similar to brushing the almost dry brush over the raised edges of a surface, as shown in Photo 15-6 on p. 196, brush into inside corners or near joints, or even near the edges of tabletops or cabinet doors.

Toning

Toning is the application of a thinned finish with a colorant added. The applied colorant is then left as is: It isn't manipulated as is done in glazing. The colorant can be pigment or dye, or it can be a combination of the two.

There are actually two terms used to describe toning. When you apply the colored finish to an entire surface, it's usually called *toning*, and the colored finish is called a *toner* (Photo 15-9). When you apply the colored finish to only a part of a surface—for example, just to the sapwood—it's usually called *shading*, and the colored finish is

Photo 15-9: The bottom half of this cabinet door has been toned using a pigmented toner. To contrast toning with staining, the top half was stained, with the excess stain wiped off. Then a finish was applied to the entire door.

Pickling

The intent of pickling is to make wood look old. Early attempts using strong acids to "gray" the wood are no longer practiced. The modern idea of pickling probably originated when someone tried to remove the paint from old paneling. Because it's almost impossible to remove all the paint from the pores of wood, what was left was a thin, uneven color, through which wood was clearly visible. Though I'm sure these results were disappointing at the time, this look is now very fashionable, and you can re-create it without having to paint, and then strip, the wood.

Pickling, in its simplest form, is nothing more than wiping or brushing either a heavily pigmented stain or a thinned paint over wood and then wiping off as much of the excess as necessary to give you the look you want. Usually the stain or paint is white or off-white in color. But it can be any color, including a pastel. You must remove enough of the color so you can see the wood underneath, or you are painting instead of pickling (top photo).

Pickling can also mean applying a white or off-white glaze over a sealed surface. Allow the glaze to lose its gloss, and then wipe off as much of the excess as you want, but enough so you can see the wood underneath (bottom photo).

If you use a stain, it should be heavily pigmented, so you can leave a significant amount of color on the surface of the wood. If you use paint, you should thin it with about 25 percent of the proper thinner (mineral spirits for oil-based paint,

There are two significantly different ways to pickle wood: by staining and by glazing. For staining, apply a white or off-white stain directly onto the wood and wipe off all or most of the excess. For glazing, apply a white or off-white glaze over a sealed surface and wipe off all or most of the excess. You can use the same product to do both, as I've done here. I used a white gel stain directly on the wood (above) and over a sealed surface (below). I could have used a white glaze on both.

water for latex paint) so it will be easy to spread.

Each type of paint has its advantages. Oil-based paint cures much more slowly, so you have more time to spread it and remove just the right amount. Oil-based paint also doesn't raise the grain of the wood. Water-based paint doesn't yellow and doesn't contain the solvent content of oil-based paint, so the air you breathe is much cleaner, especially when you're pickling large surfaces, such as paneling.

Instead of stain or paint, you could simply add a little white or off-white pigment to some varnish or water-based finish. Then brush or spray this on the wood and leave it without wiping. As long as you can still see the wood, you are pickling and not painting.

Pickling is usually done on pine, oak, ash, or elm. It's effective on pine because the underlying figure is very pronounced, so it shows through even a fairly heavy layer of color. It's effective on oak, ash, and elm because more of the color remains in the deep grain, accentuating the feel of wood underneath. In each case, enough of the color remains on top of the wood to subdue the contrasts between earlywood and latewood.

When you are happy with the appearance, apply one or two coats of finish to protect the color. Otherwise, the color will be easy to rub off. In cases where the pickling has been done with white or off-white color, water-based finish is best because it has no amber tint as other finishes have, and it doesn't yellow over time. Usually, you'll want to use a satin or flat finish, rather than a gloss, to better imitate the appearance of age.

Photo 15-10: Shading (top) means to spray a thinned coat of colored finish to just a part of the surface. This often has the effect of highlighting other parts, as in this example.

called a *shading stain* (Photo 15-10). There is no consistency in the use of these terms, however. Both toning and shading are often referred to as "toning," as I have done above. And some manufacturers of aerosol toners label their pigmented toners "shading stain" and their dye toners "toner." So be prepared for a little confusion in the terminology.

It's almost always more effective to use a spray gun to apply the toner, because it is too difficult to control with a brush. You'll leave brush marks.

Toning is not nearly as versatile as glazing, but it is much more effective for matching colors and evening the contrasts between different colored boards and between sapwood and heartwood. Toning is less forgiving than glazing because it is usually done with lacquer, shellac, water base, or two-part finish (varnish cures too slowly and collects too much dust), so you can't simply wipe it off if you get it wrong. If you get the color too dark, for example (the most common mistake), there's usually nothing you can do except strip everything and start over.

There is no rule governing how much to thin a toner. There are probably as many variations as there are people spraying toners. Here's a place to start. Using lacquer, combine one part lacquer with one part NGR dye or 1 part lacquer stain and thin it with about 6 parts thinner. Spray this and adjust your mix from there. As mentioned, the biggest risk is building the color too rapidly and getting it too dark. It's much better to "sneak up" on the color you want.

With water-based finish, it's best to use a water-based stain as your toner or shading stain because it is already thinned. You can't thin water-based finish with 6 parts water and expect it to still level out. It will bead up like water on wax. You will have to experiment with different stains. The best to use are the ones that are primarily dye (Photos 4-2 and 4-3 on p. 43 and Photo 4-4 on p. 45). Typical pigmented water-based stains from home centers will be difficult to control.

Instead of making your own toner, you can use an aerosol toner. Aerosol toners are available from a number of mail-order suppliers and from some paint stores that sell to the painting trade. You lose control of the mix with aerosols, but they are handy for many situations, including repairing damage to finishes. (See Chapter 19: "Repairing Finishes.") You can use a lacquer-based aerosol over any finish as long as you don't spray fully wet coats that might cause it to blister. You can also use an aerosol or spray gun–applied lacquer toner in between coats of water-based finishes.

Step Panel

Once you get beyond simple staining and into glazing and toning, keeping the colors and looks the same can be difficult if you are finishing numerous cabinets or pieces of furniture. It's here that a step panel comes in handy. This is a board or piece of veneered plywood on which you have performed all the steps in taped or marked-off sections so that it is easy to see what each step should look like. A step panel gives you a visual history so you can match each step to get to the correct final appearance.

To make a step panel, take a board or piece of veneered plywood that is the same species of wood as the project you want to finish (ideally scrap from the project) and apply each step as you intend to do on the project. As each step dries, and before moving to the next, tape off a section if you're spraying, or mark it off if you're brushing or wiping. In fact, if you're brushing or wiping, you can mark off sections of the board before you even start because you don't have to worry about overlaps.

Ideally, you would make each section as large as possible to produce the greatest visual impact, but I've seen step panels with sections no larger than the

Common Glazing and Toning Problems

Glazing is usually done with a brush or other hand-held specialty tool. Toning is usually done with a spray gun. Both are easy to do, but to be successful you have to have an idea of the effect you're after. Here are the most common problems that occur when glazing or toning, and their causes and solutions.

PROBLEM	CAUSE	SOLUTION
The finish turned off-white when applied over a glaze.	The glaze was too wet. The problem usually occurs with a lacquer finish and shows up most often in the wood's pores, where the glaze is thickest. The cause is applying the lacquer before all the thinner has evaporated from the glaze. The lacquer came out of solution.	You can try spraying the wood with lacquer thinner. If this doesn't clear up the problem, you'll have to strip and start over. Be sure to allow plenty of time for the glaze to dry, especially on humid or cool days.
Dark scratches appeared when you applied the glaze.	The last coat of sealer or finish wasn't hard enough when you sanded it. Or you used sandpaper with too coarse a grit.	Before the glaze cures, remove it by washing with mineral spirits (for oil- or varnish-based glaze) or water (for water-based glaze). Let the undercoat cure thoroughly, resand with fine-grit sandpaper, and reapply the glaze.
The glaze penetrated into the wood, causing a blotchy appearance.	You didn't totally seal the wood. Or you sanded through the washcoat or sealer in places.	Strip the wood and start over.
The finish separated at the glaze layer and peeled.	The glaze was applied too thickly. It didn't contain enough binder to hold it together.	Strip off the finish and start over. Don't apply the glaze as thickly, or add some varnish or water-based finish to the glaze. Experiment on scrap wood.
You got the color too dark with toner or shading stain.	You used a toner or shading stain with too much colorant, or you applied one coat too many.	Strip off the finish and start over. Build the color slowly with a very thinned-down toner or shading stain. Don't apply too much colorant.
Lap marks showed up after you sprayed a toner.	The toner had too high a concentration of colorant, causing your sprayed overlaps to show.	Strip off the finish and start over. Thin the toner more. It's better to spray more passes with a thinner toner (so there is very little build).
The match you created using a toner no longer matched when you placed the object in the room.	The lighting in the room was different than in your shop.	You have to have the same lighting in both places. Re-create one or the other to match. (See "Matching Color" on p. 58.)

width of ¾-inch strips of masking tape working in from the edge of a cabinet door (Photo 15-11).

Sometimes, step panels are made as bracketing panels, with one panel showing the lightest color acceptable and the other the darkest. For more precise control, you can write temperature and humidity conditions on the back of the panel. Both can affect the outcome of a finish. Temperature changes the thickness of a finish for application purposes, and humidity affects grain raising which can cause more or less stain to be retained after wiping off the excess.

Step panels are valuable for achieving consistent results, even over several days or weeks of work and even if different people are doing the application. Step panels can also be used to gain approval from clients or to impress them with the complexity of the work so they will better understand your charges.

Photo 15-11: A step panel shows every step in a finish so that there is a visual guide for matching. The steps in this panel are as follows: unfinished wood, light oak stain with the excess wiped off for background color; washcoat; cordovan mahogany stain with the excess wiped off; sprayed walnut toner; two coats of sprayed lacquer. The combination of steps produces a rich, deep coloring and (by using the toner selectively) will even the slight color variations in the wood on this child's chair.

CHAPTER 16

Finishing
the Finish

The difference between a quality finish and a flawed finish has less to do with how you apply the finish than with what you do to it afterwards—with how you finish the finish. To finish a finish, you rub it with abrasives, such as sandpaper, steel wool, rubbing compounds, or a combination of these, sometimes using a lubricant such as wax, mineral spirits, oil, or soapy water. The idea is the same as sanding wood. You level and smooth the surface using increasingly finer abrasives until you are happy with the way it feels and looks.

Rubbing a finish does two things. It makes the finish feel smoother, and it gives the finish a softer appearance. Both are difficult to describe and virtually impossible to capture in a photograph.

Whenever you apply several coats of a film finish (a finish that you build to a thickness on the wood), you will always get some roughness caused by embedded dust. You will also get brush marks or orange peel, depending on the tool you used to apply the finish, and there may be other flaws. No matter how careful you are, you can't apply a perfect finish.

Rubbing a finish cuts off (or at least rounds over) dust nibs, and it removes (or at least disguises) brush marks and orange peel. Rubbing does this by putting fine scratches in the surface. The

In Brief

- **Cutting Through**
- **Additional Factors in Rubbing a Finish**
- **Synthetic Steel Wool**
- **Rubbing with Steel Wool**
- **Comparison of Rubbing Lubricants**
- **Leveling and Rubbing**
- **Machine Rubbing**

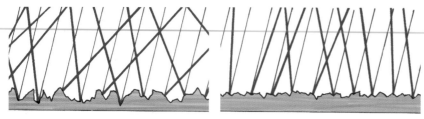

Figure 16-1: The larger the scratches you put into a finish, the more the light is scattered and the lower the sheen (left). The finer the scratches, the more clearly an image is reflected back to you and the higher the sheen (right).

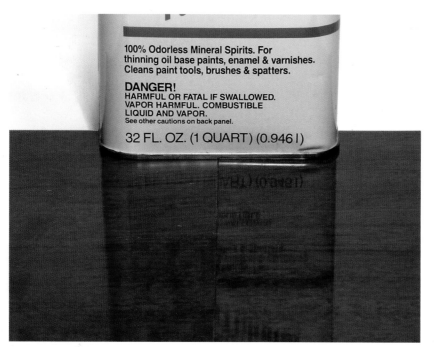

Photo 16-1: The amount of sheen that you rub into a finish is easy to see when you look at the reflection of an object in the surface. A rubbed high-gloss finish (right) shows a clear reflection of the can of mineral spirits. A rubbed satin finish (left) obscures the reflection.

> **TIP** If you have problems with dust settling on your wet finish and becoming embedded, plan to rub the finish using sandpaper for the first step. Then you won't have to worry so much about the dust.

scratches become what you feel and see, thus replacing the problems. By making scratches too fine to feel, you make the surface feel smooth. Depending on how fine you make the scratches, you also control the amount of shine. The finer the scratches, the higher the gloss. The coarser the scratches, the lower the gloss. The word for degree of gloss is *sheen*. A high sheen is a higher gloss. A low sheen is satin or flat (Figure 16-1 and Photo 16-1).

Rubbing a finish also creates a surface that is easier to repair than a non-rubbed finish. You can usually match the sheen perfectly by rubbing the repaired area with the same grit abrasive. (See Chapter 19: "Repairing Finishes.")

Many woodworkers avoid rubbing a finish because they don't understand the process, or they consider it too complicated. This is usually a mistake. There's not much to understand, and the complication is only in the number of ways to do it. If you've never rubbed a finish before, I suggest you begin simply by rubbing with steel wool. (See "Rubbing with Steel Wool" on p. 210.) You will smooth and disguise flaws in your finish and produce a satin sheen. Next, try sanding a finish level before rubbing with steel wool. This will eliminate flaws and produce a satin sheen. From there, if you want, you can begin rubbing with finer or coarser abrasive compounds to raise or lower the sheen. (See "Leveling and Rubbing" on p. 214.) You can do this using different rubbing abrasives as many times as you want—until you finally cut through the finish to the wood.

Cutting Through

You are, of course, worried about cutting through. This is always a risk, no matter how experienced you are. I wish I could tell you how many coats to apply to avoid cutting through, but there are just too many variables. These include the wood you are working on, whether or not you filled the pores with paste wood filler, and whether you are leveling the surface before rubbing or just rubbing. In addition, everyone levels and rubs a little differently and applies finishes differently, and the finishes themselves build differently. (See "Solids Content and Mil Thickness" on p. 108.) Just like sanding veneer or sanding out the coarser scratches in wood created by the previous grit of sandpaper, it's more a feel than anything else.

Rubbing a finish without leveling doesn't cut off much finish, so the worst problem you usually experience is cutting through the edges. You can reduce the chance of doing this by softening, or "breaking," the edges with sandpaper before finishing and by applying an extra coat or two to the edges.

Leveling cuts off more finish. If you have never leveled and rubbed a finish before, I suggest that you make up a practice panel on veneered plywood and apply the finish you normally use in the way you normally apply it. Apply a couple of extra coats—maybe four or five total. Then use one or more of the methods described in this chapter to level and rub the finish. See how much it takes to cut through to the wood. Very quickly you will get the feel.

You don't have to rub the finish. But you will always improve the results if you do (Photo 16-2).

Additional Factors in Rubbing a Finish

The results you get by rubbing a finish are influenced by a number of factors in addition to avoiding cutting through. These include:

■ the type of finish you are rubbing
■ how thoroughly the finish has cured
■ the type of rubbing abrasives you use
■ the type of rubbing lubricants you use
■ the rubbing schedule
■ the cleanup
■ the final waxing or polishing

Type of Finish

Hard, brittle finishes are easier than tough finishes to rub to a smooth, even sheen because hard finishes yield a clean, sharp scratch pattern when rubbed. Tough finishes are difficult to scratch, and the scratches you do make are un-

even tears rather than smooth, clean cuts. The evaporative finishes, shellac and lacquer, are the best rubbing finishes. (The most expensive rubbed dining tables, for example, are usually finished with lacquer.) The reactive finishes—varnish (including polyurethane) and two-part finishes—are more difficult to rub to an even sheen. Water base is also more difficult. You can still rub these finishes, of course, but the results won't be as nice.

Keep in mind that there are variations within each type of finish depending on how the particular finish is made. It's possible, for example, to make a varnish with good rubbing qualities and a lacquer with poor rubbing qualities. (See Chapter 8: "Introduction to Film Finishes" and the chapters on each of the finishes.)

> If you want to rub a tabletop to a satin sheen in order to improve the look and feel but don't want to spend the effort on the table legs or chairs, apply a gloss finish to the tabletop (for the best clarity and so you can see pitting easily during the rubbing) and a satin finish to everything else. Rub out the tabletop and leave everything else as is. The two will blend for an even appearance.
>
> **TIP**

Photo 16-2: Think of a film finish as a layer of plastic on the surface of the wood. As long as the layer is thick enough, you can eliminate virtually all flaws simply by sanding the surface level and then rubbing it with finer and finer abrasives until you achieve the sheen you want. Here, I poured on a thick layer of lacquer and let it begin to set up. Then I smeared it around with a cloth and let it dry hard to create worse flaws than you will ever encounter. Finally, I sanded the right side level and rubbed it up to the grade of rottenstone. The surface on the right side is now perfectly level with a perfectly even gloss sheen. Virtually any flaw in a film finish can be fixed.

Photo 16-3: Clogged or "corned" sandpaper will mar the finish. Change the paper if corns begin to develop.

Thoroughness of Cure

A finish begins as a liquid and becomes a solid when it cures. Between these extremes, it goes through various stages of hardness. If you try to abrade a finish before it has adequately cured, the scratch pattern will be uneven, and the scratches you do make may disappear in places as the finish continues to cure. This will cause a blotchy sheen. In addition, because finishes shrink as they cure, pores that you have filled and leveled may open, leaving a pitted surface again. (See Chapter 7: "Filling Pores.")

There are no absolute rules for how long you should let a finish cure before you rub it, but the longer the better. With all solvent-based finishes, you can get a good indication that the finish is ready to be rubbed by pressing your nose against the dried finish and taking a whiff. If you can smell any of the solvent, give the finish more time. It is still shrinking.

NOTE

It's difficult to compare degrees of coarseness among the three types of abrasives. It's often difficult even within one of the types. Standardization between manufacturers is fairly good with sandpaper. It's not bad with steel wool. But it's completely nonexistent with rubbing compounds. Among the abrasive types, it's my observation that #0000 steel wool, pumice, and 600- and 1000-grit sandpaper produce about the same sheen.

Choice of Abrasives

There are three types of abrasives for rubbing finishes:

- sandpaper
- steel wool (including synthetic steel wool)
- rubbing compounds

Sandpaper is used to cut back the surface and eliminate irregularities such as orange peel, brush marks, and dust nibs. You can back the sandpaper with your hand or with a flat rubber, cork, or felt block. Using a block will produce a more level surface. I like to use cork or felt because they are softer. (See the drawing of my sanding block on p. 11.)

Stearated (dry-lubricated) and wet/dry sandpaper used with a liquid lubricant are best for sanding finishes because they don't clog easily. (See "Sandpaper" on p. 12.) Stearated sandpaper is available up to 600-grit. Wet/dry sandpaper is available up to 2500-grit. Both types may still clog when used on a finish, particularly if the finish hasn't totally cured. The finish rolls up into tiny balls, called *corns,* and sticks in the sandpaper grit (Photo 16-3). You should check the sandpaper often and remove these corns with a dull scraper, or change to fresh sandpaper. If you don't, the corns will put visible scratches in the finish that you will then need to sand out.

You have to be especially careful that you are using the grit sandpaper you intend to use when sanding finishes. A lot of suppliers are now stocking "P" grade sandpapers, which vary significantly from traditional sandpaper in the higher grits. (See "Sandpaper" on p. 12.)

Steel wool is used to put an even satin scratch pattern in the finish without much risk of clogging, or corning. You can buy steel wool in natural or synthetic ("non-woven" fiber) form, and in various degrees of coarseness. (See "Synthetic Steel Wool" at right.) The finest commonly available traditional steel wool is #0000. You should use this or #000 when rubbing a finish. Both produce a satin sheen.

Rubbing compounds are very fine abrasive powders suspended in a paste or liquid. These powders are almost always finer than the finest steel wool, so they usually produce sheens higher than that produced by #0000 steel wool. It's often difficult to compare degrees of coarseness among brands, so it's best to stay within one brand if you're rubbing to a progressively higher sheen (Photo 16-4).

Pumice (very hard, finely ground lava) and rottenstone (very soft, finely ground limestone) are inexpensive abrasive powders that you can make into your own rubbing compounds by mixing one or the other with water or mineral oil. With water the abrasive cuts faster and leaves a slightly duller sheen. Oil lubricates better, so the cutting is slower and the sheen a little higher. If you find that the oil is too thick to work with, thin it with mineral spirits or use mineral spirits alone.

You can make the paste right on the finish by sprinkling some of the powder onto the surface and then pouring on a little water or oil. The consistency (ratio of powder to lubricant) is not important. Alternatively, you can mix either pumice or rottenstone with one of the lubricants in a plastic squeeze container and use it to dispense the compound (Photo 16-5 on p. 212).

Pumice and rottenstone are often used together in phrases such as, "I rubbed the finish with pumice and rottenstone." In fact, they don't work well together. Pumice is about as course as #0000 steel wool or 600-grit sand-

Synthetic Steel Wool

Synthetic steel wool is a fibrous, "non-woven" nylon coated with abrasive powders. The most commonly available brands are 3M's Scotch-Brite and Norton's Bear-Tex.

The abrasiveness of synthetic steel wool is attributable to abrasive powders glued to the fiber, not to the fiber itself. When these powders wear off, the pad becomes largely ineffective. In this regard synthetic steel wool resembles sandpaper more than traditional steel wool. The fiber pads are color-coded according to the grade of abrasive powders used. In the consumer market gray is roughly equivalent to #000 steel wool, green is roughly equivalent to #00 steel wool, and maroon is roughly equivalent to #0 steel wool.

You can substitute synthetic steel wool for traditional steel wool when you rub a finish or when you rub between coats. Anytime you are using water-based products and there is a possibility that you may apply another coat, you should make this substitution. Any pieces of steel from traditional steel wool that remain in pores or cracks will rust and cause dark spots when you apply the next coat. Otherwise, the principal limitation of traditional steel wool (rounding over dust nibs instead of cutting them off) and the principal advantage of traditional steel wool (reduced clogging) hold for synthetic steel wool.

Photo 16-4: Rubbing compounds come in three different forms: pumice and rottenstone abrasive powders that you can mix into a compound with oil or water (left); synthetic abrasive powders already in a compound and sold for use on wood (center); and synthetic abrasive powders in a liquid made especially for high-speed buffing on automotive and wood finishes (right). Products in this third category are sometimes called glaze, but they are not at all related to glazes used for coloring wood.

paper; it produces a satin sheen. Rottenstone is much finer and produces a gloss. The relative abrasiveness is too different to jump successfully from one to the other. You will have to work too hard to eliminate the relatively deep scratches produced by the pumice. Therefore, if you intend to finish with rottenstone, it's best to sand up to 1500-grit or 2000-grit and then go straight to rottenstone. In other words, don't use the pumice at all.

Rubbing with Steel Wool

You can rub any finish with steel wool to smooth it and to even its sheen. You should use #000 or #0000 steel wool. (Synthetic steel wool, also known as Scotch-Brite, can be substituted.) Steel wool will lower the sheen (reduce the gloss) of most finishes, but it will raise the sheen of some film finishes that contain a lot of flatting agent. (See "Controlling Sheen with Flatting Agent" on p. 110.) Here's how to do it:

1 Give the finish time to cure hard—at least several days. Several weeks are better.

2 Arrange your work so you can see what's happening in the reflection of a light source.

3 On flat surfaces, using one or both hands and medium-to-heavy pressure, rub in long straight strokes with the grain of the wood. Avoid making arcs with your strokes. Keep the pressure even over the entire surface, and overlap each stroke by 80 to 90 percent. Be very careful not to rub over the edge, or you will cut through the finish and expose bare

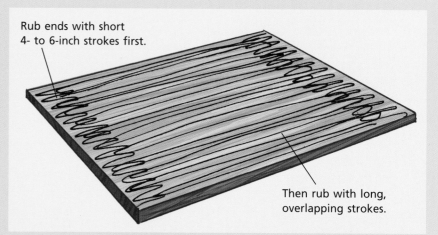

Rub ends with short 4- to 6-inch strokes first.

Then rub with long, overlapping strokes.

To keep from cutting through the edge of flat surfaces, rub the last 4 to 6 inches first with a series of short strokes right up to the edge. Follow with overlapping strokes running the entire length, stopping just short of the edge.

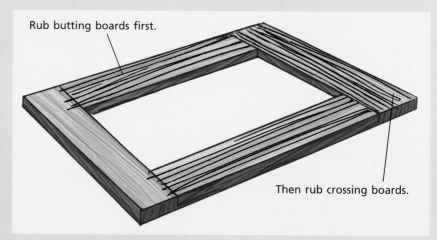

Rub butting boards first.

Then rub crossing boards.

To keep scratches in line with the grain when rubbing boards that butt together cross-grain, rub the butting boards first, then the crossing boards. Remove any cross-grain scratches in the crossing boards.

wood. To avoid cutting through the edge, rub right up to the edge first with short strokes. Then rub the rest of the surface with long strokes, stopping just short of the edge, as shown in the drawing above (top).

On boards that are joined cross-grain, rub the butting boards first, then the crossing boards, removing any cross-grain scratches you may have made while rubbing the first boards (drawing above, bottom).

You can usually find the largest selection of supplies for rubbing a finish in auto-body supply stores. You'll also find some of these supplies in woodworking catalogues and stores. Home centers and paint stores rarely stock much.

Choice of Lubricants

Lubricant is used with sandpaper and steel wool to reduce corning and to float away grit and abraded material, maintaining the abrasive's effectiveness. The lubricant also holds down dust and steel-

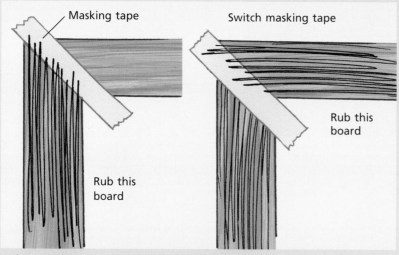

To keep rubbing-scratches from crossing over a mitered joint, you can rub one board while masking tape protects the second, then switch the masking tape and rub the second board.

TIP You can lower the sheen on difficult-to-reach carvings, turnings, and moldings by brushing pumice powder into the recesses with a shoe brush. The pumice will scratch the finish to a satin sheen.

For mitered boards, stop short of the joint, or use masking tape to protect one board while rubbing the other (drawing above).

On turnings, rub around the cylinder, just as you would sand on the lathe.

4 Carefully clean off the dust. It's best to vacuum or blow it off with compressed air and then wipe lightly with the grain using your hand to be sure no dust remains. Otherwise, wipe lightly using a tack cloth or a cloth dampened with mineral spirits. Wipe with the grain. If you wipe across the grain, you may put noticeable cross-scratches in the surface.

5 If you're not happy with the appearance, determine what is wrong (for example, incomplete rubbing, an irregular scratch pattern caused by uneven pressure, or arcing strokes caused by an arced scratch pattern) and begin rubbing again to correct the problem.

6 If you rub through the finish, repair that spot with more finish or recoat the entire surface. Then allow the finish to cure thoroughly and rub again. If you rub through a stain, apply more of the same stain to the area unless it will dissolve the finish. If the area is bigger than an inch in diameter, you may not be able to disguise it successfully.

You can vary this schedule as follows:

- Sand the surface lightly to remove protruding dust nibs before you begin rubbing with steel wool.
- Use a lubricant with your steel wool. (See "Choice of Lubricants" in the text above.) A lubricant will disguise rub-throughs, however, until the damage becomes worse. So practice a few times without a lubricant.
- Substitute a commercial rubbing compound or pumice for the steel wool, and use a rubbing pad to do the rubbing. (See "Making a Rubbing Pad" on p. 22.)
- Use a satin finish on any parts you're not rubbing to imitate the rubbed effect.
- Apply paste wax or a silicone furniture polish to raise the sheen and protect the surface from scratches. (See "Applying Paste Wax" on p. 90 and "Applying Liquid Furniture Polish" on p. 251.)

Photo 16-5: I find plastic squeeze containers very useful for dispensing my own pumice or rottenstone compound. I usually fill the container with about an inch of the powder, then add about a third mineral oil and two-thirds mineral spirits to the top. I shake the container before dispensing.

CAUTION

▼

Mineral spirits and naphtha may soften water-based finish enough to prevent your getting an even gloss, so you should use oil or soapy water when rubbing water base. Though I've never found it to be a problem, mineral spirits and naphtha also have the potential of slightly softening lacquer and varnish if these finishes aren't totally cured. Softening could produce an uneven scratch pattern.

wool particles so you don't breathe them, and some lubricants reduce the size of the scratches. There are four types of lubricant for rubbing finishes:

■ mineral spirits or naphtha

■ liquid or paste wax

■ oil

■ water or soapy water

In addition, there are commercial rubbing lubricants usually made with a petroleum distillate that evaporates more slowly than mineral spirits.

Each of these lubricants is effective and has its advocates. To use a lubricant, wet the surface liberally and keep it wet as long as you are rubbing. Mineral spirits evaporates much more slowly than naphtha, so mineral spirits is usually the better choice between the two. Mineral spirits allows for fast cutting with very little or no corning. Liquid or paste wax and non-curing oils, such as mineral oil and vegetable oil, almost totally eliminate corning but significantly slow cutting. You can mix mineral spirits with wax or oil to blend the characteristics.

Soapy water works well with steel wool, but it is not very effective at preventing corning on sandpaper. Using water, with or without soap, can cause its own problems. If you cut through the finish, the water may raise the grain of the wood, a defect that will be very difficult to repair. You don't have to worry about rust unless you intend to apply another coat of water-based finish on top, in which case, be sure to first clean the surface well. Some manufacturers sell paste soap under names like "Wooling Wax," "Wol Wax," "Wool Lube," and "Murphy's Oil Soap." None of these products has anything to do with wax or oil, and the reference to wool means they will lubricate steel wool. (See "Comparison of Rubbing Lubricants" on facing page.)

Any of these lubricants will reduce the scratching of the steel wool a little, and the liquid will keep the steel-wool particles from circulating in the air you breathe. But the lubricant will disguise rub-throughs so you won't know they're there until the lubricant has evaporated. By then you've usually done considerable damage. A lubricant also makes it difficult to judge the sheen being produced. You can't see what you're doing.

I suggest you use a lubricant with sandpaper to reduce corning, but not with steel wool until you've rubbed a few finishes without it. Then you'll have a better feel for how much you can rub without cutting through and for the effect you're creating.

Rubbing Schedule

There are two procedures, or schedules, you can use to rub a finish:

■ Level the surface with sandpaper before rubbing with steel wool and rubbing compounds.

■ Skip the leveling step and just use steel wool or rubbing compounds.

If you skip the leveling step, your finish will include imperfections such as orange peel, brush marks, and dust nibs, all slightly visible in reflected light. Leveling with sandpaper removes these imperfections. But leveling is an extra, time-consuming step, and it's not always needed. If you're not aiming for perfection, you can often skip the leveling step and simply rub with steel wool. The satin sheen it produces will disguise all but the most severe imperfections. Also, you can usually skip the leveling step on curved, turned, molded, and carved surfaces, as well as on chairs or table legs.

If you don't have enough experience to judge whether a finish should be leveled, try rubbing it first with steel wool. If the surface is too uneven for your taste, start over with leveling.

If you have to sand a lot to level a finish, you run the risk of cutting through the top layer of finish and exposing the layer underneath (Photo 16-6). You may see a clear line separating the two layers. This phenomenon is called *layering* or *ghosting* (you see the "ghost" of the layer below). It rarely occurs with evaporative finishes, where the layers dissolve into each other. It almost always occurs between coats of varnish and polyurethane, and it often occurs between coats of water-based finish.

You can usually disguise layering by rubbing with an abrasive equivalent to the coarseness of #0000 steel wool. If this doesn't work, or if you want to rub to a higher sheen, you need to apply another coat of finish. To keep the layering from occurring again, sand the surface level, so you won't have to sand the next coat so much that you cut through.

If you want a less fragile rubbed surface (one that doesn't show scratches

Comparison of Rubbing Lubricants

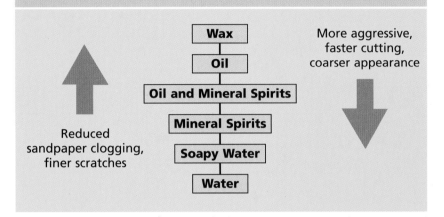

The more oily or waxy a rubbing lubricant, the better it lubricates and reduces the scratching, as well as sandpaper clogging. The less oily or waxy a rubbing lubricant, the faster and more aggressive the abrasive cuts.

Reduced sandpaper clogging, finer scratches

More aggressive, faster cutting, coarser appearance

Wax
Oil
Oil and Mineral Spirits
Mineral Spirits
Soapy Water
Water

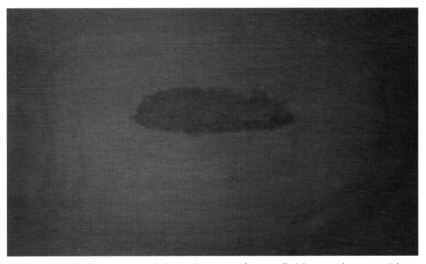

Photo 16-6: When you sand through coats of some finishes, such as varnish (including polyurethane), and water base, you may notice the "ghost" of the underlying coats showing through. This is called layering or ghosting. Here, I've sanded through several coats and all the way to the wood in the center. Disguise ghosting by rubbing with #0000 steel wool, or apply another coat of finish and don't sand through.

easily) and also a surface as level as possible, sand the next-to-last coat level. Then apply the last coat as evenly and smoothly as possible. It will flatten well.

Cleaning Up

If you use several grits in your rubbing, clean the surface well between each grit. The reason is the same as in sanding

Leveling and Rubbing

On flat surfaces, sand with a backing block and lubricant. Apply the lubricant generously.

Rubbing a finish with an abrasive merely smooths and rounds over imperfections such as dust nibs, brush marks, and orange peel. (See "Rubbing with Steel Wool" on p. 210.) To remove the imperfections, you have to cut them off and level the surface using sandpaper, and a backing block if you're working on a flat surface.

Sanding a film finish is just like sanding wood, except you almost always use much finer grits—320 and finer—and you have to use a lubricant to keep the sandpaper from clogging and damaging the surface. If you've never leveled and rubbed a finish before, try it on a sample finished panel. (See "Cutting Through" on p. 206.)

You'll find it very satisfying, and it will increase your confidence in your ability to control a finish. Here are the steps:

1 Allow the finish to cure hard—at least several days. Several weeks is better.

2 Arrange your work so that you can see a light source reflecting off the surface. This will make it easier to see what's happening.

3 Choose a grit sandpaper that removes the flaws efficiently without creating more work than necessary to remove the sanding scratches. In most cases, this will be 400-grit or 600-grit sandpaper.

Because a finish doesn't have grain like wood has, it doesn't make any difference in what direction you sand or rub until the final rubbing. You will remove the scratches of each grit with the next grit anyway. So it's actually an advantage to sand or rub in a different direction each time you change to a finer grit. This way you can clearly see when you've sanded or rubbed enough. You can also sand or rub in circles, which I find easier, as well as straight lines.

TIP

4 If the surface is flat, back the sandpaper with a cork, felt, or rubber block to keep it flat (photo, facing page). If the surface is not flat, use your hand to back the sandpaper. Either way, wet the surface generously with mineral spirits, liquid or paste wax, oil, or soapy water to lubricate the sanding. (See "Choice of Lubricants" on p. 211.) On large surfaces, it's usually easier to work in sections.

5 Check the sandpaper often to be sure it's not clogging (corning). Remove any corns, or change to fresh sandpaper.

6 Remove the sludge and dry off the surface every so often so you can see if the sheen is even. For a quick check, use a plastic spreader or squeegee to scrape off the sludge from a small area (photo at right). If you used a gloss finish, which is the best practice, any pitting left will stand out as shiny spots. Continue sanding until you have removed all of these. Drop back to a coarser grit if you feel it will be more efficient. If you decide to leave some pitting, rubbing with steel wool or pumice is usually effective at dulling the pits along with the surface.

7 When no shiny spots remain, clean all the sludge off the surface.

8 At this point the surface is level, and you just need to rub in the sheen you want. It's usually most efficient to use sandpaper grits to work your way up close to the particular rubbing compound you want to use. (Rubbing compounds always leave a more even sheen than

A quick way to check your progress in eliminating the pitting caused by the pores is to scrape off the rubbing sludge from a portion of the surface using a plastic spreader. As long as you have used a gloss finish, any pitting that remains will show up clearly in contrast to the flat rubbed sheen on the surface.

sandpaper, even if they are equivalent to the sandpaper grit.) If the surface has been sanded to 600-grit and you want to finish with #0000 steel wool or pumice, you can jump directly to the steel wool or pumice. (See "Steel wool" and "Rubbing compounds" in "Choice of Abrasives" on pp. 208–209.) But if you want to rub to a higher sheen, it's better to sand with finer-grit sandpaper to get up close to the grade of the rubbing compound.

9 It's wise to apply a paste wax or a silicone furniture polish to a rubbed surface to fill in and disguise the tiny rubbing scratches and to protect the finish from additional, unwanted scratching. (See Chapter 18: "Caring for the Finish.")

CAUTION
▼

Cleanliness is critical when rubbing to a high sheen. Any large particles of dust or dirt lodged under your rubbing pad will scratch the surface and force you to drop back a grade or two to remove the scratches.

wood: Particles from a previous grit will scratch the finish more than the grit you're switching to.

When you've finished rubbing, you will have dust or sludge on the surface. You should vacuum the dust or blow it off with compressed air. Otherwise, wipe lightly with the grain using a tack cloth or a cloth dampened with mineral spirits. Wipe with the grain to avoid cross-grain scratches from the loose grit. If you have sludge left over from using a lubricant, wash it off quickly after you've finished rubbing. (Use naphtha or mineral spirits for sludge made with mineral spirits, oil, or wax; use water for sludge made with water.) Sludge remaining in scratches, pores, and recesses may dry opaque and cause a haze on flat surfaces or put solid color into recesses. Use a toothbrush to get the sludge out of narrow recesses.

If you have a problem with the sludge drying in recesses and coloring them (usually white), add some darker pigment to the rubbing compound before rubbing.

Waxing and Polishing

It's almost always a good idea to apply paste wax or a silicone furniture polish to a rubbed surface to reduce wear. Rubbed finishes show scratches more easily than non-rubbed finishes. This is because the ridges created in the rubbing are so easily flattened.

Paste wax protects much longer than furniture polish because paste wax doesn't evaporate. Dark-colored paste wax can be used to advantage on dark woods because it reduces hazing by coloring any rubbing residue. Furniture polish is effective only until it evaporates. Dark-colored paste wax can also be used to disguise any white residue that may have gotten into recesses. (See Chapter 18: "Caring for the Finish.")

Machine Rubbing

Just as with all operations in woodworking and finishing, rubbing can be made more efficient with the use of machine tools. There are three possibilities:

- random-orbit sanders
- in-line pad sanders
- sander/polishers

Random-Orbit Sanders

You can rub out a finish using a random-orbit sander and Abralon abrasive pads. These are composed of silicon-carbide grit bonded to soft foam pads. The grits range from 180 to 4000. You should level the surface with sandpaper before beginning with the sander and pads (Photo 16-7).

Using a random-orbit sander to rub a finish is essentially the same as using it to sand wood. The difference is that you use a lubricant when rubbing finishes. You can use any of the lubricants already discussed (see "Comparison of Rubbing Lubricants" on p. 213), but you should be especially careful of using water or mineral spirits with an electric sander. Be sure the motor is double insulated, and avoid splashing any of the liquid onto the housing.

Once you have leveled the finish, begin sanding with a 1000- or 2000-grit Abralon pad. Don't bear down on the sander. If these grits don't produce enough gloss, you can advance to a 4000-grit pad. With each of these grits, the sander leaves little squigglies, just like the coarser grit sandpapers do on wood. An easy way to remove these marks is to take the pad off the sander and use it to rub lightly with the grain. Alternatively, you can use a rubbing compound.

In-Line Pad Sanders

By far, the best machine tool to use is an in-line pad sander (Photo 16-8).

Photo 16-7: You can use a random-orbit sander, together with Abralon pads, to rub out a finish. If you use an electric sander instead of a pneumatic sander, you should be very careful to keep the lubricant from splashing onto the sander housing.

Photo 16-8: The most efficient machine tool for both leveling and rubbing a finish on a flat surface is an in-line pad sander. The most useful of these are the dual-pad sanders. The one I'm using here is a small one. The large one weighs 30 pounds and is used widely in the furniture industry.

These sanders are available in several sizes, ranging from single-pad and small two-pad machines to a large 30-lb. two-pad machine, which is used in industry to level and rub dining and conference tabletops. The downside of all these machines is that they are expensive, and they require a large compressor to operate them.

Operation is easy, however. The pads are sized to accept standard sandpaper sheets cut into thirds. So it is easy to use these machines to level tabletops, working up through the grits. In addition, several companies, including 3M and Norton, provide synthetic-abrasive pads in very fine grades, and rubbing compounds in various grades, all designed especially for rubbing wood finishes.

Sander/Polishers

To achieve a high gloss, you can use a sander/polisher with a lamb's-wool bonnet and automotive rubbing compounds. (Photo 16-9). You have to keep the machine moving so it doesn't create enough heat to melt and swirl the finish. You also have to work on a perfectly flat surface without cracks or recesses (or pores) that the compound can lodge in, making it difficult to remove. (See "Cleaning Up" on p. 213.)

Sander/polishers create very light scratches in a swirl pattern, of course, so these machines can be used only for high-gloss finishes, similar to rubbed finishes on automobiles. In fact, the swirls will appear similar, showing up faintly in a reflected light, but not being a distraction otherwise.

Photo 16-9: Sander/polishers are useful for rubbing finishes to a high gloss. Smear automotive rubbing compound on the surface with the lamb's-wool bonnet. Hold the pad flat on the surface and keep it moving so you don't generate a lot of heat in one place. Buff until the compound breaks down to an almost nonexistent powder.

Finishing
Different
Woods

Understanding finishes and how to apply them is not the whole story. Woods vary in color, density, and texture. You need to consider the characteristics of a specific wood in deciding how to finish it (Photo 17-1 on p. 220).

In most cases the woods you use are the same as those used hundreds of years ago. You're not the first to struggle with the choices of how best to finish a particular wood. You can learn a great deal by looking at how previous generations solved the problems. Often an image of how a wood should look comes from having seen it in a given style. You might aim to reproduce the look of a period piece, echo a familiar effect, or present a wood differently than people are used to seeing it.

Following is a discussion of the major considerations and problems you will encounter in finishing different woods, and some choices for finishes to use. The step-by-step finishing schedules I present are only suggestions, meant to illustrate the variety of ways to finish wood. I include a photo with each schedule to show how the finish finally looks. When I think one brand of finishing material is significantly better or more widely available than others, I name it. But in most cases there's not enough difference between brands of one type of product—wiping stain, paste wood filler, nitrocellulose lacquer—to be concerned with which brand you use. Keep in mind, too, that every stain, paste wood filler, glaze, and

Photo 17-1: Unfinished woods, clockwise from top: pine, oak, ash, elm, chestnut, walnut, mahogany, hard maple, birch, cherry, soft maple, gum, poplar, aromatic red cedar, teak, rosewood, cocobolo, and ebony.

Photo 17-2: When you stain pine, the porous earlywood accepts much more stain than the dense latewood. This causes a pronounced color reversal in the grain pattern: Compare unstained pine (left) with stained pine (right).

finish can be applied to every wood. You are making aesthetic decisions, so there are no absolute rules. People will disagree about what's best and what they prefer.

Pine

Pine is often the first wood used by beginning woodworkers. It's widely available, relatively inexpensive, and one of the easiest woods to cut and shape with machine and hand tools.

Yet pine may be the most difficult of all woods to finish. The earlywood (spring growth) of both white and yellow pine is soft, porous, and off-white. The latewood (summer growth) is very hard, dense, and orange. Thus, the earlywood and latewood react differently when sanded, stained, and finished, causing an uneven appearance that frustrates beginning and experienced woodworkers alike.

When you sand pine by hand, with only your fingers backing the sandpaper, you cut away the softer earlywood much faster than the latewood. This leaves depressions and ridges that become highlighted when you apply a finish.

When you apply a liquid stain and wipe off the excess, the stain penetrates deep into the porous earlywood but very little, or not at all, into the dense latewood. This uneven stain penetration causes a color reversal in the grain pattern. The light earlywood darkens considerably, while the orange latewood stays about the same (Photo 17-2).

When you finish pine with non-building finishes, such as oil and oil/varnish blend, or highly thinned finishes, such as wiping varnish, the finish soaks deep into the porous earlywood but hardly at all into the dense latewood. This results in an uneven sheen. The earlywood appears flat, even after several coats, while the latewood becomes glossy very quickly.

Pine also varies randomly in density throughout, in addition to earlywood and latewood variations. No matter how well you sand pine before staining, you often get blotches when you apply a stain. These blotches are caused by deeper stain penetration in less-dense areas that occur at random in the growth of pine trees. (See Photo 4-13 on p. 59.)

Historically, pine has usually been painted or finished unstained. Only in the last half century, with the increase in do-it-yourself projects, has there been much interest in staining pine. Often, staining is an attempt to make pine re-semble another wood, such as walnut or mahogany. But imitating other woods is almost impossible with pine because the grain is too pronounced to disguise.

Your best option for finishing pine (other than painting) is probably to leave it unstained and apply a film finish, such as varnish, lacquer, or water base. Ap-plying several coats gives you an even sheen across the porous earlywood and the dense latewood. Unstained pine is quite attractive. The wood turns a warm amber as it ages. All finishes except water base warm and deepen the coloring even more, becoming darker and richer with age. This look on pine has been popular in northern Europe for many years and was once popular in the United States (think of the "knotty pine" look that was so popular in the 1950s).

If you do decide to stain pine, there are two ways to reduce the problems of color reversal in the grain and blotching:
■ Washcoat the wood prior to staining.
■ Use a gel stain.

The method most commonly rec-ommended is to apply a washcoat of finish, which partially seals the wood. (See "Washcoating Before Applying Stain" on p. 63.) A common product,

Pine with Brushing Lacquer

Earlywood and latewood in pine have contrasting densities, but film finishes build quickly to produce an even sheen over both. Here I'm using brushing lacquer.

1 Sand to 180-grit and remove the sanding dust.

2 Brush on a coat of brushing lacquer. (My favorite is Deft Semi-Gloss Wood Finish because I like the soft sheen it produces.) Thin the finish, adding 10 percent or more lacquer thinner if you like, to make it easier to sand. Let the finish dry for at least two hours, better overnight.

3 Sand lightly with 280-grit or finer stearated sandpaper to remove dust nibs and roughness caused by raised grain. Remove the sanding dust.

4 Apply a full-strength coat and let it dry for at least two hours.

5 Sand lightly with 320-grit or finer stearated sandpaper to remove dust nibs. Remove the sanding dust.

6 Repeat Steps 4 and 5.

7 Apply the final coat full strength in as dust free an environment as possible. (If you achieve an even sheen with three coats, you don't need the fourth. Two or three coats of varnish or water base are usually adequate.) To get the final coat to level better, thin it with 10 percent or more lacquer thinner.

Toned Pine with Sprayed Lacquer

To tone wood, add a colorant (in this case, "light walnut") directly to a thinned topcoat (or topcoats) of finish. Because the wood has been sealed by the sealer coat, it won't blotch.

1 Sand to 180-grit and remove the sanding dust.

2 Spray a coat of lacquer sanding sealer or lacquer thinned half with lacquer thinner. If the pine has resinous knots, spray a coat of shellac.

3 Sand lightly with 280-grit or finer stearated sandpaper to make the surface smooth. Remove the sanding dust.

4 Add a lacquer stain or some dye or pigment (or combination) colorant to some lacquer and thin it with 4 to 6 parts lacquer thinner to make a toner. The thinning allows you to build the color slowly to maintain control. Spray as many coats as necessary to achieve the color you want on the wood. You can spray the coats one right after another as long as you don't get the surface so wet that the toner runs.

5 Spray a coat of lacquer thinned about half with lacquer thinner, and sand it smooth with 320-grit or finer sandpaper after it dries.

6 Spray as many topcoats as you need to give you the appearance you want.

usually labeled "Wood Conditioner," is widely available and marketed for the purpose of washcoating. (See "Wood Conditioner" on p. 64.) Washcoating is unpredictable, however, because the amount of finish solids you apply varies depending on the amount of thinner added and your application technique. You usually have to practice a bit to get the finish solids just right. Therefore, using a gel stain is the best option, in

my opinion, if you are staining only one or two objects at a time. The time spent mastering washcoating is justified only if you are staining multiple objects or are staining on a regular basis. Gel stains are applied just like liquid stains, but they don't blotch because they don't penetrate. (See "Thickness" on p. 55.)

In addition to the above two options, you can seal the wood entirely with a full coat of any finish and build all

Gel-Stained Pine with Satin Polyurethane Varnish

Gel stain effectively eliminates blotching in pine because the stain doesn't penetrate. Polyurethane provides excellent wear resistance.

1 Sand to 180-grit and remove the sanding dust.

2 Apply a gel stain (in this case, "oak"), and wipe off the excess. Move rapidly, as gel stain dries fairly quickly. Make your last wiping strokes follow the direction of the grain so that any streaks you leave will be disguised. Let the stain cure overnight.

3 Brush on a coat of satin polyurethane. To make it easier to sand, thin it half with mineral spirits. Let this sealer coat cure for 4 to 6 hours, better overnight.

4 Sand lightly with 280-grit or finer stearated sandpaper to make the surface smooth. Be careful not to sand through at the edges. Remove the sanding dust.

5 Brush on a second coat of satin polyurethane full strength, or thin it with 10 percent mineral spirits to improve flow-out and reduce bubbles. Let the finish cure overnight.

6 Sand lightly with 320-grit or finer stearated sandpaper to remove dust nibs, or, if there aren't any dust nibs, scuff with #000 or #0000 steel wool or a maroon or gray synthetic abrasive. Remove the sanding dust and repeat Step 5.

7 You can stop here or apply more coats if you want. Apply the last coat in as dust free an environment as possible, and thin the finish if you want it to level better.

Photo 17-3: This sample oak door has been dye-stained, sealed, and then glazed to accent the pores, all in different colors.

the color on top. There are two ways to build the color on top:

- Use a glaze.
- Tone the wood.

To use a glaze, apply a full coat of finish and let it dry. After sanding lightly, brush or wipe glaze over the surface and remove the amount necessary to give you the appearance you want. You can use a gel stain as a glaze. (See "Glazing" on p. 194.)

To tone the wood, add a compatible dye or pigment to your finish and apply it to the wood after you have sealed it. You will get the best results if you spray this colored finish, which is called a toner. (See "Toning" on p. 199.) You can also brush a varnish stain such as Minwax Polyshades, which won't obscure the wood much because it has so little pigment. But brushing leaves brush marks, which become more pronounced because of the pigment. It's best to apply one or two coats of clear finish over the toner to protect it from being scratched off the wood.

Personally, I like pine best when it's unstained and finished with a film finish.

Oak

Oak is almost as difficult to finish as pine. Like pine, oak varies greatly in density between earlywood and latewood. In contrast to pine, however, the earlywood pores of both red oak and white oak are very large—large enough to see with your naked eye. These pores give plainsawn oak, the most commonly used type, its coarse appearance.

When you sand plainsawn oak by hand with only your fingers backing the sandpaper, you cut away more of the porous earlywood than the dense latewood. You may not notice this while you're sanding, but when you apply a finish, you will see pronounced depressions in all the earlywood areas. (See Photo 14-3 on p. 183.)

Even when you sand with a flat backing block or power sander, a thick finish still rounds over somewhat in the porous earlywood areas producing a look that resembles plastic. Before the age of plastic this look may have been attractive, but I don't think it is now. You can create a more level appearance by filling the pores, but it takes a lot of work to make the surface truly level. Usually, the earlywood areas still dip somewhat. I find oak most attractive with a relatively thin finish that sharply defines the pores.

When you apply a common wiping stain to oak and wipe off the excess, the colorant lodges heavily in the large pores of the earlywood, but the colorant is almost all removed from the dense, latewood areas. The large-pored areas are thus highlighted in a way that accentuates the coarseness of the wood. This is especially the case with plainsawn oak. (See Photo 4-3 on p. 43.) I don't find this effect attractive.

On the other hand, the deep pores of oak offer certain advantages for decoration not found in most other woods. Colored paste wood filler or glaze can be used to make the pores a different color than the surrounding dense wood, which can be stained another color or left natural. (See "Filling Pores with Paste Wood Filler" on p. 96 and "Glazing" on p. 194.) Any color combination, for a wide range of effects, can be used (Photo 17-3).

Three very popular furniture styles feature oak: Old English and Mission (which are very dark), Golden (an even brown), and Modern (natural, unstained). These styles have one important characteristic in common: The earlywood/latewood contrast in the wood is deemphasized.

Oak with Satin Lacquer

Oak looks its best with a thin finish so the pores don't become rounded over. Any finish can be made to be thin on the wood. Just apply fewer coats, or thin the coats before applying them.

1 Sand the wood to 150- or 180-grit and remove the sanding dust.

2 Spray on a coat of lacquer sanding sealer or lacquer thinned half with lacquer thinner. Let it dry for several hours, better overnight.

3 Sand lightly with 280-grit or finer stearated sandpaper to remove dust nibs and any roughness caused by raised grain. Remove the sanding dust.

4 Spray on a coat of satin lacquer, and let it dry for several hours.

5 Sand lightly with 320-grit or finer stearated sandpaper if you need to remove dust nibs. Otherwise, sanding is not necessary.

6 Spray on a second coat of satin lacquer. Add additional coats if you want.

Oak with Walnut Oil/Varnish Blend

You can achieve a fairly even coloring on oak, despite its uneven grain, by using an asphaltum-based stain-and-finish combination.

1 Sand to 180-grit and remove the sanding dust.

2 Wipe or brush on a wet coat of walnut-colored oil/varnish blend. (I like to use either Watco or Deft black walnut Danish Oil.) Keep the finish wet on the surface for at least five minutes by applying more finish to spots that soak up the finish.

3 Wipe off all the excess finish before it becomes tacky. (Hang rags to dry and harden before throwing them in the trash.) Let the finish cure overnight in a warm room.

4 Apply a second coat of black walnut oil/varnish blend and sand it lightly with 600-grit wet/dry sandpaper while the surface is still wet with finish. Then wipe off the excess.

5 Repeat Step 3.

6 If the surface doesn't have a pleasing, even sheen, apply a third coat in the same manner as Step 4. Wipe off the excess finish.

Old English furniture was made with English brown oak, a variety that is darker than American red or white oak. The oak then became even darker over the centuries as the soot from open wood fireplaces and coal-burning stoves penetrated the commonly used wax finish.

Both Mission and Golden oak furniture from the early twentieth century were commonly made with quartersawn oak—that is, oak sawn radially, with the growth rings perpendicular to the face of the boards (Figure 17-1). Quartersawn oak has much more evenly spaced pores than plainsawn oak and a distinctive grain feature called *ray fleck* (Photo 17-4). *Rays* are hardwood cells that extend radially in a tree stem; in quartersawn oak they appear as elongated, dense, light-colored flecks. The rays resemble tiger stripes, so quartersawn oak is also known as "tiger oak." Sometimes the oak was colored by a process known as *fuming*. The furniture was placed in a room filled with the fumes of ammonia, which reacted with the tannic acid in the wood to darken it chemically. Fuming produces an even brown color in both earlywood and latewood, and also in the rays, which dye doesn't color as well.

You can imitate the even coloring of Old English Oak and Mission Oak by using a dye stain. Dyes penetrate everywhere in oak (except the rays), so the dense latewood is colored almost as completely as the porous earlywood. Any type of dye stain will work, but water-soluble dye doesn't color the pores well. Add color to the pores by applying a wiping stain of similar color over the dye stain (after it has dried) and wiping off the excess. The colorant will lodge in the pores, evening the color over the entire surface. To maintain the exact coloring produced by the dye stain, seal or washcoat the wood

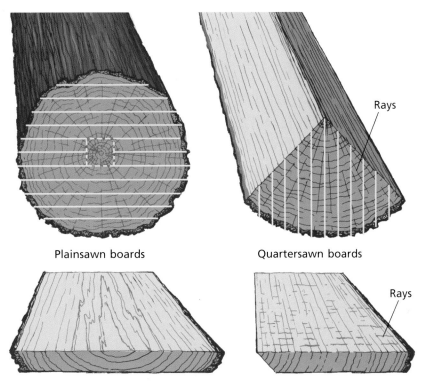

Plainsawn boards   Quartersawn boards

Figure 17-1: Logs can be plainsawn or quartersawn. In oak, quartersawing exposes the wood's rays as a "tiger-stripe" pattern on the face of the boards.

Photo 17-4: Because of oak's pronounced grain pattern, it's easy to distinguish a plainsawn board (left) from a quartersawn board (right). Note the ray flecks crossing the grain in the quartersawn board.

Pickled Oak with Satin Water Base

Pickling can be done by applying a white stain or water-thinned white latex paint directly to the wood and wiping off most of the excess or leaving it if you have brushed or sprayed it out evenly. Water-based finish doesn't add a yellow tint as other finishes do.

1 Sand to 150- or 180-grit and remove the sanding dust.

2 Wipe, brush, or spray a water-based, white pickling stain onto the wood. Alternatively, thin some white latex paint with up to 25 percent water and apply it to the wood. Wipe off most of the excess or leave it if it gives you the look you want. Let it cure overnight.

3 Brush or spray on a coat of satin water-based finish. Let it cure for at least two hours, better overnight.

4 Sand lightly with 220-grit or finer stearated sandpaper to smooth the raised grain. Don't sand any more than necessary to make the surface feel smooth. Remove the sanding dust.

5 Apply another coat of satin water-based finish.

6 Apply additional coats if you want more thickness. Sand between coats if necessary to remove dust nibs.

before applying the wiping stain. Alternatively, you can use an alcohol, oil, or NGR (non-grain-raising) dye stain to avoid the problem. Another alternative is walnut-colored Watco or Deft Danish oil. The colorant in these oil/varnish blends is asphaltum (tar), which penetrates much like a dye. You will achieve a fairly even dark walnut coloring.

You can imitate fumed oak in the same way, by applying an amber dye stain. It helps to then seal or washcoat the wood and apply and wipe off a brown wiping stain. This adds the correct color to the grain without shifting the color elsewhere. Remember, however, that early twentieth-century fuming was almost always done on quartersawn

Stained and Pickled Oak with Satin Lacquer

You can pickle only the grain of oak if you seal or washcoat the wood over the stain. A satin lacquer topcoat softens the effect.

1 Sand to 150- or 180-grit and remove the sanding dust.

2 Wipe, brush, or spray on a background color (in this case, "French Provincial") using an oil- or lacquer-based stain. Wipe off the excess.

3 Seal or washcoat the wood with lacquer or clear shellac. Let it dry for at least two hours, better overnight.

4 Apply a white pickling stain or thinned paint. You can use latex or oil paint. Remove the excess before it dries, and let it cure overnight.

5 Sand lightly with 280-grit or finer stearated sandpaper until smooth to the touch. Leave the pickling color only in the grain. Remove the sanding dust.

6 Spray on a coat of satin lacquer, and let it dry for several hours, better overnight.

7 Sand lightly with 320-grit or finer stearated sandpaper if you need to remove dust nibs. Otherwise, sanding is not necessary.

8 Apply additional coats if you want.

oak. You'll never achieve the same look using plainsawn oak.

Personally, I like oak best when the coarseness of the contrasting grain is deemphasized and the pores are left sharply defined. So I usually finish oak unstained, or stained with a dye or asphaltum. For a finish, I usually use an oil/varnish blend or wiping varnish, or I keep my film-finish coats thin on the wood. I also like oak pickled, with white in the pores.

Walnut

Walnut is America's supreme native furniture hardwood. It is a hard, durable wood with beautiful figure and rich,

Walnut with Oil/Varnish Blend

Oil/varnish blend is very easy to apply and provides some protection without building a noticeable film on the surface.

1 Sand to 180-grit and remove the sanding dust.

2 Wipe on a wet coat of oil/varnish blend. If any areas lose their wetness within several minutes, apply more finish.

3 Wipe off the excess after about five minutes.

4 Let the finish cure overnight in a warm room.

5 Sand lightly with 400-grit or finer sandpaper or rub with steel wool to remove the raised grain. Remove the sanding dust.

6 Wipe on a second coat of oil/varnish blend and wipe off the excess.

7 If the sheen is even and pleasing, you can stop here. Otherwise, apply another coat or two with one day's curing time between each.

dark coloring. It has a smooth, medium-porous texture that accepts all stains evenly, and it finishes nicely with any finish. The coloring of air-dried walnut heartwood is a warm reddish brown. The coloring of kiln-dried heartwood, which is commonly steamed to reduce heartwood and sapwood color variations, is a cooler, grayish brown. As steamed walnut ages, the gray warms, gaining a slight reddish tint. The reddish tint in aged walnut makes it difficult to distinguish from mahogany in old furniture.

There are two finishing problems presented by walnut: The color contrast between the dark heartwood and the almost-white sapwood, and the coolness of steamed walnut.

There are five ways to overcome the color contrast between heartwood and sapwood:

■ Cut away all the sapwood so you're using only heartwood.

- Arrange your boards so you use the color differences to decorative advantage.
- Bleach the wood to a uniform off-white color and then stain it back to whatever color you want. (See "Bleaching Wood" on p. 50.)
- Use a toner to bring the sapwood to the color of the heartwood. (See "Toning" on p. 199.)

- Apply an almost black dye stain (called a *sap stain*) to the sapwood before the other coloring and finishing steps.

Woodworkers making one-of-a-kind furniture usually choose one of the first two methods: They cut away the sapwood, or they use it decoratively. Bleaching walnut was common in factories in the 1950s when blond furniture was popular. Today furniture factories

Walnut with Orange Shellac and Wax

The amber color of orange shellac warms and enriches walnut's rather cool coloring. Use this finish on furniture or accessories not subject to heavy use; a tabletop finished this way should be protected with a tablecloth or coasters.

1. Sand to 150- or 180-grit and remove the sanding dust.

2. Brush or spray on a coat of 1-pound-cut orange shellac. (It can be either waxed or dewaxed shellac.) Let it dry at least two hours, better overnight.

3. Sand lightly with 280-grit or finer stearated sandpaper. Remove the sanding dust.

4. Brush or spray on a coat of 2-pound-cut orange shellac. Let it dry at least two hours, better overnight.

5. Rub with #00 or #000 steel wool in the direction of the grain. (If there are a lot of dust nibs, sand first with 320-grit or finer sandpaper.) Remove the dust.

6. Repeat Step 4.

7. Rub with #000 steel wool. Remove the dust.

8. Apply a coat of paste wax and remove the excess when it loses its shine. Leave overnight and wax again.

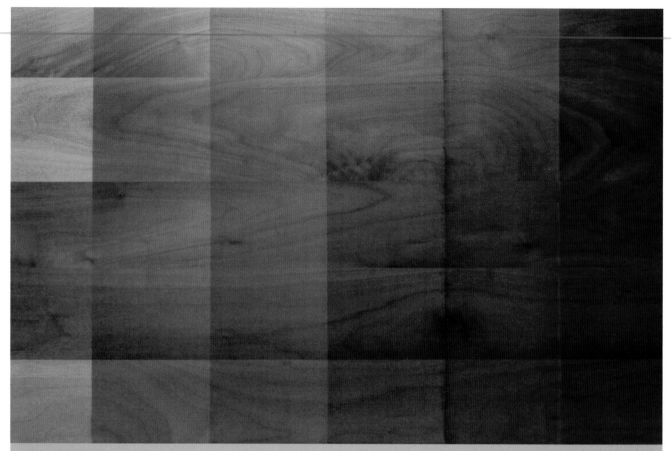

Walnut with Sap Stain and Lacquer Finish

You can bring the sapwood in walnut to the color of the heartwood by first applying a walnut sap stain. Then apply a background color and stain the wood with a wiping stain to further even the coloring. Finally, apply a finish. Here I'm demonstrating each step in turn, as might be done on a step panel. (See "Step Panel" on p. 202.)

1 Sand to 150- or 180-grit and remove the sanding dust.

2 Spray or brush (it's best to spray) a walnut sap stain onto the sapwood, "feathering" into neighboring heartwood. You can use a commercially available non-grain-raising (NGR) walnut sap stain, or you can make your own. Add between 10 and 20 percent black dye to a walnut-colored dye and adjust from there. The percentages will depend on the strength of the dyes you use. Practice on scrap wood first.

3 Spray on an NGR dye stain to bring coloring to the background color you want.

4 Apply a washcoat to separate the dye from the next step.

5 Wipe on an "American Walnut" wiping stain (burnt umber, or "walnut" with a slight reddish tint) and wipe off the excess.

6 Spray on a lacquer sanding sealer or lacquer thinned half with lacquer thinner. Let it dry for two hours, better overnight.

7 Sand lightly with 280-grit or finer stearated sandpaper and remove the sanding dust.

8 Spray on a coat of satin lacquer. Let it dry for at least two hours, better overnight.

9 Repeat Steps 7 (to remove dust nibs) and 8 if you want to add more coats.

use stains and toners to blend sapwood and heartwood.

You can warm the tone of walnut by staining or toning. Most finishes contain a natural amber tint that warms the wood a little. Orange shellac contains the most color, and it is often used on walnut for this reason, though it's not a durable finish for tabletops. Water-based finishes are totally devoid of color, so if you use water base on walnut, you may want to stain it first. (See Photo 13-1 on p. 172.)

Personally, I like just about any finish on walnut. I've used oil/varnish blend, wiping varnish, and film finishes. To warm the color of the wood, I typically stain with a dye or wiping stain that has the color of burnt umber. These stains are often labeled "American Walnut."

Mahogany

The mahogany available in the eighteenth and early nineteenth centuries was considered at the time to be the premier furniture hardwood. This mahogany was very dense and had a rich reddish brown color. It was generally known as Cuban or Santo Domingan mahogany, because it came from those islands.

Cuban and Santo Domingan mahogany were generally left unstained and unfilled. The natural color was so rich that the wood didn't need stain, and the wood was so dense (its pores are smaller than those of walnut) that it had a pleasing appearance without being filled. Because of the great widths available, new styles of tabletops were developed—most notably, large pie-crust tables.

Unfortunately, this mahogany is no longer available. The best mahogany commonly available today is Honduran mahogany. Though Honduran maho-

gany is the same botanical species as Cuban and Santo Domingan mahogany, it is softer, less rich in color, and it has larger pores—the result of different soil and growing conditions. Still, Honduran mahogany is a fine furniture wood.

Honduran mahogany grows in Honduras and other countries in Central America and northern South America. Right after being milled, it is pink in color. It darkens in air and light to a rich coppery red. Honduran mahogany is very stable and works well, though it does have an interlocking grain that can be tricky to plane. The interlocking grain is the result of the tree

Photo 17-5: Figure in mahogany varies from plain (left) to ribbon stripe (right), which is the result of quartersawing.

Mahogany with Wiping Varnish

Wiping varnish is an easy finish to apply, and it maintains mahogany's natural look. Because the finish is thin on the wood, it doesn't round-over the pores. The wood darkens significantly after a few years.

1 Sand to 180-grit and remove the sanding dust.

2 Wipe or brush on a coat of wiping varnish. Wipe off most of the excess if it is thick and uneven. Let it cure overnight. (See "Wiping Varnish" on p. 155.)

3 Sand lightly with 280-grit or finer sandpaper until the surface feels smooth. Remove the sanding dust.

4 Repeat Steps 2 and 3.

5 Repeat Step 2 in as dust free an environment as possible.

6 If the sheen is more glossy than you want, lower it by rubbing lightly with #0000 steel wool.

growing in alternating spiral annular rings. When the wood is quartersawn, a distinct ribbon-stripe pattern is revealed (Photo 17-5 on p. 233). Quartersawn mahogany that has a pronounced pattern is typically sliced into veneer.

Other mahoganies available are African mahogany and Philippine mahogany. Though neither of these woods is a true mahogany in the botanical sense, both resemble Honduran mahogany and are commonly sold as mahogany.

African mahogany is coarser, less stable, and weaker than Honduran mahogany. The grain patterns are somewhat wilder, with more contrast, though the overall coloring and the way it darkens with age are the same.

Philippine mahogany, which is more commonly called lauan (pronounced loo-ahn), is coarser and weaker than either Honduran or African mahogany. Its pores are much larger, making it a more difficult wood to finish nicely. Hollow-core doors used in house construction

Stained and Filled Mahogany with Rubbed Lacquer

This finish involves some extra effort, but the result is elegant: a mirror sheen with great depth.

1 Sand to 150- or 180-grit and remove the sanding dust.

2 Apply a water-soluble dye stain (in this case, "brown mahogany") and wipe off the excess before it dries, or spray on a non-grain-raising (NGR) dye stain and leave it. Let the water-soluble dye dry overnight.

3 Brush or spray on a washcoat of shellac or lacquer. (See "Washcoats" on p. 64.) Let it dry for several hours.

4 Brush on a coat of oil-based paste wood filler. (See "Using Oil-Based Paste Wood Filler" on p. 100.)

5 When it loses its shine, remove the excess filler by wiping across the grain with clean burlap. Then wipe lightly in the direction of the grain with a soft cloth to align any streaks with the grain. Let the filler cure overnight, or longer if the weather is humid or cool.

6 Repeat Steps 4 and 5.

7 Sand lightly with 320-grit or finer stearated sandpaper to smooth the surface. Remove the sanding dust.

8 Repeat Steps 3 and 7.

9 Spray on four to six coats of lacquer, no more than three per day.

10 Let the lacquer harden for up to two weeks, or until you can

no longer smell lacquer thinner when you press your nose against the surface.

11 Level and rub the top surface following the instructions in "Leveling and Rubbing" on p. 214. Rub the surface to whatever sheen you want.

12 Because you seldom see reflections on lower vertical surfaces, you can usually get adequate results on the sides, aprons, and legs by simply rubbing with the rubbing abrasives you used on the top. You don't have to level these surfaces first.

13 Apply a silicone furniture polish or paste wax.

Stained and Glazed Mahogany with Lacquer

Glazing can be used to accentuate depth and emphasize the sculptural quality of molded, carved, or turned pieces by darkening the hollows and crevices.

1 Sand to 150- or 180-grit and remove the sanding dust.

2 Wipe or spray on a lacquer stain and wipe off the excess while it is still wet. Let it dry for about an hour.

3 Spray on a coat of lacquer sanding sealer and let it dry for two hours, better overnight.

4 Sand lightly with 280-grit or finer sandpaper and remove the sanding dust.

5 Wipe, brush, or spray on an oil-based glaze. When it loses its shine, wipe off the excess from all high places, leaving glaze in the recesses. Spray a mist coat of lacquer within two hours, or let the glaze cure overnight in a warm room.

6 Spray two or three coats of satin lacquer, allowing at least two hours between coats. Let the finish dry overnight.

are commonly veneered with lauan. Though lauan also darkens with age and can be made to look fairly elegant by filling the pores, it is not a quality furniture wood like Honduran and African mahogany.

The high-quality mahogany available in the eighteenth and early nineteenth centuries was usually left unstained and unfilled. When mahogany came back in style in the late nineteenth century and again in the 1920s and 1930s with Duncan Phyfe reproductions, only the poorer-quality Honduran and African varieties were available. Furniture made of these mahoganies was almost always stained with dye stain, and the pores were almost always filled.

Both Honduran and African mahogany take all types of stain evenly. Before deciding to stain mahogany, however, remember that the wood will darken considerably within a couple of years. If you stain the wood to the color you want, you may find that it soon becomes darker than you want. Consequently, you might decide to stain the wood only half way to the color you want.

Woodworkers today often finish mahogany without staining or filling. They often apply an oil/varnish blend or a wiping varnish. The wood darkens and reddens in time, and both finishes can be kept thin enough so that the pores don't take on a rounded-over, plastic appearance.

Personally, I like mahogany better with a rich brown dye stain, not too red (there being enough red in the wood already), the pores filled (at least on tabletops), and a lacquer finish rubbed to an even semigloss. This finish makes the lesser-quality Honduran and African mahogany resemble Cuban and Santo Domingan mahogany.

Dyeing brings out the maximum beauty of maple, especially curly and bird's-eye maple. A film finish deepens the coloring.

1 Sand to 150- or 180-grit and remove the sanding dust.

2 Dewhisker the wood. (See "Dewhiskering" on p. 14.)

3 Apply an amber-colored water-soluble dye stain: for example, Lockwood's "Honey Amber Maple." Wipe off the excess stain before it dries. To achieve better "pop" in the curls or bird's eyes, apply several highly thinned coats of dye (try five or ten parts thinner) and sand or scrape off the color between the curls or bird's eyes after each coat. Leave the color in the curls or bird's eyes. The color there will darken with each application. Slowly increase the darkening of the curls or bird's eyes until you get the effect you want while the wood is damp with dye. Then intensify the effect even more with an application of boiled linseed oil after the dye dries.

4 Brush or spray on a coat of 1-pound-cut blond shellac. Let it dry for several hours. (If you applied linseed oil, let it cure for a week before applying the shellac or any other finish.)

5 Sand lightly with 320-grit or finer stearated sandpaper to remove raised grain. Remove the sanding dust.

6 Brush or spray on a coat of 2-pound-cut blond shellac. Let it dry for several hours.

7 Sand lightly with 320-grit sandpaper and remove the sanding dust.

8 Repeat Steps 6 and 7.

9 Apply a final coat of 1-pound-cut blond shellac and leave it, or rub the finish with #0000 steel wood lubricated with wax.

Dyed and Shellacked Maple

Photo courtesy of the maker: Chris Christenberry

Maple with Wiping Varnish

For decorative objects made of maple, wiping varnish gives a pleasing gloss and warms the color of the wood.

1 Sand to 400-grit or finer on the lathe and remove the sanding dust.

2 Wipe on a thin coat of wiping varnish and let it cure for at least four hours, better overnight. (See "Wiping Varnish" on p. 155.)

3 Sand lightly with 320-grit or finer stearated sandpaper to remove dust nibs and any roughness caused by raised grain. If the sandpaper doesn't conform well to the shape, use #00 or #000 steel wool. Remove the sanding dust.

4 Wipe on a second coat of wiping varnish. Let it cure overnight.

5 If the second coat will not be your last coat, buff with #000 or #0000 steel wool or with 400-grit sandpaper.

6 If the sheen is not even or if you want to build a thicker finish, wipe on additional coats. Between coats, rub with steel wool or sand lightly to remove dust nibs.

7 If the final coat is glossier than you want, wait a day or two and rub lightly with #0000 steel wool. Use an oil or wax lubricant to soften the scratching.

Hard Maple

Maple is an excellent wood for woodworking. It is strong and wear-resistant, and it works well. It makes very good flooring because it wears slowly, smoothly, and evenly without splintering. It is also the best wood for kitchen cutting boards because it is dense, fine-grained, and free of any odor or taste that might be imparted to food. Hard maple comes from the sugar maple tree, the same tree that produces the sap that is made into maple syrup. Unusual growth patterns in sugar maple result in the distinctive and attractive figures of *curly* and *bird's-eye* maple (Photo 17-6). Maple with a tightly curled figure is called *fiddleback* maple because it is often used for the backs of violins.

Maple is more difficult to finish than most woods. The problem is that most maple is so light and its figure so subtle that it is uninteresting without stain. The exceptions are curly and bird's-eye maple, though these grain variations are also greatly enhanced with stain. To successfully stain maple, you must use a dye stain. Many woodworkers and finishers use pigment or wiping stains on maple and are unhappy with the results.

The reason for the problem is the density of the wood. The pores in maple are not large enough to accept much pigment. So pigment stains don't have much effect unless you build the pigment on top, which obscures the wood. This goes for curly and bird's-eye maple as well. Though pigment stain highlights the curls and bird's eyes, it doesn't do so nearly as effectively as dye stain. With dye stain you can make maple any color you want and as dark as you want, without obscuring its figure. You can even make the wood black. (See "Ebonizing Wood" on p. 55.)

When maple was used in the eighteenth and early nineteenth centuries, it was generally left unstained. That maple

now has a warm amber color, but age alone can't account for this color change. I suspect that linseed oil was applied to the wood, and it is the darkening of the linseed oil that produces this color. You can, of course, achieve the same thing with linseed oil, but it will take a number of years for the color to develop. (See Photo 5-6 on p. 86.) It's much quicker to imitate this color with an amber dye.

Maple does have a tendency to blotch when stained, however (though not nearly as much as cherry or birch does). So when amber-colored maple became popular in furniture in the 1950s, factories usually toned rather than stained the wood. They added a little pigment to the lacquer finish.

More recently, handmade maple furniture has been left unstained, largely, I

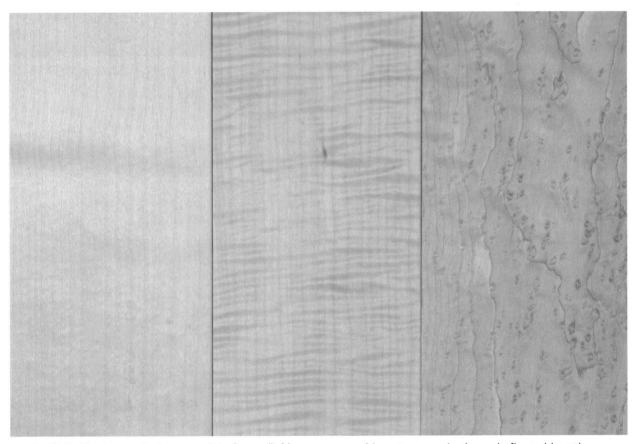

Photo 17-6: Maple can display very plain figure (left) or more graphic patterns, as in the curly figured board (center) or the bird's eye (right).

Maple with Water Base

To keep maple as close to its natural color as possible with a protective finish, use a water-based finish.

1 Sand to 150- or 180-grit and remove the sanding dust.

2 Brush or spray on a coat of water-based finish. (To reduce the grain raising this will cause, you can dewhisker the wood first. See "Dewhiskering" on p. 14.)

3 Let the finish cure for at least two hours, better overnight, then sand it with 220- to 320-grit sandpaper to remove the raised grain. Stearated sandpaper will work best.

4 Remove the sanding dust, and apply a second coat. Let it cure for at least two hours and sand with 320-grit or finer stearated sandpaper to remove dust nibs.

5 Brush or spray on a third coat of satin water-based finish in as dust free an environment as possible.

believe, because woodworkers haven't understood the results that could be achieved with dye. But unstained maple does have its own appeal.

I believe that maple has much more character with a dye stain. I also like maple better with a film finish, though I don't object to maple finished with an oil/varnish blend. Film finishes bring out more of the wood's character, because the thickness adds depth.

Cherry

Cherry has been a popular furniture wood since the eighteenth century. It was often used as a native American substitute for imported mahogany. Cherry was sometimes stained to accelerate the darkening process, but it was usually left unstained to darken naturally. In the 1950s cherry became very popular in mass-produced furniture. Factories would usually tone the cherry rather than stain it. Toning evens the color differences between heartwood and sapwood without causing blotching.

In recent years cherry has become one of the most popular woods used by woodworkers making one-of-a-kind furniture. Its popularity is so great that it is now among the most expensive domestic hardwoods. Cherry is popular for several reasons. Most important is its association with the warm, translucent, rust-red color found on antique cherry furniture. Also, cherry is an easy wood to work. It has a pleasant scent when being machined, especially when contrasted with the smell of most other woods. And it has a familiar name that is associated with a tasty fruit (even though the cherry trees that produce the wood don't produce that fruit).

In spite of its popularity, cherry is a difficult wood to finish. Freshly milled cherry doesn't have the warm, even,

Cherry Aged Naturally with Gel Varnish

Exposure to light and oxygen causes cherry to darken naturally. Noticeable darkening occurs very quickly, but it takes many years or decades to reach the widely appreciated warm, rust-red color common on cherry antiques. Gel varnish is easy to apply without blotching and produces a soft satin sheen.

1 Sand to 150- or 180-grit and remove the sanding dust.

2 Wipe on a coat of gel varnish and wipe off most or all of the excess before the varnish cures. Let it cure for 4 to 6 hours, better overnight. (Gel varnish cures to a non-workable state fairly rapidly, so it's best to complete one section of a large object at a time.)

3 Sand lightly with 280-grit or finer sandpaper to remove dust nibs.

4 Repeat Step 2 several times until you get the look you want. Sand between coats if there are any flaws you want to remove.

Toned Cherry with Rubbed Lacquer

Toning (adding a colorant to the topcoats of your finish) can be used to even the coloring between sapwood and heartwood without highlighting blotching. Rubbing to a satin sheen gives the finish a more refined appearance.

1 Sand to 150- or 180-grit and remove the sanding dust.

2 Spray on one or two coats of thinned non-grain-raising

(NGR) dye stain to bring out the figure in the wood. Use a cherry color. Let the dye dry for an hour.

3 Spray on a coat of lacquer sanding sealer or a coat of lacquer thinned half with lacquer thinner. Let it dry for several hours, better overnight.

4 Sand with 280-grit or finer stearated sandpaper until

smooth. Remove the sanding dust.

5 Spray on several coats of toner composed of a cherry-colored pigment/dye combination mixed 1:1 with lacquer and thinned with 4 to 6 parts lacquer thinner. You can use a commercial lacquer stain for the colorant, or you can use NGR dye and industrial tinting colorants (pigment). Mix a

little yellow and black with red.

6 If there is sapwood mixed in with the heartwood, spray more toner on the sapwood to blend it in. Let the toner dry for several hours, better overnight.

7 Sand very lightly with 400-grit or finer stearated sandpaper if you need to remove dust nibs. Remove the sanding dust.

8 Spray on 4 to 8 coats of lacquer. Sand lightly between coats if you need to remove dust nibs. Use any sheen of lacquer, but the last coat should be approximately the sheen you will rub into the top.

9 Sand the topcoat with 600-grit wet/dry sandpaper using a mixture of mineral oil and mineral spirits as a lubricant. Or use a commercial rubbing lubricant. Back the sandpaper with a flat block, and sand until you have removed all orange peel.

10 Clean off the surface with a soft cloth and naphtha.

11 Repeat Steps 9 and 10 using 1000-grit sandpaper.

12 Rub with #0000 steel wool and a wax or oil lubricant. Rub the apron and legs if you want.

rust-red, coloring of old cherry. New cherry is usually pink to light red in color. But the color can also have a grayish cast. Different boards vary in color, and the color often varies significantly even in the same board. In addition, the figure is far more pronounced in newly cut cherry than in old cherry, which has mellowed considerably. Because the look of old cherry takes many years to develop naturally, many woodworkers try to imitate it immediately using stain.

The problem with staining is that cherry often blotches. In this way, cherry resembles pine and birch. In addition, even if you do achieve an even, rust-red color with stain (Lockwood's "Antique Cherry" water-soluble dye stain is the best stain I've found to accomplish this), the cherry may continue to darken through its natural process until it becomes too dark. Therefore, it's usually best to choose your boards very carefully so they match well and contain little or no sapwood. Then let the cherry darken naturally. (You can accelerate the natural darkening by applying a coat of boiled linseed oil and letting it cure for a week before applying the finish.) If you do decide to color cherry, try to use boards either without a blotchy figure or with an attractive blotchy pattern. To color cherry while minimizing the blotchiness, use gel stain or tone the wood.

Gel stain has a good track record as a stain for cherry. The early Bartley cherry-furniture kits included this stain, and users had great success with it. The downside is that the stain doesn't add a lot of color, nowhere near enough to approximate the deep color of antique cherry.

Toning requires that you have access to spray equipment, but applying a toner gives you great control over the

NOTE

Despite the information provided here, old cherry that has darkened naturally is actually quite impossible to match exactly with stains or toners. The color can be matched well, but neither the stain nor toner can recreate the translucence of naturally aged cherry.

coloring process. Use a dye toner when your primary goal is to make the wood darker without obscuring the figure. Use a pigment toner when your primary goal is to mute the figure. When applying toner to an entire surface, I find that it's usually best to use a combination of dye and pigment, just as factories do with almost all contemporary cherry furniture. But boards vary, so make your decisions as you proceed.

You will sometimes encounter the suggestion to use lye or potassium dichromate to make cherry look old. Both do darken cherry considerably, and it is sometimes possible to approximate the look of old cherry quite closely with either. There are several problems, however, in addition to the obvious one that the cherry will continue to darken on its own.

Both chemicals are somewhat hazardous to use, so protect your eyes and skin well. Lye can be reactivated to become a stripper if water gets through a finish and into the wood. So be sure to neutralize the lye with an acid such as vinegar. (See "Lye" on p. 294.) Also, using any chemical to color wood is somewhat unpredictable. The color may come out uneven, or you may get the color too dark and then not be able to lighten it short of sanding it out or bleaching the wood.

Because of these problems, I don't recommend lye or potassium dichromate as stains for cherry. I prefer to let the cherry age naturally or use a dye stain (if blotching isn't a problem), gel stain, or toner. I also prefer a film finish on cherry rather than oil or oil/varnish blend, because a film finish provides more depth and richness. But many woodworkers like to use an oil/varnish blend, probably because it's so easy to apply, and I don't find the results objectionable.

NOTE

It's almost always best to use a dye toner when coloring sapwood to match heartwood. A pigment toner applied just to the sapwood will muddy it and make it look noticeably different than the heartwood, where the figure will be bright and well defined.

Ash, Elm, and Chestnut

The grain structure of ash, elm, and chestnut is very similar to that of oak. Furniture manufacturers have often substituted these woods for oak or mixed these woods with oak. After staining, it takes a trained eye to identify which is which.

When you stain ash, elm, or chestnut with a pigment stain, the same problem occurs as with oak: The natural coarseness of the woods is made even more pronounced. But the problem is not as severe as with oak because the latewood growth of these woods is not as dense. The latewood of ash, elm, and chestnut retains more pigment than the latewood of oak, so the overall coloring is more even. Nevertheless, the techniques for minimizing the coarse look of oak work well with ash, elm, and chestnut.

I like ash, elm, and chestnut finished in the same ways I suggest for oak: no stain, a dye stain, toned with pigment, or pickled; then a thin finish to leave the pores sharply defined.

Aromatic Red Cedar

Aromatic red cedar is commonly used in cedar chests because its odor repels moths. On the inside of a chest the cedar is seldom, if ever, stained or finished because it has beautiful natural color, and finishing would seal in the odor that makes the wood effective. When it's on the outside of a chest, the cedar is usually finished but not stained.

Problems occur when you finish any part of the inside of a cedar chest, whether the part is cedar or not. The cedar's aromatic solvents build up

Toned Ash with Satin Lacquer

Toning is an effective way to evenly color any uneven-grained wood or to mute the contrast created by stain. Satin lacquer further quiets the effect.

1 Sand to 150- or 180-grit and remove the sanding dust.

2 Wipe or spray on a coat of lacquer stain. Wipe off the excess before it dries. Let it dry for one hour.

3 Spray on a coat of lacquer sanding sealer or lacquer thinned half with lacquer thinner. Let it dry for two hours, better overnight.

4 Sand with 280-grit or finer stearated sandpaper until smooth. Remove the sanding dust.

5 Spray on a toner made of lacquer and lacquer stain or pigment thinned with 4 to 6 parts lacquer thinner. Spray the toner until you get the color and effect you want.

6 Spray on two or three coats of satin lacquer. Sand lightly between coats with 320-grit or finer stearated sandpaper if you need to remove dust nibs or other flaws.

enough gas inside the chest to soften most finishes, causing them to become sticky. To avoid the problem, leave all inside parts unfinished.

I think aromatic red cedar on the outside of a piece of furniture looks best unstained and finished with a film finish.

Soft Maple, Gum, and Poplar

Soft maple, gum, and poplar are easy-to-work, relatively inexpensive hardwoods that are traditionally used in furniture as "secondary" woods. Factories as well as custom furniture makers use them for the structural parts of tables, chests, and chairs, using a nicer wood or veneer for more prominent parts. Utility woods are usually dye-stained (when visible) to resemble the better-quality wood, and many people don't realize the difference.

There are two problems with finishing soft maple, gum, and poplar: their plain figure and their low density, as compared with woods such as hard maple and walnut. The plain figure is usually uninteresting unless it is stained. You can use pigment or dye, but you'll be able to get much darker colors with dye. The low density usually requires that you apply a film finish rather than an oil/varnish blend to give the woods enough sheen to look nice.

I like these woods finished with a film finish. I use either pigment or dye, depending on how dark I want the wood to get.

Birch

Birch can look similar to maple and is sometimes mistaken for maple. Birch has the same characteristic of high density, so it also doesn't accept much pigment stain. But birch usually has a more swirly grain, so it blotches more than maple. If the blotching is more than you can tolerate, build the color on top using a

Dyed Poplar with Water Base

Poplar has very little character unless stained to resemble another wood, often walnut. Water-based polyurethane is a tough finish, well suited to high-wear applications.

1 Sand to 150- or 180-grit and remove the sanding dust.

2 Brush on a walnut-colored, oil-soluble dye stain in long strokes with the grain. You can substitute Watco or Deft black walnut Danish oil, in which case, wipe off all the excess stain and let it cure a week before applying the water-based finish. (Don't use a water-soluble or NGR dye under water base if you are brushing; you may lift and smear the color.)

3 Brush on a coat of satin, water-based polyurethane. Let it cure for at least two hours, better overnight.

4 Sand lightly with 320-grit or finer stearated sandpaper if you need to remove dust nibs or other flaws. Remove the sanding dust.

5 Repeat Steps 3 and 4.

6 Brush on a final coat in as dust free an environment as possible.

Dyed Birch with French Polish

You can make birch resemble mahogany by applying a dye stain. (The top drawer of this birch chest is veneered with mahogany.) Shellac applied with the French polishing method creates a deep mirror-gloss finish.

1 Sand to 150- or 180-grit and remove the sanding dust.

2 Dewhisker the wood. (See "Dewhiskering" on p. 14.)

3 Wipe on a coat of water-soluble dye stain (in this case, "mahogany") and wipe off the excess before it dries. Let it dry overnight.

4 Sand very lightly with used 400-grit stearated sandpaper. Be careful not to cut through the stain, especially on the edges.

5 Remove the sanding dust.

6 Brush on a coat of 1-pound-cut blond shellac. Let it dry for two hours, better overnight.

7 Sand lightly with 320-grit or finer sandpaper to remove raised grain and dust nibs. Remove the sanding dust.

8 Repeat Steps 6 and 7.

9 French polish the surface, covering all parts three or four times, or until the surface has an even gloss. (See "French Polishing" on p. 131.)

10 Remove the oil by wiping with a naphtha-dampened cloth.

11 Apply a silicone furniture polish or paste wax.

toner instead of trying to put it in the wood. If you use a dye in your finish, you'll get an even color without obscuring the wood.

Birch, along with maple, was often dye-stained red and used to imitate cherry and mahogany in furniture made at the turn of the twentieth century. I like to finish birch the same way I finish maple. If blotchiness will be a problem, I use maple instead.

Rosewood with Wax

Wax has a minimal effect on the natural color of rosewood.

1 Sand to 400-grit or finer on the lathe and remove the sanding dust.

2 Apply a coat of paste wax. Remove the excess when the shine disappears. Let the wax dry overnight.

3 Apply a second coat of paste wax. Remove the excess when the shine disappears. (On less-dense woods, apply additional coats to achieve an even satin sheen.)

4 Buff the surface by hand or machine with a lamb's-wool pad until all streaking is removed and the sheen is even.

Oily Woods

Many woodworkers like to use colorful exotic hardwoods such as teak, rosewood, bubinga, cocobolo, and ebony for decorative purposes, sometimes as accents to other woods, but also for whole pieces of furniture. It's rare that these hardwoods are stained; their natural beauty is the reason these expensive woods are used in the first place. But they are almost always finished, and the oil they naturally contain can cause problems.

The most common problem is that the finish sometimes takes a long time to cure. This can occur when you use oil, oil/varnish blend, or varnish. The oil in these woods gets into the finish and retards the curing.

The other problem occurs with lacquer, two-part finishes, and water base. The oil prevents these finishes from establishing a good bond with the wood.

You can prevent both problems by wiping the surface of the wood with a cloth dampened with a fast-evaporating solvent such as naphtha or lacquer thinner. This cleans the oil off the wood surface. Apply the finish quickly after the solvent evaporates so the oil doesn't have time to bleed back to the surface.

On objects made entirely from exotic woods, I use an oil/varnish blend or wiping varnish when I want the pores sharply defined. I build a thicker film finish when I want more protection. I sometimes use only wax when the object is decorative and won't be handled much. On objects where exotic woods are used as trim or decorative accent, I use whatever finish is appropriate for the object as a whole.

Caring for
the Finish

Of all finishing subjects, caring for the finish is by far the most misrepresented by product manufacturers. Claims range from half-truths, such as "Furniture polish preserves the finish," to outright absurdities, such as "Furniture polish replaces the natural oils in wood." The success of the furniture polish industry in convincing millions of consumers that there's oil in wood that needs replacing has to rank among the great scams of American marketing.

Deceptive marketing has shifted the emphasis away from the real benefits of furniture polish as an aid in dusting, cleaning, and adding scent to a room. In addition, some furniture polish manufacturers have totally misrepresented the beneficial role of wax. Instead of pointing out its long-lasting shine and wear resistance, they've made wax into a problem, claiming that it keeps wood from breathing by stopping up its pores, and that it builds up to create a smeary surface.

Enough confusion has been created to spawn a thriving sub-industry, which specializes in miracle remedies and operates out of antique and home-and-garden shows. This "snake oil" business markets essentially the same substances as the primary industry at three to four

Photo 18-1: Bright ultraviolet light, especially direct sunlight, causes colors to fade and finishes to crack and craze. Crazing is evident everywhere on this 100-year-old drawer front, except in the center, where a drawer pull blocked the light. There, the finish is like new.

MYTH

Furniture polish feeds or moisturizes wood.

FACT

To do this, the oily solvent in furniture polish would have to penetrate a finish whose primary purpose is to keep liquids such as soft drinks, perspiration, water, and "oily solvent" out of wood. When furniture looks dull or dry, it's not because there's something wrong or missing in the wood; it's simply because the finish has deteriorated. When the shine from the furniture polish you've applied disappears, it's not because the polish has gone into the wood; it's because the polish has evaporated.

times the price. Its success demonstrates that there are serious misunderstandings about furniture care.

To get a grasp on what you're trying to accomplish in caring for the finish on your furniture, you need to understand why finishes deteriorate in the first place and how the deterioration can be slowed. It also helps to understand exactly what paste wax and liquid furniture polish are and what they do. Then you can make intelligent decisions about how you want to care for your furniture—or how you advise your clients.

Causes of Finish Deterioration

Finishes deteriorate as a result of the following conditions:

- exposure to strong light
- oxidation
- physical abuse, including contact with heat, water, solvents, and chemicals

Strong Light

Light, especially sunlight, is the natural element most destructive to finishes. Consider how much faster paint deteriorates on the south side of a house than

Applying Liquid Furniture Polish

Applying liquid furniture polish is simple, but the method can vary depending upon whether you are just removing dust or are using the polish to raise the sheen. In either case, make sure the surface of the finish is not dirty. If it is, wash it with a mild soap such as dishwashing liquid or Murphy's Oil Soap.

If you are using the polish solely to remove dust, lightly dampen a soft cloth with the liquid and wipe over the finish. Dust will cling to the dampened cloth. You should not be leaving a significant wetness on the surface.

If you are using the polish to raise the sheen of the finish or to make the surface slick to reduce scratching, apply enough polish to the soft cloth to make it wet. Wipe the finish. Alternatively, you can spray the liquid directly on the finish and wipe it around with the cloth: Wet the finish with polish, then remove all the excess.

If you don't remove the excess each time, you may get a buildup of dust and dirt mixed with wax or silicone, if either wax or silicone is contained in the polish. You will notice that the finish starts showing fingerprints and is sticky. (This is often referred to incorrectly as "wax buildup.") To remove the stickiness, wash the surface with a mild soap, or wipe over with naphtha or mineral spirits. Your cloth will become dirty, and the finish underneath may be dull. The dullness has been caused by age, not by the furniture polish. Reapply your furniture polish. It will raise the sheen again, as long as the finish is still in good shape. If there is no finish underneath, you should refinish.

MYTH

Furniture polish replaces natural oils in wood.

FACT

Common furniture woods never contained natural oils, and no wood "needs" oil. Even the few exotics such as teak and rosewood that do contain natural oil don't need it replaced, especially not with the petroleum-based solvents contained in furniture polishes. In fact, the oil in these woods causes problems for the finish, as I've pointed out in earlier chapters.

on the north side. Or how much faster the paint on a car dulls when it's parked daily in the sun instead of under cover. Even indoor light eventually takes its toll on a finish (Photo 18-1).

Oxidation

Oxidation is the second most destructive natural element. Oxygen combines with almost all elements, changing them into their oxides. The process is slow, but it's an important factor in the deterioration of materials. Oxidation causes most finishes to darken, and all finishes eventually to crack, even without the accelerating effect of light.

Physical Abuse

All finishes can be physically damaged by coarse objects, heat, water, solvents, acids, and alkalis. Some finishes, such as polyurethane and catalyzed finishes, are more resistant than others, but still they can be damaged.

Preventing Finish Deterioration

So what can you do to prevent deterioration caused by light, oxidation, and physical abuse? Actually, most of what you can do is fairly passive. Active care accomplishes relatively little. (See

CAUTION

Some soap manufacturers suggest you wash your furniture regularly with soap and water. Though mild natural soaps, such as Ivory (made from animal fat and lye) and Murphy's Oil Soap (made from vegetable oil and lye), won't damage a finish, excessive contact with water will. If there are any cracks in the finish, water will get underneath and cause the finish to peel from the wood. Excessive contact with water will also cause concave warping in tabletops if the finish has deteriorated or been worn off. Use soap and water on furniture only when the furniture is dirty!

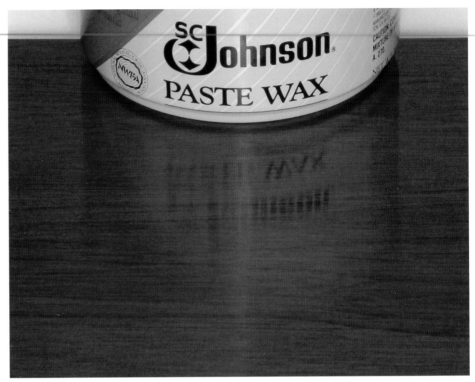

Photo 18-2: A primary function of paste wax and furniture polish is to raise the sheen of dull surfaces. Paste wax does this fairly permanently; liquid polishes are usually more temporary. Paste wax has been applied to the right side of this panel.

MYTH

Furniture polish moisturizes the finish, slowing the process of drying out and cracking.

FACT

Furniture polish has no effect on cured finishes, good or bad, except to add shine and scratch resistance. To have an effect would actually be disastrous, because "moisturizing" would cause the finish to soften and turn gummy. When a finish does soften, it's usually because of repeated contact with acidic body oils, or strong soaps or other chemicals, over an extended time.

"Deterioration Causes and Preventions" on facing page.)

Passive Care

The best way to care for the finish on your furniture is to keep it covered or away from destructive elements. Here are few examples:

- To shield furniture from strong light, place it away from direct sunlight, make use of curtains and shades, keep your tabletops covered with a tablecloth, and throw a sheet over your better furniture when on vacation.
- To slow oxidation, don't store furniture in an attic or other area that gets extremely hot. Heat accelerates oxidation.
- To minimize physical damage, use hot pads, coasters, place mats, and tablecloths. (But don't keep your tables covered with plastic; the plastic and the finish may stick together.)

Active Care

Active care entails applying paste wax or a liquid furniture polish to your furniture regularly. (See "Applying Liquid Furniture Polish" on p. 251.) But neither paste wax nor furniture polish retards the destructive forces of light or oxidation. Nor does wax or polish protect against damage from heat, solvents, or water. Though both cause water to bead up and run off of vertical surfaces, neither stops the penetration of water on horizontal surfaces. The film of wax or oily solvent is too thin, and there are always pores or scratches large enough for water to pass through.

Paste wax and liquid furniture polish protect only against wear. They reduce friction, so objects tend to slide over rather than dig into the finish. (See "Furniture Polish Overview" on p. 254.)

In addition to wear protection, paste wax and liquid furniture polish add shine

Deterioration Causes and Preventions

CAUSES	PREVENTIONS
Exposure to light	Place furniture away from windows.
	Make use of curtains and shades.
	Cover critical surfaces, those subject to the most exposure, when not in use.
Oxidation	Don't store furniture in a hot attic; heat accelerates oxidation.
Everyday wear and abuse	Reduce surface friction with paste wax or furniture polish.
Excessive contact with heat, water, solvents, acids, or alkalis	Use hot pads, coasters, placemats, and tablecloths.

CAUTION
▼
Some paste waxes, such as Briwax, contain toluene (it will be listed on the can). This solvent is strong enough to dissolve and remove many finishes if they haven't thoroughly cured. It will also damage water-based finishes even when thoroughly cured.

to dull surfaces and conceal minor damage (Photo 18-2). They do this by filling tiny voids in the finish caused by scratches or natural finish deterioration. When you look into the finish, light reflects back at you instead of scattering in all directions. This makes the wood underneath the finish appear richer and deeper, and makes the finish appear less damaged. (To some people it might even look as if you've put oil in the wood, underneath the finish.)

Paste wax doesn't evaporate. Liquid furniture polishes that don't contain wax do evaporate. (If a liquid polish contains wax, it will usually be packaged in a clear container and you will see the solid wax settled at the bottom.) That's the most significant difference between paste wax and liquid polish. It means that paste wax will continue to provide wear protection and shine until it is worn or washed off the surface. Waxless polish, on the other hand, will provide wear protection and shine only until it evaporates.

Liquid furniture polish is a far better cleaner than paste wax, because it is better at picking up dust and dirt. Most liquid polishes also add a pleasant scent to the room.

If the furniture polish goes through the finish into the wood, the finish is badly deteriorated and you should consider refinishing. Neither the finish nor the furniture polish is protecting the wood.

Paste waxes used for finishing bare wood are the same as those used for polishing over other finishes, and they are applied in the same manner. (See Chapter 6: "Wax Finishes.")

Liquid furniture polishes are made from four primary ingredients:
- petroleum-distillate solvent
- water
- silicone
- wax

MYTH
Lemon-oil and orange-oil furniture polishes are made from lemon or orange oil.

FACT
These polishes have a lemon or orange scent added to a petroleum-distillate base. If these polishes were really made from the tiny amount of oil that exists in the peels of lemons or oranges, not only would the price be exorbitantly high, the price would skyrocket every time there was a freeze in Florida!

Petroleum-distillate solvent is the primary ingredient in most furniture polishes and is often referred to as "oil." Actually, it is a form of mineral spirits with a slower evaporation rate and would more accurately be described as an *oily solvent*. This liquid adds shine and scratch resistance, but only until it evaporates. This usually happens within a few hours. The liquid also helps pick up dust, and it removes grease and wax, but it has no cleaning effect on water-soluble dirt. (See "Turpentine and Petroleum-Distillate Solvents" on p. 158.)

Water is added to many polishes because it is the best cleaner for most types of dirt. (Water is an even better cleaner, of course, when combined with a mild soap such as dishwashing liquid or "oil" soap, but this degree of cleaning is rarely needed.) When water is combined with petroleum-distillate solvent to make an *emulsion* polish, the polish appears milky-white when first applied. This is how you can identify an emulsion polish.

Silicone is a very slick synthetic oil that produces the appearance of great depth in wood when applied to a finish. The oil remains on the surface for a week or longer, providing excellent scratch resistance due to its slickness. Despite claims insisting otherwise, silicone is totally inert and causes no damage to the finish or the wood, but it *does* cause refinishing problems that require extra effort to overcome. (See "Fish Eye and Silicone" on p. 146.) As a result, many refinishers and conservators discourage the use of silicone polishes. Nevertheless, these polishes are very popular with consumers.

Wax is a solid at room temperature and does not evaporate from the furniture's surface, so there is no reason to apply it often. Wax is thus not effective for dusting, cleaning, or adding scent. (To dust a waxed surface without removing the wax, wipe with a water-dampened cloth or chamois rather than with furniture polish.) Sometimes wax is added to liquid polishes. These are easy to identify since the wax settles in the container.

How to Choose

Choosing an active-care approach to furniture care is not nearly as complicated as the large number of products on store shelves would make you think. There are

Furniture Polish Overview	
Furniture Polishes Do:	**Furniture Polishes Don't:**
■ Add temporary scratch resistance. ■ Temporarily conceal light scratches. ■ Add temporary shine. ■ Aid in picking up dust. ■ Clean grease, wax, and water-soluble dirt from the surface. ■ Fill the room with a pleasant scent.	■ "Feed" the wood by replacing "missing oils." ■ "Feed" the finish. ■ Protect against heat, water, solvent, or chemical damage. ■ Slow deterioration caused by light or oxidation.

Types of Furniture-Care Products

All furniture-care products can be grouped into four types. Choose the type of care product you want to use. Then choose within that type for scent and for evaporation rate (if you even notice a difference). Choose a colored product if you want to disguise nicks and scratches. (Refer to "Applying Liquid Furniture Polish" on p. 251 and "Applying Paste Wax" on p. 90 for application instructions.)

EXAMPLES	DESCRIPTION	REASON TO CHOOSE
	**Clear Polishes** are petroleum distillates such as mineral spirits. Sometimes related solvents, such as citrus or turpentine, are included. These polishes are usually packaged in clear plastic containers. Clear polishes clean grease and remove wax, but they don't clean water-soluble dirt such as dried soft-drink spills or sticky fingerprints.	Choose a clear polish if you want an inexpensive, pleasant-smelling liquid to aid in dust removal.
	**Emulsion Polishes** are a combination of water and petroleum distillates and have a milky-white color when first applied. These polishes are usually packaged in aerosol spray cans. The advantage of emulsion polishes over clear polishes is their ability to clean both grease and water-soluble dirt.	Choose an emulsion polish if you want a polish that aids in dusting *and* cleans well.
	**Silicone Polishes** have a small amount of silicone added to a petroleum-distillate (clear) or emulsion (milky-white) carrier. The silicone, which is an oil, doesn't evaporate from the surface. You can identify silicone polishes by the telltale marking they leave when you drag your finger over a surface—even after several days.	Choose a silicone polish if you want long-lasting shine and scratch resistance along with a dusting (and sometimes cleaning) aid.
	**Wax** is the most permanent furniture-care product and also the most difficult to apply because of the extra effort required to remove the excess. On deteriorated surfaces, wax has the advantage over liquid polishes of not highlighting cracking and crazing.	Choose a wax polish if you want fairly permanent shine and scratch resistance on old, deteriorated finishes, or on newer finishes without using a silicone polish.

MYTH

Wax applied as a polish builds up, making the surface smeary.

FACT

Wax builds up only if you don't remove all the excess after each application. Each time you apply a new coat of paste wax, the solvents in it dissolve the existing wax, making one new mixture. Remove the excess and you're back to the wax that is stuck to the surface. For effective removal of the excess, rub with a clean cloth. To remove wax that has been allowed to build up, wipe the surface (hard if necessary) with mineral spirits, naphtha, turpentine, or a clear furniture polish.

only four types of furniture-care products: clear polishes, emulsion polishes, silicone polishes, and wax (see "Types of Furniture-Care Products" on p. 255). Within each type the only significant differences are scent, evaporation rate, and, sometimes, added color (to help color in nicks and scratches).

Keep in mind that you don't have to use any of these products on your furniture or cabinets. Simply dust with a damp cloth or chamois, as is commonly done everywhere else in the world. Whatever you decide to do, always follow the passive-care suggestions outlined earlier in this chapter. These methods will provide the best long-term protection for the finish.

Dusting can be accomplished with electrostatic cloths such as Grab-It. But the other benefits of furniture polishes—adding shine, adding scratch resistance, concealing light scratches, cleaning dirt stuck to the surface, and creating a pleasant scent—are lost. Because there is no oily lubricant in the cloths, the dust that is picked up by the cloth can scratch the surface you are dusting. Washing the cloths or applying furniture polish to them destroys the static charge.

Caring for Antique Furniture

Unless recently refinished, the finish on antique furniture is typically dull and cracked. In addition, the joints holding the parts together may be loose, and veneer may be lifting. Overall, the furniture is just more fragile than new furniture, and you should treat it as such.

All the information pertaining to the care of new furniture applies also to the care of antique furniture, only more so. In other words, it is more important to keep the furniture away from bright light, and it is more important to protect the finish from scratches because it is brittle and will damage easily. Paste wax does this best.

It is also best to keep the relative humidity in your home as constant as possible, because wide swings cause further loosening of joints and lifting of veneer. Beyond this simple care, no further steps need to be taken—other than to enjoy the furniture.

These simple and rather intuitive instructions probably run contrary to what you are used to reading in magazines and hearing from various sources. It's unfortunate, but a great deal of fear has been introduced into the care of antique furniture. Many people have been intimidated from doing anything to their furniture, lest they do something wrong and destroy its value. (See "Deterioration of Finishes and *Antiques Roadshow*" on p. 294.)

If you are one of these people, or if you have a client who is, keep two facts in mind. First, very few antiques possess any great value to begin with. Second, you can't cause damage to paint, finish, or wood with any commonly available paste wax or furniture polish unless you were to apply it roughly. Except for the substitution of paste wax for furniture polish on badly deteriorated finishes, active care of antiques doesn't vary from active care of new furniture.

Repairing
Finishes

In Brief

- **Removing Foreign Material**
- **Repairing Superficial Damage**
- **Repairing Color Damage in the Finish**
- **Touching Up the Color**
- **Filling with a Burn-In Stick**
- **Filling with Epoxy**
- **Repairing Deep Scratches and Gouges**

Finishes deteriorate, they get damaged, and they can be repaired. Some finishes are easier to repair than others, as I've explained in previous chapters, but most damage that occurs to most finishes can be fixed. Within the furniture industry a specialty—distinct from finishing itself—is dedicated to repairing finishes. It's concentrated in furniture factories, furniture stores, and moving companies, where most damage to finishes occurs.

There are five broad categories of damage that occurs to finishes, and sometimes through the finishes into the wood beneath:

- foreign material stuck to the surface of the finish in the form of candle or crayon wax, Magic-Marker marks, latex paint spatter, or adhesive from stickers and tape

- superficial damage to the surface of the finish in the form of light scratches, light cracking (called *crazing*), dullness, and packing (or *press*) marks from furniture being stacked in hot trucks or storage buildings

- damage to the color in the finish
- damage to the color in the wood
- damage deep into a thick finish or through the finish and into the wood in the form of deep scratches or gouges

Superficial damage to clear, penetrating finishes (oil and oil/varnish blends), and to any finish applied very

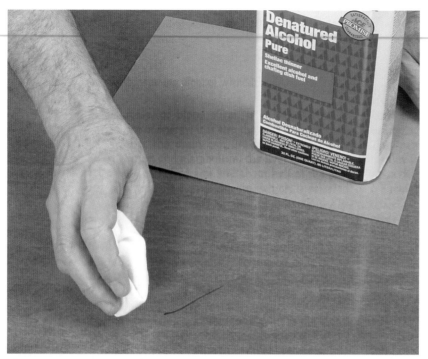

Photo 19-1: It's usually easy to remove marks made by Magic Markers by wiping with an alcohol-dampened cloth. If this doesn't work, try wiping with lacquer thinner, but use as little as possible because lacquer thinner will damage most finishes.

thin on unstained wood, is easy to repair. Simply wipe on an oil or oil/varnish blend and wipe off the excess. More substantial damage to these finishes (color problems, gouges, and deep scratches) is difficult to repair, because there is no film thickness to work with. Once damaged, the surface will probably never look undamaged. All types of damage to film finishes, on the other hand, can be repaired, but concealing color problems, gouges, and deep scratches often requires a high degree of skill.

Removing Foreign Material

All foreign material stuck to the surface of a finish can be removed by abrading. But abrading damages the finish, so it's usually best to remove the foreign material with a solvent that doesn't damage the finish.

- *Candle wax* can often be released from the surface by freezing it with an ice cube. Otherwise, scrape off the bulk of the wax and remove the rest by rubbing with mineral spirits, naphtha, or turpentine. You can also use a blow dryer to heat the wax and melt or soften it so you can wipe or rub it off. Don't get the finish so hot that it softens. If the wax is colored and some of the coloring has penetrated into the finish or the wood below, you won't be able to remove it without stripping and refinishing.
- *Crayon wax* can be removed by wiping with mineral spirits, naphtha, or turpentine.
- *Marks from Magic Markers* can usually be removed with denatured alcohol. Dampen a cloth and wipe lightly. Don't soak the finish. If alcohol doesn't work, lacquer thinner will, but you risk damaging the finish (Photo 19-1).
- *Latex paint spatter* can be removed with toluene, xylene, or DBE (di-basic esters). Dampen a cloth and rub lightly. Several commercial products, including Goof Off and Oops!, are marketed to remove this type of spatter. Each brand offers several choices. The stronger is xylene and the weaker is DBE, the same solvent used in weak paint-and-varnish removers. (See "N Methyl Pyrrolidone" on p. 290.) DBE is safer to use on water-based finishes and is often promoted as "environmentally safe." Read the ingredients on the label to determine the solvent in the can.
- *Adhesive from stickers and tape* can present a problem. Lacquer thinner will always remove the adhesive, but it may damage the finish. Before resorting to lacquer thinner, try rubbing with naphtha, turpentine, toluene, or xylene. Toluene and xylene usually

work. (See "Turpentine and Petro-leum-Distillate Solvents" on p. 158.)

Repairing Superficial Damage

Superficial wear, light scratches, press marks, and surface deterioration are common and usually easy to repair. There are four ways to repair this kind of damage:

- Apply a coat of paste wax to the surface and wipe off the excess.
- Cut through the damage or dullness using sandpaper to expose unaffected finish below. Or rub with steel wool or a rubbing compound in order to disguise the damage with a fine scratch pattern.
- Apply another coat or two of finish to cover up the problem. This can be done right on top of the damage or after cutting off the damage using abrasives.
- Amalgamate or "reflow" the finish. This can be followed by abrading to level the finish.

Applying Paste Wax

Applying paste wax to a finish is the easiest of all repairs. It is very effective at disguising light wear and scratches and raising the sheen of dull surfaces. (See "Applying Paste Wax" on p. 90.) Colored paste waxes can be helpful for coloring in light scratches. Keep in mind that paste wax can be streaked and removed with furniture polish, so the surface should be dusted with a dry or water-dampened cloth.

Cutting Back the Finish

If the finish is thick enough, you can cut it back to expose a better surface. You do this in exactly the same way you rub out a new finish. (See Chapter 16: "Fin-ishing the Finish.") You can begin by leveling the surface with sandpaper and a lubricant, or you can skip this step and simply rub with steel wool or rubbing compounds. Always choose the finest abrasive available that removes the damage efficiently. In most cases, this is 400-, 600-, or 1000-grit sandpaper, #0000 steel wool, gray abrasive pad, or pumice. You want to reduce the risk of cutting through the finish, and you don't want to put scratches deeper than necessary into the finish.

Applying More Finish on Top

You can always apply more finish over an existing finish, even when you don't know what the existing finish is. (See "Finish Compatibility" on p. 120.) You can sand or rub the surface with steel wool to smooth it before applying the new coat, just as you might do normally between coats. If you finished the piece originally and can remember what you used, it's best to apply another coat of the same finish. (Using the same brand is not important.) Otherwise, you have three broad choices: Wipe on an oil/varnish blend or wiping varnish; French polish the surface; or apply a film finish that will provide the characteristics you want—for example, polyurethane that provides good durability. Many refinishers spray a light coat of lacquer after cleaning the surface because it's fast and effective. (See Chapter 8: "Understanding Film Finishes.")

Oil/varnish blend isn't going to do any more good than paste wax because you have to wipe off all the excess. But sometimes a colored oil/varnish blend can be very effective for coloring in lighter areas, and oil/varnish blend is more permanent than paste wax. (See Chapter 5: "Oil Finishes.") It's seldom a good idea, however, to apply oil/varnish blend to tabletops that have a mirror-flat

CAUTION
▼

Many finishes, especially factory-applied finishes, have color in them—in the form of a toner or glaze. So in cutting back a finish, you may begin to remove some color even before you get down to the wood. You can usually see the color of the surface getting lighter, which will give you an early warning to stop abrading.

finish. The surface will show every flaw, and the oil/varnish blend, being soft, will damage easily. It's usually better to use paste wax or one of the other methods for repairing this type of surface.

French polishing is a wonderful technique for repairing lightly damaged surfaces. (See "French Polishing" on p. 131.) It was used widely in the nineteenth century and is still used a lot in Europe and on finer antique furniture in the United States to "shine up" old finishes. Because modern furniture wasn't finished originally with shellac, it is very important that the surface being French polished is clean and dull. It's wise to sand or rub with steel wool to create scratches that give the shellac a rough surface to bond to.

Brushing or spraying a film finish, whether or not the same you applied originally, is always risky over an existing finish. Unpredictable things can happen, from poor flow-out to blistering to fish eye. (See "Fish Eye and Silicone" on p. 146.) It's also often inconvenient: You have to move the furniture to an area set up for finishing, and the furniture may be out of use for some time. If you choose this repair technique, be sure to read "Finish Compatibility" on p. 120 before beginning.

Often the alternative to cutting back a finish or applying more finish on top is stripping and refinishing. So, little is lost in attempting the repair.

Amalgamating

Shellac and lacquer are evaporative finishes, so it's possible to redissolve and reflow the surfaces of these finishes by applying the appropriate solvent

Photo 19-2: Crazed finishes can often be amalgamated or sanded back and renewed by applying more finish on top. But the finish on this piano is too far gone. The most obvious clue is the missing finish—the crazing has gone so deep that pieces of the film have flaked off. Unfortunately, you'll have to learn the limits of renewal by trial and error, but it never hurts to try if the alternative is stripping.

(alcohol for shellac; lacquer thinner for lacquer—see Chapter 8: "Introduction to Film Finishes"). Reflowing is called *amalgamating*, and you might choose to do it to preserve an existing finish and its coloring.

There are two ways to amalgamate a finish: Spray or brush a solvent onto the finish, or rub a solvent into the finish using the French-polishing method. Spraying or brushing simply soaks the finish so it reflows. Rubbing additionally burnishes the surface to help smooth it. Both methods renew the shine and improve the smoothness if done well. But rarely does either method repair the finish all the way through to the wood. To do so would mean putting the finish back into solution totally, and it would run, sag, and puddle. Short of that, if the cracking or crazing is deep, you'll still see it when you look straight into the finish.

With shellac, you don't have a choice of solvent—there's only denatured alcohol. With lacquer, you can choose between lacquer thinners for evaporation rate, with the slowest usually producing the best results. (See "Lacquer Thinner" on p. 140.) The closer you come to putting the shellac or lacquer back into a liquid state without it sagging, the deeper and more complete the repair.

Amalgamating a finish is risky. Don't try it unless you are willing to refinish if it doesn't work (Photo 19-2).

Repairing Color Damage in the Finish

Damage to the color of the finish is of three sorts:

- damage caused by water (water rings)
- damage caused by heat
- damage caused by scratching or rubbing off part of the color

Photo 19-3: An alcohol-dampened cloth is very effective at removing water rings. Use just enough alcohol to leave the appearance of a vapor trail behind the cloth as you gently wipe, so you don't damage the finish.

Removing Water Rings

Water rings occur when moisture gets into the finish, obscuring the transparency of the film. The film appears cloudy or white, usually in the shape of a ring because it's most commonly caused by a wet drinking glass or a hot cup under which moisture condenses on the finish. Heat accelerates the penetration. Water rings are more common on finishes that have aged and developed minute cracks. The cracks allow moisture to enter. Alcohol can also cause water rings by taking moisture along with it as it penetrates into a finish.

It's usually possible to remove white water rings, though damage to very old finishes can be difficult (Photo 19-3). Here are several ways to do it, each more aggressive, and thus potentially more damaging, than the previous.

MYTH

Water rings are often in the layer of furniture polish or wax.

FACT

Neither furniture polish nor wax will develop water rings. This myth has become popular because the water ring sometimes fades when you wipe the surface with an oily solvent such as mineral spirits, as you might do to remove furniture polish or wax.

CAUTION

If water has gotten through the finish and separated it from the wood, you will have to remove the lifted finish and repair it and any color damage, or strip and refinish. Often this type of damage appears as fissures in the finish. If water has gotten through the finish and darkened (stained) the wood, you will have to strip the finish and bleach out the dark stain with oxalic acid. (See "Using Oxalic Acid" on p. 286.)

- Apply an oily substance, such as furniture polish, petroleum jelly, or mayonnaise, to the damaged area and allow it to remain overnight. This rarely works, but it sometimes fades the coloring a little and it does no damage.
- Wipe over the damage with a cloth very lightly dampened with denatured alcohol—no more than will leave the appearance of a vapor trail as you wipe. Wetter is not better, because it may soften and streak the finish, or it may cause a water mark itself. Don't rub hard, and don't get the surface wet.
- For most finishes, especially lacquer, mist on a glycol-ether solvent. This solvent, usually butyl Cellosolve, is available in aerosol spray cans for this purpose. Brand names include Blush Eliminator, Blush Control, and Super

Blush Retarder. (A water ring is similar to "blushing" in lacquer or shellac.) This product is available to nonprofessionals from www.woodfinishing supplies.com.

- For all finishes, cut through the damage by rubbing with a mild abrasive. The damage is usually right at the surface of the finish, so a lot of rubbing isn't usually necessary. The trick is to avoid rubbing in a sheen that stands out against the rest of the finish. Toothpaste, or cigarette ashes mixed with water or oil, leaves a gloss sheen and sometimes works. Rottenstone mixed with water or oil is a little coarser but still produces a gloss sheen. Pumice and #0000 steel wool create a satin sheen and almost always work. Lubricate them with oil or wax so they scratch less. If the sheen in the rubbed area is then too dull, rub it with finer abrasives or spray a finish with the correct sheen onto the dull area using an aerosol. You could also rub the entire surface to an even sheen.

Repairing Heat Damage

Heat damage usually looks similar to water damage. The film becomes cloudy and off-white in color. Heat may also cause an indentation in the finish. Heat damage can go all the way through a finish and be impossible to repair short of stripping and refinishing. But it's worth trying the methods used to remove water rings. Treat indentations as you would press marks, described under "Repairing Superficial Damage" on p. 259.

Replacing Missing Color

Mild color damage is usually in the form of nicks, scratches, and rub-throughs. There are four possible situations, each requiring a different repair procedure.

Photo 19-4: If you want to know which repair procedure will work best on color damage to a finish, dampen the damaged area with some mineral spirits or some liquid from your mouth. If the color returns, simply apply a clear finish. If the color returns a little but not enough, apply a stain. If there is no color change, paint in a colored finish. If the color becomes too dark, apply a clear paste wax.

(continued on p. 266)

Touching Up the Color

Colorants in powder form are easier to work with than colorants in liquid form. A small tackle box provides a convenient carrying case, though you have to be careful in transit to keep the colorants from spilling over and mixing. I have included both dyes and pigments in this box. Film canisters provide a convenient container for the binder.

Wood grain and color can be painted into areas where the color has been rubbed or scratched off, and onto solid-colored wood-putty, burn-in, hard-wax, and epoxy patches, as well as glue splotches. In all cases it's best to work in the same type of light in which the object will be placed (incandescent, fluorescent, or natural daylight). It's also best to seal the surface with an aerosol or with shellac or padding lacquer (shellac dissolved in lacquer-thinner solvents—see "Padding Lacquer" on p. 136) before doing the painting. Sealing reveals the true color of the surface and makes removing your repair easier if you get the colors wrong.

For colorants, you can use pigment or dye, depending on how much transparency you want. If the colorant doesn't already include a binder, add one. Most repair specialists use a fast-drying shellac or padding-lacquer binder, but you can combine oil or japan colorants with varnish to give yourself more working time if you

Touching Up the Color *(continued)*

1 If you are coloring a solid patch to match an open-pored wood such as oak or mahogany, cut some grain into the patch with the tip of a knife.

2 A glass plate is useful for mixing colorants because it allows see-through visibility to the color you are matching. I'm using the green pigment on this plate to "kill" some of the red in the burnt-umber pigment and create a better match with the grain in this oak. (See "Matching Color" on p. 58.)

3 Paint in the grain lines with a fine artist's brush. Connect the lines with the surrounding grain, matching the pattern of the pores. Pigment (with a binder) is usually best for this task. You can also use a graining pen to draw these lines. Graining pens are the same as artist's pencils and are easy to use but are limited in colors.

like. You'll just have to wait considerably longer between steps.

Though less effective because of limitations in color matching, artist's pencils can be substituted for colorants and binders. You will have to use an aerosol to seal in the color between steps.

If you are working in a home or office environment, you may meet with objection to the odors created by the solvents you are using. You can substitute a water-based aerosol, which probably won't work as well as solvent-based, or a water-based padding lacquer, such as Finish Up from Mohawk Finishing Products, which works almost as well. (Be sure to wipe the nozzle of the aerosol to keep it from clogging.) There is no universally accepted solution to the problem of solvent smells associated with finish repair.

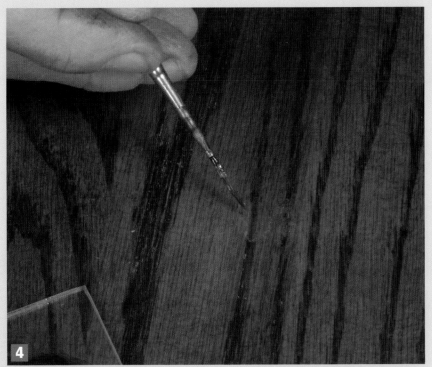

4 When the grain lines are dry, "seal" them in by dusting on an aerosol lacquer or padding on some shellac or padding lacquer with a rubbing pad. (See "Rags" on p. 22.) Then, complete the coloring by fine-tuning the background color (the lightest color in the surrounding wood), dabbing in many short lines using an artist's brush. Alternatively, you can pad rapidly back and forth across the repair with shellac or padding lacquer until the surface becomes tacky, and then dab in a tiny amount of dye or pigment powder with your finger. When you have completed the repair, apply a protective coat of finish using an aerosol or rubbing pad. Blend in the sheen using the appropriate aerosol sheen, or rub with abrasives. Or, if you made the repair between coats of finish, continue applying the finish.

You can use a spray gun or an airbrush to "feather in" missing color to any damage or patch. **TIP**

Method 1: Just above the problem, hold a piece of cardboard with a hole cut into it about the size of the damage or patch. Then spray a short burst through the hole from several inches above the cardboard.

Method 2: Set the spray gun or airbrush to spray a fine mist in a narrow pattern. Pull the trigger back just enough to turn on the air, and begin moving across the surface toward the area with the missing color. As the gun passes over this area, pull the trigger further, flick your wrist in a pendulum motion, then release the trigger. Thin the color enough to require several passes so you can adjust it between passes if it isn't exactly right.

- Enough color remains in the wood, either from the natural color of the wood itself or from remaining stain, so that all you have to do is apply a clear finish to the damage to blend it in. The finish will darken the damage enough.
- Not enough color remains in the wood, so you have to add some color to repair the damage.
- The wood is still sealed, preventing added color from penetrating. You have to apply a colored finish on top.
- The fibers of the wood are so damaged that any liquid you apply makes the color too dark. You have to use a neutral-colored paste wax, water-based finish, or a very fast-drying finish.

Because the fix for each of these situations is different, you need to test in

Filling with a Burn-In Stick

A burn-in stick is solid finish in stick form. The finish is always some form of evaporative finish—for example, shellac or lacquer—because evaporative finishes can be melted and easily manipulated with heat. (See Chapter 8: "Introduction to Film Finishes.") Here are the steps for doing "burn-ins." You apply hard wax using the same techniques, except that often you can scrape the excess level.

Prepare the damaged area by removing any roughness around the edges using sandpaper or a scraper. If the damage is a cigarette burn, cut away the char. Choose a colored burn-in stick (you can use a combination of sticks) that closely matches the background color (the lightest color) in the surrounding wood. If the correct color is already in the damaged area, choose a clear burn-in stick. Melt the solid finish into the damage using a hot burn-in knife or an electric or butane knife. Alternatively, you can use a soldering gun or a screwdriver held over a flame, but be sure to wipe off the soot. Slightly overfill the damage.

Melt the solid finish into the damage using a hot burn-in knife or an electric or butane knife. Alternatively, you can use a soldering gun or a screwdriver held over a flame, but be sure to wipe off the soot. Slightly overfill the damage.

advance to learn which is most likely to work. Here's the easy test: Apply some clear liquid to the damage and see what happens. Does the liquid make the mark disappear, darken the damage but not enough, do nothing, or make the damaged area too dark?

The best liquid to use is mineral spirits, but you might be away from your shop on a job site or simply visiting a friend, and it's not available. So use liquid from your mouth instead. Simply dab it onto the damage with your finger (Photo 19-4 on p. 262). You will know the situation within seconds, depending on how the liquid affects the color:

■ *If the liquid restores the color,* all you need to do is apply a clear finish. Your best choices are oil/varnish blend, clear shellac, or varnish. Oil/varnish

3

When the burn-in cools, level it with the finish. One way is to sand it level using 320-grit or finer wet/dry sandpaper and an oil lubricant. Back the sandpaper with a cork block barely larger than the repair you're sanding. Keep the cork block level on the repair so you don't remove the surrounding finish.

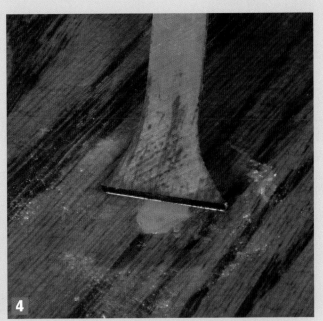

4

An alternative method to leveling the burn-in is to remove the excess by melting it with heat from your burn-in knife. Ideally, you want the knife to be hot enough to melt the burn-in, but not so hot that it damages the surrounding finish. You should first apply a special "burn-in balm" (or some petroleum jelly) to the surface to prevent the melted repair from sticking to the surrounding finish. Be sure your knife is clean. Lightly drag the heated knife over the burn-in, transferring some of the solid material to the knife. Wipe the finish from the knife with a cloth. Continue removing the excess burn-in until the patch is almost level with the surrounding surface. Then finish off by sanding, as shown in the photo at left. Finish by coloring the repair. (See "Touching Up the Color" on p. 263.)

Photo 19-5: To repair color damage to an edge, use a touch-up marker, which is similar to a Magic Marker but in wood tones. Simply draw the felt tip of an appropriately colored marker along the damaged edge.

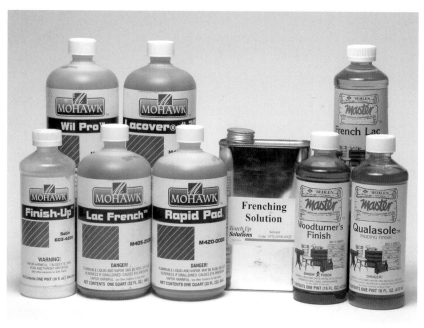

Photo 19-6: Padding lacquers are primarily shellac, often with other resins added to improve water resistance, and with stronger lacquer-thinner solvents used in place of alcohol. Padding lacquers are easier to use on small repairs because the lubricant is built in and evaporates after application, eliminating the need to remove it.

MYTH

If you get the color right, damaged areas will be invisible to passersby.

FACT

Actually, getting the sheen and levelness right is more important. The color can be a little off, and people will regard the damage as a natural anomaly in the wood, so long as the surface is level and the sheen is even.

will darken more then clear shellac. Varnish will be in between.

■ *If the liquid doesn't darken enough,* apply a stain. An oil-based wiping stain or water-soluble dye stain is easiest because you can wipe off the excess without causing any damage to the surrounding area. You could also use a commercial product marketed for this purpose, such as Howard's Restor-a-Finish or a colored paste wax.

■ *If the liquid has no effect,* the wood is still sealed with finish. The color you are replacing was in the finish, so you will need to paint it back in. You can do this with a touch-up marker (Photo 19-5), or you can brush on any colorant that includes a binder. Typical binders include shellac, varnish, and water base. Padding lacquer, which is shellac dissolved in lacquer-thinner solvents, can also be used. (See "Padding Lacquer" on p. 136, and Photo 19-6.) In effect, you are painting with thinned paint. Use universal tinting colorants (UTCs) and pigment powders with shellac, padding lacquer, and water-based finish, and oil or japan colorants with varnish. (See "Touching Up the Color" on p. 263.)

Filling with Epoxy

Any epoxy can be used successfully to fill a scratch or gouge, but the easiest epoxy to work with is stick, or "Tootsie-Roll," epoxy. This is a cylindrical stick with one of the epoxy parts inside the other. You can combine the epoxy stick with almost any colorant except oil or japan colors as you are kneading the epoxy, or you can use a pre-colored stick. Most epoxy sticks have an 8- to 10-minute working time after mixing. Until the epoxy cures, you can remove the excess the same as with a burn-in stick, using a hot knife, or you can use the following technique.

1 Select an appropriate epoxy stick to match the background color of the wood you are repairing, or use a neutral stick and blend in a colorant. Slice off enough of the epoxy to make the repair and knead it in your fingers until it becomes a single color. It will help to wet your fingers.

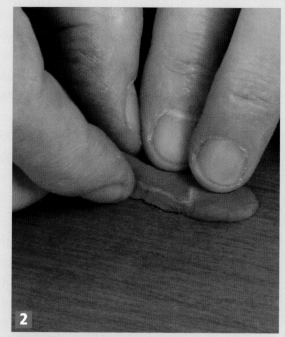

2 Press the kneaded epoxy into the damage, leaving it slightly overfilled.

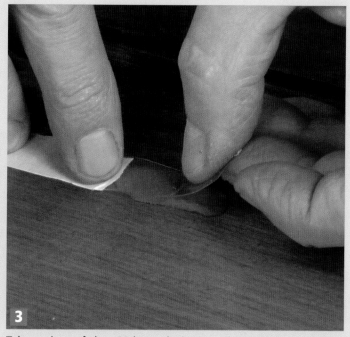

3 Take a piece of clear Mylar and trim it so that it just covers the area of the epoxy fill. Lay the Mylar over the fill, securing one end with a piece of masking tape.

(continued on p. 270)

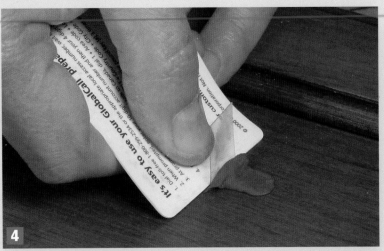

Take a credit card or similar object and, beginning at the end of the Mylar secured with the masking tape, squeegee out the excess epoxy fill. The credit card should bridge the area of the fill so that the card levels the fill with the surrounding surface.

Remove the Mylar carefully so that you don't pull the fill out of the damaged area.

Before the epoxy hardens, use a cloth dampened with rubbing (isopropyl) alcohol to clean off any excess from the surrounding area. Then color in the fill, if necessary, using the techniques described in "Touching Up the Color" on p. 263.

■ *If the liquid makes the color too dark,* this usually indicates that the wood has been roughened, and too much of the liquid is being retained. If you can't smooth the surface, apply a clear paste wax, which will darken the least, or apply shellac or water base.

Repairing Deep Scratches and Gouges

Scratches and gouges that go deep into a finish or through the finish into the wood have to be filled. It's very difficult to do this successfully with wood putty because the putty sticks to the finish everywhere it comes in contact, and it is difficult to remove without causing more damage. It's better to fill the damage with solid finish (in the form of a "burn-in" stick), epoxy, or wax, which is available in several hardnesses. (See "Filling with a Burn-In Stick" on p. 266 and "Filling with Epoxy" on p. 269.) Burn-in sticks, epoxy, and hard wax work well on tabletops because they become very hard. Epoxy and hard wax are easier to use, and thus better for cabinet doors and other vertical surfaces. Both also have a lower sheen than burn-ins, and are easier to match to the surrounding sheen. Epoxy is best for patching table edges, carvings, and turnings because it cures tough. Burn-ins and hard wax are brittle.

Some imported furniture and pianos are finished with polyester, which requires a special polyester repair material to totally disguise the damage. A polyester repair kit, along with instructions, is available to nonprofessionals at www.woodfinishingsupplies.com.

Exterior Finishing

Wood is a beautiful material. If you put a clear finish on it to bring out its color, it's even more beautiful. It's not surprising, then, that there is a widespread desire among consumers to preserve this beauty on decks, doors, outdoor furniture, fences, and other wooden objects with exterior exposure. The desire is strong enough that an entire industry has grown up to satisfy it—the industry that supplies exterior finishes.

Wood will last indefinitely if it's protected from ultraviolet (UV) light and moisture. The proof lies under any well-maintained paint on old buildings. Re-move the paint, and the wood is like new. But expose the wood to the ravages of sunlight and rain for a year or so, and the wood will turn gray and start to split and warp. It might begin to rot. You know this is true because you see it all around you. Furthermore, if the wood is in a moist climate, and especially if it is in the shade and sheltered from air movement, fungus in the form of mildew begins growing, usually showing up as a dark discoloration on the wood. In this chapter, I'm going to explain how sunlight and moisture degrade wood and then tell you how you can prevent, or at least slow, the damage.

Wood Degradation

When exposed for long periods to sunlight and rain, wood degrades. It does this in four principal ways:

- It loses its color.
- It rots.
- It splits and warps.
- Mildew grows.

Color Loss

Wood changes to a silvery gray color fairly rapidly in sunlight and rain because these elements combine to destroy the lignin and extractives at the surface of the wood. UV light breaks down the lignin, and rain washes it and the extractives away. *Lignin* lends rigidity to cellulose wood cells and acts as a glue that holds them together. *Extractives* give wood its interesting yellow, brown, pink, and red coloring. When the lignin and extractives disappear, so does the color. Only the gray cellulose, which is resistant to UV degradation, is left.

If you like the gray color and you aren't having problems with rotting or splitting, you can leave the wood unprotected. The grayed surface is actually very effective at blocking further degradation below (Photo 20-1). Softwoods erode at only about $1/4$ inch per century.

If you don't like the gray color, you can usually remove it (by removing the surface cellulose) with a commercial deck brightener or oxalic acid. Oxalic acid is very effective, but you should be sure to protect nearby plants and grass by covering them or wetting them down before and after hosing off the acid. (See "Using Oxalic Acid" on p. 286.) Only in the most severe cases will you need to sand the surface to remove the degraded wood.

Rot

Wood rot is the result of fungi consuming the cellulose in the wood (Photo 20-2). A visually similar decay is caused by insect infestation. Both need moisture to spread, so water is the indirect cause of rotting and insect damage. (The term "dry rot" is a misnomer usually applied to wood that has decayed so much that it crumbles to a dry powder; water is still required to cause it.)

The heartwood of some woods such as redwood, cedar, and teak contains extractives that resist rotting. So these woods are often chosen for exterior use. Wood from old-growth trees is more resistant to rot than wood from second-growth trees.

Rot is rare in dry western climates, because moisture is necessary for rot to develop. As a result, it's often possible to leave non-rot-resistant woods completely unprotected and expect them to hold up well for many decades. They will turn silvery gray on the surface, of course, but the wood underneath will be unaffected.

Most softwoods don't resist rot. But they are essential to the construction industry, and they are regularly used in applications (such as sills and decks) where they are liable to rot. To make them rot resistant, they (most commonly Southern yellow pine) are pressure injected with a chemical such as alkaline copper quaternary (ACQ) or copper azole (CBA). (Until recently, chromated copper arsenate, or CCA, was standard, but this was removed from the market for safety reasons.) Wood treated this way almost never rots, as long as the chemical has saturated the wood all the way through. The wood is sold as "pressure-treated" or "PT" and has a familiar dull-green or dull-brown coloring.

To some extent, rotting can be retarded by applying a commercial preservative, or a water repellent or stain that contains a preservative, to the surface of the wood. But compared to the natural

---

CAUTION

▼

Household bleach (sodium hypochlorite or chlorine bleach) is very effective at killing mildew spores, but it also destroys lignin, thereby removing a lot of color from the wood and roughening the surface wood fibers. Reduce the bleach with up to three parts water and wash it off the wood within about 10 minutes to minimize the damage. Use household bleach only when you want to kill mildew. Never mix household bleach with lye (sodium hydroxide). They combine to create a poisonous gas.

preservatives in some woods, and to pressure treating, the protection offered by these products is temporary and very superficial. The preservative has to be applied often, and rotting can still occur if it can get started below the surface of the wood.

The application of a preservative is essential in moist climates on non-rot-resistant woods that aren't pressure treated. Preservatives are also very helpful on rot-resistant woods that contain some sapwood. Preservatives are somewhat useful on the heartwood of rot-resistant woods, especially on second-growth woods. Preservatives are useful only for mildew resistance (they commonly contain a mildewcide) on pressure-treated woods because these woods are very resistant to rot anyway.

Rot isn't altogether bad. Without wood-consuming fungi and insects such as termites, forest ecosystems couldn't function. Rot is nature's way of recycling dead wood.

Splitting and Warping

Even if you are willing to live with graying and you use a wood that resists rotting, you still have to deal with splitting and warping. These are caused by both sunlight and rain. Sunlight heats and dries out the exposed surface of the wood, causing it to shrink and split and the wood to warp. Rain soaks the exposed side, causing expansion, which the wood's thickness prevents. The resulting compressed cells retain their shape even after drying, and after a number of cycles, the wood splits and warps. This is called "compression shrinkage." (See "Splits, Checks, and Warps" on p. 2.)

Splitting shows up first on end grain at the tops of boards in fences, on the ends of boards on decks, and at the bottom of shingles and shakes. Splitting and warping occur significantly less on

Photo 20-1: UV light and rainwater destroy and remove the surface lignin in wood. With it, the extractives that give wood its distinctive coloration are also washed away, leaving the wood silvery gray in color. The change occurs only at the surface of the wood.

Photo 20-2: Rot is caused by fungi and other organisms consuming the cellulose of the wood. The indirect causes are moisture and oxygen because the organisms can't survive without them.

Photos 20-3: Plainsawn wood splits much more quickly than quartersawn wood. The boards in the top of this cedar table were exposed to sunlight and rain for about eight years with no protection. You can see that the plainsawn board (top) has developed numerous splits, while the quartersawn board (bottom) is in perfect shape, except for the graying.

boards that are quartersawn (cut on the radius of the tree) than on boards that are plainsawn (cut tangential to the growth rings). (See Figure 17-1 on p. 227.) For this reason it is best to use quartersawn wood on outdoor projects when you can get it (Photos 20-3).

Mildew

Mildew is a gray, dark green, brown, or black discoloration that grows on wood or coatings, especially in moist climates or behind trees or shrubs where air movement is restricted. Mildew does not seriously damage the wood or the coating; it just looks bad (Photo 20-4).

The easy test for mildew (to distinguish it from dirt) is to splash a few drops of household bleach onto the discoloration and see if it lightens. The bleach will kill the mildew, and the wood will return to its natural color or become lighter.

Some coatings are more vulnerable to mildew growth than others. Especially vulnerable are linseed oil and any coating containing linseed oil. Mildew feeds on linseed oil. Also vulnerable are alkyd paints. Latex paints using titanium dioxide pigment are more vulnerable than latex paints using zinc oxide. Mildewcides can be added to any coating by the manufacturer or by you to improve resistance. (Mildewcides in concentrated form are often available at paint stores, especially those located in damp and humid areas.) A wood preservative can also be applied on a regular basis to raw wood or to a coating on the wood to retard mildew growth.

Slowing Degradation

To prevent or slow the degradation of wood placed outdoors, you have to block UV light and seal the wood from contact with water. In moist climates you may also need to apply a preservative if you want to prevent the growth of mildew. For movable objects such as furniture, you can keep them under cover (for example, on a covered porch or in a garage) when not in use. For exterior doors, the best protection is an overhang. (See "Finishing Exterior Doors" on p. 277.) For these and everything else, you can also apply paint, stain, clear finish, or water repellent to protect the wood.

Paint

Paint is the most effective coating for protecting wood. The thick film blocks water penetration, and the pigment blocks UV light. You can find wood siding that is in perfect shape after 200 years because it has been protected continuously with well-maintained coats of paint.

There are two categories of paint you can choose between: oil-based and water-based (latex). Because oil-based paints wear better than latex paints, they are best for objects such as chairs and picnic tables.

Oil-based primers are also best when you are painting wood that has been exposed to the weather for a month or longer, especially if the wood has grayed. The graying is evidence that the surface

Photo 20-4: Mildew is a dark discoloration on wood or a coating that looks bad but doesn't cause great harm to the wood. Test to distinguish mildew from dirt by splashing some household bleach on it. If it's mildew, the discoloration will lighten considerably.

fibers are unattached to the fibers below, because the lignin has been destroyed. Oil-based primers penetrate deeper than latex primers, so they are better able to penetrate the degraded wood and bond to good wood underneath. If the wood is freshly milled or sanded, acrylic-latex primers perform well.

Latex paint is best for wood siding and trim, because it is better than oil paint at allowing moisture vapor to pass through (Photo 20-5 on p. 276). What you might think of as a shortcoming is actually a benefit because moisture that is generated inside buildings from cooking, showers, and so on has to be able to get out when the building is closed up for heating or air-conditioning. The moisture vapor works its way through the walls, through the insulation, and through the wood siding. If it can't get through the paint layer, it will

TIP Be sure to caulk all areas where water might get through and work its way underneath the paint. The areas most vulnerable are where siding butts up against trim. If you are installing the siding and trim yourself, you can improve water resistance for several years by applying a paintable water repellent to the end grain of the boards before installing them. You still need to caulk.

Photo 20-5: Latex paint is best for exterior siding because the paint "breathes." It allows moisture generated inside a building from cooking and showers to pass through in vapor form. Alkyd oil paint is better at blocking the moisture, so it builds up behind the paint and causes it to peel.

MYTH

You should wait at least six months after installing siding, a deck, or a fence in order to let the wood dry before painting or staining it.

FACT

Unless the wood is soaking wet (your saw blade sprays water during cutting), you should apply a paint or stain within a month. Waiting longer will result in a weaker bond and accelerated paint or stain failure because of wood degradation caused by exposure to sunlight and rain.

build up behind the paint and cause it to peel. (A primer coat of oil-based paint applied under latex paint is not thick enough to stop moisture penetration.)

Paint is great for siding and house trim because you can caulk where the two join together, and for furniture and exterior doors if they don't get a lot of exposure to moisture. But paint is a poor choice for decks and often for fences because they do get a lot of exposure, and it's rarely possible to seal off or caulk all the end grain effectively. Water will find a way under the paint causing it to peel, and then it will be a huge job to sand or strip for repainting. Paint requires too much work to keep up, so it is seldom used on decks and fences.

Note the differences in the way water vapor and liquid water cause coatings to peel. Water vapor works its way through siding from inside a building. In vapor form the water can pass through latex paint. Liquid water finds a way to get under a coating from the outside. It is too concentrated to pass through a thick coating.

Pigmented Stain

Pigmented stain is the next most effective coating for exterior wood. Just as with paint, it resists both moisture and UV-light damage because it contains both a binder and pigment. But because there is much less of each and very little or no film build, pigmented stains are not as protective as paint. Nor do they last as long. On the other hand, the lack of film build makes maintenance easier. Usually, all that is required is a fresh application of the stain every year or two, depending on the climate and how much exposure the wood gets. There's seldom a reason to scrape or sand. (See "Staining Wood Decks" on p. 278.)

For wood decks, fences, and unpainted cedar, cypress, or redwood siding, pigmented stain is usually the best choice.

There are three types of binder and two types of pigment among which to choose. The binders are oil-based, water-based, and alkyd-based. The pigments are semi-transparent and solid color.

Oil-based stains are the most common, the most popular, and the easiest to use. You can brush, spray, or roll on a coat, and enough of it will either soak into the wood or evaporate so that you end up with very little or no film build. With no film build, there is nothing to peel, so recoating is easy. Usually, all you have to do is clean the wood of dirt and mildew and apply another coat.

Water-based acrylic stains are popular because of their lack of odor, easy cleanup, and reduced amount of polluting solvents. But water-based stains leave a build that obscures the wood somewhat and may peel if water gets underneath. Water-based stains also show

Finishing Exterior Doors

Exterior wood doors present a special problem because they are often made of beautiful hardwoods that are chosen particularly for their visual appeal. These hardwoods gray and split when exposed to sunlight and rain just as do softwoods used for decks and fences.

Because of the way these doors are made—usually frame-and-panel, sometimes individual boards positioned in decorative patterns attached to a solid core—it's virtually impossible to prevent water from getting underneath a coating and causing it to peel. The panels or individual boards expand and contract as the seasons change, so that cracks open up in any coating.

The only way exterior doors can survive in good condition for many years without graying or splitting is if they are shielded from sunlight and rain. On the north side of buildings where the sun is not a problem, all that might be needed is a storm door. Where the sun does shine on such a door, the best solution is to build an overhang or covered porch. The overhang has to be large enough to shield the door completely not only from sunlight but also from rain if no storm door is used.

In a case such as the example shown in the photo at right, where an overhang would detract from the design of the building, the next best solution would be to finish the door with a marine varnish (to resist UV damage) and to protect against water damage with a storm door. Without a storm door, you will have to scrape and reapply the finish on a fairly regular basis to keep the door looking nice.

Even with a storm door or overhang, and without any exposure to sunlight, the door should be finished with a flexible spar varnish because the wood will shrink and expand considerably as a result of humidity changes. UV absorbers won't be needed.

This front door faces west with no trees or other obstructions to block afternoon sunlight, so the door has very little protection from sunlight or rain. You can see that the door is in good shape at the top where the deep recess of the framing protects it, but the condition worsens progressively from there down because of exposure to both sunlight and rain.

Staining Wood Decks

Staining decks involves two steps, the first of which is all too often ignored. The first step is to clean the wood, even if the deck is newly installed. Decks get dirty very easily because most of the boards are horizontal. The second step is to apply the coating you have chosen. As explained in the accompanying text, the best coating for most decks is a stain.

CLEANING

The following cleaning instructions can be used on any surface and with any coating. To clean the wood, follow these directions, depending on the situation.

Wood that is newly installed

1 Check for *mill glaze* or wax. Mill glaze is a condition created in the milling process that causes liquids to bead rather than soak in. Wax is sometimes used in the pressure-treating process and has the same effect. Check by splashing some water on various areas to see if the water penetrates. If it beads, do one of the following:

- Let the wood weather for a couple of weeks.
- Pressure-wash the wood.
- Apply a commercial deck brightener, and scrub with a stiff bristle brush or broom.
- Sand the wood.

2 Wash the wood if it is dirty and let it dry.

Wood that was previously coated with water repellent

1 Clean off all dirt using a pressure washer, or a garden hose and a stiff-bristle scrub broom.

2 If mildew remains, apply a commercial deck brightener using a pump sprayer, roller, or brush, and scrub the wood or wash with a pressure washer. (Deck brighteners contain sodium hypochlorite, oxalic acid, or oxygen bleach and often a detergent.) For more even flow-out, wet the wood first with a garden hose.

NOTE
▼

A pressure washer is a pump that puts water from your faucet under very high pressure. It can be rented from any equipment rental store. Begin with 500 or 1000 psi and increase the pressure if necessary, but not so much that the water damages the wood.

3 If tannin or rust stains remain, apply a solution of oxalic acid and water or a commercial deck brightener or bleach that contains oxalic acid. (See "Using Oxalic Acid" on p. 286.)

4 Rinse the wood thoroughly and let it dry.

Wood that was previously stained

1 Follow the instructions for cleaning wood that has been treated with a water repellent.

2 If you want to remove the existing stain, apply a deck stripper, which is usually a mild concentration of sodium hydroxide. (See "Lye" on p. 294.)

3 Rinse the wood thoroughly and let it dry.

Wood that was previously painted

1 Strip the paint using a deck stripper (usually sodium hydroxide), a heat gun, or a solvent stripper (See Chapter 21: "Removing Finishes.") Sanding is rarely a good idea because of the nails or screws in the wood.

2 Rinse the wood thoroughly and let it dry.

A stain is usually the best finish for a deck because stains rarely peel. The pigment in the stain provides some UV protection and the binder provides some water resistance.

APPLYING

To apply a deck stain or water repellent, follow these steps.

1 Work on a warm day. (Temperatures should not fall below 40 degrees Fahrenheit for oil-based products or 50 degrees Fahrenheit for water-based products for 24 hours.)

2 Check that rain isn't predicted for at least 24 hours.

3 Brush, roll (using a short-nap roller), or pad (using a paint pad) the stain or water repellent onto the wood. If you use a roller or paint pad, *back-brush* for best results. That is, brush back over the coating you have applied. Brush with the grain of the wood. (You can also use a spray gun, but be careful not to apply the coating too thick.)

4 Work from end to end on several boards at once and maintain a wet edge so you don't leave lap marks.

5 Coat the end grain (if you can get to it) of all the boards.

6 With water-based, solid-color, and semitransparent stains, and with water repellent and any type of oil, apply only one coat and don't leave it thick. You want as much of the product as possible to soak into the wood so you create little or no build. With alkyd stain, which is designed to be built on the wood, be sure the wood is completely clean to reduce the chances of peeling.

7 Clean and recoat whenever the deck begins to show wear or look dry.

TIP Protect plants, grass, and other growth with plastic or wet them down both before and after applying bleach or stain.

traffic patterns more easily than oil-based stains because the thin build wears through.

Alkyd-based stains make use of a very long-oil varnish to glue the pigment to the wood. This stain is meant to build on the wood, but it resists peeling because it attaches so well to the wood and it is so flexible. Often, manufacturers recommend as many as three coats and instruct you to clean the surface and apply an additional coat every year or two. The most widely available brand is Sikkens. The disadvantages of these stains are that they will peel anyway if the wood isn't nearly perfectly clean during initial application or recoating, and visible wear is common in high traffic areas. It's very difficult to blend these areas with others without stripping and starting over.

The primary difference between semitransparent and solid-color stains is the amount of pigment included. Solid-color stains contain more pigment, so they are better at blocking UV light. But they obscure the wood more than semitransparent stains do. Semitransparent stains, especially those that use the more transparent trans-oxide pigments, are the most common and most popular stains. They are also easier to apply because lap marks are easier to avoid.

Clear Finish

Clear film-building finishes, including water base and all types of varnish, resist water penetration well, but not ultraviolet light. Destructive UV light penetrates the film and causes the wood to degrade. The lignin that glues the cellulose fibers together loses its strength, and the surface fibers separate from the rest of the wood. When this happens, the finish, which is bonded to these surface fibers, peels. Clear finishes exposed to sunlight usually peel

MYTH Manufacturer's claims concerning the functional life of their stains are credible.

FACT I've never understood how a manufacturer can claim a single working lifetime when a product can be applied in locations with such diverse weather conditions as those, for instance, in Minneapolis, New Orleans, and Tucson. You would be wise to shorten the recommended recoating times considerably the farther south you live.

long before the finish film deteriorates enough to disappear.

The trick to getting a clear finish to survive in UV light is to add UV absorbers, and many manufacturers supply finishes with these added. There is, however, a great deal of difference in effectiveness. (See "UV Protection" at right.)

Clear finishes sold for exterior use can be divided into three categories: marine varnish, spar varnish, and oil. Water-based exterior finishes are also available, but they have not found much acceptance thus far. Marine varnish is a long-oil varnish with UV absorbers added. (See "The Mix of Oil and Resin" on p. 153.) Spar varnish is a long-oil varnish without UV absorbers added. Oil may or may not have UV absorbers added, but even if it does, an oil finish is too thin on the surface to provide much protection from sunlight. An oil finish will disappear from the wood very rapidly if the wood is exposed to either sunlight or rain.

Linseed oil, whether raw or boiled, is also ineffective at blocking sunlight and water. Worse, it is susceptible to mildew growth. In fact, mildew feeds on the fatty acids in linseed oil, so mildew develops faster than if no linseed oil had been applied. Only in very dry climates should linseed oil be considered as a finish for exterior wood.

Marine varnishes are the best clear finishes to use outdoors. They are always very glossy (for better light reflection), relatively soft (for better flexibility), and require eight or nine coats to reach maximum UV resistance. In addition, because the UV absorbers in these finishes don't prevent the finish itself from deteriorating, you will need to sand off surface deterioration (dullness, chalking, and crazing) and apply a couple of additional coats whenever the surface begins to deteriorate. This might be as often

> **TIP**
> There are three good ways to give a glossy marine varnish a satin sheen:
> ■ Rub with steel wool.
> ■ Add flatting agent from the bottom of another can of varnish. (See "Controlling Sheen with Flatting Agent" on p. 110.)
> ■ Apply a coat of interior satin varnish on top. (This coat will deteriorate faster, so you will have to replace it more often, but the UV absorbers in the coats of marine varnish below will block UV light from reaching the wood.)

UV Protection

Ultraviolet light, primarily from sunlight but also from fluorescent light, causes colors in wood, stain, and even paint to fade and finishes to dull and eventually peel. Pigment is the best UV blocker available for coatings. It works by absorbing UV light, thereby preventing it from reaching the wood. But pigment hides, or at least obscures, the wood.

Chemicals called *UV absorbers* can be added to clear finishes by manufacturers to block UV light. These chemicals don't obscure the

Even through window glass, which partially blocks UV light, sunlight can bleach wood and stain, and cause finishes to peel. The back of this cabinet was exposed to a west-facing window for five years.

There is a big difference between marine varnishes sold at marinas and marine varnishes sold at home centers and paint stores. This red-dyed board was coated with five coats of four different varnishes and placed in a west-facing window for six months, the top part protected with newspaper. The left panel was finished with a marine varnish bought at a marina. The two middle panels were finished with popular marine varnishes commonly available at home centers and paint stores. The right panel was finished with a standard interior alkyd varnish. The varnish bought at a marina was fairly effective at preventing UV light from penetrating and fading the dye. The home-center/paint-store marine varnishes were just a little more effective than the interior varnish, which contained no UV absorber.

wood. They work like sunscreen, turning light energy into heat energy. Just as with sunscreen, however, UV absorbers wear out in time. So UV protection from any clear finish is only temporary.

Many manufacturers claim UV protection for their clear exterior wood finishes, but common consumer brands available in home centers and paint stores tend not to contain enough of the expensive UV absorber to be effective. The most effective UV-resistant clear finishes are available from marinas. Other products often marketed for

their UV resistance are applied too thin to be effective. These include water repellents and oil finishes, including so-called "teak" oil. (See "Additional Confusion: Teak Oil" on p. 80.) Neither of these coatings builds on the wood, so no matter what percentage of UV absorber is added to the finish, there isn't enough thickness for the absorber to do much good. It quickly loses its effectiveness.

To be effective for several years or longer, a thick film has to be built on the wood. Wooden boat finishers apply 8 to 12 coats of very

high quality, UV-resistant marine varnish and expect it to last up to 10 years or more—as long as they maintain the finish. Maintenance means sanding off the top coat or two every year or so when the finish dulls and applying another couple of coats. You should do this also whenever you have used a marine varnish on any exterior surface (a door, for example) that has dulled. The dullness indicates that the surface of the finish has deteriorated and there is no more UV resistance to the depth of the dullness.

TIP
If you are willing to expend the effort, you can maintain the original color of wood in your deck or fence by following this procedure. Beginning with new wood, apply a water repellent that contains UV absorbers. As soon as the wood begins to turn gray, wash it with a deck brightener or oxalic acid to return it to its original color. Then apply another coat of water repellent with UV absorbers. Use one that contains a preservative if you live in a moist climate. You may have to recoat as often as every three to six months, depending on your location and the exposure the deck gets. This procedure will prevent graying for many years, but it won't prevent splitting or warping.

as once or twice a year if the finish is exposed to bright sunlight in southern exposures.

Water Repellent

Water repellents are usually mineral spirits with low-surface-tension wax or silicone added to repel water. Sometimes, they are simply thinned water-based finish. Though short-lived, water repellents are fairly effective at reducing water penetration into the wood. If they contain UV absorbers, they block some of the UV light, but only for a short time. The coating is too thin, and the small amount of UV absorber that can be contained in that thin layer quickly wears out. The result is that wood coated with a water repellent and exposed to rain and sunlight grays, splits, and warps at almost the same speed as wood left uncoated.

Water repellents provide the least protection of any exterior wood coating, but they are easy to apply because they never leave lap marks and they don't peel.

How to Choose

Based on the above discussion, choosing a coating for an exterior surface is not difficult. Use paint on exterior siding, trim, doors, furniture, and possibly fences. Be sure to caulk siding and coat all areas, such as end grain, where water could get in and work its way under the paint. Use latex paint on siding and oil paint on surfaces you want to wear well.

Use stain on decks, fences, cedar-shingle siding, and possibly on furniture and doors. Choose among alkyd, solid color, semitransparent, and water base. Alkyd, solid color, and water base tend to build on the wood, which makes them vulnerable to peeling. Semitransparent is less resistant to UV light and water, but there is no peeling, so recoating is easier.

Use a clear film finish on doors and furniture, and use linseed oil on anything if you are in a desert-dry climate. Use marine varnish on objects where you want maximum UV resistance with a clear finish. Use spar varnish if UV resistance isn't critical. Remember that any film-building finish will peel if water can find a way underneath.

Use water repellent on decks if you don't mind the wood graying or if you are willing to keep it up, as described in the tip at left. Use water repellent with a preservative included if you live in a damp climate. Use paintable water repellent on the end grain of siding and trim before installation.

CHAPTER 21

Removing
Finishes

Removing the finish brings us full circle. In the first chapter, "Why Finish Wood, Anyway?" I explained why it is important for wood to have a finish in good shape. In subsequent chapters, I explained all the various means of applying finishes, how to choose among them, and how to repair and care for them. Now I'm going to explain how to take the finish off.

Since writing the first edition of this book, removing finishes has become quite controversial—due mostly to the popularity and resulting influence of the *Antiques Roadshow* and similar TV programs. The rationale for even including a chapter on this subject is now being questioned by some. You'll find my thoughts on this subject in "Deterioration of Finishes and *Antiques Roadshow*" on p. 294.

Throughout this book, I've argued that finishes and finishing can be understood—that finishing is not, as the editor of a major woodworking magazine once said to me, a craft that "we don't take seriously because no one can understand it." No subject better illustrates the basic understandability of finishing than paint-and-varnish removers. This is because all the principal ingredients in these products are bad for your health, and manufacturers therefore list the ingredients right on the containers. With strippers, it's easy to know what you're getting, so you can choose intelligently among the offerings. (See "Breaking the Code—An Overview of Strippers" on p. 288 and "Quick Stripper Identification" on the facing page.)

There are only three primary solvents, or solvent groups, used in strippers, so the task of learning the names and how each works is not very difficult (spelling and pronunciation aside). The three solvents differ in effectiveness, price, and potential danger to your health. Pairs of these solvents, or groups, are sometimes combined, alkalis or acids are sometimes added to increase the stripper strength, and one alkali (lye) is sometimes used alone. Solvent strippers are supplied in either liquid or semi-paste consistency, and some have a detergent that is added to make them water-washable.

You should choose among the categories for solvent strength, safety, and price. Within each category you should choose for ease of use and also for price. You won't notice any significant difference in solvent strength, speed of removal, or safety within each category.

Other means of stripping—sanding, scraping, and removing with a heat gun—are usually too harsh for furniture. Mechanical processes (sanding and scraping) are often effective for removing paint from exterior siding and from interior woodwork, but they can't help but remove some of the surface wood along with the paint or finish. This damages the aged character that makes old furniture appreciated and sometimes valuable. Sanding also rounds over the crisp lines of carvings and turnings and risks cutting through veneer. Heating the paint or finish hot enough to cause it to blister risks scorching the wood and dissolving the glue that holds veneer on and furniture joints together.

Stripping Solvents and Chemicals

There are three solvents, or solvent groups, commonly used in strippers. These solvents or groups are used alone or combined with one of the others. Because the names of the solvents are long and sometimes difficult to remember, I'm including abbreviations:

- methylene chloride (MC)
- acetone, toluene, and methanol (ATM)
- n-methyl pyrrolidone (NMP)

There are also two very strong alkalis used for stripping—sodium hydroxide (lye) and ammonium hydroxide (ammonia). Lye is often used alone. Both are sometimes combined with one of the solvents to increase the stripper strength. Lye and ammonia darken most hardwoods. Lye, which is used alone in a water solution, also breaks down old glue and turns wood into pulp if left in contact long enough. So you should avoid using lye unless you need its strength.

Oxalic acid is also sometimes added to increase stripper strength. Because the acid can eat its way through metal cans, strippers containing oxalic acid are available only to professionals. (See "Professional Stripping" on p. 291.)

Methylene Chloride

Methylene chloride has been the primary active ingredient used in most paint-and-varnish removers for the past four or five decades. It's the most effective stripping solvent available to the general public as well as to commercial stripping shops. It's also non-flammable. But methylene chloride is toxic and, unfortunately, it has been classified as a probable carcinogen. (See "Stripper Safety" on p. 286.)

You can buy methylene chloride strippers in liquid or semi-paste consistency and in four different formula strengths. The consistency (or thickness) of the stripper is an important consideration if you're working on non-horizontal surfaces—liquid will run off; semi-paste will cling. But consistency has very little to do with the strength of the stripper.

The solvents in both liquid and semi-paste strippers of all four strengths evaporate very rapidly, so paraffin wax is added to retard the evaporation. The wax rises to the surface of the stripper and forms a skin that holds the solvents in. If you disturb this wax covering, you allow the release of some of the solvents. (See "Using Strippers" on p. 295.)

You must remove all the wax before you apply a new finish. If you don't, the new finish won't bond well, and it may wrinkle on the wood or not dry well. Many instructions tell you to "neutralize" the stripper to remove the wax. This is a very misleading instruction. Wax can't be neutralized; it is not an acid or alkali. It has to be washed off the wood using clean cloths and plenty of solvent—mineral spirits, naphtha, or lacquer thinner. Many refinishing problems are caused by not thoroughly removing the wax before applying a new finish.

Some methylene chloride strippers in each of the formula strengths are made to be water-washable by the addition of a detergent to the formula. Water washing makes the wax, the stripper, and the gunk it creates easier to remove by hosing the wood. But hosing introduces water, which can raise the grain, remove water-soluble dye stains, and potentially lift veneer and loosen joints.

The strength of methylene chloride strippers depends primarily upon the formulation. All four classes contain a small percentage of methanol as an "activator" to increase the effectiveness:

Quick Stripper Identification

Here's a quick method of identifying the main categories of strippers. For a more in-depth method, see "Breaking the Code—An Overview of Strippers" on p. 288.

	MC	MC/ATM	ATM	NMP
In a plastic container				X
Labeled biodegradable				X
Labeled flammable		X	X	
Labeled non-flammable	X			
Noticeably heavier	X			

MC = METHYLENE CHLORIDE
ATM = ACETONE, TOLUENE, AND METHANOL
NMP = N-METHYL PYRROLIDONE

- methylene chloride and methanol
- methylene chloride and methanol strengthened with an alkali
- methylene chloride and methanol strengthened with an acid
- methylene chloride and methanol thinned with acetone and toluene (actually a combination of two categories: MC and ATM)

Methylene chloride/methanol strippers are strong enough to rapidly remove all but the most solvent-resistant paints and finishes. They are less effective on two-part finishes. You can improve the effectiveness by scuffing the finish with 60- or 80-grit sandpaper before applying the stripper. These strippers are also non-flammable and non-polluting. (Methylene chloride, which makes up 75 to 85 percent of the formula, is non-flammable and not considered an ozone depleter or smog producer by the Environmental Protection Agency.) The primary disadvantages are potential health hazards and cost. Methylene chloride is a moderately expensive solvent, so strippers made with high percentages of methylene chloride are also moderately expensive.

CAUTION
▼

Methylene chloride metabolizes into carbon monoxide in the blood stream, causing the heart to pump harder to get enough oxygen to the body. As a result, methylene chloride could trigger a heart attack in someone with an existing heart condition. If you have a heart condition, *don't* use methylene chloride strippers.

Alkali-fortified methylene chloride strippers are stronger than methylene chloride strippers because of the added alkali. The alkali is usually ammonium hydroxide (ammonia) and sometimes sodium hydroxide (lye), and it's usually, but not always, listed on the container.

Alkali-fortified strippers are available in most paint, boat, and auto-body supply stores. They are often sold as marine strippers. The advantage of these strippers is their increased effectiveness on exceptionally tough paints and finishes. The drawbacks are their moder-

Using Oxalic Acid

Oxalic acid can be used to bleach out dark stains caused by alkalis, such as lye and ammonia, which are contained in some strippers, and rust marks (black water rings) caused by water and metal residue.

Dissolve some oxalic acid crystals, available at pharmacies and many paint stores, to a saturated solution in warm water. (A solution is saturated when the crystals will no longer dissolve in the water.) Brush the solution over the entire surface, not just over the stains; otherwise, you may create lighter spots in these areas, and you'll have to recoat the entire surface anyway to even the color. Let the oxalic acid dry. Wash the crystals off the wood with a hose or well-soaked sponge or cloth. (Don't brush the crystals into the air, or you may breathe them.) Wash the surface well with water. Then add to clean water some baking soda, a small amount of household ammonia, or some other mild alkali, and wash once again to neutralize the acid.

Oxalic acid will seldom bleach the wood itself, but it should remove the stains. Sometimes a second or third application helps, but the first usually does the job. If a light brown mark remains, you can usually sand it out easily. The mark is usually superficial.

CAUTION
▼

Oxalic acid is highly toxic, capable of causing severe skin and respiratory problems. Wear gloves and eye protection when using it, and don't generate airborne dust.

Stripper Safety

All stripping solvents are bad for your health. How could it be otherwise when even mineral spirits can cause dizziness and irritability? But it needs to be clearly stated anyway, because some manufacturers advertise their strippers as safe. Some even put the word "safe" in the name, enhancing the deception.

The issue of stripper safety came to the forefront in the mid-1980s, when it was discovered that high doses of methylene chloride (MC) caused cancer in a certain strain of experimental mice and caused benign tumors in rats. Despite four major human studies failing to come up with any evidence that methylene chloride caused cancer in humans, methylene chloride was listed as a probable human carcinogen by the Environmental Protection Agency (EPA). These four studies involved over 6,000 workers, exposed to methylene chloride all day every day for their entire working careers.

The mere possibility that methylene chloride was carcinogenic was enough to encourage manufacturers to look for other solvents that could remove paint and finish. ATM (acetone, toluene, methanol) strippers already existed, but these strippers are highly flammable and quite toxic (though not carcinogenic) in their own right. Manufacturers settled on N-methyl pyrrolidone (NMP) as the most likely candidate. What distinguishes NMP is not reduced toxicity but slow evaporation. High concentrations of NMP vapors are extremely toxic. But evaporation is so slow it would take days for NMP to reach the same levels of concentration in the air that MC and ATM achieve in minutes. By then, normal air movement should have cleaned the air in a room many times over.

It's important that you understand this distinction so you can make sense of manufacturers' sometimes vicious claims and counterclaims. Makers of NMP strippers have to convince you that MC and ATM strippers are bad for your health. Otherwise, you probably wouldn't buy their strippers, because they are considerably slower and more expensive. On the other hand, makers of MC and ATM strippers can legitimately claim (and they do) that NMP strippers are actually more toxic than MC or ATM at equal levels of vapor concentration.

All solvents, whether stripping solvents or thinning solvents, are bad for your health. The more we learn about solvents, the more we discover problems with them. (For example, in the 1970s methylene chloride, which at the time was thought to be safe, replaced benzene in strippers after it was discovered that benzene was carcinogenic.) Expose yourself as little as possible to the fumes of all solvents by working outside or in a room with good cross-ventilation. Wear a NIOSH-approved organic-vapor respirator mask, but don't rely on it alone. (Respirator masks have very short-lived effectiveness against methylene chloride fumes.) Arrange good airflow, and rely primarily on breathing fresh air.

ately high price, the health hazards associated with methylene chloride, and their tendency to stain hardwoods such as oak, mahogany, cherry, and walnut. The staining is caused by the alkali, which reacts with the tannic acid contained naturally in these woods. You can use oxalic acid to remove the staining. (See "Using Oxalic Acid," at left.)

Acid-fortified methylene chloride strippers are available to professional stripping shops for use on catalyzed lacquers and conversion varnish. The acid makes the stripper especially effective on these coatings. You can make your own acid-fortified stripper by adding oxalic acid to a methylene chloride stripper. Make up a saturated solution of oxalic acid (no more will dissolve) and warm water and add about 5 percent to a water-washable methylene chloride stripper. Alternatively, make up a saturated solution of oxalic acid and lacquer thinner and add about 5 percent to a methylene chloride stripper that is not water-washable. Don't store either in a metal or plastic container.

Methylene chloride/acetone, toluene, methanol (MC/ATM) strippers are the weakest of the four types that are based on methylene chloride. But they are strong enough to strip almost all old finishes and paints. They are also the least expensive of the four MC types. The downside of adding ATM to methylene chloride is that it introduces solvents that are flammable and which also cause air pollution.

Sometimes methyl ethyl ketone (MEK) or other ketones are substituted for the acetone, and xylene (xylol) is substituted for the toluene. These solvents, which evaporate a little more slowly than acetone and toluene, will be listed on the container.

> **TIP** Manufacturers sometimes add a small amount of toluene, xylene, or a ketone to what is technically still a strong methylene chloride stripper. This can cause you some confusion when you are reading labels. Here are two alternative methods of identifying strippers high in methylene chloride content:
> - "Non-flammable" will be listed.
> - The can will be noticeably heavier (MC weighs more than other solvents used in strippers).

Breaking the Code—An Overview of Strippers

Manufacturers commonly list on the container all the solvents used in strippers. Though they aren't required to list the percentages, these are well established in the industry and can be deduced from the combination of solvents listed.

LISTED CONTENTS	APPROXIMATE PERCENTAGES	
Methylene chloride Methanol	75%–85% MC* 4–10% Methanol	
Methylene chloride Methanol Ammonium hydroxide (not always listed)	75%–85% MC* 4%–10% Methanol 1%–5% Ammonium hydroxide	
Methylene chloride Acetone Toluene Methanol (Other ketones may be substituted for acetone. Xylene may be substituted for toluene.)	25%–60% MC 10–40% of each of the others	
Acetone Toluene Methanol (ATM stripper) (Other ketones may be substituted for acetone. Xylene may be substituted for toluene.)	10%–40% of each	
Acetone Toluene Methanol (ATM refinisher)	10%–40% of each	
N-methyl pyrrolidone (NMP)	40%–80% NMP	

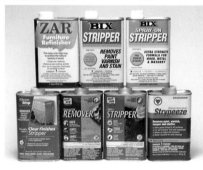

Strippers with a high methylene chloride content are non-flammable (always mentioned on the container) and noticeably heavier than all other strippers.

RELATIVE STRENGTH	POTENTIAL PROBLEMS	SAFETY CONCERNS	COMMENTS
Effective on all but the toughest coatings.	Contains wax, which must be removed before applying a finish.	Fumes are a health hazard.	Work outside or in a room where you've arranged cross-ventilation.
Strongest of all over-the-counter paint-and-varnish removers.	Contains wax, which must be removed before applying a finish. Ammonium hydroxide will darken many hardwoods.	Fumes are a health hazard.	Work outside or in a room where you've arranged cross-ventilation. Use on unusually tough coatings.
Will remove most old paint and finish.	Contains wax, which must be removed before applying a finish.	Fumes are a health hazard. Fumes and liquid solvent are a fire hazard.	Work outside or in a room where you've arranged cross-ventilation. A good, inexpensive choice for removing most old paint and finish.
Will remove most old paint and finish.	Contains wax, which must be removed before applying a finish. Some contain unlisted ammonium hydroxide, which will darken many hardwoods.	Fumes are a health hazard. Fumes and liquid solvent are a fire hazard.	Work outside or in a room where you've arranged cross-ventilation. A good inexpensive choice for removing most old paint and finish.
Will dissolve shellac, lacquer, and water base. Ineffective on everything else.	Very inefficient as a stripper, because refinisher doesn't contain wax to slow solvent evaporation.	Fumes are a health hazard. Fumes and liquid solvent are a fire hazard.	Work outside or in a room where you've arranged cross-ventilation. Many people become discouraged when refinisher doesn't work.
Works much more slowly than methylene chloride strippers.	Trying to rush it.	Fairly safe to use because of slow evaporation rate.	Most expensive of all stripping solvents.

CAUTION

The vapors of all three solvents—acetone, toluene, and methanol—are highly flammable and toxic. Toxic fumes in concentrated amounts can impair your central nervous system, cause illness, and in extreme cases, kill you. So you should take the same precautions when using ATM strippers and refinishers as you do with methylene chloride strippers. (See "Stripper Safety" on p. 286.)

Acetone, Toluene, and Methanol (ATM)

Acetone, toluene, and methanol (including their ketone, xylene, and alcohol substitutes) are three of the basic ingredients in lacquer thinner. If you have ever put lacquer thinner on a finish, you're familiar with the damage this blend of solvents can cause. It will dissolve shellac, lacquer, and water base, and it will soften and sometimes wrinkle varnish. Manufacturers take advantage of this solvent strength to make non–methylene chloride strippers. There are two types:

- strippers that contain wax to retard evaporation, and usually contain thickeners to make them into a semi-paste
- refinishers that contain neither wax nor thickeners

ATM strippers are used in the same way as the four methylene chloride strippers, and are available in liquid or semi-paste consistencies and in varieties that are water-washable or not water-washable. ATM strippers work well on most old paints and finishes. The strippers are effective because the wax holds the solvents in contact with the coating long enough for them to penetrate. Their advantages: They are cheap and perform well without the added health risks of methylene chloride. Their disadvantages: They are weaker than methylene chloride, highly flammable, and air-polluting, and some brands contain an alkali that will stain many hardwoods.

ATM refinishers don't contain wax, so they evaporate very rapidly—before the solvents have time to penetrate and thoroughly soften or blister the finish. As a result, refinishers are ineffective on paints and all finishes except shellac, lacquer, and water base. Even on these finishes, refinishers are inefficient. The solvents evaporate so rapidly that you have to scrub the finish with steel wool to get it off. You can't just wipe off the finish as you can with strippers. This largely mechanical removal of the softened film is the procedure usually recommended by manufacturers.

The ineffectiveness of refinisher on old varnish (despite manufacturers' claims to the contrary) and on all two-part finishes, together with the universal lack of instructions for identifying the type of finish you're stripping, is the most serious deficiency of this product. Many people become discouraged because of the great amount of effort they have to expend scratching off the finish with steel wool. In addition, considering that refinisher is simply lacquer thinner (you can use lacquer thinner instead), many brands are unreasonably overpriced. On the other hand, because refinishers leave no wax residue on the wood to interfere with the new finish, there's no need to wash the wood with a solvent after stripping. You save a step.

N-Methyl Pyrrolidone (NMP)

N-methyl pyrrolidone is not as effective as either methylene chloride or ATM for removing paints and finishes. But NMP evaporates very slowly, so fumes don't build up in the air as quickly. As a result, NMP is less toxic to work with, and it is not highly flammable. It is also not classified as an air pollutant by the EPA. Because the solvent evaporates so slowly, the stripper doesn't require the addition of wax to keep it in contact with the finish. There is, therefore, no wax that has to be removed after stripping. On the other hand, NMP is expensive, so strippers based on NMP are expensive.

To reduce the cost, other slow-evaporating and weaker solvents are blended in. These include di-basic esters—that is, esters of adipic, succinic, and glutaric acids (DBE)—ethyl-3-ethoxypropionate (EEP), and gamma-butyrolactone (BLO). You will see these listed on the container.

NMP has been around since the 1940s and has been used primarily as a cleaning solvent. In the early 1990s, as methylene chloride was coming under attack as a probable carcinogen, companies introduced NMP as an alternative. It became widely available, with several brands carried by almost every paint store. Unfortunately, NMP has turned out to be a case study in how not to market a product, and it is often difficult to find now.

Professional Stripping

Professional stripping shops use basically the same solvents and chemicals that are available to amateurs for stripping paints and finishes. The big difference is that these shops have more efficient equipment and methods for doing the stripping.

There are two principal stripping systems: flow (commonly called "flow over") and vat. The *flow system* uses a hose and pump to flow stripper (usually methylene chloride, but any stripper can be used) continuously over an item placed in a metal tray. The item is simultaneously scrubbed with a stiff bristle brush. (Many bristle brushes are equipped with a hose connection so the brush can dispense the stripper while brushing.) For stubborn paints and finishes, the stripper is flowed on and allowed to soak for a period of time before scrubbing begins. The sludge runs off and down a drain where it flows through a screen, which catches paint and other solids. The cleaned stripper is then recycled by the pump.

When all the paint or finish has been removed or loosened, the item is placed in a booth where it is hosed with a pressure washer to clean it. After drying, sanding and finishing can begin.

The *vat system* uses two large vats, one filled with a solution of lye and the other with a solution of oxalic acid. The item is first placed in the lye vat and allowed to remain until the paint or finish is loosened and can be scrubbed off. When clean, the item is placed in the oxalic-acid vat to neutralize the lye and bleach out the usually darkened coloring caused by the lye. The object is removed from the oxalic acid, hosed clean, and sanded and finished after drying.

Both systems are efficient, but they usually require fairly heavy sanding because the water raises the grain. The flow system is less damaging to wood, but the strippers are fairly expensive. The chemicals used in the vat system are much cheaper, but the lye can severely damage wood and dissolve old glues if furniture is allowed to remain submerged too long.

The vat system has given refinishers a bad reputation, though in trained hands, this system is not very destructive. Most wood furniture should be stripped using the flow system. Metal furniture and wood trim can usually be stripped safely using the vat system.

Strippers based on NMP work slowly, but they take days to evaporate from the surface. Therefore, you can leave them for several days if necessary, and they will work through many coats of paint or finish. If you aren't in a hurry, you can accomplish your stripping with a great deal less work than is necessary with the fast-evaporating strippers, which often require several applications. I find myself often going to this stripper rather than the faster ones

Common Problems Using Strippers

If you've ever done any stripping, you know that it's seldom as easy as the step-by-step instructions suggest. (See "Using Strippers" on p. 295.) Here are some of the most common problems, their causes, and solutions.

PROBLEM	CAUSE	SOLUTION
The stripper doesn't work.	You're not allowing enough time.	Allow more time. When the temperature is below 65 degrees Fahrenheit, the stripper will work much more slowly. When the temperature is above 85 degrees, the stripper will evaporate much more quickly. Keep the surface wet with more coats of stripper, or cover the surface with plastic wrap.
	Your stripper is not strong enough. (It may strip one coat, but not the next, because that is a different sort of paint or finish.)	Change to a stronger stripper (see "Breaking the Code— An Overview of Strippers" on p. 288). Scuff the surface with 60- or 80-grit sandpaper to increase the surface area for the stripper to act on.
	You are mistaking stain for finish. You have removed all the finish. What's left is stain. Few stains are removed totally by a stripper.	Allow the wood to dry. If there is no shine in reflected light, either on the wood or in the pores, the finish is off. The wood should feel like bare wood.
You can't get the paint out of the pores.	Oil-based (reactive-curing) paint doesn't dissolve. It swells and blisters. This is sometimes true for latex paint also. Since there is no place in the pores for the paint to swell, it remains there until it's scrubbed loose.	Apply more stripper to the wood. Scrub the wood in the direction of the grain with a soft brass-bristle brush. Remove the gunk and repeat if necessary. This may not work on tight-grained woods, such as pine and poplar. Try stripping with lye before you resort to sanding.
You can't get the stain out of the wood.	Stains can be dyes based on various solvents, or pigment using different binders. No stripper will remove them all. (See Chapter 4: "Staining Wood.")	You don't have to remove all the stain to restain an equivalent or darker color. You can partially remove water-soluble dye stain, the most common stain used on old furniture, with water. Your stripper should have partially removed solvent-soluble dye stains. You can remove most of the dye coloring with chlorine-type (household or pool) bleach, but you may also turn the wood white. (Protect yourself from the fumes.) You can remove pigment stains (thinned paint) lodged in the pores using the procedure described above for paint.

precisely because of the reduced effort required.

But NMP strippers weren't marketed this way. They were (and still are) marketed as working in 30 minutes. The result is that the stripper has gained the reputation, "It doesn't work," and this is the reason so few paint stores and home centers stock it.

These strippers are also labeled "biodegradable," and this is terribly misleading. The faster-evaporating strippers

PROBLEM	CAUSE	SOLUTION
The stripper streaks and darkens the wood.	Lye and strippers that contain an alkali darken many hardwoods.	Bleach out the dark stains with oxalic acid. (See "Using Oxalic Acid" on p. 286.) Oxalic acid will seldom bleach the wood itself, but it will take out alkali stains. It will also remove rust stains (brown or black water stains).
The stain won't take evenly after the wood has been stripped.	The wood itself is the problem.	See "Common Staining Problems, Causes, and Solutions" on p. 68 for ways to solve this problem.
	You didn't remove all of the old finish. Some of it is still in the wood, preventing the stain from penetrating evenly.	Restrip the wood. Sand it lightly with 180- to 280-grit sandpaper to be sure all finish has been removed.
The new finish won't dry, or it peels after it has cured.	You didn't remove all of the wax contained in the stripper.	Strip the poorly dried finish, and wash the wood thoroughly with mineral spirits, naphtha, or lacquer thinner. Refold and turn your cloth often to remove the wax from the wood rather than smear it around.
Your sandpaper clogs up when you sand the stripped wood.	The stripper (NMP) hasn't totally evaporated.	Allow more time for evaporation, heat the wood with a heat lamp, or wash the wood with alcohol or lacquer thinner to speed the drying.
	You didn't remove all the finish.	Strip the wood again, or, if you aren't concerned about preserving the patina, continue sanding until the sandpaper stops clogging and there's no more finish on the wood.

don't have to be biodegradable. They evaporate so fast that they simply aren't there anymore when it's time to dispose of the stripped coating. And the NMP stripping sludge, which can remain moist for a considerable time, is considered hazardous waste almost everywhere because of what was in the coating being stripped! So you wouldn't want to throw it in the trash until it dried out anyway.

Lye

Lye (sodium hydroxide or caustic soda) is probably the oldest chemical paint stripper. It is effective but dangerous to use and damaging to the wood. It's often used by commercial strippers, who dip furniture into a heated vat filled with lye and water. The lye removes the paint or finish, but it also dissolves glue and damages the wood. The wood's surface becomes soft and punky and requires heavy sanding to get through to good wood underneath. Much furniture has been ruined by being stripped with lye, and stripping shops have gotten a bad reputation because of their often indiscriminate use of this chemical for stripping.

Lye is not all bad, however. It can be used sparingly to dissolve stubborn paint out of pores without doing too

Deterioration of Finishes and *Antiques Roadshow*

You may find it ironic that television shows like *Antiques Roadshow,* which do so much to educate people about antiques and their value, are also responsible for the destruction of an enormous amount of antique furniture. This is the consequence of the appraisers on these shows discouraging people from refinishing their antique furniture, even their old-but-not-yet-antique furniture. As I explained in Chapter 1, "Why Finish Wood, Anyway?" the inevitable result of a deteriorated finish, besides unsightliness, is loose joints, peeled veneer, warping, and splitting—to the point that the furniture will probably be thrown away at some time.

The misleading message of these shows is that refinishing lowers value. The message goes like this: "If this furniture had not been refinished, it would be worth X dollars. But now that it has been refinished, it's worth only Y

dollars." The difference in dollars is usually quite significant, and the comparison is with furniture in near-perfect condition. Reasons for the furniture having been refinished are rarely discussed.

Why is furniture refinished? Because the existing finish is in very bad shape, of course. What would the furniture be worth if it had not been refinished, if the deterioration had been allowed to continue? This should be the comparison—not to furniture in near-perfect condition. If the furniture had survived in very bad condition, it would be worth less than it is now, refinished and in good condition. The message from the appraisers should instead be as follows:

"Apparently, this furniture was in very bad shape at some time, and it was refinished. This is good, because it survived and is now worth Y dollars. Had this furniture not been refinished, it would be

worth considerably less. On the other hand, had this furniture sat in some dark corner of a room (light destroys finishes) and not been moved or used (wear destroys finishes) for generations, it might have survived in pristine 'original' condition and be very rare. Then it would be worth X dollars. But no one would have gotten the pleasure of having used the furniture."

Except for a few rare furniture survivors that have value precisely because of their rareness, and will be preserved in ideal temperature and humidity conditions, there is nothing wrong with refinishing furniture suffering from a badly deteriorated finish. In fact, the furniture should be refinished, ideally so as to preserve as much of its aged appearance as possible, or to restore it to its original appearance. Both practices have their advocates (and their buyers) in the marketplace.

Using Strippers

Stripping paint or finish requires no particular skill, but it can be messy and bad for your health, and some strippers are flammable. Here are steps for how to use all common strippers except refinisher (see "ATM refinishers" on p. 290) and lye (see "Lye" on p. 294 and "Common Problems Using Strippers" on p. 292):

1 Work outdoors in the shade or in a room where you have arranged good cross ventilation. Work in warm temperatures; strippers lose potency when they are cold. Don't work near an open flame or source of sparks if you're using a flammable stripper.

2 Remove hardware and difficult-to-get-to wood parts that can be disassembled easily. If the hardware requires stripping, soak it with stripper in a coffee can.

3 Wear a long-sleeved shirt, solvent-resistant gloves (butyl or neoprene), and glasses or safety goggles.

4 Shake the container of stripper. Use a cloth to cover the cap, and open it slowly to allow for a gradual release of pressure. Pour the stripper into a wide-mouth jar or can.

5 Brush a thick layer of stripper onto the wood using an old or inexpensive paint brush. (Some synthetic-bristle brushes will dissolve in methylene chloride–based strippers.) Brush in one direction rather than back and forth; this helps to lay on a thick coat and reduces solvent

Scrape dissolved or blistered paint or finish off flat surfaces with a plastic scraper or wide putty knife.

evaporation by not disturbing the wax that has risen to the surface of the stripper.

6 Allow the stripper time to work on the paint or finish. Test it now and then with a putty knife to see if the film can be lifted from the wood. Add more stripper if the original has mostly evaporated. (You can cover the stripper with plastic wrap to slow solvent evaporation.) All strippers will lift many layers of paint at one time if kept wet and allowed time to penetrate.

7 Remove the dissolved, blistered, or softened film in one of the following ways, depending on the situation:

- Scrape the film off flat surfaces into a bucket or cardboard box with a plastic spreader or a wide, dull putty knife. The putty knife should be clean and smooth; round its corners with a file so it doesn't scratch the wood.

- Soak up and wipe off dissolved film with heavy-duty paper towels.

Brush a thick layer of stripper onto the wood using an old or inexpensive paint brush.

Use wood shavings to soak up dissolved or blistered paint or finish.

- Soak up dissolved or blistered film by rubbing the wood with handfuls of wood shavings (from a jointer or planer). Then brush them off with a stiff-bristle brush.

- Break blistered or softened film loose from moldings, turnings, and carvings with #1 natural or synthetic steel wool (Scotch-Brite).

- Pull a coarse string or rope back and forth around the recesses of turnings to work out blistered paint or finish.

- Pick the softened paint or finish out of cracks and recesses with sharpened sticks or dowels, which won't damage the wood as sharp metal picks will.

It's not necessary to sand the wood after stripping unless there are problems in the wood, such as scratches or gouges, that you want to remove. Sanding removes the characteristics of age that make old furniture sought after. These characteristics include natural color changes at the surface of the wood, called patina, and normal marks of wear. In most cases, the only reason you should consider sanding after stripping is to ensure that you've removed all the finish. Any remaining old finish will clog sandpaper. Use a fine-grit sandpaper (180- to 280-grit), and sand lightly. If you find there is still finish on the wood, it's usually easier and better to strip again rather than sand it off.

8 Coat the wood with more stripper, and scrub out any paint or stain left in the wood pores with a soft brass-bristle brush. Scrub with the grain of the wood.

9 Wash the wood with mineral spirits, naphtha, or lacquer thinner to remove wax residue left from strippers containing wax. It's not necessary to take this step on refinishers, or strippers based on NMP, because they don't contain wax. It is necessary to allow NMP several days to evaporate out of the pores of wood, however, before applying a finish. If you want to speed the evaporation, apply heat using heat lamps or wipe with alcohol or lacquer thinner.

Scrub the wood shavings out of recesses with a stiff-bristle brush.

Remove dissolved or blistered paint or finish from recesses of turnings by pulling a coarse string or rope around the recesses.

If you need to use steel wool or an abrasive pad to aid in the removal of a finish, you will probably remove the coloring unevenly, and this may cause color problems during the refinishing. It's always best to use rags or paper towels, and plastic (not metal) spreaders, to remove finishes if at all possible.

10 Let the solvent evaporate out of the stripping sludge, then dispose of it in the trash unless local laws forbid this. (The dried sludge is the same thing that was on the furniture before you stripped it. Sending dried paint sludge to the landfill is no more polluting than tossing the entire painted object into the landfill.)

Scrub out any paint or unwanted stain that remains in the wood pores with a soft brass-bristle brush. Scrub with the grain of the wood.

much damage to the wood. It can be used effectively to strip metal objects (except aluminum) without causing damage to the metal. It can be used to strip milk paint, a casein-based paint sometimes used in the eighteenth and nineteenth centuries that is particularly difficult to remove with other strippers. And it is a cheap, effective stripper for large surfaces of exterior woodwork, masonry, and concrete, and on indoor plaster and softwood trim.

To make a lye stripper, dissolve about $1/4$ pound of lye (available at paint stores) in a gallon of warm water. Don't use an aluminum or plastic container. Be sure to pour the lye into the water, not the other way around, because the sudden chemical reaction may boil over and burn you. The lye and water mixture will get hot from the chemical reaction, so don't hold the container.

Brush the dissolved lye onto the finish using a natural-bristle brush. Let the lye work just long enough to dissolve the finish but not damage the wood. After stripping the finish, you'll need to wash the wood with a 50/50 solution of white vinegar and water to neutralize the lye. If you don't neutralize the lye, it could be reactivated later by moisture penetrating the finish in that area, and reactivated lye can strip the finish.

Which Stripper to Use

How do you choose among all these types of strippers? First decide whether you're willing to accept the health risks of using a methylene chloride stripper. If you are, choose the cheapest type that will do the job. The weakest formula

class—methylene chloride and methanol reduced with acetone and toluene—is the cheapest and will strip most old paints and finishes. Tougher finishes, such as polyurethane, will require strippers that are made with only methylene chloride and methanol. The toughest coatings, such as catalyzed finishes, polyester, and baked-on coatings, will require an alkali- or acid-fortified, methylene chloride stripper, and you can improve your chances of success by scuffing the coating with 60- or 80-grit sandpaper.

If you don't know what type of paint or finish you're stripping but you want to be relatively sure the stripper you use will work, use a methylene chloride/methanol stripper. It will take off almost all coatings without staining the wood.

If you don't want to expose yourself to methylene chloride, use an ATM stripper. While not as strong as methylene chloride strippers, ATM strippers will remove most old paints and finishes.

If you want to limit your exposure to toxic solvents as much as possible and you are willing to pay more, use an NMP stripper. Just be sure to give it the time it needs to work through the coating.

If you are stripping metal (not aluminum), or you are not worried about damage to the wood, and if you can protect yourself well, you could use lye. When stripping wood with lye, try to leave the lye in contact with the paint or finish just long enough to dissolve it but not so long that it harms the wood underneath.

If all else fails, you will need to remove the coating by scraping or sanding or with a heat gun.

Afterword

You have now been exposed to all of beginning and intermediate wood finishing and some advanced techniques. You have surely realized that this is not a difficult subject if you begin with an accurate understanding of the materials and the few simple tools. Of course, mastering the craft of wood finishing does require a good deal of experience. Unfortunately, wood finishing has been made infinitely more difficult by misleading and often incorrect information from manufacturers and by the vast amount of contradictory information that circulates in magazines and books.

Since the publication of the first edition of *Understanding Wood Finishing* in 1994, I've seen no movement on the part of manufacturers to give us better and more accurate information about their products. And though some of the woodworking magazines and publishers of woodworking books have made an effort to improve the accuracy of the information they print, they are the exception.

When I teach seminars, I usually finish by making a plea to participants to speak up when they encounter inaccurate or misleading information—complain to the manufacturer or the publisher, or inform the store clerk or mail-order company of the problem and ask them to take the issue to the manufacturer. I make this same plea to you. I've become convinced that nothing short of a "consumer revolt" on our part is going to bring about the necessary change. Otherwise, the inertia will prevail.

* * *

I was honored to be asked to write the first edition of *Understanding Wood Finishing*. The opportunity to write a second edition is an even greater honor, and I owe it to Chris Reggio and Dolores York at Reader's Digest. Thank you for believing in me.

In writing this book, I have been extremely fortunate to work with the same two exceptional people, Rick Mastelli and Deborah Fillion, who put together the first edition. The success of a how-to book is every bit as dependent upon the presentation of the information as on the information itself, and Rick (as editor and photographer) and Deborah (as designer and layout artist) are the best at presenting this kind of information. If you find this book attractive and accessible, you owe it to them.

A lot of people have helped me improve my knowledge of wood finishing. Primary among them is Jim McCloskey who allowed me to edit *Finishing and Restoration* (formerly *Professional Refinishing*) magazine for four years. I learned so much during those years from my close association with a wonderful group of highly skilled refinishers from all over the country. Also important were the editors at a number of magazines, including *Woodshop News*, *Popular Woodworking*, *Woodwork*, *Maine Antique Digest*, *The Paint Dealer*, and *American Painting Contractor*, who gave me the opportunity to explore hundreds of finishing topics in their magazines. I have incorporated into this book much of what I learned writing those articles.

I am privileged to count as friends a number of people who have helped me over the years with technical information. Foremost are David Bueche, Mike Fox, Jerry Hund, David Jackson, Lloyd Haanstra, Russ Ramirez, and Greg Williams.

I am also fortunate to have a wonderful local support group of woodworkers and finishers who are always available with encouragement and advice when I need it. For this I would like to thank Randall Cain, Matthew Hill, Bill Hull, Alan Lacer, and Bryan Slocomb. Alan Lacer and Bryan Slocomb, along with Chris Christenberry, Charles Radtke, and Michael Puryear, allowed me to include photos of some of their work. Jim Roberson let me use some photos he had taken of me at work.

Finally, I want to acknowledge and thank the most important person of all, my wife Birthe, who has always believed in me and supported me as I've chosen to pursue one risky endeavor after another. ■

Sources of Supply

Though local paint stores and home centers stock most of what you need to paint your house, few carry more than the basics for wood finishing. Distributors and the few paint stores that cater to the professional finishing trade carry lacquers, two-part finishes, NGR stains, and other more specialized products. You may be able to locate these stores in the Yellow Pages of your telephone book.

You will find quality spray equipment and the widest selection of supplies for rubbing-out finishes at auto-body supply stores, which will also be listed in the Yellow Pages.

For other items that you can't find locally, you should turn to mail-order suppliers. Listed below are reliable suppliers who will send you a catalogue on request.

If you are not a professional finisher, be sure to check out www.woodfinishingsupplies.com, an Internet-only source of finishing materials not otherwise available to non-professionals.

Many suppliers carry finishing materials from H. Behlen Bros., the consumer arm of Mohawk Finishing Products, which sells to professional finishers. Catalogues that carry a large number of Behlen products are marked with a (B).

Many also carry a wide color selection of powder dyes from W. D. Lockwood. These are marked with an (L).

A few carry hard-to-find resins, pigments, and chemicals. These are marked with a (C).

Benco Sales, Inc.
PO Box 3649
Crossville, TN 38557
(931) 484-9578
(800) 632-3626
www.bencosales.com
Supplier of finishing and stripping materials to the refinishing trade.

Besway Systems, Inc.
305 Williams Ave.
Madison, TN 37116
(615) 865-8310
(800) 251-4166
www.besway.com
Supplier of finishing and stripping materials to the refinishing trade.

The Chemistry Store.com
520 NE 26th Court
Pompano Beach, FL 33064
(800) 224-1430
www.chemistrystore.com
Many hard to find chemicals. (C)

Constantine's
1040 E. Oakland Park Blvd.
Ft. Lauderdale, FL 33334
(954) 561-1716
(800) 443-9667
www.constantines.com
Wide assortment of finishing materials. (B) (L)

Garrett Wade
161 Avenue of the Americas
New York, NY 10013
(212) 807-1155
(800) 221-2942
www.garrettwade.com
Wide assortment of finishing materials. (B)

Goff's Curtain Walls
1225 E. Wisconsin Ave.
Pewaukee, WI 53072
(262) 691-4998
(800) 234-0337
www.goffscurtainwalls.com
Heavy plastic curtains for spray booth.

Highland Hardware
1045 N. Highland Ave. NE
Atlanta, GA 30306
(404) 872-4466
(800) 241-6748
www.tools-for-woodworking.com
Wide assortment of finishing materials. Classes offered. (B)

Hood Finishing Products
PO Box 97
Somerset, NJ 08875
(732) 828-7850
(800) 229-0934
www.hoodfinishing.com
Supplier of finishing and stripping materials to the finishing and refinishing trade.

Homestead Finishing Products
PO Box 360275
Cleveland, OH 44136
(216) 631-5309
www.homesteadfinishing.com
Wide assortment of finishing materials. (B)

Klingspor's Woodworking Shop
PO Box 3737
Hickory, NC 28603
(828) 327-7263
(800) 228-0000
www.woodworkingshop.com
Wide assortment of finishing materials. (B)

Kremer Pigments
228 Elizabeth St.
New York, NY 10012
(212) 219-2394
(800) 995-5501
www.kremer-pigmente.com
Wide assortment of finishing materials, including many specialty items. (C)

Lee Valley Tools, Ltd.
1090 Morrison Dr.
Ottawa, Ontario, Canada K2H 8K7
(613) 596-0350
(800) 461-5053 from USA
(800) 267-8767 from Canada
www.leevalley.com
Wide assortment of finishing
materials. (B) (L)

W. D. Lockwood & Co.
81-83 Franklin St.
New York, NY 10013
(212) 966-4046
(866) 293-8913
www.wdlockwood.com
The largest supplier of water-,
alcohol-, and oil-soluble powder dyes
to the wood finishing trade. (L)

Merit Industries
1020 North 10th
Kansas City, KS 66101
(913) 371-4441
(800) 856-4441
www.meritindustries.com
Wide assortment of finishing and
touch-up materials. (B)

Mohawk Finishing Products
PO Box 22000
Hickory, NC 28603
(828) 261-0325
(800) 545-0047
www.mohawk-finishing.com
Supplier of finishing and touch-up
materials to the professional finishing
and refinishing trade. Touch-up
seminars offered around the country.

Olde Mill Cabinet Shoppe
1660 Camp Betty Washington Rd.
York, PA 17402
(717) 755-8884
www.oldemill.com
Wide assortment of finishing and
touch-up materials. Classes offered.
(B) (L) (C)

Refinisher's Warehouse
13 Amy Elsey Dr.
Charleston, SC 29407
(843) 556-4538
(800) 636-8555
Wide assortment of finishing and
refinishing materials. (B)

Restorco (Kwick Kleen products)
PO Box 807
Vincennes, IN 47591
(812) 886-0556
(888) 222-9767
www.kwickkleen.com
Supplier of finishing and stripping
materials to the refinishing trade.
Training courses offered.

Rockler Woodworking and
Hardware
4365 Willow Dr.
Medina, MN 55340
(763) 478-8200
(800) 279-4441
www.rockler.com
Wide assortment of finishing
materials, especially at the many
Rockler stores around the country.
Classes offered at the stores. (B)

Touch Up Depot
5215 Sjolander Rd.
Baytown, TX 77521
(866) 883-3768
www.touchupdepot.com
Supplier of finishing, stripping, and
touch-up materials to the refinishing
trade. Training courses offered.

Touch Up Solutions
PO Box 9346
Hickory, NC 28603
(828) 397-6206
(877) 346-4747
www.touchupsolutions.com
Supplier of finishing and touch-up
materials to the finishing and
refinishing trade.

Van Dyke's Restorers
39771 SC Hwy 34 E.
Woonsocket, SD 57385
(605) 796-4888
(800) 558-1234
www.vandykes.com
Largest supplier of all types of
restoration materials.

Woodcraft
560 Airport Industrial Park
Parkersburg, WV 26102
(304) 422-5412
(800) 225-1153
www.woodcraft.com
Wide assortment of finishing
materials, especially at the many
Woodcraft stores around the country.
Classes offered at the stores. (B)

Wood Finish Supply
PO Box 929
Fort Bragg, CA 95437
(707) 962-9480
(800) 245-5611
www.woodfinishsupply.com
Wide assortment of finishing
materials including many specialty
items. (B) (L)

Wood Finishing Supplies
855 38th St. NW, Suite B
Rochester, MN 55901
(507) 280-6515
(866) 548-1677
www.woodfinishingsupplies.com
Internet source of finishing and
touch-up materials for professionals
and non-professionals.

Wood Finisher's Supply
(Master's Magic)
2300 Holloway Dr.
El Reno, OK 73036
(405) 422-1025
(800) 548-6583
www.woodfinisherssupply.com
Supplier of finishing, stripping, and
touch-up materials to the finishing
and refinishing trade.

Woodworker's Supply
5604 Alameda Pl., NE
Albuquerque, NM 87113
(505) 821-0500
(800) 645-9292
www.woodworker.com
Wide assortment of finishing
materials. (B) (L)

Index